Changing language teaching through language testing: A washback study

Changing language teaching through language testing: A washback study

Liying Cheng

CAMBRIDGE
UNIVERSITY PRESS

CAMBRIDGE UNIVERSITY PRESS
Cambridge, New York, Melbourne, Madrid, Cape Town, Singapore, São Paulo

Cambridge University Press
The Edinburgh Building, Cambridge CB2 2RU, UK

www.cambridge.org
Information on this title: www.cambridge.org/9780521544733

First published 2005

Printed in the United Kingdom at the University Press, Cambridge

A catalogue record for this publication is available from the British Library

ISBN-13 978-0-521-83614-2 hardback
ISBN-10 0-521-83614-X hardback

ISBN-13 978-0-521-54473-3 paperback
ISBN-10 0-521-54473-4 paperback

Dedication

This study is dedicated to my parents who have, to their best knowledge and ability, encouraged me to reach the highest level of education possible throughout my life, for which I am greatly indebted to them.

Contents

List of figures

Chapter 5 Phase II – Teachers' perceptions of the change

Chapter 6 Phase II – Students' perceptions of the change

**Chapter 7 Phase III – Teachers' and students' actions and reactions
    to the change**

List of tables

Chapter 6 Phase II – Students' perceptions of the change

**Chapter 7 Phase III – Teachers' and students' actions and reactions
to the change**

Acknowledgements

Bringing this book to print has been something of a labour of love. I would like to express my gratitude to a number of people in the field of language testing who have supported and encouraged me throughout the process.

In particular, I am most grateful to Dr Peter Falvey, my doctoral supervisor, for his patient guidance, thought-provoking advice and constant support. I would like to thank Professor Kathleen Bailey and Professor Lyle Bachman for their constructive feedback during the time of research and the years thereafter. I must also thank Dr Andy Curtis for his unfailing support and constant encouragement. He is always the first reader of my work.

I am indebted to my friends – Peter Gu, An-e He, Sima Sengupta, Qiufang Wen and Liz Walker – who served as the research hotline throughout the whole research process. I wish to express my sincerest thanks for their academic and emotional support.

I would like to take the opportunity here to acknowledge several individuals from the Hong Kong Examinations Authority for insights into this washback study. My heartfelt thanks go to Rex King, Christina Lee and John Fullilove.

Particular thanks goes to my case study teachers – Sister Matthew, Yeo Shu Hoon and Mandy Ho Man Yan – for their ardent professional belief in this research and for letting me into their classrooms to analyse and investigate every aspect of their lessons over the two year period. Thanks also to the teachers in my baseline study who offered such generous assistance and allowed me to bring video cameras into their classrooms. I am truly indebted to all the teachers and students who participated in my survey studies.

I would like to thank the detailed work of Calvin Bowry and Ying Yu at Queen's University for proofing the manuscript.

And finally my heartfelt thanks goes to my family for their unshakeable belief in me and their unselfish support. They have encouraged me throughout this washback study right up to the point of going to print. Special thanks to my beloved son, Jack, for his tremendous understanding of his mother's work, even at a very early age in his life.

Series Editors' note

It is now commonplace to regard validity as a unitary concept with theory based, content and criterion related validation processes all having a part to play in contributing evidence in respect of the interpretation of test scores. High stakes test providers such as Cambridge ESOL are also concerned with the ethical dimension of testing in terms of the impact of a test on individuals and society and place equal emphasis on social values and social consequences in any considerations of the validity of test scores.

Test impact is concerned with the influence of a test on general educational processes and on the individuals who are affected by the test results. It is recognized that examination boards have a major impact on educational processes and on society in general because their examinations often have widespread recognition and 'cash in' value. Washback is an important element of test impact. While impact may occur at a 'macro' or social and institutional level, washback occurs at the 'micro' level of the individual participant (primarily teachers and students).

There is now a clear consensus on the need for a concern with, if not agreement on, the effects of what has been termed 'washback/backwash'. Washback is considered a 'neutral' term (which may refer to both (intended) positive or beneficial effects and to (unintended) harmful or negative effects and is broadly defined as the effect of a test on teaching and often also on learning. It has been associated with effects on teachers, learners, parents, administrators, textbook writers, classroom practice, educational practices and beliefs and curricula although the ultimate effects on learning outcomes should perhaps be the primary concern.

Given that language teachers have to equip students with the skills that tests are intended to provide information about, it seems likely the closer the relationship between the test and the teaching that precedes it, the more the test is likely to have washback on both staff and students. Some authors caution that although the test may influence the content of teaching this may not be uniformly positive and more critically tests may have little impact on methodology, how teachers teach. Liying Cheng found such a situation following the exam reforms in Hong Kong but her research clearly indicates that if adequate training for teaching the new test is not provided we should hardly find it surprising that old methodologies persist. The same is true in the Sri Lankan washback study described by Wall to be published in a later volume in this series where additionally a debilitating civil war was hardly conducive to change.

This volume looks at the impact of the 1996 Hong Kong Certificate of Education in English (HKCEE), a high stakes public examination, on the classroom teaching of English in Hong Kong secondary schools. Liying Cheng investigates the effects from the decision-making level of the Education Department (ED), the Curriculum Development Committee (CDC), and the Hong Kong Examinations Authority (HKEA), down to the classroom levels of teaching and learning, with reference to aspects of teachers' attitudes, teaching content, and classroom interaction.

The study addresses the following research questions:
(1) What strategies did the HKEA use to implement the examination change?
(2) What was the nature and scope of the washback effect on teachers' and students' perceptions of aspects of teaching towards the new examination?
(3) What was the nature and scope of the washback effect on teachers' behaviours as a result of the new examination in relation to:
   (a) Teachers' medium of instruction, teacher talk, teaching activities,
   (b) Teaching materials used in teaching, aspects of lesson planning,
   (c) Assessment and evaluation in relation to their teaching.

Despite widespread lip service to the mantra of 'washback' in the international testing community, until recently only a limited number of research studies have been undertaken to study the effects of high stakes language tests on teaching and learning and even fewer were based on samples as adequate as the one employed in this study in Hong Kong.

An important strength of Liying Cheng's work is the use she made of both quantitative and qualitative methods to investigate these effects. A balanced combination of quantitative and qualitative research methods is employed to explore the meaning of change in the Hong Kong context as a result of the new examination. Phase I utilized interviews, observation, and initial surveys of teachers and students. Phase II involved two parallel survey studies of teachers and students. The major research methods used in Phase III were classroom observations and follow-up interviews. The triangulation of the methodology (multi-method methodology) and inclusion of comparable student and teacher data is of interest to all those contemplating researching in this area.

The overt aim of the HKEA, in introducing the examination, was to bring about positive washback effects on teaching and learning in schools. However, the study shows the washback effect of the new examination on classroom methodology to be limited in many respects although the content of lessons shows marked change. Of particular interest is the identification of washback intensity (potential areas in teaching and learning that experience more washback effects than others within the given context of the study).

Two forthcoming volumes in this series on washback by Wall on the O level English examination in Sri Lanka and Green on IELTS should further enrich our understanding of this under-researched area of validity and help further ground the methodologies for investigating it.

Cyril Weir
Michael Milanovic
2004

Section One:
Education on the change

Rapid change has long been a phenomenon
of modern times. And it is a phenomenon that is
universal; no one and nowhere has escaped.

Lord & Cheng (1987: vii)

This section lays out the research background for an impact study of a major public examination change on English language teaching in Hong Kong secondary schools. The focus of this study was to determine whether or not any washback effect was evident on the teaching and learning of English in Hong Kong secondary schools as a result of a change to its public examination system. The examination under study was the 1996 Hong Kong Certificate of Education Examination (HKCEE) in English language.[1] This section consists of two chapters. Chapter 1 provides background information on the Hong Kong education system and its secondary school English language teaching and learning context. Chapter 2 reviews relevant research studies related to the educational phenomenon known as and referred to as *washback*.

1. The 1996 HKCEE in English language, also described as the revised HKCEE in this book, refers to the official 1996 HKCEE English examination syllabus, and the examination itself. Changes were made to the original HKCEE syllabus in 1993. The official 1996 HKCEE syllabus was put into effect in secondary schools in 1994. The 1996 HKCEE English examination was taken by students for the first time in May 1996.

1 The Hong Kong research context

Hong Kong is an examination-mad town. Public examinations dominate its secondary education system with students preparing for 'O' level examinations taken at the end of secondary 5 and 'A' level examinations, which they sit after secondary 7. Teachers plan and conduct their lessons with an eye fixed firmly on the requirements of the examinations in their subjects.

Fullilove (1992: 131)

The problem

As is well known among educators, assessment practices are currently undergoing a major paradigm shift, which can be described as a reaction to the perceived shortcomings of the prevailing paradigm's emphasis on standardized testing (Biggs, 1995, 1996; Genesee, 1994). Alternative assessment is built on current theories of learning and cognition and is grounded in futurists' views of what skills and abilities students in our society will need for future success. This kind of assessment has been initiated as a result of current educational reform movements and accountability (Herman, 1992; Oller, 1979). This assessment reform further reflects a trend towards using assessment to reform curriculum and improve instruction at the school level (Linn, 1983, 1992; Noble & Smith, 1994a, 1994b; Popham, 1983, 1987). Assessment is used by and has an impact on schools, colleges, and employers. In addition, assessment is also expected to have an impact on what and how teachers teach. According to Linn (1992), each of the above-intended consequences needs to be evaluated, the process of which should start with identifying the assessment system's intended effects on teaching and learning.

An important assumption behind the current beliefs about examination consequences is that deleterious effects on teaching and learning can be overcome by switching to alternative assessments. Those deleterious effects are associated with the traditional assessment paradigm of standardized testing. Alternative assessments such as performance-based assessment, on the other hand, are more closely linked to curriculum frameworks. It is argued (Baker, Aschbacher, Niemi, & Sato, 1992; Honig, 1987; Linn, 1992; Noble & Smith, 1994b; Popham, 1987,1991) that performance-based assessment can be designed to be so closely linked to the goals of instruction as to be almost indistinguishable from them. Rather than being a negative consequence, as the impact is now with some high-stakes uses of existing standardized tests, it is asserted that teaching to these proposed performance-based assessments would be considered a virtue.

The current study is situated along this line of the debate. Hong Kong is in line with the overall worldwide assessment paradigm shifts in education. English language teaching is moving towards a target- and task-based approach to curriculum and assessment. In 1993, the Hong Kong Examinations Authority (HKEA) introduced major changes to its existing fifth year Secondary (S5) English examination syllabus, which is known as the Hong Kong Certificate of Education Examination (HKCEE) in English language.[2] These changes were made in accordance with the Target Oriented Curriculum initiative in Hong Kong, and were reflected in two sections of the examination. One section is the integrated listening, reading, and writing exam paper, which requires students to perform simulated 'real life' tasks rather than just multiple-choice questions as in the previous paper. The other section is the oral paper, which presents brand new exam formats and has an increased weighting. The goal of this exam change was to improve the current English language teaching and learning standards in Hong Kong secondary schools. The intended impact was to positively influence the teaching of English by moving away from traditional behaviourist approaches towards the new philosophy of constructivist models of learning. Examples of this new approach include a change from non-interactive teacher dominated talk to more practical and task-based teaching approaches.

This major public examination change reflects a change towards a more task-based and integrated approach to assessment in Hong Kong. The intention was particularly evident at the policy-making level.[3] The focus of the

---

2. The HKCEE in English language offers alternative syllabuses to cater for two different groups of candidates. Candidates may enter for Syllabus A or Syllabus B, but not both. The skills covered by the two syllabuses are broadly comparable. However, a higher standard is expected of the candidates taking the Syllabus B examination. This study focuses only on Syllabus B of the HKCEE in English.

3. Interviews were conducted with the Deputy Secretary and three senior English subject officers from the HKEA.

current study, however, was to determine whether the effort of the Hong Kong Examinations Authority to change this public examination into a more appropriate assessment had changed teaching in Hong Kong secondary schools to become more integrated and task-based. The changes made to the HKCEE represent only one step towards assessing students' abilities to carry out real life language tasks using integrated and task-based approaches. However, the HKCEE is still norm-referenced, with its major function still being to select students rather than to educate them (Biggs, 1995: 1-2).

Purpose of the study

The purpose of the study was to:

- study the phenomena of the washback effect[4] in the light of measurement-driven instruction
- understand how the main participants within the Hong Kong educational context reacted to changes made in the HKCEE – a major public English examination
- explore the nature and scope of the washback effect on aspects of teachers' and students' perceptions, and teachers' behaviours, within the context of the examination change
- identify areas of washback intensity[5] in teaching and learning.

As mentioned above, the public examination studied was the Hong Kong Certificate of Education Examination in English language (1996). The primary purpose of the HKCEE is to measure the attainment [sic] in all subject areas of students who have completed a full-time secondary school course of five years' duration (Hong Kong Examinations Authority, 1992/93). This series of examinations is taken by the majority of secondary students at the end of their fifth year of secondary school. Students either proceed to further studies at the sixth form level, or leave school and seek employment.

The Hong Kong Certificate of Education examinations are conducted annually in April and May by the Hong Kong Examinations Authority. Forty-two subjects (including practical subjects) are examined; English language is one of them. Candidates' performance in individual subjects is assessed on the basis of six grades: A, B, C, D, E, and F, where A is the highest and F the lowest (a fail). Achievement below grade F is designated as 'unclassified'. Grade E represents a basic level of achievement in a subject and syllabus. Grade C or above is recognized as the equivalent of an O level pass in a British G.C.E. overseas examination.

---

4. The washback effect in this book is sometimes referred to as the effect of washback, or simply as washback. Although it is used in the singular, it is taken to include all of the different effects of washback collectively.
5. Washback intensity refers to the degree of washback effects in one area, or in a number of areas in teaching and learning affected by an examination (see Cheng, 1997).

As mentioned earlier, in 1993 the Hong Kong Examinations Authority introduced major changes to its existing HKCEE in English, in format and in weighting, in an attempt to 'narrow the gap between what happens in the exam room and the real world' (HKEA, 1993). The former HKCEE consisted of five examination papers: *Paper I – Composition, Comprehension, and Usage; Paper II – Comprehension and Usage; Paper III – Listening Comprehension; Paper IV – Oral English; and Paper V – Summary, Directed Writing, and Comprehension.* The revised 1996 HKCEE consists of four papers instead of five (see Table 1 below). They are *Paper I – Writing; Paper II – Reading Comprehension and Usage; Paper III – Integrated Listening, Reading, and Writing; and Paper IV – Oral.* Major changes were made to *Paper III* and *Paper IV* in relation to the previous syllabus, which will be discussed in full in a later part of this chapter.

Definition of key research terms

For the purpose of this study, the following research terms are operationally defined.

Washback is a common notion in educational and applied linguistics literature. *Backwash* is also used in the literature bearing the same definition (Biggs, 1995; Fullilove, 1992; Spolsky, 1994, 1995). *Washback* is defined as 'the impact of a test on teaching, and...tests can be powerful determiners, both positively and negatively, of what happens in classrooms' (Wall & Alderson, 1993: 41). The term *washback* is preferred in this study and used throughout

Table 1 Comparison of the weighting of each component on the old and new HKCEE

OLD HKCEE (from 1983 to 1996)		NEW HKCEE (from 1996 onwards)	
Paper I – Composition, Comprehension, and Usage	25%	Paper I – Writing	26%
Paper II – Comprehension and Usage	20%	Paper II – Reading Comprehension and Usage	24%
Paper III – Listening Comprehension	15%	Paper III – Integrated Listening, Reading, and Writing	32%
Section A – Short Items		Part A – Short Tasks	
Section B – Extended Listening		Part B – Extended Tasks	
Paper IV – Oral English	10%	Paper IV – Oral	18%
Section A – Reading and Dialogue		Part A – Role Play	
Section B – Conversation		Part B – Group Interaction	
Paper V – Summary, Directed Writing, and Comprehension	30%		

the book to indicate an intended direction and function of curriculum change by means of public examinations, as was the case for this study on Hong Kong schools. The researcher has retained the use of the term *washback* or *backwash* in its original form when quoting directly from the authors.

Public examinations are used in this book to refer to large-scale standardized tests. The public examination under study is the 1996 revised Hong Kong Certificate of Education Examination (English). It is a large-scale standardized examination taken at the end of Secondary Five, its 'primary purpose being to measure the attainments of students who have completed a full-time secondary school course of a five-year duration' (HKEA, 1994a: 6). The examination known as HKCEE is issued by the Hong Kong Examinations Authority and conducted annually in May.

Curriculum change normally refers to pedagogical and policy-based changes, often initiated by an education body. Curriculum changes, in more recent times, also occur at the grassroots level when teachers feel that the curriculum they are following requires reform. However, in this study, the term *curriculum change* refers to those changes to the curriculum that are driven by assessment; that is, as a result of changes in a public examination syllabus and format.

Classroom teaching is where 'The classroom can be defined as a place where more than two people gather together for the purpose of learning, with one having the role of teacher' (Tsui, 1995: 1). Teaching and learning are studied together as they are interactive processes in the classroom.

In this study, classroom teaching is defined and studied at the following levels:

- basic theoretical or philosophical level
- policy level
- behavioural or surface level (c.f. Stern, 1989).

This study investigated the washback effect of the public examination change upon the above levels of classroom teaching.

Task-based and integrated approach is where a task is referred to as 'some kind of activity designed to engage the learner in using the language communicatively or reflectively in order to arrive at an outcome other than that of learning a specified feature of the language' (Ellis, 1994: 595). It can refer to a real life activity or a contrived, pedagogical activity (Nunan, 1989b). In this study, a task-based and integrated approach to language teaching and learning involves learners in using the language communicatively and reflectively, and involves the integration of the four major language skills to carry out real life type tasks in the classroom. Such an approach is specified in the new 1996 HKCEE and constitutes the major changes made to the exam syllabus, and is the driving force behind the impact it intended to bring about.

Context of the study

This section will provide important background information on the Hong Kong education context. It will address the main features of the Hong Kong education system and the language teaching context, and describe the situation of English language teachers in Hong Kong secondary schools.

The Hong Kong education system

Hong Kong's education system has moved from being a highly selective, elite system to one providing nine years of universal, free, and compulsory education. Since 1978 there has been a massive expansion in the provision of post-secondary places at all levels, from craft courses to postgraduate degrees. The transition of secondary education in the 1970s and 1980s witnessed successive reforms of different stages of the system, which touched both on the quantity and quality of education. By 1980, most (87%) of the student population chose to continue beyond the nine years of mandatory schooling, with 40% studying in government or government-aided schools and the rest in self-financing private schools (see Postiglione & Leung, 1992: 11).

With these educational opportunities available, the next need was to further improve the quality of education for all learners. In Hong Kong, as in other modern knowledge-based societies, there is a recognized necessity for:

*   quality education for all learners, which enables them to think, to learn how to learn, and to respond to the rapid changes in society and the economy
*   a fair and quality-focused system of assessment and evaluation that ensures that all learners and the school curriculum are meeting these unprecedented challenges (Falvey, 1994; Hong Kong Curriculum Development Council, 1995).

Hong Kong's education system is typically one with a selection bias. The government places students according to the *Primary One Admission Scheme* after kindergarten, *the Secondary School Places Allocation System (SSPA)* after primary school, and the *Junior Secondary Education Assessment (JSEA)* after junior secondary school. Students who remain in secondary schools until Secondary Five (also known as Form Five) will sit for the Hong Kong Certificate of Education Examination (HKCEE). About one third of these students go on to study for two more years in the sixth and seventh form and then sit for an advanced level of examinations for entry into tertiary education.

Furthermore, the Hong Kong education system is centralized (see Figure 1.1 below). Two centralized agencies coexist within the Hong Kong education system, namely the *Curriculum Development Council (CDC)* and *the Hong Kong Examinations Authority (HKEA)*. They are mainly responsible for the identification and promotion of new or revised educational programmes. While the HKEA's official function is primarily to oversee the creation and administration of examinations, it has frequently been used as the primary agency of both initiating and constraining curriculum changes. The main result of these two agencies is the production of the CDC's *teaching* and the HKEA's *examination* syllabuses. The HKEA is an independent statutory body, but there is an overlapping membership with the Education Department (ED) – the Hong Kong governmental education organization.

Figure 1.1 Governing structure and curriculum development (Source: Morris, 1990a: 6)

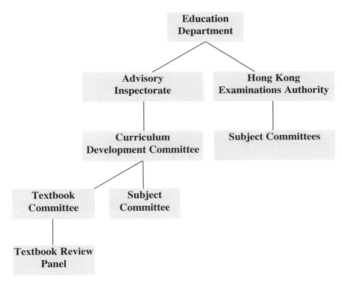

As mentioned above, the examination syllabus devised by the HKEA (Hong Kong Examinations Authority) and the teaching syllabus devised by the CDC (Curriculum Development Council) coexisted in Hong Kong secondary schools. The official syllabuses published by various subject committees under the CDC usually contain statements like the following (CDC English Syllabus):

> The Curriculum Development Council, together with its subject committees, is widely representative of the local education community, with membership including heads and teachers from government and non-government schools, university and college of education lecturers, officers of the Advisory Inspectorate, and officers of other divisions of the Education Department (1983: 5).

Moreover, it is stated in the teaching syllabus for English Language (Hong Kong Curriculum Development Council) that:

> It must be recognised that for both these groups of students [students either proceed to Secondary Six for further studies or leave school or seek employment after Secondary Five], the Hong Kong Certificate of Education examination assumes critical importance. For almost all of them, the results they achieve in this examination will be the prime factor determining their future careers. It seems vital, then, that the teaching syllabus at this stage and the examination syllabus should be in step (1983: 12-13).

While the CDC focuses on teaching materials and methods and the HKEA runs the public examinations, the curriculum in practice continues to be defined by the publications of the latter body, particularly the public examination scripts and their accompanying marking schedules (Morris, 1990a: 19). The textbooks in use locally, too, generally reflect the examination syllabus in their format, emphasis, and approach (Fullilove, 1992: 134). Preparing students for the HKCEE is still regarded as the major teaching focus at the Secondary Four and Five levels in Hong Kong secondary schools. Given the importance of the HKCEE in Hong Kong secondary schools, it is natural that schools, teachers, and students all work towards a better pass rate in the HKCEE. Morris (1990a) points out that the influence of the public examination and its exam syllabus on teachers constrains the teaching approach used in Hong Kong secondary schools.

Following the 1989 publication of the *Education Commission Report No. 4*, the Target Oriented Curriculum (TOC) and relevant assessment initiatives have been planned and implemented initially in all primary schools, since 1995. The TOC was planned to be extended to secondary school education in the year 2001. The curriculum is to be target-based, and assessment practice is designed to determine whether or not the targets have been met.

The TOC was designed to set clear guidelines for learning in order to connect more closely with learning and its assessment, thereby promoting the individual progress of all primary and secondary school learners. This initiative was prepared by the CDC and issued by the Hong Kong Education Department in 1992. The philosophy behind the *Education Commission Report No. 4* was that students should be given the chance to demonstrate they can make use of certain learning strategies. The individual targets for some students may be different from the academic targets necessary for entry into tertiary education. Anyone who does not achieve that goal should not be labelled a failure. The Education Department wishes to ensure that all students are able to demonstrate that they are capable of achieving genuine learning targets and of mastering certain skills. These skills can be assessed and a report of the outcomes can be produced as evidence of learning at specified levels.

Under the TOC, levels of achievement are being set for Hong Kong students in Chinese, English, and Mathematics. They are described in the official handbook as learning targets that are designed for four key stages.[6] As a result of the concern over multiple-choice test formats in the Hong Kong educational context, the HKEA has determined that in the future, each subject area will require students to be assessed, partially, by questions that require a written response. This means that students will have to express themselves in continuous prose, create and organize ideas in text, and communicate with the examiner. This decision is expected to have implications for the teaching and learning of all subjects. The HKCEE in English, the focus of this study, is one of the attempts made by the HKEA to incorporate the principles of TOC and to bring about a positive washback effect on teaching and learning in schools.

In reality, major changes proposed in the Hong Kong curriculum context over the last ten years are expected by the Hong Kong Education Department to affect, in particular, the teaching and learning of Chinese, English, and Mathematics. However, these planned changes, especially those relating to pedagogy, in most cases have not been implemented in the classroom (c.f. Morris, 1990a, 1990b).

According to Morris (1990a: 5), three phases in Hong Kong curriculum development are commonly distinguished: Phase I – Initiation (or policy-making), Phase II – Implementation, and Phase III – Institutionalisation. Initiation and policy-making is most evident in the Hong Kong educational context. The activities and organizational structure of the two centralized agencies, the CDC and the HKEA, are mainly intended to identify and promote new or revised educational programmes. Both the structure and the official rhetoric of these organizations stress and portray a picture of local participation and problem solving in the production of the CDC teaching and HKEA examination syllabuses.

While the structure of the CDC reflects an attempt to encourage a 'problem solving' strategy, the reality is more akin to a 'power coercive' strategy such as official directives and requirements. Teaching approaches recommended by the CDC are sometimes viewed cynically by teachers, who tend to believe that those approaches would be wholly ineffective in enabling students to pass the public examination, which is controlled by the HKEA. The effective control of ED (the Education Department), and the HKEA officials over the processes of curriculum policy-making means that they are the main sources of 'expertise'.

The implementing processes involved are intricate because real changes, as distinct from verbal or 'changes on paper', are involved. Unfortunately,

---

6. In Hong Kong, the eleven-year programme is divided into four key stages in the CDC teaching syllabus; Stage One – Primary 1-3, Stage Two – Primary 4-6, Stage Three – Secondary 1-3, and Stage Four – Secondary 4-5.

resources in Hong Kong have mainly been directed to the initiation stage of curriculum development and have largely ignored what students and teachers do in the classroom. A lack of real change, especially in terms of methods in teaching and learning, cannot be explained solely in terms of the knowledge or skills of teachers, which might be true to some extent (Falvey, 1991b, 1996; Johnson, 1992, 1993/1994; Lord, 1987, and Morris, 1990a, 1990b, 1991, 1995). Teachers are willing to express agreement with the rhetoric around innovations, especially those relating to changes in teaching methods, but they generally do not, and are often unable to, implement the desired approach. The centralized nature of curriculum development in Hong Kong means that the government is in de facto control of both the nature and the variety of curriculum made available to students. Given that teachers often do not understand what the particular innovation requires in practice, or that they do not have the skills to implement it, the absence of any systematic attempt to provide in-service training or resources is surprising (Morris, 1990a).

Indeed, many secondary school teachers in Hong Kong have no subject training. Schools have few teaching resources, the curriculum is dominated by public examinations, and most classes have more than forty students. The fact that teachers were seen to have positive attitudes towards curriculum innovations in Hong Kong suggests that innovations are successfully implemented. Moreover, the main criteria for evaluating teachers' performance are the percentage of students who pass, and syllabus coverage. Teachers do not view examinations as a wholly alien phenomenon. They actually view them as a normal and natural part of their work, which give a purpose and a framework to the tasks of teaching and to the functioning of schools. As the primary function of education is one of selection in Hong Kong, changes are unlikely to occur unless teachers perceive them to be necessary for students to pass the public examination. In fact, in the course of a Hong Kong student's school career, he/she may go through as many as eight sets of examinations over and above diagnostic classroom assessments, all of which play a significant role in opening up or closing off future options for the student, not only in education but ultimately in life.

The teaching of English in Hong Kong secondary schools

Hong Kong is an international centre of trade, finance, and commerce with a population of over six million, 98% of whom are Chinese, with Cantonese as the predominant language. As such, English serves a unique and important role. Although English is used with varying degrees of proficiency among the Chinese population, ranging from native-like to minimal or non-existent, it has traditionally been the principal language of government, education, and business, as well as an important medium for communication, media, tourism, and the arts (Falvey, 1991a, 1991b; Harrison, 1990; Johnson, 1983; Richards, Tung, & Ng, 1992). English has therefore always played a crucial role within Hong Kong's education system.

English is taught as a subject in Hong Kong secondary schools for some eight periods[7] a week. The English curriculum has reflected general trends in language teaching over the years, with a movement away from a structural approach in the 1970s to a more communicative one in the 1980s. However, in practice, both students and teachers see the primary goal of English teaching at the secondary level as passing the public examinations, which are administered in the fifth and seventh forms. For the majority of students in Hong Kong, English is an important school subject (Richards et al 1991: 3; c.f. Falvey, 1991b).

It is specified in the Teaching Syllabus recommended by the CDC (Curriculum Development Council) that:

> the principal objective of the English language curriculum in the schools of Hong Kong is to provide every student with the opportunity to develop the maximum degree of functional competence in English, of which he or she is capable, given the constraints inherent in the situation, in particular competence in those domains of use which are especially appropriate to the Hong Kong situation (1983: 8).

The importance of English, however, is not uniform throughout a student's school career. Initially, from kindergarten to primary school, the significance of English is not so obvious, because all the other subjects are taught in Chinese, except for a comparatively small number of students in English-medium[8] primary schools. At the end of Primary Six, students are required to sit for the *Secondary School Entrance Examination* under *the Secondary School Places Allocation System (SSPA)*. The SSPA is the process by which primary students are allocated to secondary schools. This system requires students to sit for tests in English, Chinese, and Mathematics.

The SSPA consists of two parts: *Internal Assessment* and *the Academic Aptitude Test*. The Academic Aptitude Test consists of two multiple-choice papers, Verbal Reasoning and Numerical Reasoning. The Verbal Reasoning paper is in Chinese and the Numerical Reasoning has both Chinese and English versions. A Primary Six student's chance for allocation to a school of his/her (or parents') preference depends largely on his/her position in the order of merit. This order of merit is based on the internal school assessments at the end of Primary Five, both mid-year and at the end of Primary Six. The internal assessment is formed by standardizing all the students' marks for all subjects by means of a mathematical formula. To ensure that students will receive a

---

7. The duration of a period in Hong Kong secondary schools is usually from 35 minutes to 45 minutes.
8. Schools using English as a medium of instruction are called and categorized as Anglo-Chinese schools within the Hong Kong educational context.

balanced education, all subjects taught in the school are assessed, except Biblical Knowledge and Putonghua[9] in some schools.

From Secondary One to Seven, with the last two years spent preparing for tertiary education, most students study using English as the medium of instruction for nearly all subjects (except Chinese Language, Chinese Literature, and Chinese History). There is no public examination until students reach Secondary Five. However, at the end of Secondary Three, students will be put into either a Science or an Arts stream from Secondary One to Secondary Five depending on the results of their internal school assessment. Students will sit for the Hong Kong Certificate of Education Examination (HKCEE) at the end of Secondary Five. This examination plays a key role for students who either want to get a career-oriented job or continue with further study. The *Use of English* examination *(UE)* is for those students finishing their seventh year of secondary school education who are preparing for entrance into tertiary institutions.

The existing secondary school English syllabus was mainly a major revision of a syllabus published in 1975. It explicitly sets out to encourage, as it says, a 'more communicative, purposive type of approach', rather than a structural one. In actual teaching, the HKCEE examination syllabus plays the key role. The 1996 examination syllabus was revised in 1993 and had been in effect since the 1994 – 1995 academic year.

Looking at the teaching of English in Hong Kong secondary schools, a panel chair – subject head of English, is the first person to make decisions (with or without the school principal) about various aspects of teaching and learning. His/her responsibility involves designing the Scheme of Work,[10] choosing the major teaching materials, organizing subject meetings, arranging teachers to teach at certain grades, and assessing the quality of teaching in general. Some schools appoint form coordinators to be in charge of teaching English at different key stages. Teachers are also grouped to teach accordingly, e.g. at Forms 1-3, 4-5 or 6-7. In general, the more experienced teachers will be allocated to teach higher levels. Teachers teaching Form 4-5 (Secondary 4-5), which is key stage Four, usually have a bachelor's degree (in any subject).

Normally teaching is organized either on a weekly system or a cycle system in Hong Kong secondary schools. A weekly system arrangement is based on the usual five day calendar. A cycle, however, consists of a six day calendar, which provides one of the greatest challenges to conducting any school research within the Hong Kong educational context.

---

9. Putonghua, also known as Mandarin, refers to the official spoken and written language in the People's Republic of China.

10. A Scheme of Work is an overall teaching plan for the whole academic year in Hong Kong secondary schools. It provides teachers with a time framework of what is to be taught on a particular day within a weekly or cycle system. It is usually a joint work of the English panels and teachers involved. The Scheme of Work is designed on the basis of the main textbook contents.

Teachers of English in Hong Kong secondary schools

English teachers in secondary schools have different levels of training and experience. They may be (a) non-university graduates, but holders of a teaching certificate (mainly teaching at junior secondary grades), (b) university graduates, but not necessarily in English, with or without a teaching certificate (Richards et al, 1992). A common phenomenon is that returning graduates from overseas universities are hired to teach English even though they have had no formal study of the English language, Linguistics, or Literature at their respective universities. They are hired for the sole reason that they possess some skill in speaking English, the assumption being that if they can speak English, they can teach it (Boyle & Falvey, 1994; Falvey, 1996; King, 1994).

Richards et al (1992) pointed out that, although teachers generally have a high degree of professional commitment, they must contend with large classes (up to 40 students), a heavy teaching and administrative load (an average of 30 class periods per week) and limited availability of resources. Furthermore, their performance is likely to be assessed on the performance of their students in public examinations, not on the quality of their teaching. Due to the increased demand for English speaking graduates in the workplace, they are also recruited into the private sector by major companies. Fewer English graduates are entering the teaching profession. This shortage of qualified English teachers contributes to the current teaching situation in Hong Kong. Figures 1.2 and 1.3 below show the training and qualification context of English teachers in Hong Kong secondary schools.

Figure 1.2 Survey of all graduate and non-graduate secondary school teachers of English (Source: Coniam, Sengupta, Tsui, & Wu, 1994: 353)

All Secondary School Teachers of English in Hong Kong	
Number:	5240
Subject trained:	18.9%
Subject and professionally trained:	14.2%

Figure 1.3 Survey of all graduate teachers of English in Hong Kong secondary schools (from Coniam et al, 1994: 353)

University Graduate Teachers of English in Hong Kong	
Number:	3700
Subject trained:	27%
Subject and professionally trained:	14.2%

Due to the grave shortage of qualified teachers of English, Falvey (1996) points out that the majority of English teachers in Hong Kong are unprepared either for recent changes to the curriculum or for the pedagogical changes, which had occurred in the past.

Background of the study

Rationale behind the 1996 HKCEE English Language Syllabus

Assessment in Hong Kong is geared towards providing a basis to select students (Biggs, 1993), not only in the HKCEE (Hong Kong Certificate of Education Examination) at the end of Secondary Five and the HKAL (Hong Kong Advanced Level) at the end of Secondary Seven for tertiary selection, but also in primary schools, to provide the data for banding[11] in the Secondary School Places Allocation (SSPA) exercise. The Hong Kong educational system is characterized as 'an examination-led system, …where what goes on in the classroom is largely dictated by what happens in the public examination halls' (Fullilove, 1992: 135).

Given the traditional importance placed on public examination qualifications in the Hong Kong community, the Hong Kong Examinations Authority inevitably exerts a great influence on what happens in the senior classes of the secondary schools. The Authority's staff are very conscious of the notion that 'if it is not examined, it won't be taught' (Hong Kong Examinations Authority, 1994b: 80) and much thought is given to how the examination process can be used to bring about positive and constructive change to the system – commonly referred to as *positive washback*.

Washback is a term that can be found frequently in official education documents in Hong Kong (see the Education Department 1989, 1990; HKEA, 1992/93, 1993, 1994a, 1994b; Hong Kong Government, 1984, 1986, 1990). In Hong Kong, washback is expected whenever language examinations are introduced. Some examples of a positive washback effect from public examinations in Hong Kong are reported in the literature (see Andrews, 1994a, 1994b; Andrews & Fullilove, 1993, 1994; Fullilove, 1992; Johnson & Wong, 1981). Moreover, Morris (1990a) states that any change in the Hong Kong educational system must first involve a change in the examination. Many of the major innovations of recent years have been designed with the

---

11. Banding is based on the Secondary School Places Allocation (SSPA) in Hong Kong. The SSPA is the process by which primary students are allocated to secondary schools. The SSPA consists of school internal assessment at Primary Five and Primary Six scaled by the Academic Aptitude Test (AAT). The AAT covers verbal and numerical reasoning. The SSPA covers the whole of the primary curriculum. Band One schools have the best intake of students with Band Five the lowest. However, banding is not an absolute scale. The level of students is also related to the geographical location of the schools.

expectation that the examination changes will help classroom teachers to keep a better balance between teaching and skill-building on the one hand, and examination preparation on the other. However, what is still not clear is the nature and the scope of the washback effect of public examinations in Hong Kong.

This current study was designed to investigate the washback effect on the teaching of English in Hong Kong secondary schools from the revised 1996 Hong Kong Certificate of Education Examination in English. The revised examination syllabus was used for the first time in classroom teaching in September 1994 in Hong Kong secondary schools. The first cohort of students would sit for the revised examination in May 1996. The aim of the study was to observe how the whole education system reacted in the context of the change in this assessment, and to discover the implications of the washback effect on the teaching of English in Hong Kong secondary schools.

In 1993, the HKEA introduced major changes to its existing examination syllabus in English in accordance with the Target Oriented Curriculum (TOC) initiative in Hong Kong.

> The proposed changes of the 1996 HKCEE in English aim to modernise and improve the examination syllabus as well as to incorporate some TOC principles by adopting an integrated approach and by being more task-based. It is expected that the change will narrow the gap between what happens in the examination room and the real world (Hong Kong Examinations Authority, 1993, Appendix C1).

This attempt to 'narrow the gap' is reflected in the major changes to the old examination syllabus, whereby five examination papers were merged into four to form the revised version (see Table 1 (p. 6) for a comparison of the old and the new HKCEE).

The 1996 HKCEE English Language Syllabus

The overall aim of the examination is to assess candidates' achievement of the objectives of the Syllabus for English Language (Secondary) prepared by the Curriculum Development Council and recommended for use in schools by the Education Department. The proposed changes aim to modernize and improve the examination syllabus as well as to incorporate some principles of the Target Oriented Curriculum by adopting an integrated approach and by being more task-based. It is expected that the change will narrow the gap between what happens in the examination room and the real world.

The 1996 HKCEE (see Appendix IV for the actual exam paper) consists of four papers with major changes having been made to *Paper III* and *Paper IV*. *Paper III – Integrated Listening, Reading, and Writing* consists of *Part A:*

Short Tasks and *Part B: Extended Tasks*. In *Part A*, candidates are required to select from and make use of the information they hear and/or read in order to carry out a variety of short tasks. *Part B* requires students to process information by selecting and combining data from both spoken and written sources in order to complete various writing tasks (Hong Kong Examinations Authority, 1994a). *Paper IV – Oral English* underwent significant changes, from *Reading Aloud and Guided Conversation* in the old examination paper to a task-based *Role Play and Group Discussion* in the new exam. Both papers of the 1996 HKCEE require students to take an active role and participate fully in language interaction, and to carry out tasks by using different integrated language skills.

Paper I – Writing (weighting = 26%) remained basically unchanged from the previous examination except that candidates can now select from three topics, not four. The time provided to complete this section is the same – one hour and ten minutes. The weighting of this section changed slightly from 25% to 26%. A choice of questions is given, some of which may require more than one writing task. Questions will specify or imply context, reader, and purpose for writing. They will also require candidates to do one or more of the following:

• to express their own views, feelings, and ideas, imaginative and otherwise
• to describe and discuss their own experiences
• to respond to, reflect upon, evaluate, and make use of given information.

The text produced by the candidate should be appropriate to the context, purpose, and/or audience in terms of content, style, and use of English. For assessment purposes, equal weighting will be given to content and language. Content will be assessed in terms of the interest, relevance, organization, and appropriateness to the context. Language will be assessed in terms of the extent to which the candidate's style and use of sentence structure, vocabulary, spelling, and punctuation support or interfere with successful communication.

Paper II – Reading Comprehension and Usage (24%) includes, in addition to multiple-choice items, a variety of non-multiple-choice usage items. The time provided for this section changed from one hour to one hour and 30 minutes. The weighting changed from 20% to 24%. Candidates are required to respond to a variety of written texts and to demonstrate their abilities to:

• understand the overall meaning of a text as well as extract specific information from it
• recognize, interpret and make inferences from opinions, assumptions, intentions, attitudes and feelings, which occur explicitly or implicitly in a text
• use linguistic and contextual clues and general knowledge to determine meaning

- complete a text by supplying or selecting words or phases, which are semantically and syntactically appropriate to the overall meaning of the text
- modify a written draft so that the modified text makes sense and reflects a correct use of language
- make use of information provided in a variety of texts in order to produce or complete a different type of text, such as a text written for a different audience, with a different purpose or in a different style or format.

Since this paper is objective and wide-ranging, and tests both reading comprehension and usage, the criteria for assessment vary according to the items.

Paper III – Integrated Listening, Reading, and Writing (32%) has an integrated listening, reading, and writing component, as well as traditional task-based listening items. The new paper combines the original *Paper III – Listening* (approximately 45 minutes) 15% with *Paper V – Summary, Direct Writing, and Comprehension* (one hour and 30 minutes) 30%. The time allowed for the new paper is one hour and 30 minutes. It is weighted at 32% of the total examination, with *Part A (Short Tasks)* making up 10% and *Part B (Extended Tasks)* 22%.

Paper III consists of two tasks. In *Part A: Short Tasks*, candidates are required to select from and make use of information they hear and/or read in order to carry out a variety of short tasks. In *Part B: Extended Tasks*, candidates will be required to process information by selecting and combining data from both spoken and written sources in order to complete various writing tasks. At least one of these tasks will necessitate extended writing. All the information necessary to complete these tasks will be provided.

Assessment is based on how well candidates complete the tasks, taking into account the appropriateness of their language to the purpose and context, relevance, and organization where applicable. Language will be assessed in terms of the extent to which use of sentence structures, vocabulary, spelling, and punctuation supports or interferes with successful communication.

Paper IV – Oral (18%) is task-based and will consist of role-playing and group interaction. The original paper consisted of reading and dialogue, and conversation. The time provided changed from about five minutes in the original paper to 15 minutes in the new paper. The weighting increased from 10% to 18%.

Part A: Role Play – The candidate and the two examiners will take part in a role play. The candidate will be required to perform a task with each examiner based on the instructions and information, in a manner appropriate to the role. The candidate will be assessed on conversational strategies and overall fluency.

Part B: Group Interaction – Four candidates grouped together are presented with a situation and task, which they will work on together through discussion. The task will require candidates to express, elicit, and respond to ideas, opinions and feelings. They may also need to seek and give clarification, summarize their points, and redirect the discussion.

Candidates are assessed on their conversational strategies, overall fluency, and the contribution they make to the interaction. The emphasis is on effective communication rather than on task completion.

Figure 1.4 Chronological development of the 1996 HKCEE

September 25 1992	First meeting of the HKCEE English Language Subject Committee on the proposals for revising the CE English Language exam.
March 9 1993	Second meeting of the HKCEE English Language Subject Committee on the proposals for revising the CE English Language exam.
August 1993	1. Schools received the Proposed HKCEE English Language Syllabus (1996) for comments.
	2. Textbook publishers received the Proposed HKCEE English Language syllabus (1996) for textbook revision.
January 1994	Seminars and workshops started being organised by the HKEA for tertiary institutions and textbook publishers for the Proposed English Language Syllabus (1996).
September 1994	Schools:
	1. Received the official Syllabus Handbook for the revised HKCEE English Language Syllabus (1996).
	2. Adopted new textbooks[12] for the revised HKCEE English Language Syllabus (1996) for their Form 4 students.
	3. First cohort of students started being taught under the new 1996 HKCEE syllabus while the last cohort of F5 students was still being taught under the old syllabus.
Same teachers teaching both	{taught under the new HKCEE English Language syllabus (1996)} {taught under the old HKCEE English Language syllabus (1995)}
May 1996	First cohort of students takes the new HKCEE English Language Syllabus (1996)

12. At the start of the new academic year, schools whose students would take the 1996 HKCEE in English had all adopted new textbooks for at least their Form Four students. The situation varied for the lower forms. Some of the schools changed to new textbooks from Form One – Form Four, some only with Form Four. However, there was one cohort of Form Five students in 1995, who were required to take the old version of the HKCEE.

Research time framework

This was a longitudinal study consisting of three different phases that were conducted between January 1994 and November 1996. Time played a significant role in this study. During the research into the washback effect on secondary school English teaching with reference to the 1996 Hong Kong Certificate Examination in English Language examination syllabus, there were two different cohorts of Form Five students studying English with the *same* teaching syllabus. This syllabus for English (used for Forms 1-5) was prepared by the CDC (Curriculum Development Committee) in 1982. However, these two cohorts of students were required to take different HKCEE examinations at the end of their Form Five. Therefore, even though they were subject to the same teaching syllabus, the fact that they were required to take different examinations meant that they would be taught differently in order to meet the requirements of the two different examinations. One group was the last to take the old HKCEE examination in 1995, the other the first to take the new revised HKCEE examination in 1996. This provides the basis of the research context. The research schedule is outlined in Figure 1.4.

Research questions

Based on the chronological framework outlined in Figure 1.4, the washback effect of this public examination change was observed initially at the macro level (i.e. major parties or participants within the Hong Kong educational context), and then at the micro level in schools (regarding different aspects of classroom teaching and learning). It is important to emphasize here that both teaching and learning were studied in this project as both of these constructs occur interactively in the classroom. Therefore, both teachers and students were included in the study. However, aspects of learning and learners were studied only when they related to classroom teaching.

This study explored the following research questions–operational definitions of the research questions are discussed in Chapter Three together with the research design.

- what strategies did the HKEA use to implement the examination change?
- what was the nature and scope of the washback effect on teachers' and students' perceptions of various aspects of teaching towards the new examination?
- what was the nature and scope of the washback effect on teachers' behaviours as a result of the new examination?

Overview of research methodology

To answer the above research questions, a combined research framework for this study was employed (Erickson, 1986; Erickson & Shultz, 1981; Miles, 1979; Miles & Huberman, 1994). First, the study stressed the importance of context, setting, and subjects' frames of reference (Marshall & Rossman, 1989). Second, the study emphasized the importance of multiple perspectives of the research problem as well as the characteristics of policy-makers, textbook publishers, teachers, and students. Third, the study highlighted the research strategy–watching and asking (Allwright & Bailey, 1991; Chaudron, 1988; van Lier, 1988)–using both quantitative and qualitative methods. The following figure presents an overview of the research methodology in relation to the book.

Figure 1.5 Overview of the research methodology

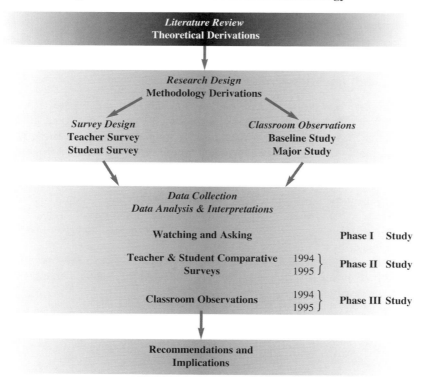

Significance of the study

This was the first large-scale empirical study of washback in Hong Kong. It was one of the few washback studies that has employed both quantitative and qualitative data. This research provided solid research evidence of the washback effect of public examinations on aspects of teaching and learning, and on the Hong Kong educational system as a whole. It identified the general characteristics of a system of testing in Hong Kong that contributes to or distracts from the systematic validity of an assessment. It explored the general life cycle of the effect of washback within the Hong Kong educational context. Although this investigation provided hard data and evidence of the washback effect in a specific educational context, it should also contribute to the general understanding of washback in education. It further offered some insights into English language teaching and learning in Hong Kong secondary schools. 'To judge the value of an outcome or end, one should understand the nature of the processes or means that led to that end. It is not just that means are appraised in terms of the ends they lead to, but ends are appraised in terms of the means that produce them' (Haladyna, Nolen, & Haas, 1991: 6).

If an examination is to have the impact intended, educators and measurement specialists need to consider a range of factors that affect how the change succeeds or fails and how it influences teachers' and students' attitudes and behaviours. Alderson and Wall (1993) have pointed out that language testers should pay more attention to the washback effect of their tests, but they should also guard against oversimplified beliefs that 'good' tests will automatically have a 'good' impact, which is the belief of the Hong Kong Examinations Authority, and probably the general public.

2 Literature review

Introduction

This chapter focuses on the theoretical underpinnings that shaped and guided this research. It consists of four interrelated parts, which substantiate the theoretical framework of the study. The first part explores the concept of washback by tracing its origin and discussing various terms that have been used to describe this educational phenomenon. It will then illustrate the function of washback in order to explore the meaning and the mechanism of washback in the study. The second part begins by exploring foundations of the beliefs of teaching and learning on which language testing is based. It will then discuss the impact of testing by reporting relevant research studies that have been carried out both in general and in language education. This part explores why and how washback influences aspects of teaching and learning within the educational system. The third part closely explores the phenomenon of washback under different educational contexts, especially within the Hong Kong educational context in which this study is situated. This section puts washback under the microscope and into specific regional educational contexts. The fourth part of this chapter reviews current models of teaching and learning research in the context of the theoretical and practical considerations of washback discussed in the first three parts.

Exploring the research concept

This part consists of three sections: the origin of washback, the definition and scope of washback, and how washback functions in practice. This part aims to construct a concept of washback from the general educational perspective and language education in particular.

The origin of washback

Washback (Alderson & Wall, 1993), together with other similar related terms such as *backwash* (Biggs, 1995, 1996), *test impact* (Bachman & Palmer, 1996; Baker, 1991), *systemic validity* (Fredericksen & Collins, 1989), *consequential validity* (Messick, 1989, 1996*), measurement-driven instruction* (Popham, 1983, 1987), *curriculum alignment* (Shepard, 1990, 1991, 1992 & 1993), and possibly other terms, all refer to different facets of the same phenomenon. The concept and study of washback has also been derived from recent developments in language testing and measurement-driven reform in the areas of general educational assessment.

Advances in language testing, especially in the past decade, can be seen through (a) the development of a theoretical view that considers language ability to be multi-componential and recognizes the influence that testing method and test taker characteristics have on test performance, and (b) the applications of more sophisticated measurement and statistical tools, and the development of 'communicative' language tests that incorporate principles of communicative language teaching (Bachman, 1990, 1991; Bachman & Palmer, 1996). One of the major preoccupations of language testers in the past decade has been investigating the nature of language proficiency in the light of 'the unitary competence hypothesis' (Oller, 1979).

Research in language testing has centred on questions about whether or not and how we assess the specific characteristics of a given group of test takers and whether and how we should incorporate these characteristics into the design of language tests. Perhaps the singlemost important theoretical development in language testing since the 1980s was the realization that a language test score represents a complexity of multiple influences. Language test scores cannot be interpreted simplistically as an indicator of the particular language ability to be measured. They are also affected by the characteristics and content of the test tasks, the characteristics of the test taker, the strategies the test taker employs in attempting to complete the test task, and the inferences we wish to draw from them. What makes the interpretation of test scores particularly difficult is that these factors undoubtedly interact with each other.

Language tests are used for a variety of purposes, including:

- making inferences or predictions about test takers' language abilities or to make predictions about their capacity for using language to perform further tasks in contexts outside the test itself
- making decisions (e.g. selection, diagnosis, placement, progress, grading certification, employment) about test takers on the basis of their test scores, which can inform the decision-makers about their ability or their capacity for language use in non-test situations.

Alderson (1986) pointed out an additional area to which language testing research needed to turn its attention in years to come–the washback effect. Alderson (1986: 104) discussed the 'potentially powerful influence offsets,' and argued for innovations in the language curriculum through innovations in language testing. Washback is often introduced in language testing courses for teachers as a powerful concept that all test designers need to strongly consider, and of which most classroom teachers are all too aware. Davies (1985) asks whether tests should necessarily follow the curriculum, and suggests that perhaps tests ought to lead and influence curriculum. Morrow (1986: 6) further used the term 'washback validity' to describe the quality of the relationship between testing and teaching and learning. He claimed that '...in essence an examination of washback validity would take testing researchers into the classroom in order to observe the effect of their tests in action.'

Messick (1989, 1992, 1994, 1996) has placed the washback effect within a broader concept of construct validity (consequential validity). Messick claims that construct validity encompasses aspects of test use, the impact of tests on test takers and teachers, the interpretation of scores by decision makers, and the misuses, abuses, and unintended uses of tests. Washback is an inherent quality of any kind of assessment, especially when people's futures are affected by the examination results, regardless of the quality of the examination (Eckstein & Noah, 1992, 1993a, 1993b). Whether the washback effect is negative or positive could be dependent on what the examination measures. If an examination is congruent with the sentiment and the purposes of the course objectives, beneficial washback can be achieved; if not, negative washback effects are bound to happen.

In short, washback is an educational phenomenon derived from research studies into (a) the relationship between teaching, learning, and testing and into the relationship between different curriculum components, and (b) into the relationship of curriculum change and innovation. These two areas are highly related to the current study.

The influence of testing on teaching and learning (*washback* or *backwash*) is rooted in the notion that tests should drive teaching and hence learning (measurement-driven instruction). In order to achieve this goal, a 'match' or an overlap is encouraged (curriculum alignment) between the content and format of the test and the content and format of the curriculum (e.g. curriculum surrogate such as the textbook). The closer the fit or match between test content and curriculum, the greater the potential improvement on the test. However, the idea of curriculum alignment has been declared unethical (see Dalton, 1988; Haladyna et al, 1991: 4). Such an alignment is particularly evident in the Hong Kong context (especially in terms of the textbooks), where new or revised examinations are introduced into the education system to improve teaching and learning (systemic validity).

The new 1996 HKCEE of the current study was designed with the intention of using the function of this public examination to influence and guide teaching and learning of English in Hong Kong secondary schools.

The definition and scope of washback

Washback is a term commonly used in language testing, yet it is rarely found in dictionaries. However, the word *backwash* can be found in certain dictionaries and is defined as 'the unwelcome repercussions of some social action' by the *New Webster's Comprehensive Dictionary of the English Language*, and 'unpleasant after-effects of an event or situation' by *Collin's Cobuild Dictionary of English Language*.

Washback, commonly used in the field of applied linguistics, refers to 'the impact of a test on teaching' (Wall & Alderson, 1993: 41; c.f. Alderson & Wall, 1993: 117). It refers to the extent to which a test influences language teachers and learners to do things 'they would not necessarily otherwise do because of the test' (Alderson & Wall, 1993: 117). Messick (1996: 241) points out that 'washback, a concept prominent in applied linguistics, refers to the extent to which the introduction and the use of a test influences language teachers and learners to do things they would not otherwise do that promote or inhibit language learning.' He continues to comment that 'some proponents have even maintained that a test's validity should be appraised by the degree to which it manifests positive or negative washback,' a notion akin to the proposal of 'system validity' (Frederiksen & Collins, 1989) in the educational measurement literature. Shohamy notes (1992: 513) that 'this phenomenon is the result of the strong authority of external testing and the major impact it has on the lives of test takers.'

Biggs (1995: 12) uses the term 'backwash' to refer to the fact that testing drives not only the curriculum, but teaching methods and students' approaches to learning (Crooks, 1988; Frederiksen, 1984; Frederiksen & Collins, 1989). However, after quoting definitions of the term *backwash* from the *Collin's Cobuild Dictionary of English Language*, Spolsky (1994: 55) commented that 'backwash is better applied only to accidental side-effects of examinations, and not to those effects intended when the first purpose of the examination is control of the curriculum.' According to Alderson and Wall (1993: 115), the notion that testing influences teaching is referred to as 'backwash' in general educational circles, but it has come to be known as 'washback' among British applied linguists, though they see no reason, semantic or pragmatic, for preferring either term.

Pearson (1988: 98) points out that 'public examinations influence the attitudes, behaviours, and motivation of teachers, learners and parents, and because examinations often come at the end of a course, this influence is seen working in a backward direction, hence the term 'washback.' He further emphasizes that the direction in which washback actually works must be forwards in time. Alderson and Wall (1993) also emphasize the fact that evidence of washback is typically demonstrated in behavioural and attitudinal changes in teachers and learners that are associated with the introduction of tests bearing important educational consequences. This is precisely the context of the current study as mentioned in Chapter One, where a major public examination change–the new 1996 HKCEE–is introduced with the aim of bringing about a positive washback effect on the behaviour and attitudes of teachers and learners (see HKEA, 1993, 1994a, 1994b).

Messick (1996: 241) mentioned that 'for optimal positive washback, there should be little, if any, difference between activities involved in learning the language and activities involved in preparing for the test.' However, 'such forms of evidence are only circumstantial with respect to test validity in that a poor test may be associated with positive effects and a good test with negative effects because of other things that are done or not done in the education system' (Messick 1996: 242). Furthermore, Alderson and Wall (1993: 116) argue that 'washback, if it exists–which has yet to be established–is likely to be a complex phenomenon which cannot be related directly to a test's validity.' The washback effect should refer to the effect of the test itself on aspects of teaching and learning. Besides, other operating forces within the education context also contribute to or ensure that the washback effect takes its place on teaching and learning.

Bailey (1996: 259) summarized, after considering several definitions of washback, that washback is defined as the influence of testing on teaching and learning, that it is widely held to exist and to be important, but relatively little empirical research has been done to document its exact nature or the mechanisms by which it works. Bailey commented further that there were also concerns about what constituted both positive and negative washback, as well as about how to promote the former and inhibit the latter.

Washback defined in this study

The term 'washback' is preferred by the researcher to indicate an intended direction and function of curriculum change on aspects of teaching and learning by means of a change of public examinations. However, it is important to point out that even when washback is used in this study to describe an intended curriculum change by means of public examination change, unintended and accidental side effects can also occur, because successful curriculum change and development is a highly complex matter. Unintended and accidental side effects are defined as 'backwash' by Spolsky (1994: 55) and as 'negative washback' by Alderson and Wall (1993: 115). The researcher has, however, retained the use of 'washback' or 'backwash' in the book in its original form when quoting directly from the authors.

It was clearly evident from this study that the introduction of the new 1996 HKCEE examination (Hong Kong Examinations Authority, 1994: 5) was a top-down attempt to elicit positive washback effects on the teaching and learning of English in Hong Kong secondary schools. It is an attempt by the Hong Kong Examinations Authority to make use of the washback effect to bring about changes in teaching and learning, though the specific areas of washback are not clearly defined, either in the Hong Kong Examinations Authority's documents or in the HKEA Subject Committee agenda.

Negative washback

Language tests are often criticized for their negative influence on teaching–so-called 'negative washback' (see Alderson & Wall, 1993: 115). Vernon (1956: 166) commented that teachers tend to ignore subjects and activities that do not directly contribute to passing the exam, and claimed that examinations 'distort the curriculum.' Davies (1968a: 125, 1968b), for example, indicates that 'all too often the washback effect has been bad; designed as testing devices, examinations have become teaching devices; work is directed to what are in effect–if not in fact–past examination papers and consequently becomes narrow and uninspired.' Alderson & Wall (1993: 5) refer to 'negative washback' as the negative or undesirable effect on teaching and learning of a particular (and, by inference, if not direct statement, poor) test. In this case, 'poor' usually means something that the teacher or learner does not wish to teach or learn. The tests may well fail to reflect the learning principles and/or the course objectives to which they are supposedly related.

Fish (1988) discovered that teachers reacted negatively to pressure created by public displays of classroom scores, and also found that relatively inexperienced teachers felt greater anxiety and accountability pressure than did experienced teachers. Noble and Smith (1994a: 3) also pointed out that high-stakes testing affected teachers directly and negatively, and that 'teaching test-taking skills and drilling on multiple-choice worksheets is likely to boost the scores but unlikely to promote general understanding' (1994b: 6). Smith (1991b: 8) concluded from an extensive qualitative study of the role of external testing in elementary schools that 'testing programs substantially reduce the time available for instruction, narrow curricular offerings and modes of instruction, and potentially reduce the capacities of teachers to teach content and to use methods and materials that are incompatible with standardized testing formats.'

Positive washback

Some researchers, on the other hand, strongly believe that it is feasible and desirable to bring about beneficial change in language teaching by changing examinations, which refers to so-called 'positive washback.' This term refers to tests and examinations that influence teaching and learning beneficially (c.f. Alderson & Wall, 1993: 115). In this sense, teachers and learners have a positive attitude towards the test and work willingly towards its objectives. Pearson (1988: 107) argued, 'good tests will be more or less directly usable as teaching-learning activities. Similarly, good teaching-learning tasks will be more or less directly usable for testing purposes, even though practical or financial constraints limit the possibilities.'

Davies maintains the view that a good test should be 'an obedient servant of teaching; and this is especially true in the case of achievement testing.' He further argues that 'creative and innovative testing...can, quite successfully, attract to itself a syllabus change or a new syllabus which effectively makes it into an achievement test' (1985: 8). To Davies, the test no longer needs to be only an obedient servant; rather, it can also be a leader. Consequently, Pearson looks at the washback effect of a test from the point of view of its potential negative and positive influences on teaching. To him, a test's washback effect will be negative if it fails to reflect the learning principles and/or course objectives to which it supposedly relates, and it will be positive if the effects are beneficial and 'encourage the whole range of desired changes' (1988: 101).

However, there are rather conflicting reactions towards washback on teaching and learning. In Wiseman (1961: 159), the term washback was used to 'describe the deleterious effects of examinations.' He described paid coaching classes which were intended for preparing students for exams, and argued that those coaching classes were not a good use of time because the students were practising exam techniques rather than language learning activities. However, Heyneman (1987: 262) commented that many proponents of academic achievement testing view 'coachability' not as a drawback, but rather as a virtue.

Furthermore, Alderson and Wall (1993: 117 – 118) stressed that the quality of the washback effect might be independent of the quality of a test. Any test, good or bad, can be said to have beneficial or detrimental washback. Whatever changes educators would like to bring about in teaching and learning by a particular assessment method, it is worthwhile to first explore the broad educational context in which an assessment is introduced. Alderson and Wall (1993) pointed out that:

> It is surely conceivable that other forces exist within society, education, and schools that might prevent washback from appearing, or that might affect the nature of washback despite the 'communicative' quality of a test (1993: 116).

Therefore, it would be worthwhile investigating, first, the nature of an examination and/or assessment in teaching and learning, and then the nature of the washback effect and the conditions under which it operates, keeping in mind the importance of the context in which it might take place in order to understand how washback functions in practice.

Heyneman (1987: 262) concluded that 'testing is a profession, but it is highly susceptible to political interference. To a large extent, the quality of tests relies on the ability of a test agency to pursue professional ends autonomously.' If the consequences of a particular test for teaching and learning are to be evaluated, the educational context in which the test takes place needs to be investigated. Whether the washback effect is positive or negative will largely depend on how it works and within which educational contexts it is situated.

The function of washback

Traditionally, tests come at the end of the teaching and learning process for evaluative purposes. However, with the advent of current high-stake public examination systems nowadays, the direction seems to be reversed. Testing comes first before the teaching and learning process in order to influence the process. This section looks at the mechanism of such a phenomenon in relation to other educational theories and practices.

Where examinations are commonly used as levers for change, new textbooks will likely be designed to match the purposes of a new test, and school administrative staff, teachers, and students will all strive to achieve good scores on tests. In addition, many more changes in teaching and learning can happen as a result of a particular new test. Often such consequences are independent of the original intentions of the test designers. Shohamy (1993: 2) pointed out that 'the need to include aspects of test use in construct validation originates in the fact that testing is not an isolated event; rather, it is connected to a whole set of variables that interact in the educational process.'

Moreover, Messick (1989) also recommended a unified validity concept, in which he shows that when an assessment model is designed to make inferences about a certain construct, the inferences drawn from that assessment model should not only derive from test score interpretation but also from other variables in the social context (see also Cooley, 1991; Cronbach, 1988; Linn, Baker, & Dunbar, 1991; Messick, 1992; Gardner, 1992; Gifford & O' Connor, 1992). As early as 1975, Messick (1975: 6) pointed out that 'researchers, other educators, and policy makers must work together to develop means of evaluating educational effectiveness that accurately represent a school or district's progress towards a broad range of important educational goals.' In this context, Linn (1992: 29) stated that it is incumbent upon the measurement research community to make the case that the introduction of any new high-stakes examination system should include more provisions for paying greater attention to investigations of both the intended and unintended consequences of the system than has been typical of previous test-based reform efforts.

Bailey (1996: 262-264) cites Hughes' (1993) trichotomy to illustrate the mechanisms by which washback works in actual teaching and learning contexts. According to Hughes, there are three aspects of 'backwash' that should be clarified.

Hughes (1993: 2) further notes:

> The trichotomy into participants, process and product allows us to construct a basic model of backwash. The nature of a test may first affect the perceptions and attitudes of the participants towards their teaching and learning tasks. These perceptions and attitudes in turn may affect what the participants do in carrying out their work (process), including practising the kind of items that are to be found in the test, which will affect the learning outcomes, the product of the work.

Table 2 The trichotomy of backwash model
(Source: Hughes, 1993: 2)

1. Participants – students, classroom teachers, administrators, and materials developers and publishers whose perceptions and attitudes towards their work may be affected by a test.
2. Process – any actions taken by the participants which may contribute to the process of learning.
3. Product – what is learned and the quality of the learning.

While Hughes focused on participants, processes, and products in his backwash model, Smith (1991a), in a discussion of examples of planned change, tried to construct a model showing five components of change: the target system, the management system (consisting of both the members of the system and the structures within the system), the innovation itself, available resources, and the environment in which the change is supposed to take place. Markee (1997) illustrated through his study of curricular innovation how change may be designed, implemented, and maintained. He employed the following model: who (participants) adopts (process) what (the innovation), where (the context), when (the time duration), why (the rationale), and how (different approaches in managing innovation). These models try to illustrate the mechanism of washback as a phenomenon of change in teaching and learning, and serve as guides for the current study of the washback effect, particularly, Hughes' (1993) and Markee's (1997) models.

On the other hand, Alderson and Wall (1993), in their Sri Lankan study, focused on aspects of teaching and learning that might be influenced by examinations. They came up with 15 hypotheses regarding washback (1993:

120-21), outlined below, to illustrate areas in teaching and learning that were usually affected by washback. In addition, the current researcher has also developed the notion of *washback intensity* to refer to the degree of the washback effect in an area, or in a number of areas of teaching and learning affected by examinations. These areas in teaching and learning were studied in the research in order to chart and understand the function of washback–the participants, the process, as well as the products of the washback effect that might be brought about due to the change of a major public examination.

- a test will influence teaching
- a test will influence learning
- a test will influence what teachers teach; and
- a test will influence how teachers teach
- a test will influence what learners learn
- a test will influence how learners learn
- a test will influence the rate and sequence of teaching; and
- a test will influence the rate and sequence of learning
- a test will influence the degree and depth of teaching
- a test will influence the degree and depth of learning
- a test will influence attitude towards the content, method, etc., of teaching and learning
- tests that have important consequences will have washback; conversely,
- tests that do not have important consequences will have no washback
- tests will have washback on all learners and teachers
- tests will have washback effects for some learners and some teachers, but not for others.

Alderson and Wall concluded that further research on washback is needed, and that such research must entail 'increasing specification of the Washback Hypothesis' above (1993: 127). They called on researchers to take account of findings in the research literature in at least two areas: (a) motivation and performance, and (b) innovation and change in the educational settings.

Wall (1996: 334), following up their above study, stressed the difficulties in finding explanations of *how* tests exert influence on teaching. She took from the innovation literature and added into her research (Wall et al 1996) areas such as (a) the writing of detailed baseline studies to identify important characteristics in the target system and the environment, including an analysis of current testing practices (see also Shohamy, Donitsa-Schmidt, & Ferman, 1996), current teaching practices, resources (Bailey, 1996; Stevenson & Riewe, 1981), and attitudes of key stakeholders (Bailey, 1996; Hughes, 1993), and (b) the formation of management teams representing all important interest groups: teachers, teacher trainers, university specialists, and ministry officials (see Cheng, 1997, and also Figure 2.1, in which key stakeholders are referred to as participants).

Fullan (1991, 1993), also in the context of curriculum innovations, discussed changes in schools and came up with two major themes:

- innovation should be seen as a process rather than as an event (p. 47)
- all the participants who are affected by an innovation have to find their own meaning for the change (p. 30).

He explained that the subjective reality that teachers experience would always contrast with the objective reality that the proponents of change originally imagined. Teachers work on their own, with little reference to experts or consultation with colleagues. They are forced to make on-the-spot decisions, with little time to reflect on better solutions. They are pressured to accomplish a great deal, but are given far too little time to achieve their goals. When, on top of this, they are expected to carry forward an innovation that someone else has come up with, their lives can become very difficult indeed (c.f. Huberman & Miles, 1984). Besides, it is also found that there tends to be discrepancies between the intention of any innovation or curriculum change and the understanding of teachers (Andrews & Fullilove, 1994; Markee 1997), which can decide the success of any reform or innovation.

Andrews (1994a, 1994b) highlighted the reality of the relationship between washback and curriculum innovation, and summarized three choices by which educators might deal with washback: they can fight it, ignore it, or use it (c.f. Heyneman, 1987: 260). By fighting it, Heyneman refers to the effort to replace examinations by other sorts of selection criteria on the grounds that examinations have encouraged rote memorization at the expense of more desirable educational practices. Andrews (1994b: 51-52) used the metaphor of an ostrich for those who ignore it. 'Those who are involved with mainstream activities, such as syllabus design, material writing, and teacher training view testers as a 'special breed' using an arcane terminology. Tests and exams have been seen as an occasional necessary evil, a dose of unpleasant medicine, the taste of which should be washed away as quickly as possible.' By using washback, the purpose is to promote pedagogical ends, which is not a new idea in education (see also Andrews & Fullilove, 1993, 1994; Blenkin, Edwards & Kelly, 1992; Brooke & Oxenham, 1984; Pearson, 1988; Somerset, 1983; Swain, 1984). This is the situation in the Hong Kong context.

In the discussion of the impact of examinations upon curriculum and innovation in Hong Kong English language teaching, Andrews (1994b) argued that:

> There does seem to be a phenomenon to which one could attach the label washback as well. As a tool to engineer curriculum innovation, however, washback seems to be a very blunt instrument, one which may have relatively predictable quantitative effects on, for example, the time allocated to different aspects of teaching and on the content of that teaching, but rather less predictable qualitative effects upon the teaching-learning process and what actually takes place in classrooms (79).

In this section, the washback research concept, the origin of washback, the definition and scope of washback, and the function of washback have been discussed. Washback, as the phenomenon is used in language testing, exemplifies the intricate relationship between testing and teaching and learning. It also illustrates the tremendous impact and power of testing on teaching and learning in schools. However, whether the impact of testing on teaching and learning is positive or negative is still debatable and needs to be studied further. Discussions in this section have focused on a number of studies on searching for the meaning and mechanism of the function of washback, such as Messick's (1975, 1989, 1996) consequential validity, Alderson and Wall's (1993) 15 washback hypotheses, Hughes' trichotomy (1993), Wall (1996), Andrews (1994b), and Markee's (1997) curricular innovation insights into washback in language education.

The above studies and all the other studies mentioned in this section help to determine the nature of washback and how washback works in education. Together, they form the central issues that are explored in the current study. Drawing on the above research, this study aims to explore how different levels of people or stakeholders within the Hong Kong educational system reacted when washback was strategically anticipated to determine possible areas of washback intensity in teaching and learning in Hong Kong secondary schools, and to define the interrelationship between who changes what, how, when, where, and why (c.f. Markee, 1997: 42-47).

Exploring the research phenomenon

This section consists of three interconnected parts: measurement-driven instruction, examinations as means of control, and the influence of high-stakes testing. It explores how and why washback could work to influence other components within the educational system, trace the rationale behind the use of public examination, and its powerful function to change teaching and learning.

Measurement-driven instruction

As early as 1877, Latham (1877: 1) characterized examinations as an 'encroaching power' that was influencing education, blurring distinctions between liberal and technical education, and narrowing the range of learning through forcing students to prepare by studying with crammers and in cramming schools. It has been asserted that this encroaching power also permitted any external body–a university or a government agency–to exert control over the internal operations of educational systems that were becoming increasingly complex (Spolsky, 1994: 58).

Popham (1987) also outlined the traditional notion of measurement-driven instruction to illustrate the relationship between instruction and assessment. Popham suggested that assessment directs teachers' attention to the content of test items, acting as powerful 'curricular magnets.' In high-stakes environments, in which the results of mandated tests trigger rewards, sanctions, or public scrutiny and loss of professional status, teachers will be motivated to pursue the objectives that the test embodies. According to Noble and Smith (1994b: 1), 'the most pervasive tool of top-down policy reform is to mandate assessment that can serve as both guideposts and accountability.' Noble and Smith also pointed out that the goal of current measurement-driven reform in assessment is to build a better test that will drive schools towards more ambitious goals. This in turn will reform them towards a curriculum and pedagogy geared more towards thinking and less towards rote memory and isolated skills–the shift from behaviourism to cognitive-constructivism in teaching and learning beliefs.

Beliefs about testing reflect beliefs about teaching and learning. 'Whatever the objectives cover, tests can be written to measure them, can be administered to all, and re-administered as necessary to those who fail' (Noble & Smith, 1994b: 2).

The traditional teaching and learning views, from which views of traditional testing are derived, are grounded in behaviourist psychology and pedagogy. According to this view, the desired performance of pupils is brought about by reinforcing successive approximations of correct performance. Academic tasks are broken down into discrete units and presented to the pupils. Rewards and progress through an ordered hierarchy of tasks and skills are contingent on correct performance. Inadequate responses result in repetition and repeating through the same material until it is mastered, with instruction in 'higher order' skills resting on a foundation of 'basic skills.' In the behaviourist model, the pupil is considered a passive recipient of knowledge. The intentions of learners are generally ignored.

However, according to the more recent psychological and pedagogical views of learning, labelled 'cognitive-constructivism', three interrelated dimensions are emphasized.

> 1. *Learning is viewed as a process of construction.* In this view, learning is not an act of recording discrete pieces of information, each piece independent of the others and needing only to be repeated until it is mastered. It is a process of interpretation and construction of meaning (Glaser & Bassok, 1989). Students are active participants in their learning, constructors of knowledge, not passive recipients of information and skills (Piaget, 1973).

> 2. *Learning is knowledge-dependent.* It is not merely an act of receiving information but one of interpreting information through earlier learning.

The role of prior knowledge and experience is given special attention, for what a pupil learns on a given occasion is dependent on what has been already learned. It is much easier for individuals to learn more about their areas of expertise than it is for them to learn about other topics outside their experiences.

3. *Learning is situated in a context* (Biggs, 1992, 1993, 1995; Resnick, 1989; Resnick & Resnick, 1992). Knowledge is not independent of the context in which it develops. Learning not only occurs in a context but is also social. Learning cannot be separated from the context in which it occurs (Gergen, 1985).

The above perspective proposes that effective instruction must mesh with how students think. The direct instruction model under the influence of the behaviourist 'tell-show-do' approach does not match how students learn, nor does it take into account students' intentions, interests, and choices. Teaching that reflects the cognitive-constructivist view of learning is likely to be holistic, integrated, project-oriented, long-term, discovery-based, and social. Thus cognitive-constructivists see performance assessment or testing as parallel to the above belief of how students learn and how they should be taught. Performance assessment based on the constructivist model of learning is defined by Gipps (1994: 99) as 'a systematic attempt to measure a learner's ability to use previously acquired knowledge in solving novel problems or completing specific tasks. In performance assessment, real life or simulated assessment exercises are used to elicit original responses, which are directly observed and rated by a qualified judge.' The new 1996 HKCEE under the current study, drawing upon the above theory, employs a task-based and integrated approach to assess students.

Furthermore, proponents of performance assessment believe that what is assessed is what gets taught. Following this belief, Resnick and Resnick (1992: 59) stated that, 1) 'You get what you assess. 2) You do not get what you do not assess. 3) You should build assessments towards how you want educators to teach'. High-stakes testing could drive reform if it followed better psychology and pedagogy and employed more appropriate measurement forms, namely the above performance assessments. If tests affect curriculum and instruction, the argument goes, performance assessment could serve as an impetus for a thinking-oriented curriculum[1] geared towards developing higher order abilities and problem-solving skills (Honig, 1987; Resnick & Resnick, 1992; Wiggins, 1989a, 1989b, 1993).

---

1. 'The thinking curriculum calls for recognition that all real learning involves thinking, that thinking ability can be nurtured and cultivated in everyone, and that the entire educational program must be re-conceived and re-vitalised so that thinking pervades students' lives beginning in kindergarten' (Resnick and Resnick, 1992: 40).

In addition, an important assumption of high-stakes testing (or public examinations), as mentioned above, is that deleterious effects associated with previous efforts for test-based accountability can be overcome by switching to performance-based assessments closely linked to curriculum frameworks. It is argued that instruction directed towards preparation for a performance-based assessment promotes better instructional practice (Aschbacher, 1990; Aschbacher, Baker, & Herman, 1988; Baker, Aschbacher, Niemi, & Sato, 1992). They argued that a better test would produce better results. Performance-based assessment can be designed to be so closely linked to the goals of instruction as to be almost indistinguishable from them. Rather than being a negative consequence, as it is now with some high-stakes uses of existing standardized tests, 'teaching to these proposed performance assessments, accepted by scholars as inevitable and by teachers as necessary, becomes a virtue, according to this line of thinking' (Noble & Smith, 1994b: 7). The rationale also lay in the belief that measurement-driven instruction was initiated due to public discontent with the quality of schooling (Popham, Cruse, Rankin, Standifer, & Williams, 1985: 629).

The current study is situated along the above line of discussion of using 'better' (task-based and integrated) assessment to bring about 'better' teaching and learning (more real-life activities and more active learning). It is also based on interviews with key informants from the HKEA and other officials within the Hong Kong educational context. The rationale and intention to bring about a positive washback effect on teaching by means of a major public examination change that adopts a more task-based and integrated approach is evident from information provided by the policy-making agencies. It aimed to find out how the efforts to change this public examination into a more constructive assessment tool, or a more appropriate assessment (Biggs, 1995), would actually have the effect of changing teaching towards a more constructive approach in the Hong Kong secondary schools.

The HKEA has a strong belief in the statement, 'We believe in washback!' and 'If it's not examined, it won't be taught' (Deputy Secretary of the HKEA, personal communication, February 7, 1996).

> Authority staff are very conscious of the fact that much thought is given to how the examination process can be used to bring about positive backwash. Many of the major innovations of recent years have been designed with this in mind, i.e. with the expectation that the examination changes will help classroom teachers to keep a better balance between teaching and skill-building on the one hand and examination preparation on the other (HKEA, 1994: 80).

However, according to the studies mentioned earlier (see Alderson & Wall, 1993; Wall, 1996), the HKEA's view might be simplistic. Furthermore, according to Noble and Smith (1994a: 1-2), their study of the impact of the

Arizona Student Assessment Program (ASAP) revealed both the ambiguous characteristics of the policy-making process and the dysfunctional side effects that evolved from the policy's disparities. However, the legislative passage of the testing mandate in May 1990 demonstrated Arizona's commitment to top-down reform and its belief that assessment can leverage educational change. Noble and Smith (1994a: 13-14) focused on the beliefs that influenced the change made to the testing mandate at the policy-making and administrative levels, and those that influenced educators' reactions to and implementations of the policy. They were particularly interested in examining the interplay between policy and practice by investigating how different parties in different kinds of settings reacted to the testing mandate and then what effects this had on curriculum and instructional practices.

According to Noble and Smith (1994a), Madaus (1985a, 1985b, 1990), and Rein (1983), the relationship between testing and teaching and learning is much more complex than just the design of a 'good' assessment tool. There is more underlying interplay within each specific educational context where assessment takes place. However, these studies focused only on the influence of the examination at the macro level of the educational context where the examination takes place. The micro level, e.g. teaching and learning, ought to be observed as well in order to achieve an overall understanding of the relationship between testing and teaching and learning, which is one of the objectives of this study.

Glaser and Silver (1994) examined how the formats of measurement interact with the formats of instruction in classrooms. They concluded that 'it is testing, not the official stated curriculum, that is increasingly determining what is taught, how it is taught, what is learned, and how it is learned,' which demonstrated the need for a detailed investigation into teachers and students in the classroom.

The situation mentioned above is quite true within the Hong Kong education system. Two syllabuses, the Teaching Syllabus of the Curriculum Development Council (CDC) and the Examination Syllabus of the Hong Kong Examinations Authority (HKEA), coexist in secondary education. However, it is clearly stated even in official education documents (c.f. Hong Kong Curriculum Development Committee, 1983: 12-13) that 'the teaching syllabus at [Secondary Four to Secondary Five] and the examination syllabus should be in step.' In reality, teachers in Hong Kong rely mainly on the HKEA syllabus rather than the teaching syllabus in their teaching (Cheng, 1997; Morris, 1995).

Proponents of testing further argue that the power of testing to influence what is taught, how it is taught, what is learned, and how it is learned is a very beneficial attribute. Its advocates believe that if the skills are well chosen, if the tests truly measure them, and if the goals of instruction are explicit, then teacher and student efforts are focused on well-defined targets, standards are clear and uniform; accountability at all levels is easier and more objective, and the public has concrete information on how well the schools are doing. The idea seemed to be linear and ideal. However, Madaus (1988: 85) pointed out:

> The tests can become the ferocious master of the educational process, not the compliant servant they should be. Measurement-driven instruction invariably leads to cramming, narrows the curriculum; concentrates attention on those skills most amenable to testing; constrains the creativity and spontaneity of teachers and students; and finally demeans the professional judgement of teachers (1988: 85).

He further pointed out (1988: 92) that if important decisions were presumed to be related to test results, then teachers would teach to the test. 'The reasons are, firstly, there is tremendous social pressure on teachers to see that their students acquit [sic] themselves well on the certifying examinations. Secondly, the results of the examination are so important to students, teachers, and parents that their own self-interest dictates that instructional time focus on test preparation.' According to Madaus (1988), there is a positive aspect as a high-stakes test can lever the development of new curricular materials. Despite the ability of the examination to encourage the introduction of new materials, the examination precedent soon takes over, so the way in which the new materials eventually come to be taught and learned is determined by the examination. Even if new materials are produced as a result of a new examination, they might not be moulded according to the innovators' view of what is desirable in terms of teaching, but rather according to the publishers' view of what will sell (see Andrews, 1994b; Cheng, 1997). This is, in fact, the situation within the Hong Kong education context of the current study.

In addition, measurement-driven instruction will occur when a high-stakes test of educational achievement influences the instructional programme that prepares students for the test (Popham, 1987: 680). The reason is that important contingencies are associated with the students' performance in such a situation. Popham also stated that:

> Few educators would dispute the claim that these sorts of high-stakes tests markedly influence the nature of instructional programs. Whether they are concerned about their own self-esteem or their students' well-being, teachers clearly want students to perform well on such tests. Accordingly, teachers tend to focus a significant portion of their instructional activities on the knowledge and skills assessed by such tests (1987: 680).

It seems that measurement-driven instruction can be a potent force for educational improvement if properly conceived and implemented. Popham (1987: 682) believes that 'creative teachers can *efficiently* promote mastery of content-to-be tested and then get on with other classroom pursuits' (1987: 631). He suggested that educators need to abandon outmoded notions that testing must follow teaching. Properly conceptualized tests to him can provide the clarity to make instruction more effective.

Following the above discussion that measurement can drive instruction in a positive way, if measurement is properly conceptualized, the current study will explore how and how effectively Popham's belief about washback (c.f. HKEA, 1994b) can be realized in actual teaching and learning in Hong Kong secondary schools.

Examinations as a means of control

Examinations have been long used as a means of control. They have been with us for a long time, at least a thousand years or more, if their use in Imperial China to select the highest officials of the land is taken into consideration (Arnove, Altbach, & Kelly, 1992; Lai, 1970; Hu, 1984). Those examinations were probably the first Civil Service Examinations ever developed by the human race. To avoid corruption, all essays in the Imperial Examination were marked anonymously, and the Emperor personally supervised the final stage of the examination. Although the goal of the examination was to select civil servants, its backwash effect was to establish and control an educational programme, as prospective Mandarins set out to prepare themselves for the examination (Spolsky, 1994, 1995).

Even in modern times, the use of examinations to select for education and employment dated back at least 300 years. Examinations were seen as ways to encourage the development of talent, to upgrade the performance of schools and colleges, and to counter, to some degree, nepotism, favouritism, and even outright corruption in the allocation of scarce opportunities (Eckstein & Noah, 1992). If the initial spread of examinations can be traced to such motives, the very same rationales appear to be as powerful as ever today. Examinations are often subject to much criticism. However, in spite of all the criticism levelled at them, examinations continue to occupy a leading place in the educational arrangement of many countries.

Such use of tests for power and control, as pointed out by Shohamy (1993: 2), is an especially common practice in countries that have centrally controlled educational agencies (c.f. Heyneman, 1987; Heyneman & Ransom, 1990; Li, 1990; Shohamy et al, 1996; Workman, 1987). Policy-makers in central agencies, aware of the power of tests, use them to manipulate educational systems, to control curricula, and to impose new textbooks and new teaching methods. Under those centrally controlled education systems, tests are viewed as the primary tools through which changes in the educational system can be introduced without having to change other educational components such as teacher training or curricula. Furthermore, Shohamy et al (1996: 299) stated, 'the power and authority of tests enable policy-makers to use them as effective tools for controlling educational systems and prescribing the behaviour of those who are affected by their results – administrators, teachers and students. School-wide exams are used by principals and administrators to enforce learning, which in classrooms, tests and quizzes are used by teachers to impose discipline and to motivate learning' (c.f. Stiggins & Faires-Conklin, 1992).

Consequently, testing has become 'the darling of policy makers' in the USA (c.f. Madaus, 1985a, 1985b). Similar statements could have been made at various times during the past century and a half, most notably during periods when schools were under attack and reformers sought to demonstrate the need for change (Linn, 1992). Furthermore, as has been true of previous educational reform efforts, assessment is central to the current educational reform debate for at least three reasons. First, assessment results are relied upon by governmental and educational organizations to document the need for change. Second, assessments are seen as critical agents of reform. Third, assessment results are used to demonstrate that change has or has not occurred.

Petrie (1987: 175) emphasizes that 'it would not be too much of an exaggeration to say that evaluation and testing have become *the* engine for implementing educational policy.' Moreover, Linn (1992) commented that educational assessments are expected not only to serve as a monitor of educational achievement, but also to be powerful tools of educational reform.

Educational reform and testing are intimately linked in America (see Resnick & Resnick, 1992: 1). First, test scores signal the need for reform. Second, tests are also widely viewed as instruments for educational improvement. They also point out that the link between testing and educational reform efforts has been a feature of efforts to improve American schools since at least the end of the 19th century (Resnick, 1982). In each new round of reform, testing theories and practices have been refined and elaborated. However, they argue that 'there is rarely sustained or widespread consideration of the possibilities that the very idea of using test technology as it has developed over the past century may be inimical to the real goals of educational reform' (Resnick & Resnick, 1992: 1).

Given the important decisions attached to examinations, it is natural that they have always been used as instruments and targets of control in school systems (Eckstein & Noah, 1993a, 1993b). Their relationship with the curriculum, with what a teacher teaches and what a student learns, and to an individual's life chances are of vital importance in most societies. Therefore, systemic and empirical study of the role and function of public examinations in teaching and learning is essential.

Influence of high-stakes testing

High-stakes testing refers to tests whose results are seen–rightly or wrongly–by students, teachers, administrators, parents, or the general public as the basis upon which important decisions are made that immediately and directly affect the student. High-stakes tests can be norm- or criterion-referenced, and internal or external in origin (Madaus, 1988: 87). High-stakes tests offer future academic and employment opportunities based upon their results. They are usually public examinations or large-scale standardized tests.

The Hong Kong Certificate of Education Examination (HKCEE), the subject of this study, is such a high-stakes test. The HKCEE is taken by students at the end of their fifth year of secondary education. Students either proceed to further studies to Secondary Six, or leave school and seek employment after Secondary Five. In both situations, the certificate (examination) is vital for them.

There are quite a number of studies, both general in nature and in language education, illustrating that high-stakes standardized testing influences teaching and learning. The major areas that have been studied are as follows (see also Borko, Flory, & Cumbo, 1994; Kellaghan & Greaney, 1992; Kellaghan, Madaus, & Airasian, 1982; Kubiszyn & Borich, 1996; Macintosh, 1986; Sproull & Zubrow, 1981):

- schools (organization, practice, and achievement; accountability pressure)
- teachers (their attitudes and responses to standardized tests; teacher attention to testing in instructional planning and delivery; teaching contents; time spent on test preparation; teachers' sense of professional pride; and teachers' general attitudes about the fairness and utility of testing etc.)
- students (their reactions, self-concepts, and self-assessment; and student learning outcomes)
- parents (familiarity with the changes in evaluation of their children's school progress, and their knowledge about and attitudes towards standardized testing).

Numerous studies have shown that high-stakes testing influences teaching and learning in the following ways. Smith et al (1990) found that pressure to improve students' test scores caused some teachers to 'neglect material that the external test does not include.' In another study, Smith (1991b) commented that teachers have negative feelings about standardized testing and the narrowing of the curriculum. Mathison (1987) discovered in his research that teachers altered their instructional materials to resemble the format of mandated tests.

Herman and Golan (1991) found that teachers adjusted the sequence of their curriculum based on what was included in the test. According to the findings of Herman and Golan's (1991) study, testing substantially influences teachers' instructional planning. Teachers tend to look at prior tests to make sure that their instruction includes all or most of the test content, and plan to ensure that they cover all test objectives. They also adjust their instructional plans and the sequence of their curriculum based on the test performance of the class they had the previous year. Herman and Golan also reported that testing affects the teaching and learning process through instructional items devoted to direct test preparation activities. They concluded that testing substantially influences teachers' classroom planning. Moreover, testing is more influential and exerts stronger effects on teaching in schools serving more disadvantaged students.

Stodolsky (1988) found that the existence of mandated testing led teachers to neglect team teaching approaches. Madaus (1985b) observed that when test score gains are tied to awards, teachers feel motivated rather than pressured to increase scores. Furthermore, Madaus (1988) noted that teachers taught to the test when they believed important decisions, such as promotion, would be based on test scores. Romberg, Zarinnia, and Williams (1989) found that, as a result of the emphasis on test results, teachers increased attention to paper-and-pencil computation, but decreased attention to project work. They concluded (1989: 4), 'that the greater the consequences attached to the test, the more likely it would be to have an impact on teaching' (c.f. Alderson & Wall, 1993).

Madaus (1988: 93) pointed out that in every setting where a high-stakes test operates, a tradition of past examinations will develop, which eventually de facto defines the curriculum. It is argued strongly that if the skills and knowledge are chosen, and if the tests truly measure them, then coaching is perfectly acceptable. However, according to Madaus (1988), this ignores a fundamental fact of life: when the teachers' professional worth is estimated in terms of examination success, teachers will corrupt the skills measured by reducing them to the level of strategies in which the examination is drilled. He also pointed out that if the examination is perceived as important enough, a commercial industry would develop to prepare students for it, which is true of most testing agencies.

Furthermore, Noble and Smith (1994b: 6) argued that 'teaching test-taking skills and drilling on multiple-choice worksheets is likely to boost the scores *but* unlikely to promote general understanding.' It is also reported in Forbes (1973) that students are forced to cram for examinations rather than prepare for a broad curriculum. High-stakes testing shapes the curriculum, but not in straightforward ways.

There are a number of studies (Cannell, 1987; Linn, Grave, & Sanders, 1989; Shepard, 1990) that raise questions about whether improvements in test score performance actually signal learning. Moreover, Pearson (1988: 103) reported that 'the result of ignoring, or giving only a token place to the testing of speaking is apparent in Sri Lanka'.

Other studies point to standardized tests' narrowness of content, their lack of congruency with curricula and instruction, their neglect of higher order thinking skills, and the limited relevance and meaningfulness of their multiple choice formats (see Baker, 1989; Herman, 1989, 1992; Shepard, 1990). According to these and other researchers, rather than exerting a positive influence on student learning, testing may trivialize the learning and instructional process, distort curricula, and usurp valuable instructional time (Bracey, 1987, 1989; Dorr-Bremme & Herman, 1986; Romberg, Zarinnia, & Williams, 1989; Smith, Edelsky, Draper, Rottenberg & Cherland, 1990; Stake, 1988).

On the other hand, Dorr-Bremme and Herman (1983) found that the teachers in their study paid little attention to standardized tests, as the teachers believed such tests were of little relevance to students, and that teachers viewed the results of such tests as relatively unreliable sources of information. Moreover, referring to testing on teacher planning and instruction, Dorr-Bremme and Herman (1983) found relatively little influence of standardized tests on teacher decision-making; for instance, on placing students, planning instruction, or grading. Hogan (1986), after analysing the two major curriculum changes (e.g. mathematics and linguistics) in the past 25 years in his context of his study, found that standardized testing has not dictated the curriculum and is not likely to dictate the curriculum in the future. Standardized tests, it seemed to him, exercise little influence upon the major curriculum change.

However, it is worthwhile pointing out that the above is definitely not the situation in Hong Kong. In Hong Kong, examinations dominate and influence the actual teaching and learning (Fullilove, 1992; Johnson & Wong, 1981). Hong Kong school classrooms are portrayed as teacher-centred, textbook-centred and test-centred. Furthermore, teachers and textbook writers follow the direction of the test although the degree of attention on the test varies according to the actual teacher, textbook writer, and publisher (Andrews & Fullilove, 1994; Cheng, 1997).

In summary, it can be seen that studies into the influence of high-stakes testing have led to a variety of results: influences at different levels (school, teachers, learners, and parents), and influences on different aspects of teaching and learning (teaching content, instructional planning, approaches to teaching, the teacher's professional worth, and student learning outcomes). The greater the consequences attached to a particular test, the more likely it is to have an impact on teaching and learning. The above studies had noted positive, negative, and no influence on teaching and learning. The current study will draw on the above findings and explore the most sensitive and intensive areas in teaching and learning that are likely to be influenced by an examination change.

Exploring washback within different educational contexts

Previous sections in this chapter have focused on investigations of the washback phenomenon from a theoretical perspective. The effect of washback has been seen to have an impact on different levels of people, and on many different aspects of teaching and learning within a given educational context. The phenomenon is related to testing, teaching, and learning theories as well as curriculum innovation (change) theories. This section situates washback within different educational contexts, and explores how washback works in a certain context. It aims to explore any regional significance of the washback phenomenon (c.f. Shohamy, 1993 for more information on the role of centrally controlled education systems). Washback studies carried out in other regional educational contexts will be discussed first, followed by washback studies within the Hong Kong educational context.

Washback within other regional educational contexts

Research into the washback phenomena in language education has involved several language projects carried out in different countries: the study of new exams in Sri Lanka (Pearson, 1988; Wall, 1996; Wall & Alderson, 1993); the Netherlands school language exams (Luijten, 1991; Wesdorp, 1982); a needs-based exam at a Turkish university (Hughes 1988); the Nepalese English exam (Khaniya, 1990a, 1990b); the national university entrance examination in China (Li, 1990); the Japanese university entrance exams (Buck, 1988; Ingulsrud, 1994; Watanabe, 1996a, 1996b); EFL and ASL exams in Israel (Shohamy, 1993; Shohamy et al, 1996); similar research in Germany (Perrin, 1996); Canada (Nagy & Traub, 1986); Australia (Dunn, 1989; Wigglesworth & Elder, 1996); and research on the various exams and exam revisions in Hong Kong (Andrews, 1994a, 1994b; Andrews & Fullilove, 1993, 1994; Cheng, 1993, 1997; Fullilove, 1992; Johnson & Wong, 1981; Lam, 1993, 1994; Smallwood, 1994; Workman, 1987).

Hughes (1988) reported, after developing tests for the British Council for two years at Bogazici University (a leading Turkish university), that an overall increase could be seen in students' language proficiency in the area of syllabus, textbooks, and also in teaching, due to changes in assessment, but he did not explain what aspects of teaching changed. Alderson and Wall (1993) reported on the Sri Lankan project, which was consciously intended to provide a 'lever for change' (Pearson, 1988). They found that there was a certain amount of washback on the teaching content, but not on teaching methods. In contrast, Wesdorp (1982), in reporting his investigation into multiple-choice testing in the Netherlands, concluded that standardized testing had no washback effect on skills that are taught, teacher activities, or students' study habits. However, he mentioned that it was necessary to follow the developments in testing to prevent an adaptation of the educational system to the testing technique.

Li (1990) studied the Matriculation English Test (MET), the English test for entrance to all universities in the People's Republic of China. She suggested that because of the sheer number of people who take this test annually (three million), it could be called 'a test of great power.' She also explored the extrinsic and intrinsic power of the test to inform significantly and influence benevolently. She pointed out that washback relies on feedback, and the power of a test manifests itself as a power both to inform and to influence (1990: 397). According to Li, washback from the MET was seen in teaching materials and lesson content, but the 'most telling changes' were outside the classroom. These changes reflected 'a new awareness of time and resources and a new enthusiasm for after-class learning of English.' Feedback from one province in China showed all simplified English readers were sold out throughout the province. Li also discovered a shift in the classroom away from formal linguistic knowledge to practising and using the language. However, she also reported that teachers felt very uncomfortable with the MET, but students were much more adaptable and often accepted new testing methods quite readily. Considering the significant influence that tests have on Chinese students' future opportunities, perhaps this was natural.

Pearson (1988) studied washback in Sri Lanka, where a considerable amount of work was carried out on developing new public examinations and on encouraging the use of new kinds of formal and informal classroom tests. He commented that 'giving the examinations such a dominant role in the whole scheme means that it is now vital, as never before, that the washback effect be beneficial, and that they encourage the whole range of desired changes' (1988: 101). He argued that, from the point of view of washback, a 'good' test should do two things: it should encompass all areas of the syllabus, and it should directly reflect the accepted view of what teaching and learning involves. Good tests are often said to increase the amount or improve the quality of learner motivation, to stimulate learning on particular occasions, and to reinforce previous learning. Furthermore, Pearson commented (1988: 107) that good tests will encourage the use of beneficial teaching-learning processes, and will be more or less directly usable as teaching-learning activities.

Shohamy (1993: 17) reported her study on the impact of three tests in Israel. She commented that these tests served as 'an effective tool for changing the behaviours of teachers and students because of their power and high stakes'. However, she said that the educational effectiveness of tests couldn't be very high as these tests narrowed the process of evaluation, 'making it merely instrumental and un-meaningful.' She concluded that:

Tests used for the purpose of improving learning can be effective only if they are connected to the educational system; they are not effective when used in isolation. But using tests to solve educational problems is a simplistic approach to a complex problem. It works on people's fear of authority. It can even be said that the testers themselves are abused by the educational leadership. Testers need to examine the uses that are made of the instruments they so innocently construct (1993: 19).

Shohamy et al (1996), in their paper *Test Impact Revisited*, pointed out that a test's impact is often influenced by several factors: the nature of the subject-matter tested, the nature of the test, and the uses to which the test scores are put. Furthermore, the washback effect may change over time and may not last indefinitely within the education system.

Studies conducted in other regions have also provided insights for the present study. Madison (1979) reported that the package of interdependent changes to an examination envisaged in Ethiopia had led to the failure to implement all the necessary related changes, which explains the new examination's ultimate failure. Somerset (1983), in his work in Kenya, Nepal, and Hong Kong, has shown that public examinations can be used constructively to bring about positive changes in the way pupils are taught, and the approaches to learning that they are encouraged to use. However, these studies reported have largely failed to link the washback effect on teaching and learning with the educational systems in those particular regions.

Washback within the Hong Kong educational context

Washback is a term that can be found frequently in official education documents in Hong Kong (see the Hong Kong Examinations Authority, 1993; Hong Kong Government 1984, 1986, 1990; Education Department of Hong Kong, 1989). For example, it was stressed in the Hong Kong Education Commission Report No. 4 (1990) that 'a project should be carried out to determine the 'washback' effect of different forms of assessment.' Moreover, Morris (1990b) argues that any change in the Hong Kong educational system must first involve a change in the examinations. Also, the Education Commission Report No. 4 (1990) stated:

The Hong Kong Examinations Authority is well aware of the fact that the syllabi for the HKCEE affect the curriculum and even the teaching methods in schools, particularly in Secondary 4 and 5...the revised HKCEE syllabi have served to improve the clarity of the curriculum objectives, which has had a positive influence on teaching (70).

Some examples of the positive washback effect of public examinations in Hong Kong have been reported in the literature (see Andrews, 1994a, 1994b Andrews & Fullilove, 1994; Fullilove, 1992; Johnson & Wong, 1981). In Hong

Kong, certain washback effects are expected whenever language examinations are introduced (c.f. Hong Kong Examinations Authority, 1993). Washback is strongly believed to have a positive effect on teaching and learning. As stated previously, the HKEA has a strong conviction about washback, as expressed by the Deputy Secretary 'We believe in washback!' (Deputy Secretary of the HKEA, personal communication, February 7, 1996; c.f. HKEA 1994b: 80). However, a search of the literature indicates that an understanding of the nature of washback and the scope of its effect on public examinations in Hong Kong is still based more on presumptions than empirical data.

Fullilove (1992: 131) reported the phenomena of washback in Hong Kong as 'the tail wagging the dog... Hong Kong is an exam-mad town–a place where language testing is a prime determinant of course design and classroom practices, as in which hundreds of *How to Pass The*...cribs are published.' It is also a place where parents sometimes present their children for one- or two-day testing programmes in an attempt to get them accepted to the 'right' kindergarten (a decision which they believe will give their children favoured opportunities in the future). In Hong Kong, approximately five per cent of those students who commence primary school education will ultimately, by successfully mastering the examination system, gain a place in one of Hong Kong's tertiary education institutes (c.f. Johnson & Wong, 1981).

Fullilove (1992) commented in detail about the washback effect on several aspects of teaching in Hong Kong:

> The examinations affect the content of the lessons taught, both in broad terms and in much more specific detail as well. This influence on course content may be direct–through what the teacher plans for her lessons–or it may be somewhat less direct, but nonetheless highly significant, through the content of the recommended textbooks used in most schools. In the broadest terms, the content of course is influenced by the weighting of the parts or subsections of the examinations (1992: 136).

Johnson and Wong (1981: 279) saw the Scaling Test in Hong Kong as an example of 'testing as a force for change in teaching' and testing 'as a potent tool for ultimately changing the classroom learning and teaching techniques of English as a second or foreign language.' They viewed the test as a way of introducing more genuinely communicative methods of teaching into the classroom, including the use of authentic materials, and thereby 'as a way of achieving syllabus revision with the resulting changes in textbook design and the classroom learning and teaching techniques' (Johnson & Wong, 1981: 277). According to Johnson and Wong, eventually the exam would 'lead to syllabus revision, the design of new textbooks with different goals and objectives from those currently in use, and as a consequence, new classroom methods and techniques which stress the use of authentic English in a purposeful and interactive way.'

However, the outcome that Johnson and Wong (1981: 285) anticipated did not take place immediately, i.e. 'English is taught as a formal, textbook-based, discursive, academic subject, the process and product of which bear little resemblance to the authentic English being used around us.' Another example of classroom innovation also reported in Johnson and Wong (1981) is a public examination change in the addition of a listening component to the HKCEE. It was explicitly expected that this new element of the examination would have a significant effect on the teaching of English in secondary schools in Hong Kong. Towards the end of the implementation, the Education Department, at considerable expense, had induction loop listening systems installed in each government and aided school to encourage schools to include lessons for improving students' listening skills. However, whether the positive washback that was expected to take place in teaching and learning was actually realized is still in question.

In addition, Morris (1990b: 49-51), in his study of teachers' perceptions of the barriers to the implementation of a pedagogical innovation, found out that teachers cite public examinations as the most important factor affecting their teaching. Teachers generally felt the need to cover the syllabus and prepare students for examination questions. In general, they believed that the most efficient way of accomplishing these two tasks within the busy school year was through the traditional teaching method of lecturing to their students. Therefore, more innovative methods were generally avoided by the teachers, even if they believed these more modern approaches were worthwhile.

Andrews & Fullilove (1994), Andrews (1994b), and Workman (1987) discovered that there are widely diverging views about the nature of changes to examinations the HKEA wanted to engineer, as well as a mismatch between the views of the HKEA and those of the teachers, even though these changes were decided by a working group of the HKEA (consisting of subject officers and teacher representatives). The contrasting views of the relative importance of different pedagogical strategies viewed by decision-makers and teachers raise as many questions as HKEA could possibly answer. This further demonstrates not only the complexity of the washback effect under the Hong Kong educational context, but also a further need for studies like this one into the washback phenomenon if curriculum alignment is to be expected, as mentioned earlier in this chapter. This current study will address the complexity of the phenomenon and explore in-depth the areas of teaching and learning within the Hong Kong educational context.

Exploring washback within current models of teaching and learning

As has been noted in the previous sections, the washback effect is a powerful educational phenomenon. It not only influences different people at different levels within educational contexts, but also has an impact on many aspects of teaching and learning in the school curriculum. Studies into such educational phenomenon ought to draw research findings about teaching and learning, make references to the existing models of teaching and learning, and also draw on theories in educational change, since the notion of change is the fundamental principle of the washback phenomenon. This section explores the theoretical background and existing frameworks of teaching and learning to guide the current study of washback.

Classroom research

Classroom-centred research (Brumfit & Mitchell, 1989a, 1989b) focuses on the classroom, as distinct from research that concentrates on the inputs to the classroom (the syllabus, the teaching materials) or on the outputs from the classroom (learner achievement scores). It investigates what happens inside the classroom when teachers and learners come together. It focuses on the process variables of the classroom and answers questions such as how and why it is that things happen as they do in the classroom. The focus of such classroom-centred research reflects the purpose of the current washback study because it investigates how washback works in the educational context and in the classrooms. This study focuses on teacher and student interaction in the classroom, practice opportunities, and time allocation of teaching and learning activities, in order to understand how these aspects of teaching and learning might have been influenced by the new 1996 HKCEE and what changes the examination actually brought about in classroom teaching and learning.

This type of research, according to Long (1980), is generally carried out by observation and/or introspection. Observation involves keeping a record of what goes on in the classrooms being observed. Introspection can involve interviewing teachers or giving them questionnaires to which they respond and reflect on their experience, or diary keeping (see also Allwright, 1983, 1988; Allwright & Bailey, 1991).

Language researchers in general have chosen to look at the classroom as a setting for language acquisition and learning in terms of the language input provided by teacher talk and classroom interaction processes (see Allen, Frohlich, & Spada, 1984; Allwright, 1983, 1988; Allwright & Bailey, 1991; Long, 1980, 1983, 1984). The classroom should be the first place to look if we really want to understand how to help our learners learn more efficiently and how teachers and students interact. The classroom is also the first place to look if we wish to know whether a proposed new examination (in this study, the 1996 HKCEE) can bring about changes in classroom teaching and learning, as intended by the HKEA, and the types of changes that may result.

Consequently, observation is essential for such classroom research, and this involves keeping a record of what is happening. Various observation instruments have been developed to explore a range of variables based on different models of teaching. However, there are no existing observation instruments available for washback studies of this kind, although there are washback studies involving classroom observations (see Alderson & Hamp-Lyons, 1996; Wall & Alderson, 1993). The study of washback on teaching and learning, firstly, ought to involve a broad classroom setting (c.f. Wall et al, 1996). Secondly, variables such as process variables, presage variables, context variables and product variables should be investigated one by one if a complete picture of the examination's effect on teaching and learning is to be seen within the local context (see Dunkin & Biddle, 1974; Hughes, 1993; Stern, 1983, 1989).

Regarding the different approaches to classroom observations (see Allwright, 1988; Bailey, 1985; Chaudron, 1986, 1988; Dunkin & Biddle, 1974; Ellis, 1984, 1994; Long, 1980; Stern, 1983, 1989, 1992), Chaudron (1988) summarized four different approaches to classroom observation into four traditions in classroom research. The first, the *psychometric tradition*, was used in the early evaluations of L2 instruction. This tradition followed, as much as possible, standard educational psychometric procedures, with comparison treatment groups and measurement of outcomes on proficiency tests. This tradition involves context, presage and product studies, which investigate the quantitative relationships between various classroom activities or behaviours and language achievement. This tradition has been criticized for its neglect of variables in the classroom and for trying to establish a linear relationship between input and output variables via quantitative analysis (c.f. Allwright, 1988). This approach is not useful for studying washback as this phenomenon is far too complex to have a possible linear input and output relationship.

The second tradition, *interaction analysis*, refers to observational schemes used to describe teacher-student interaction in the classroom. It was developed by the mid-1960s (c.f. Moskowitz, 1968, 1971), when the influence of sociological investigations of group processes led to the development of systems for the observation and analysis of classroom interaction in terms of social meanings and an inferred classroom climate. These schemes are designed to help teachers discover and evaluate their own classroom behaviours so as to become ultimately 'his [sic] own agent for change' (Moskowitz, 1971: 219). However, criticism was levelled at the capacity of those schemes to capture the complete picture of classroom interaction (Bailey, 1985). For the current study, this form of analysis is really too minute to capture and understand such a multidimensional phenomenon like washback.

The influence of the second tradition, which views interaction as a chain of teacher and student behaviours (each one classifiable into one or another category), is seen in the third tradition, that of *discourse analysis*. This third tradition arose from a linguistic perspective, an attempt to fully analyse the discourse of classroom interaction in structural-functional linguistic terms. Although this approach had the potential for being applied in a quantitative fashion, its development has largely been confined to researchers' redefinitions of the appropriate categories used to describe discourse (see Coulthard, 1977; Sinclair & Coulthard, 1975). Such analysis might also be too detailed for the purpose of this research, but it can be useful for illustrative purpose for this study.

The fourth tradition, the *ethnographic tradition*, arose from sociological and anthropological traditions, and has gained wide acceptance in first language classroom research over the last twenty years. It attempts to interpret behaviour from the perspective of the individual participant's unique understanding rather than from the observer's or analyst's supposedly objective analysis. Classroom ethnography provides extensive empirical descriptions of what is happening in the classroom by 'generating a description that approximates the knowledge of participants in a particular event, making the implicit explicit, the invisible visible' (Mehan, 1979: 176). Although ethnography is often criticized for its lack of generalization to other contexts (Chaudron, 1988), it is still a very appropriate approach to gain a feel for the context of the study.

As washback studies involve the exploration of teaching and learning in a broad classroom setting, a combined research framework would be required to draw on the various strengths of the above traditions. Any one of the approaches alone would not be adequate to satisfactorily carry out such a study of washback on teaching and learning. Furthermore, Allwright (1983: 199) noted two viewpoints on classroom-centred research, one focusing on the interactive aspects of classroom behaviour and the other focusing more on teacher talk as input. The first of these, based on a sociological view of education, has brought classroom research on language teaching and learning nearer the sociological tradition of such educational researchers as Hymes (c.f. Cazden, John, & Hymes, 1972), and the particular ethnographic work of such educational researchers as Mehan (1979). The second viewpoint, focusing on teacher talk, has brought us much closer to what is now the mainstream of second language acquisition research; one of the crucial variables is input (c.f. Krashen, 1981). The current washback study, therefore, focuses more on the above two approaches–interactive behaviour and teacher talk in the classroom–as they are very closely related to the changes made in the HKCEE.

To summarize, different traditions of classroom research have led to different approaches to data collection and analysis. They have also led to the creation of different models of teaching, which will be reviewed below. For the purposes of this current study, and taking classroom process (interaction) as a focus, various aspects of the four traditions mentioned above–interactional analysis, discourse analysis, and ethnography–have been drawn upon to serve the research purpose.

Classroom research models

The various traditions and approaches to classroom-based research mentioned above illustrate how specific areas of teaching and learning have been investigated and observed. The conceptual figures below illustrate two teaching and learning models for the study of classrooms at different levels and different issues involved, which provide theoretical and methodological guides for the current study. A model for the study of classroom teaching (see Dunkin & Biddle, 1974, p. 38; cited also in Stern, 1983, and Chaudron, 1988) serves as an initial guide for the clarification of the variables and behaviours in studies of teaching. Chaudron's (1988) model of four levels of general issues concerns the effectiveness of classroom instruction. Dunkin and Biddle's model (1974; cited also in Stern, 1983, and Ellis, 1994), and Chaudron's (1988) model have been combined to serve as the theoretical framework for this study. Issues that arise from these two models, written in **bold** typeface in Figure 2.1 below, are the focus of the current study.

Figure 2.1 Variables for classroom observations

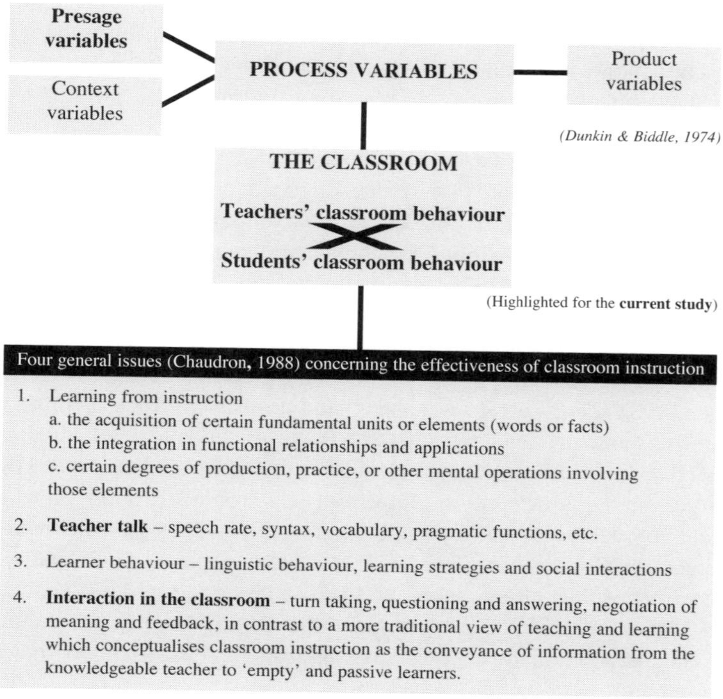

Presage variables

Context variables

PROCESS VARIABLES

Product variables

(Dunkin & Biddle, 1974)

THE CLASSROOM

Teachers' classroom behaviour

Students' classroom behaviour

(Highlighted for the **current study**)

Four general issues (Chaudron, 1988) concerning the effectiveness of classroom instruction

1. Learning from instruction
   a. the acquisition of certain fundamental units or elements (words or facts)
   b. the integration in functional relationships and applications
   c. certain degrees of production, practice, or other mental operations involving those elements

2. **Teacher talk** – speech rate, syntax, vocabulary, pragmatic functions, etc.

3. Learner behaviour – linguistic behaviour, learning strategies and social interactions

4. **Interaction in the classroom** – turn taking, questioning and answering, negotiation of meaning and feedback, in contrast to a more traditional view of teaching and learning which conceptualises classroom instruction as the conveyance of information from the knowledgeable teacher to 'empty' and passive learners.

These two models, with an emphasis on the classroom process, have been combined to guide the classroom observations for the current study. The unit of observation for this study is a lesson. This study deals primarily with the process variables of the classroom component (see Figure 2.1) where a teacher and students interact with each other–what teachers do and what students do in the classroom. Observations are conducted in depth to explore the four aspects of classroom interaction raised by Chaudron (1988). Interaction in the classroom is the focus of the current study. Teacher presage variables and student characteristics of the context variables in Figure 2.1 were studied through two comparative surveys of teachers and students. Stern (1983: 498) defined that presage variables are the characteristics, which teachers as individuals or as a group bring to teaching, their own formative experiences, their training, and their personal qualities. The context variables consist of the conditions within which the teacher must operate, the community, the school, its environment, and the students themselves. The community, the school and its environment were not chosen as the focus of this study. Product variables were not investigated in this study due to the nature of the research questions answered and the time constraints of this study. The time span of the research ranged from the time the HKCEE was changed in 1993 to after the new 1996 HKCEE was written by the first cohort of F5 students in 1996. Only limited changes could be expected in students' learning outcomes within such a short time span.

It is also worthwhile to borrow from Stern in addition to the above two models. Stern (1989) argued that the interest in studying the classroom is indeed close to the reality of language teaching practice, but there is an over-concern with the minutiae of teaching and learning in saying 'the collection of infinite and unmanageable details quickly leads to the inability to see the woods for the trees' (Stern, 1989: 207; see also Johnson, 1989; Larsen-Freeman, 1980). This point is particularly important as the current washback study involves a broader classroom setting.

Stern (1989) outlined the basic categories of a scheme for analysing language teaching, which is very useful to this washback study. His model consists of three levels. The first level, the *basic level*, relates to the basic fundamental assumptions of language learning and teaching made by the teacher, the evaluator, the administrator, the researcher, and even the learners themselves. It consists of four concepts: language, society, learning, and teaching.

The second level, the general categories of language teaching, gives language teaching its particular shape and direction. It is rooted in teaching methods and curriculum design theories. This level was called the *'policy level'* (c.f. Stern, 1989: 210), where professional planning and decision-making occur, and consists of (a) categories of content, (b) categories of objectives, (c) categories of treatment or procedures, and (d) categories of evaluation. Treatment or procedures, the most controversial aspect of language pedagogy, are linked with three strategies highly relevant to the current study of washback effect on aspects of teaching and learning. They are:

- teaching strategies: listening, reading, speaking, and writing
- timing strategies: segmenting lessons into larger or smaller chunks
- social and interpersonal strategies: teacher or student-centred/individual or class.

The third level, *language class in action*, reveals the fundamental concepts of language, learning, and teaching at the basic level, and decisions at the second level, in the area of curriculum objectives, strategies, and evaluation through the behavioural acts of teaching and learning. The three levels form a scheme of language teaching analysis, which allows researchers to recognize that observation schemes must ultimately be related to the underlying policies and fundamental assumptions of language teaching and learning. This point is closely related to the current study of the washback effect on teaching and learning as changes in the HKCEE were designed with the intention of effecting changes in teaching and learning in Hong Kong classrooms. This model serves as the guide for the data collection and analysis in the current study.

Nevertheless, the current researcher sees the model for research into classroom teaching and learning in a reverse order, shown in Figure 2.2. Washback brings changes from the top (the decision-makers) for conceptual change and decision-making, down to the school (the teaching and learning level). Washback functions on multiple levels and perhaps at different times. In this regard, the ideas of Fullan (1983) and Fullan & Stiegelbauer (1991) have been drawn upon. They strongly argue the need for teaching and learning

**Figure 2.2 A language teaching analysis scheme
(Source: Stern, 1989: 210)**

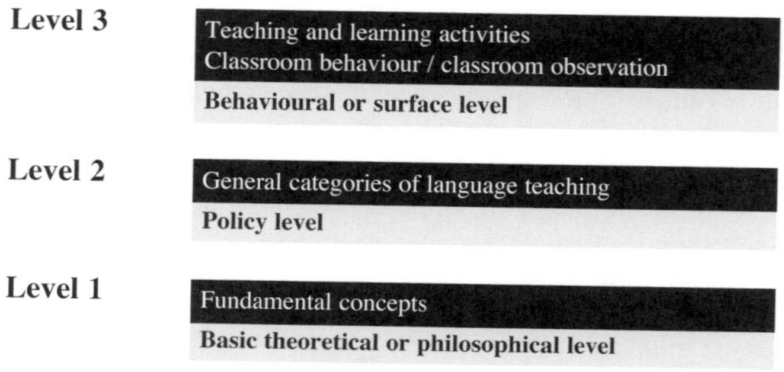

Level 3	Teaching and learning activities Classroom behaviour / classroom observation **Behavioural or surface level**

Level 2	General categories of language teaching **Policy level**

Level 1	Fundamental concepts **Basic theoretical or philosophical level**

to be studied within multiple perspectives. Fullan (1983: 36) makes it clear that educational change is multidimensional. Fullan's ideas coincide with Hughes' (1993) trichotomy of backwash model mentioned above (c.f. Bailey, 1996) and Markee's curricular innovation model (1997: 42 – 47). Hughes's trichotomy focuses on examination influences on participants, processes, and products. Bailey (1996) elaborated Hughes' trichotomy further to include different levels of influence within the trichotomy.

Moreover, Fullan (1983: 37) pointed out that objectively it is possible to clarify the meaning of educational change by identifying and describing its main dimensions. He argued that ignorance of such dimensions often explains a number of interesting phenomena in the field of educational change; for example, why some people accept an innovation they do not understand, why some aspects of a change are implemented and not others, and why strategies for change neglect certain components. Nunan (D. Nunan, personal communication, October 14, 1997) emphasizes the intricate and interlocking relationship between curriculum as planned, curriculum in action, and curriculum as outcomes. He points out the possible lack of fit between these three components.

Drawing from all sources of research in the classroom at the macro and micro levels above, the research proposes a working model below to study the complex and multidimensional nature of washback (Figure 2.3). This model serves as a theoretical and methodological guide for the current study. The curriculum as planned at Level 1 pointed out by Nunan refers to the intended changes behind the new examination syllabus. The curriculum in action and curriculum as outcomes elements are to be studied in the second and third levels. In between, there will be gaps or mismatches at each level.

Figure 2.3 Explanatory model of washback

Level 1 Decision making Agencies	**CDC** Teaching syllabus **HKEA** Exam syllabus	How do the two syllabuses work? How are the teaching and learning principles behind the exam syllabus realized as manageable tasks?
Level 2 Intervening Agencies	**Textbook publishers** Teaching content **Tertiary institutions** Teaching methods	How do teachers realize the teaching and learning theories behind the exam syllabus and the textbooks? How do teachers arrange their lessons and activities accordingly?
Level 3 Implementing Agencies	**Schools** Principals Teachers Students	How are the teaching and learning activities carried out in classrooms?

The dimensions of change that are explored in this study consist of (a) teaching materials, (b) teaching approaches, and (c) beliefs involving a dynamic interrelationship between the three dimensions. All three dimensions are investigated in the current study employing various research methods in three phases. Washback intensity within these dimensions is also investigated according to the classroom model above (see Figures 2.1 and 2.2). Washback intensity refers to the degree of the washback effect in an area or number of areas of teaching and learning affected by an examination (c.f. Cheng, 1997: 43). Moreover, Fullan (1983) points out that 'change inevitably causes anxiety, loss, and struggle for those affected once they realise that basic conceptions of education and change are involved which will affect 'their occupational identity, sense of competence, and their self-respect' (1983: 40). Schon (1971) similarly argues that real change involves passing through areas of uncertainty; which cannot be pre-empted by planning. Therefore, studies of this kind need to involve various intervening factors in teaching. The current study of the intended washback effect of the new 1996 HKCEE on teaching and learning would inevitably involve an investigation of changes in the teacher (teaching practices) from a general psychological perspective as well as a change in specific areas of teaching and learning through observations and interviews.

Summary

This chapter has reviewed washback from four perspectives: the concept itself, the mechanism of this phenomenon, washback in regional contexts, and washback within teaching and learning contexts. It has explored the theoretical underpinnings and built up a working framework for this study. What is most notable is the large proportion of studies that are essentially prescriptive. These studies deal with the phenomena of washback from different perspectives and at multiple levels. There are, however, fewer empirical analyses that have investigated the phenomena in the teaching and learning environments. There are even fewer research studies that consider washback at both the macro and micro levels, particularly in language education.

From the literature, it can be seen that using examinations as a means of control can be traced to 201 BC in China. Large numbers of studies have dealt with the influence of standardized testing since the beginning of the century. Criticisms focus mainly on the negative influence of standardized testing due to its accountability or mandating nature. Recently, performance assessment is preferred–a more appropriate assessment in terms of the current teaching and learning theories and models–to exert a positive influence on teaching and learning or to drive the teaching and learning by making using of its high-stakes assessment properties. This is known as measurement-driven instruction. However, as has been pointed out by many researchers, the relationship between testing, teaching and learning is a far more complicated issue than it might appear to be on the surface. Such an idea might be too ideal and simplistic. A study of the effects of washback needs to draw on curriculum and innovation models and explore the phenomenon within a multidimensional context.

Section Two:
Methodology for washback study

Washback needs to be studied and understood, not asserted.

Wall & Alderson (1993: 69)

Not many research studies have been undertaken to study the effects of washback on teaching and learning. Even fewer studies have employed a mixed (quantitative and qualitative) method for the investigation. In particular, the lack of classroom data in washback studies makes discussion of the phenomenon a myth. This section consists of one chapter with three major parts. The first part introduces the overall research rationale and framework, research design, and the specific research strategies adopted in this study. The next two parts describe and illustrate the two major instruments employed in this study, namely the two survey instruments and then the classroom observation study.

3 Research methodology

Part 1: Overall research design

This section will discuss the theoretical and methodological derivations that this study has drawn on for its own research agenda. It will first discuss (a) the theoretical derivations, (b) the methodological derivations, (c) the research strategies and methodology adopted in this study, and (d) the research methods used in light of the research questions.

Research questions

The purpose of the research is to investigate how a change in the HKCEE, a high-stakes public examination, influenced classroom teaching within the local Hong Kong educational context, including aspects of teachers' attitudes, teaching content, and classroom interaction discussed in Chapter 2. The washback effect of this public examination change was observed initially at the macro level (including major parties within the Hong Kong educational context), and then at the micro level in the schools (concerning different facets [aspects] of teaching and learning) (c.f. Bachman & Palmer, 1996). The following three research questions were explored in this study:

> **Research Question One: What strategies did the HKEA use to implement the examination change?**

Strategies are operationally defined as the processes and methods employed in the decision-making of the HKEA for the new 1996 HKCEE.

- how did the HKEA make the decision to change the HKCEE?
- why did they make the decision (i.e. the rationale for the change)?
- what support did they have in bringing the new 1996 HKCEE into the Hong Kong school system?
- how did different participants act in the context of the change?

Participants in this study refers to different parties or levels of people within the Hong Kong educational context reviewed in Figure 2.3 of Chapter 2. The nature of the new 1996 HKCEE might have affected their perceptions and attitudes towards teaching and learning. Therefore, this phase of the study would involve looking at the Hong Kong education system as a whole and looking at the reactions and actions of different participants in the context of change. The different participants that were studied include:

- the decision-making organizations, such as the HKEA, the CDC, and the ED
- the intervening organizations, such as textbook publishers and tertiary institutes
- implementing agents such as principals, panel chairs, teachers, and students.

To answer the above questions, the researcher chose to watch (observation) and ask (key informant interviews).

Research Question Two: What was the nature and scope of the washback effect on teachers' and students' perceptions of aspects of teaching towards the new examination?

Teachers' and students' perceptions are operationally defined as teachers' and students' apprehensions and understanding of aspects of classroom teaching in relation to the new 1996 HKCEE. The aspects of teaching that were studied include:

- teachers' perceptions of the rationale and formats of the new HKCEE
- teachers' perceptions of the added work/pressure and difficulties in teaching to the new HKCEE
- teachers' perceptions of the teaching methods, activities, the use of mock exams, and of textbooks in the context of the new HKCEE
- students' perceptions of their teachers' talk, medium of instruction, and teaching activities, as well as their own learning activities, the use of English inside and outside class, their motivation and opinions about their English lessons
- teachers' perceptions of the learning aims and motivation of students, learning strategies, activities they would like to recommend their students do in relation to the HKCEE.

The above questions were answered mainly by two comparative survey studies over two years and follow-up interviews.

Research Question Three: What was the nature and scope of the washback effect on teachers' behaviours as a result of the new examination?

Teachers' behaviours are operationally defined as what teachers do in the classroom. Teachers' behaviours in the classroom were studied in the following areas:

- teachers' medium of instruction, teacher talk, teaching activities
- teaching materials used in teaching, aspects of lesson planning
- assessment and evaluation in relation to their teaching.

The above aspects were studied through two comparative surveys as well as classroom observations. Teachers' classroom behaviours were further studied through classroom observations in terms of practice opportunities, classroom interaction, and teacher talk.

Research framework

The research stresses 'the importance of context, setting, and subjects' frames of reference' (Marshall & Rossman, 1989: 46). The methodology used in this study aimed to capture the reality, variation, and complexity of changes in day-to-day classroom practice as well as changes within the local Hong Kong educational context. For this study, the recommendations of Erickson (1986; c.f. Erickson & Shultz, 1981) as well as Miles and Huberman (1994) have been used for the design of the research methods. In order to understand action and practice, the researcher engaged directly in the local scene, spent sufficient time to understand action in its specific social context, gained access to participant meanings, and showed how these meanings-in-action evolved over time. Without careful grounding in the local context, a more general understanding was impossible. Due to the nature of this public examination and its impact on the educational system as a whole, this study investigated the educational context before investigating a particular area of teaching and learning in depth. Three levels of the washback effect of the 1996 HKCEE were identified in terms of curriculum change.

- *decision-making agencies,* consisting of the HKEA (for the exam syllabus), the CDC (for the teaching syllabus) and the ED (for educational policy)
- the *intervening agencies,* consisting of textbook publishers (for teaching materials) and tertiary institutes (for teacher education)
- the *implementing agencies,* consisting of teachers, students, and school administrators.

The HKEA made the decisions about the examination change with its subject committee, which consists of persons nominated by the Director of Education, English subject examination officers, language experts from tertiary institutions, and school teachers. The HKEA piloted the revised syllabus and went to schools to solicit opinions from teachers. It then recommended textbook publishers to revise textbook materials and informed tertiary institutions about teacher education consideration. After those stages were completed, the school and teacher level decided how they were going to carry out their actual teaching according to the syllabus. This completed a cycle for this curriculum change.

However, Smith et al (1994) found that definitions of the situation held by policy makers, i.e. the images of the problems a given policy should solve, as well as the characteristics of pupils, teachers, curriculum, assessment, and educational change, etc., are shaped and 'translated imperfectly by practitioners.' Teachers and principals redefine and reinterpret the messages about policy that they receive. They then act–adapt, teach, learn, and evaluate–according to their own definitions of the situation (Blumer, 1986; Geisinger, 1994). This study, by observing the local educational context, identified gaps from the top level down to the actual classroom teaching. The perception of those gaps by the researcher within the Hong Kong educational context greatly improved the knowledge and understanding of how and in what areas a public examination change can actually influence the school curriculum.

Three different levels of the flow of washback effect are identified above. The important intervening level was particularly teased out, since it was discovered through school visits that Hong Kong teachers mainly relied on textbooks[1] in their teaching. Textbook publishers reacted quickly to the new 1996 HKCEE exam. However, the current researcher decided to focus not only on textbooks, but rather to explore the washback effect within a broader context and more in the areas of teaching and learning behaviours in the actual classroom. This is because what teachers do reflects an accurate picture of the washback effect. Washback on textbooks itself can be a very interesting area to study. At the core of the research problem are the teachers and students who are influenced by the exam. To know whether there was any washback effect from the 1996 HKCEE, the classroom would be the place to study.

After a clear idea was gained of how the Hong Kong educational system reacted in the face of a change to its major public examination, and the interrelationship between levels of curriculum change, the main research methods of the study were then designed. Mixed methods were employed. Different levels of method triangulation were used to tackle problems at different levels and in different areas of teaching and learning. The areas of teaching and learning were chosen to be studied based on several models of teaching and learning below:

- Dunkin and Biddle (1974: 38): *Presage, context, process* and *product:* four key variables in the study of teaching
- Chaudron (1988: 5-10): *Learning from instruction, teacher talk, learner behaviour,* and *interaction:* four key issues in the study of teaching

---

1. Research findings related to textbook publishers have been discussed in an earlier paper 'How Does Washback Influence Teaching? Implications for Hong Kong' (Cheng 1997: 38-54).

- Stern (1989: 210): *Teaching and learning activities* (surface level), *categories of language teaching* (policy level), and *fundamental concepts* (basic theoretical level).

A detailed description of the above models is given in Chapter 2. These models have provided theoretical guidance in what to look for in teaching and learning in this study. They also support the researcher's beliefs and ideas about teaching and learning. Besides the language teaching model, curriculum models were also drawn upon for a broader perspective of the complex nature of washback (Fullan, 1983, 1993; Markee, 1993, 1997; Morris, 1995).

For example, Morris (1995) points out that the curriculum is not something that is wholly determined by the government. Schools and teachers are regularly making decisions about parts of the curriculum. Decision-making is made based on people's values and with reference to political considerations. Therefore, both normative and positive perspectives should be considered. A normative perspective is concerned with what should happen in schools (related to the decision-makers' intended washback effect), while a positive perspective is concerned with what actually does happen in schools (actual washback in the school setting). Therefore, washback needs to be studied in relation to the above components and at different levels of the educational context.

This research was limited by time. It started when the decision for the change to the HKCEE was made in 1993 and lasted up to 1996 when the first cohort of F5 students sat for the new 1996 HKCEE. The time framework discussed in Chapter 1 in a way restricted the researcher to start and finish the data collection within a certain fixed time, especially with respect to the comparative surveys and classroom observations. Once that certain fixed time in the research schedule passed, there would be no opportunity for the researcher to go back to collect that type of data again, which is a limitation of this study.

Methodology derivations from other washback studies

A review of washback studies showed that little empirical research has been carried out in the investigation of washback, particularly in language education (Alderson & Hamp-Lyons, 1996). Methods employed for washback studies are based on surveys, interviews, testing measures and classroom observation. A number of research studies on washback have been carried out using survey methods for data collection on the effects of standardized testing (Herman & Golan, 1991; Lam, 1994; Shohamy, 1992; Wesdorp, 1982). These studies mainly draw on findings from teachers' and/or students' self-report responses to questionnaires. Smith (1991b) investigated the effects of tests on teachers and classrooms through qualitative studies using interviews

(Andrews & Fullilove, 1994b; Watanabe, 1996a, 1996b). A few researchers (for example Hughes, 1988; Khaniya, 1990a) have administered language tests to measure washback on students' learning outcomes. Alderson and Wall (1993) used classroom observations (Alderson & Hamp-Lyons, 1996; Wall, 1996). They called for a strong observation component in the data collection in order to understand the nature of washback.

Besides a classroom observation component, the researcher thought that if the core of washback has to do with the effects of tests on teaching and learning, it would be necessary to document those effects both by asking about, and watching teaching and learning (see Bailey, 1999; Sudman & Bradburn, 1982; van Lier, 1988, 1989a, 1989b).

Bailey (1999) argues that the need for classroom observations and a combined approach can be illustrated by looking at a washback study that employs only the survey method. For example, Herman and Golan (1991) (cited in Bailey, 1999) conducted a survey among matched pairs of teachers from two different kinds of schools, and investigated schools where test scores had increased, and where test scores had decreased or remained the same. Among other things, the teachers' self-report responses to their questionnaire yielded the following findings:

- teachers felt pressure to improve students' test scores
- testing affects instructional planning and delivery
- substantial time is spent preparing students for testing
- non-tested subjects also got some attention.

Without observing the actual teaching, it would be very difficult to explore the above in full. For example, we would not know: (a) how much such pressure influences teaching, (b) in what ways tests influence planning and delivery, (c) how much time is spent preparing students for testing, and (d) what kind of attention is given to those subject areas which are not covered in the tests. Survey data alone is useful but insufficient for understanding washback.

Furthermore, Wall and Alderson (1993: 62) point out the complexity of washback and emphasize the importance of a combined method to answer questions such as 'why the teachers do what they do, what they understand about the underlying principles of the textbook and examination, and what they believe to be effective means of teaching and learning.' They concluded that 'observations on their own cannot give a full account of what is happening in classrooms.'

> It was important for us to complement the classroom observations with teacher interviews, questionnaires to teachers and teacher advisers, and analyses of materials (especially tests) teachers had prepared for classes (Wall and Alderson, 1993: 63).

Following the discussion above, the researcher felt that it would be worthwhile investigating (a) the nature of the examination within the teaching and learning context, and then (b) the nature of the washback effect and the conditions under which it operates. A study of washback cannot be carried out without considering the complex nature of the classroom, as it embodies a specific set of functions and values from the teacher and the learner, and also from the point of social setting and institutions at large (van Lier, 1988).

For this study, there are two levels of washback phenomena that lend themselves to exploration. First, the present educational context related to the teaching and learning situations in Hong Kong secondary schools should be observed. Observations would be appropriate to see which parties within the education system would react most to the examination change. Observing at this stage could provide an initial feel for the Hong Kong education setting in relation to the new 1996 HKCEE. Second, investigation could be undertaken by asking (surveying and interviewing) teachers and students on their feelings about and perceptions of the new 1996 HKCEE, and observing (classroom observations) classroom teaching and learning. Therefore, a combined approach by asking and watching is essential for this type of exploratory study.

After a combined approach had been decided for the study, the next logical step was to look at any instruments that had been developed for similar washback studies. However, no single uniform questionnaire has emerged as being widely used to survey teachers and students about washback (Bailey, 1999). The reason for the lack of a uniform questionnaire, according to Bailey, is either the advantages to surveying students in their native language, or because such studies have tended to focus on the washback from a particular local exam. In addition, neither is there an existing classroom observation scheme for observation. This might simply be due to the limited numbers of washback studies using classroom observations. The lack of existing uniform instruments for studying washback indicates that the researcher had to design her own instruments for the survey and classroom observation mentioned above. The validation and reliability of these instruments had to rely on triangulation of the data collection within the study.

To stress one point before moving on to the next section, after a review of washback studies carried out in different countries (see Chapter 2), the researcher believes that the study of washback is culturally and socially bound. The influence of certain exam(s) on teaching and learning is largely determined by the function of the examination system as well as the education system under study. Therefore, the educational context needs to be studied before studying specific areas of teaching and learning in relation to the examination. Alderson and Wall point out that:

> It is surely conceivable that other forces exist within society, education, and schools that might prevent washback from appearing, or that might affect the nature of washback despite the 'communicative' quality of a test (1993: 116).

Research strategies and methodology for this study

Drawing upon the theoretical and methodological points described in the above two sections, the researcher decided that the investigations for this study should be carried out at different levels within the Hong Kong educational context and by employing various methods.

Levels of study within the Hong Kong education system

This study explores the washback effect of the new 1996 HKCEE on classroom teaching. The investigation was carried out when a major public examination was changed in the Hong Kong secondary school system. The intended washback of the new HKCEE on teaching and learning has been well documented (see HKEA, 1993, 1994a, 1994b). What is not known is *how* the changes in the public examination would affect the classroom teaching in Hong Kong secondary schools and *what aspects* would be affected. The purpose of the study is to explore the various variables within the classroom teaching context that might be influenced by the public examination. As Fullan puts it:

> It is essential to understand both the small and the big picture. We have to know what changes look like from the point of view of the teacher, student, parent, and administrator if we are to understand the actions and reactions of individuals; and if we are to comprehend the big picture, we must combine the aggregate knowledge of these individual situations with an understanding of organisational and institutional factors that influence the process of change as government departments, universities, teacher federations, school systems and schools interact (1991).

The design of the study occurred within the specified time frame necessary to catch both the big and small picture–the macro and micro levels (see Figure 3.1). This study has adopted an approach that focuses on perceptions, values, and situational factors rather than on the classical mode of evaluation, with the study focus on inputs and outputs, to explore the teaching and learning process in the unique, complex, and varying situations in schools. It should never be overlooked that the school itself is 'the crucible of the curriculum and that the teacher is its principal agent (Fullan, 1991).' The teacher's definition of his/her own roles, his/her perception of the school and his/her judgement of what is possible within it should provide the starting point for the study of washback in relation to the new 1996 HKCEE. The reason for this starting point is that washback requires a context-based case study of curriculum change in relation to its assessment components, and classroom teaching in relation to the characteristics of individual teachers and students. Teachers and students are members of a complex interactive social system. Therefore, a form of ethnographic observation is appropriate for the study in which manifestations of changes to the HKCEE examination syllabus could be seen and experienced in their natural settings.

The aim was to observe how the Hong Kong education system reacted in the context of changes to the public examination at the macro, and then the micro levels. The observations served the purpose of discovering aspects of teaching within the Hong Kong educational context in which the most significant (or insignificant) changes occurred (see Figure 3.1 below).

Qualitative and quantitative data

Underlying the above questions is the problem of finding meaning in change. If 'changes' are to be successful, individuals and groups must find meaning concerning what should change as well as how to go about it. It is also essential to understand both the small and the big picture. We have to know what change looks like from the perspective of the teacher, student and administrator if we are to understand the actions and reasons of individuals. If we are to comprehend the big picture, we must combine the aggregate knowledge of these individual situations with an understanding of organizational and institutional factors that influence the process of change, such as the HKEA, tertiary institutions, and textbook publishers. Washback study is a multivariate endeavour that requires us to think of and address more than one factor at a time.

Combining research methods, both quantitative and qualitative data were employed based on the goals and the circumstances of the study. As discussed above, a washback study should involve what teachers *talk* about or *think* about. It also needs to involve an analysis of what teachers actually do in the classroom, and what actual changes have been made consciously and subconsciously inside the classrooms, both individually by the teachers and students and also jointly between the two parties. The goals and circumstances of the study require a multi-method methodology.

Quantitative and qualitative approaches have their own separate strengths and weaknesses. The quantitative approach usually involves a large volume of data and a large number of subjects. The results are generalizable, but are often oversimplified and show poor ecological validity. The qualitative approach can present a more accurate picture of reality and reveal more complexities, but it is time-consuming and the results are not readily generalizable (Bryman, 1992; Cohen, 1976; Cohen & Manion, 1989; Halfpenny, 1979; Hammersley & Atkinson, 1983; Patton, 1987). While we test hypotheses with a quantitative method, we have derived inferences from qualitative, conceptual considerations. The qualitative paradigm permits objectivity in the form of inter-observer agreement (Chaudron, 1986; Howe &

**Figure 3.1 The Hong Kong education system in relation to
the 1996 HKCEE**

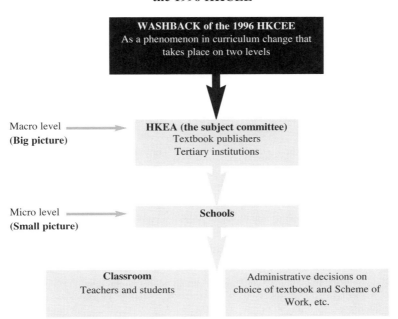

Eisenhart, 1990; Martyn, 1992; Miles, 1979). Brannen (1992) argues that quantitative and qualitative research methodologies are mutually dependent. To serve the exploratory research purpose with teaching and learning variables, neither of the single approaches would be sufficient to answer the research questions of this washback phenomenon.

The instruments adopted in this research were two survey questionnaires and classroom observations that were succeeded by follow-up interviews. The purpose of the two survey questionnaires was to explore aspects of classroom teaching related to teaching content, teachers' reactions to and perceptions of the new 1996 HKCEE, and classroom teaching and learning activities that were influenced by the change in the public examination. The aim of the qualitative part of the study, through classroom observation, was to draw from the survey results and discover further aspects of examination impact, and to explore the relationship between testing and classroom teaching activities. As Wall and Alderson (1993) point out, observations on their own can only reveal part of what is happening within the educational setting. The data makes sense only in context. The context, however, can only be acquired by study of the situation with a qualitative approach, as the situation can be more sensibly understood. Therefore, questionnaires and classroom observations with follow-up interviews were used. These three methods complement each other in this type of study. While a survey study tends to test research assumptions, classroom observation is an exploratory process of learning, which helps to shape the research design and refine the observation scheme. This type of multiple method approach provides cross-examination mechanisms, often referred to as *triangulation* (Hammersley & Atkinson, 1983: 198). They point out that 'different types of data lead to the same conclusion, one can be a little more confident in that conclusion.'

Various approaches to triangulation have been employed to increase the quality control and representativeness of the study (Allwright & Bailey, 1991; van Lier, 1989a, 1989b). The approaches used in this study are as follows:

- *data triangulation* refers to data from more than one source being brought to bear in answering a research question (i.e. data from the HKEA, textbook publishers, teachers and students, panel chairs, and others)
- *researcher triangulation* uses more than one person for data collection and/or analysis
- *methodological triangulation* is used for eliciting data (survey, interviews, and classroom observation). According to Brannen (1992: 11), method triangulation may be between-methods or within-method. A within-method approach involves the same method being used on different occasions (in this study, two-year comparative surveys and classroom observations), while between-methods means using different methods in relation to the same object of study. Thus this study has combined classroom observations with survey methods of teachers and students. Furthermore, the two research methods have been used repeatedly during the two-year study.

Ethnographic research is typically carried out in the form of a case study. The purpose of using a case study is to illuminate an issue, suggest answers to questions, describe a process, or explain a change. It is not used to establish a generalizable theory. The data collection is done in the field, usually in an unobtrusive way, i.e. letting the data unfold naturally rather than to collect responses to stimuli generated by the researcher. The 'researched' are therefore neither subjects nor respondents; they are teachers or informants. Instead of trying to test the researcher's thinking, ethnographic research aims at obtaining original perceptions. The validity of ethnographic research relies on the researcher making full use of human instruments. Ethnographic research and hypothesis testing can be mutually complementary.

In this research, it is the exploration of the nature of washback that is important, not the issue of inference or generalizability (Yin, 1984). Therefore, qualitative methods with case studies of classroom teaching in this research were used. This research started as an inductive inquiry that began with an absence of a clear hypothesis.

Figure 3.2 Data and method triangulation for the study

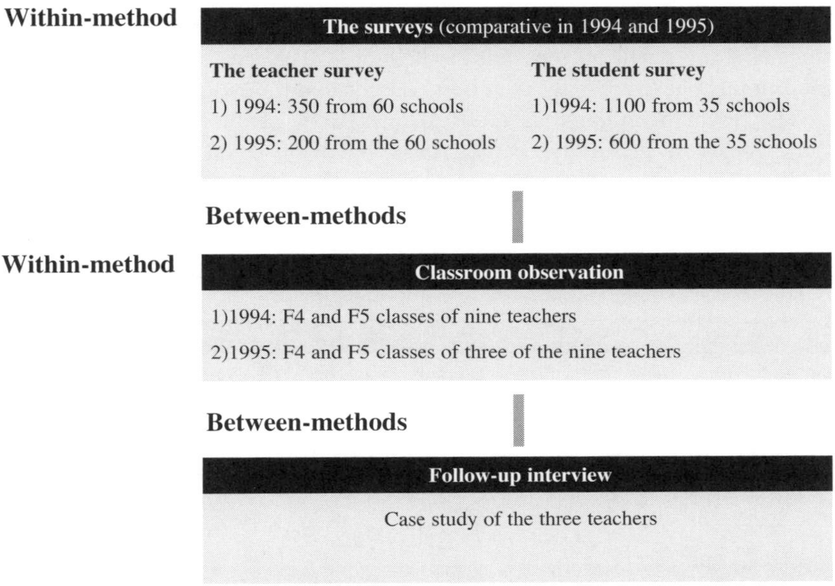

Within-method

The surveys (comparative in 1994 and 1995)	
The teacher survey	**The student survey**
1) 1994: 350 from 60 schools	1)1994: 1100 from 35 schools
2) 1995: 200 from the 60 schools	2) 1995: 600 from the 35 schools

Between-methods

Within-method

Classroom observation
1)1994: F4 and F5 classes of nine teachers
2)1995: F4 and F5 classes of three of the nine teachers

Between-methods

Follow-up interview
Case study of the three teachers

Research phases

Taking into account the time constraints on this research, this study was carried out in the following stages.

Phase I lasted from November 1993 to November 1994. This was the decision-making stage. Findings will be reported in Chapter 4. The major research methods used in this phase were:

- key informant interviews
- overall observations
- initial survey study.

Phase II lasted for another year, from November 1994 to December 1995. This period of research was in itself a time series study characterized by comparative surveys into teachers' and students' attitudes and their classroom behaviours in 1994 and 1995. This phase is the perception stage, the findings for which will be reported in Chapter 5 *(Teacher Survey)* and Chapter 6 *(Student Survey)*. The major research methods used in this phase are two parallel survey studies, the teacher and student surveys.

Phase III of the study lasted from November 1994 to November 1996, which overlapped with *Phase II* of the study. It focused on the classroom to observe closely what was actually happening inside the 'black box' (Long, 1980) in relation to the new 1996 HKCEE. Detailed follow-up interviews of case study teachers were also carried out. This phase was the implementation stage. Findings will be reported in Chapter 7. The major research methods used in this phase are classroom observations and follow-up interviews.

The research findings are reported in separate chapters according to the three stages of the study. Discussion will be presented together with the findings.

Figure 3.3 The three phases of the research study

Phase I

Stage: Decision-making of the public examination change (HKCEE)
Time: November 1993 – November 1994
Method:
- key informant interviews
- overall observations of all parties within the Hong Kong education context
- initial surveys of teachers and students.

Phase II

Stage: Implementation of the revised public examination (HKCEE)
Time: November 1994 – December 1995
Method:
- survey study of attitudinal changes toward the revised HKCEE in 1994, its introduction into teaching in 1995, and its first year of implementation in the teaching and learning of English in Hong Kong secondary schools
- survey study of F5 students' attitudinal changes towards the revised HKCEE in 1994, in relation to the activities they carry out in their English lessons.

Phase III

Stage: Restructuring of the revised public examination (HKCEE)
Time: November 1994 – November 1996
Method:
- classroom observations of teachers' behavioural changes in the actual teaching and learning contexts
- detailed follow-up interviews of the three teachers who participated in Phase II.

This part has summarized the theoretical and methodological derivations from previous research. It explains where the current study stands and the rationale for its design, and discusses the various methodological issues involved in the research design. By investigating the washback effect of the new 1996 HKCEE in English, we can explore the general characteristics of a system of testing, which can be identified as contributing to or distracting from the test's systematic validity, and to discovering any social, psychological, ethical, curricular, and educational consequences of the public examination change (Messick's 'unified validity', 1989, 1994, 1996). Validation of a system of testing in exploring its consequences on teaching and learning within an education system requires both a long time and joint efforts to achieve a beneficial effect. The validation of the assessment practices within the system also involves the participation of the whole education system regarding teaching education, material writing, and curriculum development. As only a limited amount of empirical research has been carried out to investigate the washback effect of examinations, either in the field of general education or in the specific field of language education, it is hoped that this study can provide a methodological framework for further study.

Part 2: Research design for the survey study

This section of the chapter will first present the research questions asked in the survey study. It will then describe the two questionnaires in relation to the participants, instruments, and procedures used for the data collection and analysis. Finally, it will indicate limitations of the survey study.

The instruments used in the survey study were two questionnaires. Two parallel survey studies, a teacher survey and a student survey, were carried out. The two sets of questionnaires were issued twice: in 1994 and in 1995 (see Chapters 5 and 6 for findings).

The survey questionnaires

As mentioned above, two parallel and comparative survey studies were carried out. They were conducted twice: once in 1994 and once in 1995. Both survey studies were issued in late October/early November. The two survey studies comprised *Phase II* of the study – perception of washback among teachers and students. Both studies explored the washback effect of the new 1996 HKCEE on aspects of classroom teaching and learning: attitudinal and behavioural changes in the context of the new 1996 HKCEE from teachers' and students' separate points of views. The teacher survey was conducted in English as the participants were teachers of English, whereas the student survey was in Chinese to avoid any problem caused by the use of English as a second language. Both questionnaires are reported in the following way:

- rationale and aim
- structure and content
- questionnaire design.

Teachers' questionnaire
Rationale and aim (see Appendix I)

The purpose of this questionnaire was to explore any attitudinal and behavioural changes over two academic years among teachers in relation to the new 1996 HKCEE. It investigated whether or not any washback had occurred on teachers' perceptions of aspects of classroom teaching and learning as specified and operationalized in the research questions. It should be noted here that the short administration duration of the survey over two academic years might indicate that only limited scope of changes in teachers' perceptions could be observed. When the questionnaires were administered in 1994, some teachers were still working with one cohort of F5 students scheduled to take the old HKCEE, and at the same time teaching F4–the first cohort scheduled to take the new HKCEE. When the questionnaires were administered for the second time in 1995, both cohorts of F5 and F4 students, which the teachers were teaching, were scheduled to take the new HKCEE. It is also assumed that the limited aspects of changes observed in the survey could reflect washback effects induced by the 1996 HKCEE as this exam change was the biggest change in Hong Kong Secondary school at the time of the research.

Structure, content, and sources

The Teachers' questionnaire (TQ) consisted of three parts and was designed and issued in English.

Part One consisted of eight categories[2] of teacher personal particulars related to: (a) demographic information, such as gender, age, academic qualifications, professional qualifications, and years of teaching experience, and (b) current teaching situations, such as major forms that were currently being taught, numbers of teaching periods per week, and the school banding.

Part Two consisted of 12 categories and 95 items altogether (TQ 2.1[3]-2.12). Each item was designed on a five-point Likert scale of agreement,

---

2. Refer to the Appendix I for details of the Teachers' Questionnaire (TQ). In this study, gender is operationally described as a category, which consists of two items: male and female.

3. TQ 2.1 refers to the Teachers' Questionnaire Part Two, Category One, which consists of 10 items.

Table 3.1 Structure and themes of the teachers' questionnaire

Structure	Content	Items
Theme One	Personal particulars (TQ 1.1–1.8)	8
	• demographic information, such as gender, age, academic qualifications, professional qualifications, years of teaching experience	
	• current teaching situations, such as major forms currently taught, the numbers of teaching periods per week, and the school band.	
Theme Two	Teachers' reactions and perceptions in relation to the new 1996 HKCEE (TQ 3.1 & TQ 2.1-2.5)	6
	• teachers' reactions to the new 1996 HKCEE	
	• the reasons behind the new 1996 HKCEE	
	• the new exam formats of the new 1996 HKCEE	
	• possible extra work and pressure under the new 1996 HKCEE	
	• possible difficulties in teaching the new 1996 HKCEE	
	• teaching methods teachers would like to change in the new 1996 HKCEE.	
Theme Three	Teaching materials (TQ 3.6, 3.7, 3.10)	3
	• textbook arrangements related to teaching materials (who and how)	
	• teaching and learning resources.	
Theme Four	Teachers' classroom behaviours (TQ 3.2–3.4; 3.8 – 3.9).	7
	• medium of instruction	
	• teaching arrangement (who plans and how to plan).	
	• lesson preparation	
	• teacher talk	
	• teaching activities.	
Theme Five	Assessment and evaluation (TQ 2.10–2.12)	3
	• the use of mock exams	
	• the assessment of teaching in Hong Kong secondary schools	
	• factors that influence teaching.	
Theme Six	Aspects of learning (TQ 2.6–2.9)	4
	• learning strategies	
	• learning activities	
	• learning aims	
	• motivation to learn.	

where five = strongly agree, four = agree, three = undecided, two = disagree and one = strongly disagree. The five-point Likert scale was employed as it is one of the most commonly accepted Likert scales in the education field (Cohen, 1976; Cohen & Manion 1989; Gu, Wen, & Wu, 1995; Jaeger, 1988). This part mainly dealt with teachers' perceptions of aspects of teaching, learning, and assessment and evaluation in schools in relation to the new 1996 HKCEE.

Part 3 consisted of 10 categories, which dealt with teachers' reactions to the new examination and aspects of classroom teaching and learning activities of English in Hong Kong secondary schools in the context of the new 1996 HKCEE. Categories 1 to 6 (TQ3.1 – 3.6) were designed on a multiple-choice basis. Teachers are required to choose the appropriate answers according to their own classroom teaching and learning situations. Categories 7 to 10 (TQ3.7 – 3.10) were designed on a five-point Likert scale of frequency, where 5 = always, 4 = often, 3 = sometimes, 2 = seldom, and 1 = never.

There are six main research themes designed and structured within the questionnaire. Table 3.1 presents the main themes of the teachers' questionnaire, which explored the above operationalized research questions in this study. Three main sources contributed to the development of the questionnaire. Theme Two of the questionnaire was mainly derived from interviews with members of the HKEA Subject Committee, which consists of language experts and secondary school teachers. These interviews aimed to find the main areas that might be influenced by the exam change. Themes Three and Five were derived from government documents such as the teaching and examination syllabuses (Forms I-V) and relevant documents published by Hong Kong Education Departments. Themes Four and Six were derived from talking to principals, panel chairs, form coordinators, teachers, and students. They also drew on other relevant research studies in Hong Kong (see Biggs, 1992, 1993, 1995, 1996; Hivela & Law, 1991; Johnson, 1983, 1989, 1993/1994; Morris, 1990a, 1990b, 1991, 1995; Pierson, Gail, & Lee, 1979; Richards et al, 1992).

Design and validation procedures

To emphasize the nature of the research, two main strategies, *asking and watching*, were the basis of considerations in the survey design (Erickson, 1986; Low, 1988). Both strategies were employed in the design of the questionnaire. They are reflected in the two main methods used in the survey study, namely, qualitative input and piloting procedures, which were employed in this study to ensure the validity of the items in the questionnaire. While qualitative input ensures the content validity, piloting procedures ensure the construct validity.

Stage One: qualitative input. Qualitative input consists of (a) theoretical derivations from related research studies reviewed in Chapter 2, which suggested modifications or additions to the research questions, instrument development, and plans for analysis of data, and (b) qualitative data from interviews and school visits. The qualitative input served the essential elements for this type of exploratory study. Such study is different from hypothesis testing, as here the researcher is required to go into the field to watch what is happening in the classroom and to interview teachers in order to find out what is going through their minds. It is important to get a feel for the research problem in context (Arnove, Altbach, & Kelly, 1992; Alderson & Scott, 1992). The emphasis of the qualitative input was on achieving a research focus on the research problem. For this type of exploratory study, the research problem (questions) took a long time to emerge explicitly.

Stage Two: piloting with open-ended protocols. Piloting ensures that questionnaire items are interpreted as much as possible in the same way by every survey respondent (Cohen, 1976; Cohen & Manion, 1989; Jaeger, 1988). There were two major piloting stages during the questionnaire design before the main study was carried out.

The first pilot study[4] was carried out on April 16, 1994 with 48 teachers, four months before they began teaching towards the revised examination syllabus for the first cohort of F4 students in September 1994. This was at the time that the decision was made to change the HKCEE and when the HKEA, textbook publishers, and tertiary institutions were organizing seminars and workshops for the new examination. Therefore, the first aim of this initial questionnaire was to obtain preliminary data on teachers' reactions towards the revised examination, their perceptions and understanding, and what they would like to do to prepare their students for the new examination. The second aim was to validate the construct of the questionnaire items.

The first part of the questionnaire was constructed in such a way that teachers first responded to a series of questions related to possible changes in areas of teaching and learning with a 'yes' or 'no' answer. The second part of the questionnaire was designed on a five-point Likert scale, which invited teachers to comment on their present teaching, the choice of textbooks, and the teaching methods they use.

The purpose of this questionnaire was to explore teachers' immediate attitude to the context of the revised examination. After the yes/no answers were given, the teachers were then invited to elaborate further their own views with written answers in the spaces provided. The purpose of this 'written word' data is to facilitate understanding of teachers' feelings about the examination change, and to provide qualitative input for the more structured

---

4.   The findings of the pilot study are reported in Chapter Four – Phase I of the study.

survey comparison in Phase II of the study. Such a process for the teachers to provide written data is very time-consuming, but it proved to be valuable. The most important aspect of such an amount of qualitative data, for this pilot study, was that it provided a valuable content validation for the major questionnaire study.

To reiterate here, as the nature of the survey design required the survey to be issued twice to enable a comparative study of the two-year sample, the piloting procedure was extremely important. Once the main study for the first year was issued in 1994, there was little room to allow for modifications for the second year. The procedure was pre-determined by the comparative nature of the survey. The piloting procedures also served the purpose of focusing on the research problem. In this case, the research was to explore the areas of teaching and learning that could be influenced by the changes in the HKCEE in order to explore the nature of the washback effect.

The second pilot study was carried out on October 18, 1994 with 31 teachers. This was at the time when the revised 1996 HKCEE[5] was being implemented to prepare the first cohort of students over the two year period. At that time, almost all schools whose students sat for the HKCEE acquired revised textbooks for the new 1996 HKCEE. The second study aimed to pilot and pre-test the categories and items for the questionnaire for main study and to determine what was and was not working in the questionnaire. In this way, the second pilot ensured that questionnaire items would be understood as intended. The procedure served as a method of construct validation for the main survey study. The overall structure of this version of the questionnaire was the same in format as the questionnaire for the main study. However, a number of substantial adjustments and modifications were made to the questionnaire items.

A focus group was used to allow participants the opportunity to react to various aspects of the questionnaire. Such a method was employed as another procedure for construct validation. 11 of the 31 teachers during the second pilot were selected randomly for 'cognitive interviews' (sometimes referred to as 'thinking aloud' procedures). The purpose was to determine whether (a) the question items in the survey were understood as intended by the researcher, and (b) they were understood in the same way among the teachers themselves. Such group discussions have been coupled with cognitive interviews, which are appropriate for evaluating specific question wording (Cohen & Manion, 1989). The interviews were conducted on a face-to-face basis, and sufficient time was given whenever teachers raised questions in relation to any of the

---

5. As mentioned in Chapter One, the new 1996 HKCEE syllabus was officially put into teaching in schools in September 1994. The first cohort of F5 students was required to sit for the exam in May 1996.

questionnaire items. These results from the first pilot procedure were cross-referenced with the second pilot results.

After the above procedures were finalized, expert analysis was carried out on the pre-final version of the questionnaire for the main study. In an expert analysis, a researcher reviews a questionnaire to gain an understanding of the response task and to note potential problems (Brannen, 1992; Bryman, 1992). The researcher then could classify the observations to enable a general understanding of the questionnaire, specific points where the respondents might have difficulties, and the types of misinterpretations the respondents might make. Two research colleagues, both doctoral candidates in the area of language education, were invited to complete the questionnaire and voice their opinions. Their views on the questionnaire structure, the design of the categories, items, and wordings helped to shape the final questionnaire and prepare it for the main study. Figure 3.4 illustrates the stages of the questionnaire design together with the procedures undertaken for the considerations about validity discussed above.

Figure 3.4 Stages of the teachers' questionnaire design

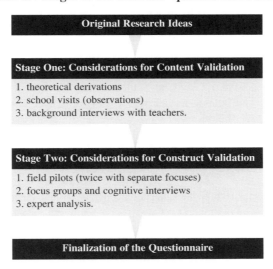

Students' questionnaire
Rationale and aim

The purpose of the student questionnaire was to explore students' attitudinal and behavioural changes that can be linked very closely with classroom teaching and learning in the context of the new 1996 HKCEE over the two years. The student survey explored the changes in relation to classroom teaching and learning activities from the students' points of view. It also investigated the role of the public examination in students' learning. It provided data from the students' points of view, but also served as valid referencing data (a triangulation) to the findings from the teacher survey. Therefore, this survey focused on the main themes designed in the teacher survey. The survey was issued to F5 students, as they were the cohort who would sit for the revised HKCEE. It was issued twice: once in 1994 to F5 students under the old HKCEE, and once in 1995 to F5 students who were the first cohort to sit for the new 1996 HKCEE.

Structure, content, and sources

This questionnaire consisted of two parts.

Part One consisted of five categories (SQ 1.1[6] – 1.5). It dealt with student demographic information in the survey and the learning contexts in which students were situated. Student demographic information included gender and the grade when students started to be taught in English. General information about the learning contexts included medium of instruction of their English lessons, the frequency with which their teachers mentioned the public examination (the HKCEE) in class, and the numbers of private tutorials they attended each week for the HKCEE. All items in this part were designed on a multiple-choice basis.

Part Two consisted of three sections with 11 categories and 78 items in total. This part deals with students' attitudes towards teaching and learning activities inside and outside their English lessons. There were three sections with a total of three themes. *Section A* (five categories, *SQ 2.1-2.5*) dealt with classroom teaching and learning activities. Items in this section were designed on a five-point Likert scale, where five = always, four = often, three = sometimes, two = seldom and one = never. *Section B* (five categories, *SQ 2.6-2.10*) invited students' opinions about aspects of learning. Items in this section were designed on a five-point Likert scale, where five = strongly agree, four = agree, three = undecided, two = disagree, and one = strongly disagree. *Section C* (one category, *SQ 2.11*) consisted of one category with 12 items. They were designed on a five-point Likert scale of agreement as well. These items are related to students' attitudes towards aspects of the public examination's influence in schools. There are two sub-themes in relation to the public examination. Items one, five, eight, 11, and 12 dealt with the impact of examinations on students themselves. Items two, three, four, six, seven, nine, and ten dealt with the impact of examinations on students' learning

---

6.   SQ 1.1 refers to Students' Questionnaire, Part One, Category One.

processes and outcomes. The categories in the student survey are described according to the main themes below in Table 3.2.

The students' questionnaire was mainly derived from the following sources:

- Hong Kong government reports (Education Department, 1990; HKCDC, 1983; HKEA, 1992/93, 1993, 1994a, 1994b)
- relevant research studies within the Hong Kong education context (Falvey, 1991a, 1991b, 1996; Lord, 1987; Lord & Cheng, 1987; Morris, 1990a, 1990b, 1991, 1995; Pierson, Gail, & Lee, 1979; Postiglione & Leung, 1992; Richards et al, 1992)
- school visits for observing classes and interviewing teachers and students.

Section C of Part Two of the student questionnaire was adapted from Gullickson (1984). His study focused on teachers' perspectives of their instructional use of tests. These perspectives were closely related to students and their learning in this study.

Table 3.2 Structure and themes of the students' questionnaire

Structure	Content and themes	Items
Part 1	Demographic information:	
	Gender, the grade when they were taught in an English learning context, medium of instruction in their English lessons, frequency with which their teachers mention the public examination (HKCEE) to them, and the numbers of private tutorials attended each week for the HKCEE.	SQ 1.1-1.5
Part 2	Theme 1: Classroom teaching and learning activities	SQ 2.1-2.5
	• their teachers' talk in class	
	• their teachers' teaching activities in class	
	• students' learning activities in class	
	• students' use of English in class	
	• students' use of English outside class.	
	Theme 2: Perceptions of aspects of learning:	SQ 2.6-2.10
	• English lessons	
	• their motivation for learning English	
	• their preferred learning strategies	
	• whether or not they are influenced by the public exam	
	• aspects of examination influences on students.	
	Theme 3: Students' attitudes towards the public exam.	SQ 2.11

Design and validation procedures

To match the research questions asked in the teacher survey, the student questionnaire was designed parallel to the teacher questionnaire. Therefore, the basic considerations for validation were the same as for the teacher survey. For example, the two main strategies–asking and watching–and the two stages of design–qualitative input and the piloting procedure–were undertaken for both student and teacher surveys.

Stage One: Qualitative Input was performed in the same way as the teacher survey, which consisted of (a) theoretical derivations and (b) school visits (observations and interviews). Stage Two: Piloting and Translation was carried out rather differently from the teacher survey as the student survey was issued in Chinese rather than English. Piloting was carried out in November 1994 with 83 students in one class of the first cohort of F4 students studying for the new examination, and one class of the last group of F5 students sitting for the old examination. Both classes were in a subsidized school in the New Territories. The questionnaire was designed on a five-point Likert scale. The section relating to students' attitudes towards learning activities inside and outside the classroom (Section A) was scaled according to frequency, while the sections relating to aspects of their learning and public examinations (Sections B & C) were scaled according to the degree of agreement. The pilot was carried out in class in the presence of their teacher and the researcher, to enable students to ask questions about the questionnaire while they were doing it. This approach helped the researcher to note any unseen problems with the questionnaire. Part of the findings from this piloting was reported in *Phase I* of the study.

Translation procedures

The student questionnaire was originally designed in English, while it was being co-developed with the teacher questionnaire in the study. It was, however, issued to the students in Chinese. The rationale behind this was to minimize misunderstanding and reliability and validity problems caused by the language factor (Geisinger, 1994). Therefore, in addition to using the same procedures that were used in the teacher survey, extra efforts were made in the validation procedure of the translated version.

The Chinese version of the questionnaire, which was translated from the English version developed alongside the teacher questionnaire, was widely read by research colleagues, especially Cantonese[7] speaking colleagues in the

---

7. The Chinese used within the Hong Kong education context is called Cantonese for the spoken and modern Chinese for the written form. Written Chinese in Hong Kong is largely the same as written Chinese in mainland China, except complicated characters are used instead of simplified characters in China. However, there are certain regional variations. Therefore, it is a valid procedure to avoid any misunderstanding by consulting persons who grew up and were educated locally.

Faculty of Education at the University of Hong Kong. To enhance the validity of the questionnaires, the Chinese version was retranslated back into English to see whether anything was missing or could be misinterpreted. The translation was carried out by fellow doctoral researchers within the Faculty. This approach minimized the differences between the use of the written Chinese language in Hong Kong and in mainland China.

The design stages and validation procedures of the student questionnaire are summarized and illustrated in Figure 3.5.

Figure 3.5 Stages of the students' questionnaire design

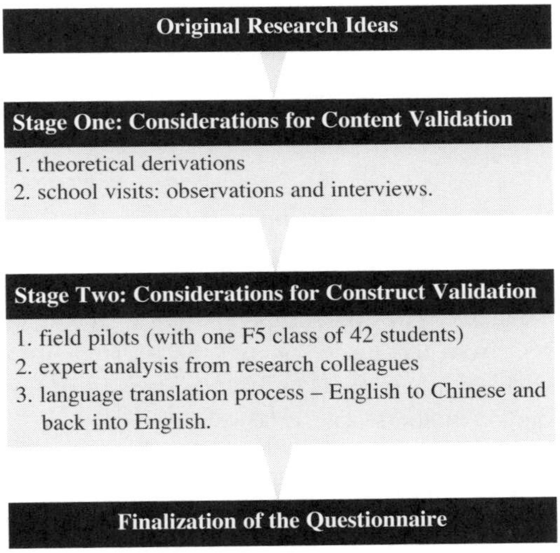

Original Research Ideas

Stage One: Considerations for Content Validation

1. theoretical derivations
2. school visits: observations and interviews.

Stage Two: Considerations for Construct Validation

1. field pilots (with one F5 class of 42 students)
2. expert analysis from research colleagues
3. language translation process – English to Chinese and back into English.

Finalization of the Questionnaire

Sampling for both teacher and student surveys

There are 448 secondary day schools (versus evening schools) in Hong Kong, located in 19 districts. Figure 3.6 shows the types of secondary schools in Hong Kong. They are, on one hand, categorized as government, aided, and private schools (horizontal row in Figure 3.6). The main reason for the existence of different types of schools is historical and political in nature. The other category of school types (vertical column in Figure 3.6) is related to the medium of instruction. *Anglo-Chinese* refers to English medium instruction; that is, all courses are delivered in English except Chinese and Chinese history. *Chinese* refers to Chinese medium of instruction. The third category, *Anglo-Chinese & Chinese,* refers to a combination of both mediums of English and Chinese. As the study focuses on the washback effect of the new 1996 HKCEE, only schools whose students would sit for the HKCEE were explored. Therefore, no international or English schools were included in the study. Evening schools and pre-vocational schools[8] were also excluded. Students in those schools do not sit for the HKCEE.

Figure 3.6 Distribution of Hong Kong secondary schools 1993/94 (Source: Hong Kong Government, 1993: 55)

	Government	Aided	Private	Total
Anglo-Chinese	33	299	56	388
Chinese	2	14	7	23
Anglo-Chinese & Chinese	3	5	4	12
English	1	5	15	21
Others	–	–	2	2
English & others	–	–	2	2
Total	**39**	**323**	**86**	**448**

Both surveys focused on teachers and students from 323 aided schools out of the 388 Anglo-Chinese schools. The rationale for this choice was the fact that students in these schools usually opt for Syllabus B of the HKCEE, which is the focus of the study. The specific population of the survey consisted of teachers of English from those schools and the F5 students in their classes. Teachers of English were surveyed in 1994 and in 1995 from the same 60 Hong Kong secondary schools. These 60 schools comprise 15% of the total secondary school population in Hong Kong.

F5 students taking the old HKCEE in 1994 and F5 students in 1995 who would take the new 1996 HKCEE responded to the student survey. They were sampled from 35 out of the 60 secondary schools. These 35 schools comprised 7.8% of the above school population. F5 students were surveyed in 1994 and 1995 from the same 35 schools. All teachers who taught those students were included in the teacher survey in both years.

The teacher survey

In 1994, 350 teachers were sampled. The return rate was 40% (140 out of 350 questionnaires issued that year). In 1995, 200 teachers were sampled. The return rate was 47% (94 out of 200 questionnaires issued in that year). The 1995 sampling was smaller compared to that in 1994, the rationale being that this sampling served as a focus study. This was also due to resource

8. Students in those schools can sit the HKCEE, if they wish to, as independent adult candidates.

constraints. The following table provides detailed information about both years' samplings.

Table 3.3 Sampling of teachers' questionnaires in 1994 and 1995

Teachers' Perspectives on Public Examinations in Hong Kong Secondary Schools

1994 Sample Size	Returned	Percent	1995 Sample Size	Returned	Percent
350	140	40%	200	94	47%

The teacher survey was conducted with similar groups of teachers in both years. The sample was from the same schools survey in 1994 (see also teachers' demographical information survey in 1994 and 1995 in Tables 3.5 and 5.1). The population of teachers in Hong Kong secondary schools changes immensely from year to year, due to the current nature of Hong Kong as a rapidly changing society, seen through such examples as the change of profession and movement into commercial sectors, emigration to other countries, etc. Another constraint on the research was the fact that it was almost impossible to trace the same groups of teachers and issue the questionnaires to them over a two year period. Therefore, the questionnaires were issued to similar groups of teachers in 1994 and 1995.

The student survey

In 1994, 1100 student questionnaires were issued to F5 students taking the old HKCEE. The return rate was 76.7% (844 out of the total 1100 questionnaires issued that year). In 1995, 600 questionnaires were issued to F5 students who would take the new 1996 HKCEE. The return rate was 73.8% (443 out of 600 questionnaires issued that year). The rationale behind the smaller sample in 1995 is the same as that for the situation with the teachers mentioned above.

Table 3.4 Sampling of students' questionnaires in 1994 and 1995

Students' Perceptions of Public Examinations in Hong Kong Secondary Schools

1994 Sample Size	Returned	Percent	1995 Sample Size	Returned	Percent
1100	844	76.7%	600	443	73.8%

Data collection procedures

After the sampling procedures were finalized, a random list of the 60 schools was generated from the school database. The procedure was carried out at the Faculty of Education, University of Hong Kong. Data collection procedures were carried out using the same approaches for the surveys in both years. The following section will explain the data collection procedures for the teacher survey and the student survey.

Teachers' questionnaires

The teacher questionnaires were distributed through many channels: (a) P.C. Ed in-service teachers or INSTEP[9] teachers studying at the University of Hong Kong, whose schools were on the sampled school lists, brought the questionnaires to their colleagues in their own schools. Their colleagues either took the questionnaires back to the University of Hong Kong by themselves or returned them by mail. Stamped self-addressed envelopes were prepared for these people. (b) The majority of questionnaires were mailed to the school principals and panel chairs (heads of the respective English department) with stamped self-addressed envelopes. Mutual agreement about return procedures via telephone and letter correspondence was reached before the mailing. These school administrators subsequently arranged for the surveys to be carried out in their schools and mailed back.

Students' questionnaires

Student questionnaires were distributed mainly by three methods. The detailed procedures were: (a) questionnaires were mailed to F5 teachers. Consent was obtained from their principals and themselves. In this case, questionnaires were administered directly by the F5 teachers who were teaching those F5 students at the time of the research who would sit for the HKCEE. Alternatively, they arranged appropriate times for their students or their colleagues' students to complete the questionnaires in their schools. They then brought them back or sent them back using self-addressed return envelopes. (b) Questionnaires were mailed to the school principals after the principals gave consent. They would arrange for the survey to be carried out in their schools and for the questionnaires to be sent back to the researcher. (c) Questionnaires were issued to students in class when the researcher was in their classroom.

---

9. INSTEP refers to the In-Service Teacher Education Programme offered by the University of Hong Kong.

Data analysis procedures

As the two questionnaires were designed using parallel procedures, the data analysis procedures were the same for both the teacher and the student surveys. Data from both questionnaires were edited, sorted, and filed on to a TOPCON computer at the University of Hong Kong. Firstly, frequency distributions were calculated for all the questionnaire items, and missing values of each item–missing completely at random (MCAR)–were replaced by the items' mean value. All percentages were reported as valid percentages with missing data excluded. The survey data was analysed using SPSS[10] (DOS version in 1994 and Windows version in 1995). Figures to illustrate the findings were created in Microsoft Excel 5.0 and the tables were created in Microsoft Word 6.0.

To emphasize the comparative nature of the survey studies, both questionnaires were issued twice during the two years to explore possible attitudinal changes among teachers and students brought about by the new 1996 HKCEE in relation to aspects of classroom teaching and learning. Therefore, the comparative study was the key to this study. The major aim of the parallel surveys was mainly to find out the *differences* between findings over the two year period. The differences of the survey findings were tested for statistical significance by using two statistical methods, namely, the chi-square test and the independent sample t-test. A probability of less than 0.05, as commonly used in educational research (Cohen & Manion, 1989; Jaeger, 1988), was taken as statistically significant for both surveys for the findings in each year.

The chi-square test was performed initially to find the similarities between the two groups of teachers and students according to the survey demographic information. The statistical rationale behind the chi-square procedure was the nature of the nominal variables designed in this part. Chi-square is used to evaluate the discrepancy (the degree of relativity) between the means of the teachers' and students' demographic information in the samples over the two different years. A significance level ($P < 0.05$) from the chi-square statistical analysis provides a valid basis for further sample mean comparison by independent t-tests. A note of caution is that the possibility of error increases with the number of chi-square tests being carried out (Woods, Fletcher, & Hughes, 1986: 149). Consequently, a multiple method design and method triangulation (see Figure 3.2) was employed in the study to complement each method used and to guide against errors rising from the data collection and analysis.

The results in Table 3.5 show that there is no significant difference among the seven categories of the teachers' demographic information ($P > 0.05$)

10. SPSS stands for Statistical Package for Social Sciences.

except one category, *forms currently taught by teachers,* which had a significant difference at the .00016 level.[11] The findings showed that the two samples of teachers were very similar despite being different groups of teachers.

Table 3.5 Teachers' demographic information

Items	Variables	Chi-square Significance
Gender	Male or Female	.37266
Age	20-30 or 31-40;	.66865
	41-50 or above	
Academic qualifications	B.A. or B.Sc.	.18192
	Masters or others	
Professional qualification	Teacher Certification	.22437
	P.C. Ed/Dip. Ed	
	Advanced Diploma	
	RSA or M.Ed.	
Years of teaching	1-3 or 4-6 or 7-9	.49256
	10 or more	
Major forms currently taught	F1-F3; F4-F5; F6-F7	.00016
Teaching periods per week	16-21 or 22-27	.18056
	28-33 or above 33	
School band	Band 1 or Band 2	
	Band 3 or 4 or 5	.18852

Chi-square tests were also carried out for the student survey. Results showed there were no significant differences in student demographic information between the 1994 and 1995 samples (see Table 3.6).

The student sample was similar to samples in 1994 and 1995 from the above table. As mentioned above, the student survey compared the differences between two groups of F5 students – one group of F5 students taking the old HKCEE in 1995, and one group of F5 students taking the new 1996 HKCEE. After the 1994 survey, the 1994 F5 group did not exist anymore. They left school or went on to study at F6. Therefore, it was not possible to issue the survey to the same group of F5 students over the

11. In retrospect, the 1994 sample should have avoided F6-7 teachers as they are not directly related to HKCEE teaching. It was hypothesized at the time of the research that this group of teachers might show a more positive attitude to the 1996 HKCEE due to a similar task-based exam change in the Use of English examination at the end of Form 7. This uneven sampling might contribute to the mixed picture seen from the results reported in Chapter Five.

**Table 3.6 Students' demographic information and
their learning contexts**

Items	Variables	Chi-square Significance
Gender	Male or Female	.67864
The grade when English was first taught	P 1-2 or P 3-4 or P5-6	.83762
	S 1 or S 2	
Medium of instruction	English only	.00000
	English supplemented with Chinese	
	Half English and half Chinese or Mainly Chinese	
Frequency with which their teacher mentioned the public exam	Never or seldom	.00000
	Sometimes or often	
	Always	
Private tutorials per week	None, once or twice	.00005
	3-4 times or 5 times & above	

following year. The survey, however, was indeed carried out with F5 students in the same 35 schools in both years. Furthermore, the other three aspects of the student survey regarding the learning context showed significant differences over the two year period, which indicated a change in their learning context with the new 1996 HKCEE (the 1995 sample being the first cohort taking the new exam), even though these students came from the same 35 schools in 1994 and 1995. The variables regarding which language (Chinese = L1, English = L2 or a mixed mode of L1 and L2) students were taught in their English classes, the frequency their teacher mentioned the public exam per week, and the number of private tutorials students attended showed significant changes. This part of the data could show the changes in relation to the 1996 HKCEE. An independent sample t-test was carried out to test differences in the students' attitudes between the 1994 and 1995 samples. A probability of less than 0.05 was taken as statistically significant.

Part 3: Research design for classroom observations

This section will expand on the discussions in the literature review, presented in Chapter Two. It presents the major considerations that were taken in the research design for the classroom observations in this study. The purpose of the classroom observations was to find out whether the new 1996 HKCEE brought about any changes in classroom teaching in Hong Kong secondary schools. Where the findings show changes, the nature of those changes is discussed. This section also describes the rationale behind the research design, the classroom observation scheme, the teacher and student participants in the study, and the procedures used for data collection and data analysis.

The combined framework for the current inquiry

This section describes the main reasons behind the choice of a combined framework for the classroom observations in this study.

Rationale

Classroom observation has been long employed as a research method into teaching and learning. 'Classroom observation views the classroom as a place where interactions of various kinds take place, affording learners opportunities to acquire the L2' (Ellis, 1994: 565). Allwright (1984: 156) sees interaction as 'the fundamental fact of classroom pedagogy' because 'everything that happens in the classroom happens through a process of live person-to-person interaction.' This perspective has led researchers to observe and describe the interactional events that take place in a classroom in order to understand how learning opportunities are created.

This study deals with possible changes that the new HKCEE might bring about in the teaching and learning of English in Hong Kong secondary schools over a period of time. Thus, observation is an essential element in this type of study. However, this study is different from the classroom studies, which focus only on what happens inside the classrooms. This study not only focuses on what happens inside classrooms, and levels of teaching (c.f. Stern, 1983), but also observes washback within the educational context. This aspect of the classroom research data and the teacher survey data complement each other, and they combine to answer the research questions of the study. Observations in this study were carried out at the decision-making level first (see Figure 2.3 in Chapter 2). The observed changes (reported in Chapter 4) showed the reactions of different parties (participants or stakeholders) in the Hong Kong education system to the examination changes, and the necessary support offered to schools at the lower grade level. Detailed classroom observations were then carried out to investigate teaching and learning interaction.

As highlighted in Chapter 2, observation is always selective. It needs a chosen object, a definite task, an interest, a point of view, or a problem. Selection is usually directed by prior decisions as to what is relevant and significant to a particular study. These decisions are derived from theoretical or value assumptions. Furthermore, Long (1980: 12) comments that 'observation instruments are, in fact, more (or less) theoretical claims about second language learning and teaching' (see also Haggstrom, Morgan, & Wieczorek, 1995; Stern, 1989).

However, others may not share the assumptions that determine the observer's selection. As a result, they could contest the selection on the grounds of bias (Weir & Roberts, 1994: 165). For this reason, observation data should be obtained by a system capable of being described to others, to minimize reflection of the observer's personal expectations and achieve as much independence and objectivity of the data as possible.

The review of the literature on classroom observation methodology in Chapter 2 illustrates four traditions and two different approaches to classroom observation: the systematic observation approach and the ethnographic approach. The systematic approach (see Flanders, 1970: Interaction Analysis Categories) used an observational system designed to reduce classroom behaviour to small-scale units under pre-determined categories suitable for tabulation and statistical analysis. This methodology focuses on objectivity of the data, in the sense that the observer is not required to make inferences during the data collection process. Therefore, low inferencing, and with well-trained observers, high inter-rater reliability, can be achieved.

The ethnographic approach, on the other hand, uses participant observation, in which observers immerse themselves in the situation they are observing for a certain duration, interacting with the participants (also called informants) and interviewing them formally or informally (see Allwright & Bailey, 1991; Breen, 1989; Byrne, 1987; Mehan, 1979; Nunan, 1989a, 1989b). The data collection process often involves recording detailed field notes including notes on the physical setting, and the way that different parties interact. This methodology acknowledges the complexity of the classroom situation and uses a holistic framework, basing the observation not on pre-determined categories but according to the context in which the teaching is occurring. Observers have to interpret and even make judgements during the observation and recording process. The ethnographic approach is, therefore, termed 'high-inference' recording, although high validity cannot be achieved.

The merits and limitations of the two approaches have been debated (Allwright, 1983; Allwright & Bailey, 1991; Chaudron, 1988). It seems to the researcher that the *systematic approach* should be used only when a researcher, backed up by well-established educational theories, is very clear about what exactly to observe, and possesses a well-tested observation scheme. In such systematic observation, the influence of other factors on the variables under observation is ignored during the observation process because if the observer takes further factors into consideration he or she is making inferences, which affects the objective recording process. In an ethnographic approach, researchers can be less sure about what exactly the focus of the observation is at the beginning and try to clarify what behaviours to look for as they gain experience during the observations. They are less interested in quantifying behaviours, and can feel free to infer and try to gain meanings out of the observations.

The two approaches discussed above represent two different research paradigms, but they are not mutually exclusive. It has been pointed out (Tsui, 1995) that there is not necessarily a conflict between these two dimensions of description. The two approaches to classroom observation–systemic observation and ethnographic study–should be used complementarily rather than exclusively. Furthermore, the investigation into the washback effect of the new 1996 HKCEE on teaching and learning presented a very complicated research situation. There were many intervening factors that interacted in teaching and learning as a result of the changes to the examination. Therefore, the nature of the research questions posed in this study required a combined approach of two research paradigms, as neither single research paradigm could answer the research questions thoroughly. Allwright and Bailey (1991: 67) referred to this type of approach as 'quantify only what can be usefully quantified, and utilize qualitative data collection and analysis procedures wherever they are appropriate' (c.f. Halfpenny, 1979).

Therefore, the researcher first employed the ethnographic approach of classroom observation to develop an understanding of the washback effect on teaching, as there were no preconceived notions as to the variables to be studied or hypotheses to be tested. At that stage, the purpose of observation was hypothesis generating rather than hypothesis testing (Long, 1983; Nunan, 1988, 1989a, 1989b; van Lier, 1988).

A systematic classroom observation scheme was later designed based on the baseline study. The classroom observation approaches used in the study drew upon and were developed from three main sources:

- theoretical models in the study of second language teaching and learning
- the non-participant observations made during school visits and by talking to teachers and students
- preliminary findings from the survey studies and interviews.

Theoretical models

This study has drawn on several theoretical models (c.f. Chapter 2). A model for the study of classroom teaching (Dunkin & Biddle, 1979: 38) served as an initial guide for the clarification of the variables and behaviours in this study. The current study focuses primarily on the process variables within the classroom box below (see Figure 2.1). The researcher tried to relate teacher presage variables and student characteristics of the context variables to the classroom process, and these variables are explored further in the survey study. Product variables were not investigated in the study due to the time constraints on the research. The time span of the research ranged from the change in the HKCEE exam syllabus to the time when the 1996 HKCEE was issued. The data collection covered two and a half years, from January 1994 to June 1996, which is a relatively short period. Consequently, as no dramatic changes were expected in students' learning outcomes, product variables were not considered necessary.

Figure 3.7 Variables focused on in the main study during classroom observations

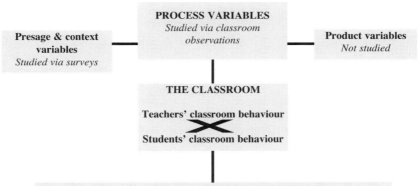

PROCESS VARIABLES
Studied via classroom observations

Presage & context variables
Studied via surveys

Product variables
Not studied

THE CLASSROOM

Teachers' classroom behaviour

Students' classroom behaviour

Two of Chaudron's four general issues (1988) concerning the effectiveness of classroom instruction served as the focus of this study:

- teacher talk
- interaction in the classroom – turn taking, questioning and answering, negotiation of meaning and feedback in contrast to a more traditional view of teaching and learning, which conceptualizes classroom instruction as the conveyance of information from the knowledgeable teacher to the 'empty' and passive learners.

As discussed in Chapter 2, a number of observation instruments have been developed based on recent developments in language teaching (Allwright & Bailey, 1991: 202-223; Chaudron, 1988; Matthews, Spratt, & Dangerfield, 1985). They derive from four major traditions in classroom research: psychometry, interaction analysis, discourse analysis, and ethnography. The current study first employed an ethnographic approach that served as a qualitative, process-oriented approach to the study of classroom interaction. The value of such qualitative insights lies in the power to alter perspectives on the variables of interest and to aid in the development of theoretical constructs and relationships within the current inquiry. A process-oriented approach was adopted in this study to explore the inter-subjective and context-dependent nature of classroom events as they occur, noting the regularities and idiosyncrasies in the events. Consequently, drawing on the four issues raised by Chaudron (1988), a classroom observation instrument was designed for the purposes of the research. This observation scheme was partially based on the Flint (Moskowitz, 1971: 213) and Brown Interaction Analysis System (Brown, 1975), and partially on the COLT (Communicative Orientation of Language Teaching) category (Frohlich, Spada, & Allen, 1985: 53-56).

Many classroom observation instruments are in existence. Such observation schemes may differ with respect to the type and number of content categories, coding procedures, units of analysis, as well as the purposes for which the instruments have been designed. The major observation schemes are concerned with teacher-student interaction. They are essentially adaptations, extensions, or simplifications of Flanders' original categories (c.f. Malamah-Thomas, 1987). These comprise two main categories, teacher talk and pupil talk (c.f. Brown, 1975). Descriptive frameworks in the Interaction Analysis tradition aim to analyse classroom verbal interaction in order to find out something about the sort of teaching and learning that is occurring. Moskowitz's Flint (Moskowitz, 1968, 1971) was directly inspired by Flanders, but adapted to make it more relevant to practice in the language classroom. The Flint instrument consists of twelve basic categories; seven for teacher talk and two for student talk. The remaining three categories are silence, confusion, and laughter. Brown's Interaction Analysis System (Brown, 1975) is not designed specially for analysis of language classrooms, but it is a useful tool for analysing verbal interaction (Harrison, 1996). It consists of six categories: three for teachers, two for students and one for an unclassifiable category–silence (Brown, 1975, cited by Malamah-Thomas, 1987: 48). Such instruments examine the classroom climate and the degree of direct and indirect teacher influence (Flanders, 1970). The Interaction Analysis System was drawn on in this study at the baseline stage for the analysis of interaction patterns in this study. These are the categories included in the study:

Teacher:	a.	lecturing, describing, explaining, narrating, directing
	b.	initiating questions
	c.	answering
Student:	a.	initiating questions
	b.	answering questions.

However, after a trial analysis of the interaction patterns in the first round of observations, the interaction analysis produced disconnected tallies of behaviours, and failed to describe the interaction pattern of the classroom. The scheme proved to be too small for exploring the washback phenomenon for this study and not relevant to the research questions posed.

The COLT observation scheme was, consequently, adopted for this study, as it tends to pay closer attention to what teachers and students actually do in the classroom and how they interact (Allen et al, 1984: 232). It consists of two parts. Part A describes classroom events at the level of episode and activity. Part B analyses the communicative features of verbal exchanges between teachers and students or among students themselves as they occur within each activity (Frohlich, Spada, & Allen, 1985: 57; Mitchell, 1988; Mosback, 1994; Naiman, Frohlich, Stern, & Todesco, 1978; Simon & Boyer, 1967 – 1970; Spada, 1989).

Part A of the COLT scheme was drawn upon for this study as the researcher felt that the classroom analysis at the level of episode and activity best fitted the nature of the research questions to be answered. For example, one of the intended washback effects of the new 1996 HKCEE was the addition of group work (role-play and group discussion in the new format). The rationale was that highly controlled, teacher-centred approaches are thought to impose restrictions on the growth of students' productive abilities. Part B was not drawn upon, as an analysis of the communicative features of verbal exchanges between teachers and students or among students was not directly relevant for this investigation of the new 1996 HKCEE's washback effect on classroom teaching and learning. The categories are too detailed and fine to catch washback, much like using a butterfly net to catch an elephant (K. Bailey, personal communication, 1997).

To summarize, the main rationale for employing combined research approaches and drawing upon the above two observation schemes, rather than employing any single or existing scheme, was based on the complex nature of the washback effect as well as the lack of existing observation schemes for washback studies (Alderson & Hamp-Lyons, 1996; Bailey, 1999). As mentioned above, few washback studies have employed classroom observation as part of their data analysis (see Alderson & Hamp-Lyons, 1996; Wall & Alderson, 1993).

Development of the classroom observation scheme

The classroom observation method used in this study was based on an approach as an inside the 'black box' perspective (Long, 1980: 1; c.f. Gaies, 1983). This perspective views the classroom as a place where interactions of various kinds take place. It leads to attempts to demonstrate the effects of different types of interactional opportunities on L2 learning.

As discussed above, the classroom observation scheme adopted in this study was first drawn from various observation schemes. It was also developed from various data sources over a period of time. Unstructured observation was used at the initial stage of the study, as the researcher was becoming familiar with the Hong Kong education context and Hong Kong secondary schools. The purpose of this initial approach was to explore aspects of teaching and learning that might be influenced by the new 1996 HKCEE and to develop the research focus.

In this part of the observation, various secondary schools with different characteristics were visited. The types of secondary schools observed consisted of government, aided, and private schools, and schools with different mediums of instruction, with Anglo-Chinese schools as the focus of the study.

Observing classroom teaching and learning activities within those schools enabled the researcher to identify variables related to the study, and a structured classroom observation scheme was designed. Such structured observation led to quantification and comparison of individual teachers teaching under the old and new HKCEE. Unstructured observation at the initial stage, however, provided a valid procedure in developing the structured classroom observation instrument (to be discussed later).

As was discussed in Chapter 2, observations alone only reveal part of what happens within the educational setting. Therefore, data from survey studies and interviews as well as lesson transcriptions were employed to validate the observation scheme as part of the process of triangulation, in which independent measures are made of the same subject, and their degree of consistency assessed (Cohen & Manion, 1989).

Research focuses for the 1996 HKCEE washback on classroom teaching

This study explored whether or not, and how, the new 1996 HKCEE would bring changes to the teaching and learning of English in Hong Kong secondary schools. As described earlier, a combined methodology was selected based on an understanding of the complex nature of such study. The combined approach was also dependent on the researcher's understanding of the nature of classroom teaching as well as of the contextual variables involved in relation to the exam change. As a result of the work of researchers from various disciplines, knowledge of classroom instruction in relation to the exam change has been studied more recently. Such knowledge, reviewed in Chapter 2, provided the researcher with a basis from which to make certain assumptions about the nature of classroom instruction in relation to the examination change, and thus derive research questions and select appropriate techniques for inquiry. One word of emphasis is needed here. The nature of the new 1996 HKCEE aimed to narrow the gap between what happens in the language classroom and the real world. The changes in the examination reflect a curriculum change, namely, TOC, as well as assessment paradigm changes from behaviourism to constructivism. The specific exam changes are reflected mainly in an integrated listening, reading, and writing paper, as well as the oral paper. The following research focuses were decided on for exploring the washback effect of the new syllabus on classroom teaching in 1996. Compared to teaching under the old syllabuses in 1995:

1. The teacher will assign more practice opportunities to students. A practice opportunity is defined in this study as the opportunity for students to engage in activities for the development of their knowledge about the language and their ability to communicate in the language. If washback does occur, the rationale for the new 1996 HKCEE would lead to a change from highly teacher-centred classroom teaching to a more student-oriented classroom. In this study, practice opportunities are measured by a percentage of class time assigned by the teachers to their students for them to carry out language tasks or activities.

2. The teacher will assign more class time to student activities involving group work, such as role-playing and group discussion, which will increase language practice opportunities. Such activities improve the quality of the student talk, help to individualize instruction, promote a positive affective climate, and motivate the learner to learn. Group work provides the kind of input and opportunities for output that enables rapid L2 acquisition (see Long & Porter, 1985). Also, role-play and group discussions are the two new exam formats in the new 1996 HKCEE oral paper. If washback occurs, the change of oral formats to role-playing and group discussions, as well as the increased percentage of time devoted to the oral component would lead to the teacher assigning more time to these activities.

3. The teacher will talk less. The students will talk more. This part of the observation will show how much students or the teacher contribute to classroom interaction. If there is a tendency for students to contribute more and more to the classroom interaction, it can be assumed that students have taken a more active part in learning than before. This is also related to the rationale for the new 1996 HKCEE, especially the increased importance of students' activities such as role-playing or group work, which would probably lead to less teacher talk and more student talk.

4. There will be more frequent and shorter teacher turns in class. 'A turn is defined as off-stream (i.e. discontinuing), introducing something new, or denying/disputing a proposition in a previous turn' (van Lier, 1988, cited in Ellis, 1994: 579). The rationale for the study of turns lies in the assumption that whether students are actively involved in classroom interaction is largely determined by the turn-allocation behaviour of the teacher and turn-taking behaviour of the students (c.f. Tsui, 1995: 19). To allocate turns to all students is something that all teachers strive to achieve, and which they often believe they have achieved.

5. The teacher will use more authentic materials from real-life sources. In this study, 'authentic materials' refers to materials taken from real-life sources rather than textbooks or exam practice books. This assumption is explored at two levels: the type and the source of the teaching materials. The type refers to the material: written, audio or video. The source refers to whether the materials are pedagogical (main textbook specifically designed for L2 learning); semi-pedagogical (mock exam papers) or non-pedagogical (materials originally intended for non-school purposes).

The observation scheme

The categories were designed to (a) capture significant features of classroom events in Hong Kong secondary school English classrooms, and (b) provide a means of comparing episodes of classroom interaction with natural language as it is used outside the classroom (c.f. Allen, Frohlich, & Spada, 1984: 232). The observation scheme in the study consists of five major categories as follows.

1. *Time:* How is time segmented within the lesson as a percentage of class time?

This category relates to instructional behaviours in the classroom. The unit of analysis chosen was a 'segment.' A segment is defined by Mitchell, Parkinson, and Johnstone (1981: 12-14) as 'a stretch of classroom discourse having a particular topic and involving participants (both the teacher and students) in carrying out an activity or task through interaction. A change of topic/activity type or a mode of interaction indicates a completion or the start of a new segment.'

The segment was selected as the basic unit of analysis because it has distinctive features, both linguistic and pedagogic and therefore can be readily divided into categories as a percentage of class time. Segment boundaries were identified on the basis of 'focusing moves' and 'framing moves' (Sinclair & Coulthard, 1975), which are indicators of the completion of one stage of a lesson and the beginning of another. These moves are realized through linguistic markers such as 'ok,' 'right,' 'now,' 'well,' 'today,' etc. Therefore, the first step in analysing any lessons observed was to segment the lesson into activities by using the moves.

2. *Participant organization:* Who is holding the floor/talking during the segments of the lesson as a percentage of class time?

'Participant organisation describes three basic patterns of organisation for classroom interactions' (Allen, Frohlich, & Spada, 1984: 235; Edelsky, 1981). Is the teacher working with the whole class or not? Are the students divided into groups or are they engaged in individual seatwork? If they are engaged in group work, how is it organized? The various subsections are:

- whole class – teacher to students or to class; student to student; choral work by students (the whole class or groups participate in the choral work, repeating a model provided by the textbook or teacher)
- group work
- individual work.

These categories are low-inference. They are descriptive of how a lesson is carried out in terms of the participants in the classroom interaction (the teacher or the students). The categories also reflect different theoretical approaches to teaching. For example, group work is considered to be an important factor in the development of fluency skills (c.f. Allen, Frohlich, & Spada, 1984: 236). The reason for this claim is that highly controlled, teacher-centred approaches are thought to impose restrictions on the growth of students' productive ability:

> In classes dominated by the teacher, students spend most of their time responding to questions and rarely initiate speech. Moreover, student talk in a teacher-centred classroom is frequently limited to the production of isolated sentences, which are assessed for their grammatical accuracy rather than for their communicative appropriateness or value. Because the emphasis in group interactions is more likely to be on the expression of meaning, and less likely to be on the linguistic accuracy of utterances, classes which can be shown to provide more group activities may affect the L2 development of learners in ways which are different from those that represent a teacher-centred lock-step approach to instruction (Allen, Frohlich, & Spada, 1984: 236).

The participant organization of classroom interaction patterns has a significant meaning for the washback effect of the new 1996 HKCEE. The participant organization is one of the rationales behind the new exam to encourage more practice opportunities for students. After the videotaped lessons were segmented according to classroom activities, using framing and focusing moves as indicators, these classroom activities were analysed according to the above three categories. The findings then enabled a comparative investigation of the interaction patterns in both F5 classes under the old and the new HKCEE syllabus, to see whether there would be any changes seen comparing the two academic years' teaching in schools.

3. *Activity type:* What teaching and learning activities are realized through various activities as a percentage of class time?

After each lesson was segmented and interaction patterns of classroom activity were analysed, it was possible to look more closely at the types of activities carried out within the segments. 'Activity type' was an open-ended construct with no predetermined descriptor. Each activity was separately described, such as discussion, drilling, or singing. Frequently, activities consisted of two or more episodes: (a) the teacher reads the words of a song aloud, (b) the students repeat the words after the teacher, and (c) the students sing the song.

4. *Content:* What the teacher and the students are talking, reading, or writing about, or what they are listening to.

'Content' describes the subject matter of the activities. It is studied in relation to two areas in this study, management and language. 'Management' refers to (a) classroom procedures and (b) disciplinary routines. 'Language' refers to language input focusing on form, function, or discourse.

5. *Materials used:* What types of teaching materials are used and for what purpose?

(i) Types of materials:

 • written or audio-visual?

(ii) Purposes of materials:

 • pedagogical (main textbooks specifically designed for L2 learning)
 • semi-pedagogical (mock exam papers)
 • non-pedagogical (materials originally intended for non-school purposes).

Teacher participants involved

Based on the nature and the methodological considerations of this study, criteria for identifying potential teachers who were teaching F5 classes both in 1994 and 1995 were selected:

• teachers who were willing to accept observations of their teaching
• teachers who agreed to have their lessons video-recorded
• teachers who were willing to encourage their students to ignore the video camera
• school administrators (principals and panel chairs[12]) who had a positive attitude towards observations

Initially nine teachers agreed to participate in the first year (1994) observation. The majority of them were female teachers, except for one male teacher. They were all qualified teachers in that they either possessed a teacher certificate or were doing a P.C.Ed. (Postgraduate Certificate of Education). This group of teachers was not meant to be representative of teachers of

---

12. A panel chair is the subject head in Hong Kong secondary schools.

English in Hong Kong secondary schools. The teachers were selected using purposeful sampling (Patton, 1987), and the main purpose was to select teachers based on whether they could provide a rich variety of information about classroom teaching and learning activities in schools in relation to the new 1996 HKCEE. This group of teachers has been trained to look at their own teaching and that of other colleagues. They had the meta-language to articulate how they felt about teaching and learning. They might also have been more aware of the theoretical underpinnings of teaching and learning in relation to examinations since they had undertaken some kind of teacher education. As they had been exposed to new and challenging ideas in theories of teaching and learning, they might also be more willing to make changes in their teaching. As this sample is very small, it will be appropriate to look at each teacher as an individual case (Hargreaves & Fullan, 1992).

Among these nine teachers, there was one panel chair. The rationale for including the panel chair is that the role of a panel chair (the subject head of English) is usually crucial to the general planning of teaching and learning in Hong Kong secondary schools. The choice of teachers for this study was less by specific selection and more by mutual agreement. One of the biggest problems of this type of independent research, compared with funded research, lies in the difficulty of getting teachers' cooperation. It was extremely difficult to find teachers who were willing to allow the researcher to go into their classroom for the observation. Teaching is a private activity individually performed by teachers. Classroom research is a sensitive business, and being investigated in any way provokes anxiety. Teachers feel the intrusiveness of outsiders, in this case the researcher (c.f. Allwright & Bailey, 1991; Chaudron, 1988; Larsen-Freeman, 1980). Indeed, teachers often feel far too busy to offer help to researchers.

As mentioned above, the first year classroom observations (1994 academic year) started with nine teachers. The recording methods were either tape- or video-recording. After the first round of observations, video-recording was chosen as the recording method for the main study. Video-recordings can reveal the maximum amount of information about the interaction patterns of teaching, and also allow the researcher to explore those lessons in full and retrospectively. When videotaping was discussed with the nine teachers, two teachers refused to allow their classes to be video or audio taped. Therefore, only field notes are available for those two. When the second year data collection was about to begin, two teachers dropped out. One teacher's teaching schedule was altered by her principal–she no longer taught F5 students, who ought to have been observed. Another teacher refused to be observed for the second year (1995) as she thought it would be rude and disruptive for her students to be observed. In the end, only three teachers remained willing to be observed in the second year and willing to be video-recorded.

These three teachers were chosen for the main study. They were all female[13] teachers. Two had obtained teaching certificates and one teacher was attending a Postgraduate Certificate of Education programme at the time of the research. Two of them were pursuing further degrees. They were very enthusiastic teachers and loved teaching. The most encouraging aspect of the classroom observations was that all three teachers made use of the video-recorded lessons for their own teaching and research purposes. One teacher used the taped lesson to motivate her students. She and her students watched some of the taped lessons together to identify areas of language improvement. In addition, the three schools where the teachers were teaching were different with regard to banding, religious affiliation, and geographical locations. One school was a top ranked school, one was in the middle, and the other was a lower ranked school.

Data collection strategies

This section discusses the data collection strategies used for the classroom observations and describes the data collection and data analysis procedures.

The nature of the data collection

Due to the complex nature of the study and lack of existing research models, this study of the washback effect on classroom teaching is not linear, but cyclical. The research questions took some time to formulate while different variables within the Hong Kong education system were being explored. Each of the processes gave new insights into the washback phenomenon. Data collection was carried out using a 'recycling' process, but with a spiral motion (see Figure 3.8). The recycling data collection process helped the researcher to understand the nature of the research data in relation to the research questions under study. This process of gradual understanding brought the researcher closer to the heart of the research problems.

This type of interactive data collection and analysis is typical in exploratory studies such as this one with a defined time line (see Bailey & Nunan, 1996; Calderhead, 1996). Two interactive stages of observation, consisting of both baseline study and main study, were carried out in the different phases of this study (see Figure 3.9). According to Allwright and Bailey (1991: 73–75), 'baseline data provides information that documents the normal state of affairs

---

13. Efforts were made to include both male and female teachers for the study, but none of the male teachers who were approached agreed to be observed. They gave various reasons for not wishing to be observed such as a heavy workload and difficulty in arranging their schedule.

as well as the basis against which researchers make comparative claims about how different or unusual the phenomena being observed is.' To the current researcher, a baseline study not only provides base-line data (c.f. van Lier, 1988: 5), but also helps to refine the observation scheme and procedures for the study. In that sense, it serves as a piloting and validation mechanism similar to what had been undertaken in the survey studies. Findings of the two stages of observation are reported in Phase I (Chapter 4) and Phase III (Chapter 7).

Figure 3.8 Cyclical nature of the data collection

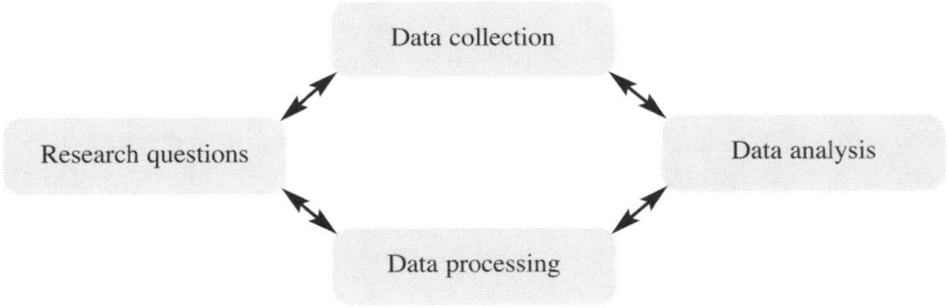

Data collection

Research questions

Data analysis

Data processing

Based on the above methodological considerations, a comparative study of classroom observation frameworks was formulated for the main study (see Figure 3.10). The figure below illustrates the comparative nature of the present study. The control variables are the old and the new HKCEE syllabuses. Classroom observations were carried out to observe the same teachers in the same schools teaching the same forms of students.

Figure 3.9 Stages of classroom observations

Stage One

Basline Study

Nine teachers in nine schools
23 lessons observed, consisting of both F4 and F5 lessons

Stage Two

Main Study

Three teachers in three schools from the baseline pool
22 lessons observed, consisting solely of F5 lessons

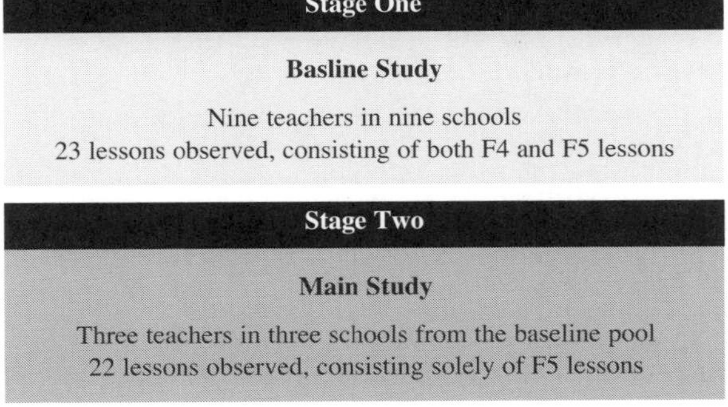

**Figure 3.10 Comparative nature of the classroom observations
for the main study**

For the current study, F5 lessons were the main focus. To interpret such a complex educational phenomenon, however, depends on a faithful description of what is happening in the classroom as well as of the contextual variables within the Hong Kong educational context. Erickson (1986) suggested two main strategies, namely, *asking* and *watching*. Allwright (1984) used other similar terms: *observation* and *introspection*. Observing or watching may have influenced the researcher's bias, whereas introspection might minimize the bias by seeking other explanations through asking, distributing questionnaires, and interviewing with participants and informants (see Section One for more information).

This study employed both 'observing' and 'asking' approaches. Asking (i.e. interviewing) was carried out at a later stage after the classroom observations. The major aim of the follow-up interview was to invite the participants to open up and reveal their words and actions in the video-recordings (why they do certain things in certain ways in the classroom) rather than seeking responses to specific questions.

Furthermore, as the purpose of the study was to find out what was going on in the 'black box' (Long, 1980) in the context of a major examination change, non-interference observations were decided upon to enable the researcher to observe closely the natural occurrences in the classroom. Therefore, non-participant observations were the most appropriate way for this study to record all relevant information from the lessons. The researcher's intention was to minimize her intrusiveness in the classroom in order to minimize interference with the subtle behaviours of the teacher and students. Therefore, fixed video-recordings were employed.

Data collection procedures

Permission to collect data

Non-participant classroom observations were carried out during a one-and-a-half year period. Permission to collect data was obtained first from the school principal and panel chair and then from the individual teacher. The researcher first consulted teacher schedules to locate any Form Five classes that could be visited. Scheduling of each classroom observation was agreed between the teachers, students, and the researcher. Decision and agreement was reached initially upon the actual days of teaching according to the weekly or rotary system. All school visits were pre-arranged with the teachers and schools involved. Telephone calls were made one day before each school visit. Usually teachers needed to inform their principal and the school general office in order to avoid unnecessary difficulties in getting into the school premises.

Seasonality of data collection

The majority of classroom observations were carried out between October and December, both in 1994 and in 1995, in the winter term when a long and continuous stretch of teaching was occurring. The HKCEE takes places annually in May, and intensive exam practice starts as early as February each year. All observations were carried out before the start of such exam practices.

The observation time was selected on the principle that the classrooms should, as much as possible for the observations, reflect as their normal and natural conditions for learning. Neither the very beginning of the term or the end of the term would provide such a condition. Periods for classroom observations were normally scheduled around October to December each year. The relationship between washback and the time of teaching has been documented in similar studies (see Freeman, 1996; Shohamy et al, 1996; Wall & Alderson, 1993; Watanabe, 1996a, 1996b). Bailey (1999) employed the term 'seasonality' to indicate the relationship between time and washback.

The choice of these time periods for observation assumed major significance for observing this particular phenomenon. First, consideration had to be given to the school time-tabling. F5 teaching is different in that preparation for the upcoming HKCEE plays a particularly dominant role in teaching at this level. The school year usually starts in September. After a period of around three months of teaching, schools will arrange an internal examination in the format of the HKCEE. After the Christmas break, there is very limited time for teaching before the Chinese New Year in Hong Kong secondary schools. The remaining months of February, March and April are spent on mock exam practice. Students can stay at home to prepare for the HKCEE examination. May is the examination season for the HKCEE. Therefore, September, October, and November are the most 'normal' months for teaching at the F5 level. September, at the beginning of the term, is busy for both the teachers and the schools. October and November, therefore, were chosen for classroom observations.

Figure 3.11 Flowchart of yearly timetabling for F5 students

September	school starts
October November December	longest stretch of 'normal' teaching; main classroom observations
January	winter holiday
February March April	mock exam practice at school and/or home teaching is carried out according to the HKCEE exam papers (format)
May	HKCEE for all school subjects (c.f. Chapter 1)
June July August	summer holiday students prepare for further study or employment

Methods of recording

After the initial school visits and baseline classroom observations of 32 lessons, detailed procedures for classroom observations and the observation scheme were decided upon. Thirty-one 70-minute lessons (double lessons[14]) of the selected three teachers were observed in 1994 and 1995 respectively. Double lessons were chosen in order to observe a longer stretch of lessons without interruption. Seventeen lessons were observed in 1994, which were in the baseline study pool. Fourteen lessons were observed in 1995.

Both audio-recording and video-recording were employed for the baseline study. Only video-recording was employed for the main study. The observed lessons were video-recorded since videotaped classroom activities could reveal the maximum amount of information about the interaction patterns of the teaching and learning. They also allowed the researcher to explore those lessons in full and retrospectively.

During the observations, a video camera was set up before each lesson in one corner of the classroom, facing the students. The rationale for fixing the video camera in one corner, without an operator, was to minimize any interruptions and disturbance of the lesson, as well as to ensure normal teacher and student interaction. Students got used to the camera very quickly. As the camera was usually set up before they entered the classroom and before the

14. A double lesson usually refers to two 35-minute lessons together without a recess in between.

lesson began, students tended to forget it and ignore it. In addition, facing the camera at the students captured as much as possible of what was happening in the classroom between the teacher and students. The researcher sat at the back of the classroom and made field notes on the interaction in the classroom as lessons progressed. The purpose of the field notes was to provide additional contextual information on the lesson being observed. They were also used as a way of recording anything that might not have been recorded by the camera. Typical field notes included the following:

• features of teaching materials employed in terms of the main textbook, exam practice book, and/or materials taken from real life sources, regardless of whether these materials were written, audio-video, etc.
• features of activities undertaken, namely, whether they were prescribed by textbooks
• features of interaction between the teacher and students in regard to who was holding the floor (talking), who initiated the questions, and who responded to the questions.
• features of outstanding occurrences of a particular classroom such as shared laughter

Data analysis for observation

Procedures for data analysis in this study consisted of (a) coding videotaped lessons according to the observation scheme and (b) transcriptions of sampled

Figure 3.12 Procedures for the analysis of videotaped data

Stage 1:	Global viewing: brief notes to index the tapes were taken and transitions between occasions of interest were noted. Field notes were double checked.
Stage 2:	General coding of all twenty-two lessons observed were carried out for the main study. A stopwatch was used for coding time in relation to the observation scheme. A general pattern of those lesson interactions was achieved. Sorting and putting the interaction patterns into tables was performed for individual teachers.
Stage 3:	Selected occasions were copied onto secondary tapes. Excerpts were timed, and junctures were described in detail. Participants and other researchers were invited to view the lessons together or separately for coder agreement, as well as for their own views of the occasions.
Stage 4:	Detailed descriptions of the participant organization structures and interactions were developed. Transcriptions were made of representative parts of the lesson.
Stage 5:	An exploratory scheme was constructed showing the interaction pattern of the lesson observed in relation to the research questions.
Stage 6:	Follow-up interviews were carried out about issues arising from the data analysis. All interview data was transcribed verbatim.

lessons, both of which required 'intensive immersion in the data' as Edelsky puts it (1981: 385).

Procedures for the analysis of the videotaped data are illustrated in Figure 3.12, which is adapted from van Lier (1988: 65; see also Erickson & Shultz, 1981).

Reliability and validity of classroom observations

Reliability for classroom observations is concerned with consistency (Allwright & Bailey, 1991: 46). There are two issues involved. 'One is concerned with whether or not an independent researcher could achieve consistent results if working in the same or similar context. The other aspect is concerned with the consistency of the procedure of data collection, analysis and interpretation' (He, 1996: 108).

To enhance the reliability of the data collection and analysis, the researcher employed two approaches: (a) cross checking with existing data, and (b) inviting inter-coders. Cross checking involved going back to the video-taped lessons and recoding a previously analysed lesson. The purpose of this approach was to make sure that the researcher was consistent with the criteria for analysis. Inter-coders in this study consisted of codings of teacher participants and of a research colleague who is an experienced classroom observer. The purpose of inter-coding was to ensure consistency in the units of analysis. Inter-coding was carried out first with teacher participants. Both the researcher and the teachers would watch one of the observed lessons together (about 16% of the lessons observed in both years). Each coder would segment the lesson based on aggregating similar activities that occurred during the lesson. Greater than 90% agreement was achieved with all three teachers' lessons inter-coded. Secondly, inter-coder agreement was carried out with the experienced observer with a random sample of observed lessons–10% of the total lessons observed in the main study. Agreement was reached for about 95% of the segments of classroom activities.

Validity is concerned with 'the extent to which the observational apparatus and inferences drawn from it will be meaningful, significant, and applicable to further studies' (Chaudron, 1988: 23). For Chaudron, an essential element in achieving validity is consistent reliability, in which others agree on the categories and description and the frequencies attributed to them.

The researcher has focused in this study on what it is that should be looked for in relation to the washback effect of the new 1996 HKCEE. This involved first a theoretical derivation based on assumptions (beliefs, ideas, and theories) about both language teaching and learning and about assessment models and paradigms. Second, it involved exploring the intended washback effect and rationale behind the new 1996 HKCEE examination. Third, it was essential to have a good baseline study 'to let the data lead the way' (van Lier, 1988: 87). This aspect of the data, together with the above theoretical derivations and exploration of the new 1996 HKCEE, has enhanced the researcher's understanding of the research problem and ensured the validity of the classroom instrument, its data collection, and analysis.

Summary

By investigating the washback effect of the new 1996 HKCEE in English, we can explore the general characteristics of a system of testing that can be identified as contributing to or distracting from the test's systematic validity, as well as discover any social, psychological, ethical, curricular, and educational consequences of the public examination change (Messick's 'unified validity,' 1989, 1994, 1996). Validation of a system of testing in exploring its consequences to teaching and learning within an education system requires a long time and joint efforts to achieve a beneficial effect. The validation of the assessment practices within the system also involves the participation of the whole education system regarding teacher education, material writing, and curriculum development.

The first part of this chapter summarized the theoretical and methodological foundations for this study. The second part described the development of the two questionnaires that were employed in this study. The design and validation procedures, as well as the rationale, aim, structure, content, and sources of the two surveys were discussed. Part Two also discussed the sampling for the teacher and student surveys, and the data collection and analysis procedures. The final part of this chapter discussed the rationale for a combined framework used for classroom observations in relation to the washback effect of the new 1996 HKCEE. It introduced the teachers who participated in this study and the processes and procedures of getting them involved, and it described details of the procedures for data collection and analysis. In the end, the issues of reliability and validity concerned with the classroom observations were discussed.

As only a limited amount of empirical research has been carried out to investigate the washback effect of examinations in the specific field of language education, it is hoped that this study can provide a methodological framework for further studies.

Section Three:
Teachers and students on the change

All real change involves loss, anxiety, and struggle.

Marris (1986)

Due to the nature of this study, research findings in this section will be reported in relation to the time line of the research. There were three phases of the research as discussed in Chapter 3.

Phase I lasted from November 1993 to November 1994, and was classified as the decision-making stage. Findings from this phase will be reported in Chapter 4. The major research methods used in this phase were:

- key informant interviews
- overall observations
- initial survey studies.

Phase II lasted for another year, from November 1994 to December 1995. This period of research was made up of comparative surveys on teachers' and students' attitudes and their classroom behaviours in 1994 and 1995. This phase was classified as the perception stage. Findings from this phase will be reported in Chapter 5 (teacher surveys) and Chapter 6 (student surveys). The major research methods used in this phase were:

- Two parallel survey studies–the teacher and student surveys

Phase III of the study lasted for approximately two years, which overlapped in part with Phase II, from November 1994 to November 1996. It focused on the classroom to observe closely what was happening inside the 'black box' (Long, 1980) in relation to the new 1996 HKCEE. Detailed follow-up interviews of case study teachers were also carried out. This phase was classified as the implementation stage. Findings will be reported in Chapter 7. The major research methods used in this phase were:

- classroom observations
- follow-up interviews.

The research findings are reported in separate chapters according to the three stages of the study. Discussion will be carried out together with a presentation of the findings.

4

Phase I – The decision-making stage of the examination change

Introduction

This chapter reports Phase I of the study, the decision-making stage of the public examination change (HKCEE). This stage lasted from November 1993 to November 1994. The major research methods employed were (a) key informant interviews of different parties involved, (b) overall observations of those parties at the macro level of the Hong Kong educational context, and (c) initial survey findings from teachers and students at the micro level in Hong Kong secondary schools.

The washback exploratory model in context

Phase I started at the same time as the introduction of the revised HKCEE examination syllabus. The researcher worked as an outsider and observer to record anything that might have occurred due to the introduction of the examination change. Observation was therefore a key element in this exploratory study, with two levels of washback phenomena being observed within the Hong Kong educational context.

The first level was the general educational context in which teaching and learning took place in Hong Kong secondary schools (see Figure 4.1). The purpose of exploring this level was to identify the reactions to the examination change of different parties at the macro level in the Hong Kong educational system, the support these parties offered to teachers, and the preparation they used to promote the examination change in schools at the micro level. Secondly, an in-depth investigation was carried out into the particular areas of teaching and learning affected by the examination in schools. I would like to use the term 'washback intensity' here to refer to the degree of the washback effect in an area or a number of areas of teaching and learning that are affected by an examination.

**Figure 4.1 Flowchart of washback in the Hong Kong
educational context**

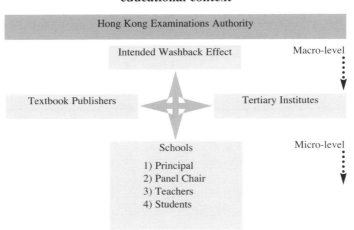

The above figure illustrates the direction in which the revised HKCEE syllabus was communicated to each party at each level within the Hong Kong educational context. Based on these two levels of washback phenomena–macro and micro–a general exploratory investigation was carried out using overall observation at the first macro level. This involved (a) unstructured key informant interviews in person and by phone and (b) initial school visits, which were followed by preliminary survey studies and classroom observations. Survey studies were employed to obtain a general picture of how teachers and students reacted to the revised syllabus. Classroom observations provided detailed information as to what teachers and students actually did in the classroom. The preliminary investigations in Phase I illustrate the degree of washback effect in the following areas of teaching and learning in Hong Kong secondary schools as a result of the changes in the HKCEE.

The Hong Kong educational context at the macro level

On September 25, 1992, the HKEA English Subject Committee[1] held its first meeting and made the decision to change the HKCEE. A second meeting was held on March 9, 1993. The proposals for revising the HKCEE were

1. There were 58 subject committees within the HKEA at the time of the research.

documented. Then, in August 1993, the proposed 1996 HKCEE English Language Syllabus was passed to major textbook publishers for textbook revision and schools for comments and feedback.[2]

From January 1994, a series of seminars and workshops on the proposed English Language Syllabus (1996) was organized by the HKEA, tertiary institutions, and textbook publishers. This situation was unique, as the Hong Kong education context seemed to react positively and collaboratively towards this examination change. Hong Kong seemed to provide a favourable ground for washback to occur.

In September 1994, all schools received the official Examination Handbook for the revised 1996 HKCEE, and adopted new textbooks[3] for their Form Four students. Hence, the first cohort of F4 students was taught under the new 1996 HKCEE starting in September 1994 while the last cohort of F5 students was still being taught under the old HKCEE. This first cohort of students would be required to take the revised HKCEE in May 1996.

The Hong Kong Examinations Authority

One of the important findings in the Hong Kong educational context is the important role of public examinations in schools, hence, the influential role of the Hong Kong Examinations Authority (HKEA). The HKEA is an independent statutory body whose membership overlaps with the Education Department (ED). The main reasons for establishing the Authority in 1977 were based on the need to improve and rationalize the examination system in Hong Kong, as well as to make more efficient use of human and technical resources.

> It was believed that centralization would lead to greater cost effectiveness by standardizing procedures and pooling the limited and specialized human and technical resources available. The aim was also to maintain a more stable and dedicated workforce. (HKEA, 1994b: 1)

The Authority has frequently been used as the primary agency for both initiating and constraining curriculum changes, though its official function remains to be an agent of implementation. In reality, the Curriculum

2. The HKEA carried out a survey in about 600 Hong Kong schools in November 1993 after its second meeting of the English Subject Committee concerning the proposed 1996 HKCEE English Language Syllabus. Among those 183 schools that replied, 51% showed a positive attitude towards the change, 42% replied with modifications and 7% responded negatively towards the change (telephone interview with a Senior English subject officer at the HKEA on 7 March 1994).

3. At the start of the new academic year, schools whose students would take the 1996 HKCEE in English had all adopted new textbooks for at least their Form Four students, but the situation varied for the lower forms. Some of the schools changed to new textbooks from Form One–Form Four, some only with Form Four.

Development Council can also initiate a change as well as the HKEA. As Morris (1990a) points out, any change in the Hong Kong educational system must first involve a change in the examination. The change of the HKCEE English syllabus was such a change initiated by the HKEA. This examination change was also in accordance with the curriculum initiative called TOC (Target Oriented Curriculum) that was being implemented in Hong Kong primary schools. This linkage contributes greatly to the way that the Hong Kong educational system is structured. For example, the overlapping membership of the HKEA with the Education Department led to the change of the HKCEE. The overlap also illustrated further how such change was originated within the Hong Kong educational system.

The following is an excerpt from one of the interviews[4] with the Deputy Secretary of the HKEA.

> The Education Department side was working on TOC [initially called TTRA]. There were a lot of adversary committees operating, which were supposed to give guidance to ED. The original group consisted of five scholars who worked with the English Language Fund to do the preliminary work for the ED on TOC. I served on one of these committees. I represented the Authority advice. I sat through several meetings so I was in a good position to know early on the way the whole development was going. And...this is difficult, but I could see clearly that TOC was in big trouble–because it didn't seem to me to have much chance of success unless certain things happen. This was part of the advice I gave to the Committee...
>
> So I thought TOC was going to have a lot of troubles with the teachers. And in fact, this proved to be the case. They began with the primary school sector and the idea was they would move gradually up into the secondary school sector. It won't get to the HKCEE exam until 2001. But in the primary school sector, they have lost a lot of time. The teachers are not really trained and equipped...
>
> In this way, this is a pity because it seemed to me that the basic underlying concept of TOC is something I approve of. Now I looked at it and said what is the essence of the TOC approach as far as the examination is concerned, and public examination is concerned. I came to the conclusion that it was more or less the direction we have been going but that if TOC did come right through the system and reach F5, there would be certain emphasis. The main one was that I believe there should be more

---

4. The interview with the Deputy Secretary was conducted by telephone on March 7, 1994 at the Department of Curriculum Studies, the University of Hong Kong. The Deputy Secretary is one of the leading persons within the Hong Kong Examinations Authority. He is also one of the 14 ex-officio members appointed by the Governor.

integrated teaching and examining of skills instead of the skills being discrete points, they should be integrated, because it reflects real life. So I took the view that the gap between the way we test English in the exam and, therefore, the way English was taught in schools, the real world of HK where English is used as a second language, and the gap, should be narrowed. You can't close it, of course. There is always something artificial about public examinations but I thought we should narrow it. That is why the changes came about–the new papers Part III and Part IV. They stress the integration of skills...

This rather long excerpt shows how decisions about the examination change were made initially at the higher level of the HKEA. The initial line of thought was to try to incorporate the TOC principles recommended by the ED and to facilitate the implementation of the TOC teaching and learning theories in schools by means of an examination change.

Consequently, the English Subject Committee[5] of the Authority made specific changes to the existing HKCEE. The intended washback effect–as an initiative for curriculum change–was clear from the minutes of the first two meetings of its subject committee. Washback is also a term frequently mentioned in the minutes when the Committee was discussing each examination paper, though not many comments were made about washback in the specific areas of teaching and learning.

During the first meeting of the Subject Committee, it was mentioned that the *Use of English Examination*[6] at Secondary Seven 'has achieved good results and beneficial washback in the classroom' (HKEA, 1992/1993: 5). At the second meeting, during the discussion of *Paper I–Writing*, Committee members argued that the provision of specifying context, audience, and purpose in the examination questions would 'have good washback on classroom teaching, as students can learn to determine the appropriacy [*sic*] of style, content, relevance etc.' (HKEA, 1992/1993: 3). When discussing Paper III, it was noted that 'a proof-reading exercise would have good washback effect in the classroom and encourage students to check their own work.' It was expected by the Committee members that the new examination format for *Paper III (Integrated Reading, Listening, and Writing)* would have a favourable washback on classroom teaching, although it would be difficult to

5. 'The functions of a subject committee are to advise on the examination of the subject, draft examination syllabuses and make proposals to the Board concerning syllabus changes, review annually the examination of the subject with particular attention to the setting of question papers and their marking and report to the School Examinations Board, nominate setters, moderators, and examiners for appointment by the Authority' (HKEA, 1994b: 12).

6. The *Use of English* is an English Language examination taken by students at the end of Secondary Seven. 'Use of English' is one of the core components of Sixth Form education. As a continuation of the Secondary One-Five English curriculum, it provides students with the opportunity to expand and strengthen their English proficiency in order to prepare themselves for adult life or further education or both. The 'Use of English' examination is also referred as the A level examination.

administer such a test. The Subject Committee also commented that the changing of the weighting of each paper would bring about a good washback effect, e.g. the weighting of Paper I (Writing) would be higher than that for Paper II, a multiple choice paper. The integrated paper would also have a higher weighting. The weighting of the oral paper on the new HKCEE went up from 10% to 18% to focus more attention on development of oral skills.

It is clear from the above that the Subject Committee members had always intended a washback effect on teaching and learning when they made the decision about specific examination papers. This has been the case with all major innovations in recent years (c.f. Andrews & Fullilove, 1994). The HKEA staff are very conscious of the belief that 'if it's not examined, it won't be taught' (HKEA, 1994b: 80). Much thought was given to how the examination process could be used to bring about positive and constructive changes in the system, with the expectation that the examination changes would help classroom teachers keep a better balance between teaching and skill-building on the one hand, and examination preparation on the other.

The effect of washback was also evident in another overt way: the personal agenda of the Deputy Secretary of the HKEA. During the interview, he commented that:

> The public exams are very important in HK schools–the HKCEE and HKAL[7] exams, partly because CE and A level have always had a central role, partly it is historical. The HKEA was set up in 1977. We did the CE exam in 1977, A level we took in 1980. Before that, the dominant role of the examination in the public system here in the teaching in schools had already been established. This is not something the HKEA has done. It is something the HKEA has inherited. Someone like me coming along–I was the headmaster for six years in two schools–when I joined the HKEA, one of my personal agenda was to see whether or not the public examination system could influence, for good, the way that English was taught in schools. And that has always been part of my personal agenda. And I have changed the exam system. That was the first thing I did when I first came, I was the subject officer for English for two or three years. When I was the senior officer, head of the 24 officers, I continued to play the role with English. Now as a Deputy Secretary, I still do. It is a bit embarrassing. Partly it is what you are interested in; partly [it] reflects my personal interest and involvement. Despite what the system does, if there is one person who knows how to use the system, I mean me, more can be accomplished in using the exam for positive washback on classroom teaching.

This extract clearly illustrates the extent to which a key person can influence a curriculum change initiative. Furthermore, in the case of the HKCEE change, there was consensus and support within the HKEA. Through

---

7. This refers to the Use of English examination at the end of Secondary Seven.

interviews[8] with three other senior examination officers, it was discovered that the Target Oriented Curriculum initiatives and the intended positive washback effect on teaching and learning were frequently mentioned in the context of this examination change. This further demonstrates how decisions about the change were made within the Authority and within the Hong Kong educational context.

Tertiary institutions and textbook publishers

The 1996 HKCEE examination was implemented in Hong Kong secondary schools in September 1994. The first cohort of students was taught with the new exam for two years, from Secondary Four to Secondary Five, before they actually took the examination in May 1996. Half a year before the teaching of the new 1996 HKCEE began, a series of seminars and workshops was organized to help teachers implement the change in teaching:

- HKEA seminars[9]. These were organized with the aim of providing teachers with information about the changes, such as the rationale and content of the new exam, and the test formats to be employed. Issues raised by schools and teachers, including their worries about the revised examination were also discussed. Sample papers and the new test formats were introduced and demonstrated using certain sample tasks.
- Seminars[10] organized by tertiary institutions. The major aim of these seminars was to give teachers the necessary methodological strategies that they urgently required to deal with the proposed changes in the revised examination. There were lengthy discussions among the teachers as to how teaching and learning should be adjusted or modified according to the new requirements of the revised HKCEE.
- Textbook publishers' seminars and workshops.[11] These seminars and workshops received the largest teacher participation. Textbook publishers provided their understanding of the proposed changes and showed how they had integrated the changes into practical language activities in their textbooks. They demonstrated, in some detail, to the teachers how these language teaching and learning activities and tasks could be carried out in the classroom, including suggestions about how much time should be devoted to particular activities.

8. A series of interviews with the examination officers and English Subject Committee members were carried out in January, February and March 1994.
9. One of the first seminars was observed on 5 February 1994 at the Hong Kong Teachers' Resources Centre. There were about 150 teachers present at the seminar.
10. The researcher personally took part in and observed two seminars organized by the University of Hong Kong on 25 February and 5 March 1994.
11. Two initial seminars and workshops observed were organized by the Oxford University Press and the Witman Publishing Company Ltd (Hong Kong) in March 1994.

Textbook publishers are very conscious of the reasons why schools choose particular textbooks.[12] One of the strategies to make their books sell is to provide full support to teachers. They usually provide the following:

• suggested lesson plans
• a teacher's book with extensive teaching notes and answer keys
• definitions of key words and expressions
• a suggested time allocated for each activity
• ways to carry out particular tasks
• suggested composition titles, etc.

Such full support might be useful for teachers, but in some way it also shows how much the textbook publishers influence Hong Kong secondary school teachers' thinking and behaviour. For one thing, publishers in Hong Kong take part whenever there is a curriculum or examination initiative since they provide the initial change in the teaching content. If the change is not fully reflected in the textbooks, the initiative could fail. Whether the textbook publishers are able to reflect fully the theory or belief underpinning the change is itself a complicated matter.

One of the common features of these publisher seminars was that free sample books with cassette tapes were always provided, even a free lunch. For example, such an expensive seminar[13] was held by Macmillan in the Sheraton Hotel, attended by around 350 teachers. These seminars generally attracted a large teacher audience.

Another reason for those teachers and school principals to attend such seminars was to explore teaching support in terms of teaching content and material support. These textbooks were usually labelled specifically 'For the New Certificate Syllabus', which certainly helped the books sell more easily. If textbooks did not have such a label, teachers tended to be very reluctant to adopt them. One example of this was observed during the Macmillan seminar. One teacher commented to the writer of the *Impact* series of textbooks that it did not reflect the revised HKCEE. No such label was evident on the book cover, though the writer explained that the changes had been incorporated into the actual tasks. However, sales of the *Impact* series, especially *Impact 5*,[14] still fell. This not only showed that teachers relied on textbooks for direct support when there was a change; it also demonstrated an apparently cosmetic change that might be brought about by the change of the examination. Teachers tended to look for explicit labels on the cover initially, rather than for skill-building tasks in the textbooks.

---

12. Usually a set of textbooks would consist of: 1) student book 2) workbook 3) audio-cassette 4) teacher book 5) supplementary materials and 6) tests for school assessment.
13. The Macmillan ELT seminar was held on 3 October 1995 in the Silver Ballroom, The Sheraton, Tsim Sha Tsui, Kowloon.
14. Impact 5 is a textbook designed for Secondary Five. The major objective of Secondary Five is to work towards the HKCEE.

The Hong Kong educational context at the micro level

No matter how positive the washback effect of the revised HKCEE was perceived at the decision-making level, the actual changes had to take place in the school settings and be implemented in the teaching and learning context. The following section reports on the initial findings within the schools.

School administration – teaching content

A series of key informant interviews[15] was conducted with principals and panel chairs[16] in Hong Kong secondary schools. The interviews aimed to find out how school administrators reacted to the examination change, how the schools made decisions about the choice of teaching materials, and how they rearranged the teaching at an overall level. Through various school visits, it was found that in some Hong Kong secondary schools the principals made the decision on the choice of textbooks. In others, it was the English panel chairs that made the decision on this issue. In most situations, a particular series was chosen solely because publishers went to the school with whole sets of complimentary textbooks. During the interviews, panel chairs expressed their concern about whether a new textbook had provided actual teaching and learning tasks to cope with the examination change. Together with other teachers' views, they would decide which sets of textbooks were to be used.

In Hong Kong secondary schools, the overall teaching plan is designed according to the set of textbooks employed. Usually, textbooks are chosen after consultation with teachers. The reason, according to one of the panel chairs, is that if teachers do not like that textbook, they would not teach well. For F5 students, there was no main textbook for the year, only a workbook was used to prepare them for each paper of the HKCEE examination. Through the interviews in schools and with the textbook publishers, it was found that textbooks were by far the most direct teaching support teachers could obtain and rely on in their teaching. Teachers would expect textbook publishers to reflect the revised examination syllabus so that they could prepare their students well for the examination. Teachers did not rely on the CDC teaching syllabus for much of their teaching. The existing teaching syllabus for the key stage 4–Secondary Four and Five–was published in 1982 by CDC. When teachers did refer to the syllabus, they actually meant the HKEA examination syllabus, which was the syllabus they used in their teaching. This point was further illustrated in later school visits.

---

15. Some of the interviews were carried out by telephone, some in person. Most of them were carried out in early 1994. For detailed findings based on interviews with panel chairs, see Phase III Chapter 7.
16. The panel chair is the subject head in Hong Kong secondary schools.

Survey of teachers' and students' attitudes

Teachers' questionnaire[17]

The aim of the initial questionnaire was to obtain preliminary data on teachers' reactions to the revised examination, their perceptions and understanding of the revisions to the examination, and what they would like to do to prepare their students for the exam. The first part of the questionnaire was constructed in such a way that teachers first responded to a series of questions related to possible changes in areas of teaching and learning with a 'yes' or 'no' answer. This explored teachers' immediate attitudes towards the new examination. After each yes/no answer, teachers were invited to elaborate further their own views with written answers in the spaces provided (see Appendix I). Another purpose of this written word data is to facilitate understanding of teachers' feelings towards the examination change, and to provide qualitative input for the more structured survey in Phase II of the study.

The second part of the initial questionnaire was designed on a five-point Likert scale, which invited teachers to comment on their present teaching in terms of their teaching arrangement, the choice of textbooks, and the teaching methods they employed in their school.

A preliminary survey was carried out in April 1994 with 48 teachers, four months before they began teaching towards the revised examination syllabus for the first cohort of F4 students in September 1994. These teachers were from various kinds of Hong Kong secondary schools. 62% of these teachers taught in English medium schools and 29% taught in Chinese medium schools. Table 4.1[18] shows teachers' primary reactions to the new 1996 HKCEE and to different aspects of teaching and learning in their schools.

When teachers were asked about their reactions to the revised examination, 37% of the respondents were sceptical about the change, 29% were neutral, and another 21% welcomed or enthusiastically endorsed the changes, with 13% of the teachers not responding to the question. When asked whether or not they would like to make any changes in their teaching under the context of the revised examination, 84% of the teachers commented that they would change their teaching methodology. Teachers' written responses included statements such as 'I will put more emphasis on the integration of the skills,' 'Oral practice will mainly be based on facilitating discussion among students,' and 'To invite active participation from my students.'

While 66% of the teachers mentioned that the proposed changes in the 1996 examination syllabus were not contradictory to their present teaching methodology, 68% of teachers felt that coping with the extra work and

---

17. The questionnaire is in English.
18. In some cases, survey results fail to add up to 100%. This is due to the missing data, as some teachers did not provide responses to all questions.

increased number of teaching materials and aids would add pressure to their teaching. As for teaching materials, four months before the teaching of the new 1996 examination syllabus began, 55% of the respondents' schools had already changed textbooks. By the time the actual teaching started, nearly every school in Hong Kong whose students would sit for the 1996 HKCEE was using revised textbooks targeted towards the new examination. Teachers were also provided with the new teaching materials.

Table 4.1 Teachers' reactions to the revised HKCEE (n=48)

No.	Item	Yes	No
1.	Teachers knew the year in which the new exam would take place.	79%	21%
2.	Teachers knew the major skills to be tested.	63%	26%
3.	Teachers would like to change their teaching methodology.	84%	16%
4.	Teachers felt the new exam would add pressure to their teaching.	68%	32%
5.	Teachers regarded the new examination as contradictory to their teaching philosophy.	11%	66%
6.	Teachers regarded the new examination as an involvement of more teaching aids.	71%	11%
7.	Teachers would suggest that their students change their learning strategies.	76%	24%
8.	Teachers perceived that the new examination would motivate their students to learn English.	47%	18%

Although 76% of the teachers indicated that they would certainly suggest that students adopt new learning strategies for the new examination, some still worried about shy and quiet students since, in the new syllabus, students are required to initiate questions rather than just respond to them.

Looking at the teaching situation, it can be seen from Table 4.2 that 61% of the respondents stated that teachers jointly chose the textbooks, 22% and 13% of them stated that the decision was made by panel chairs and principals respectively. As for the overall arrangement of teaching content, decisions were made by teachers in the case of 60% of the respondents, and panel chairs according to 29% of the respondents.

Table 4.2 Teaching arrangements in Hong Kong secondary schools

	Selection of textbooks	Lesson arrangement
Teachers together	61%	60%
Panel chairs	24%	29%
Principals	13%	8%
Missing data	2%	3%

When the teachers were asked how they carry out language skills training in class, they replied that 61% of the English lessons were arranged for the purpose of teaching separate skills such as listening, reading, or grammar usage. Only 5% of the lessons involved integrated skills teaching. The teachers were also asked what major role the following factors played in their daily teaching. The following list shows the percentage of weighting respondents indicated in each category:

- public examinations   30%
- teaching beliefs   35%
- teaching experience   6%
- learners' expectations   19%
- principal's expectations   7%
- peers' expectations   3%

Among the factors that influence teaching, the teachers reported that examinations played a 30% role, teaching beliefs a 35% role, and teaching experience a 6% role. The rest of the influencing factors, at 19%, 7% and 3%, were attributed to learners', principal's, and peers' expectations. Although examinations are one of the factors that play a major role in teaching, 68% of the teachers, however, reported that they had never been negatively affected by their students' past test scores. The reasons behind this were explored more during school visits discussed in Phase III of the study.

Students' questionnaire

A student questionnaire was issued with the primary aim of investigating the role of the public examination on students' learning. The students were also invited to comment on the actual teaching and learning of English in their schools. The questionnaire was designed on a five-point Likert scale. The part related to students' attitude towards public examinations was scaled according to the strength of agreement, while the part related to their learning activities inside and outside the classroom was scaled according to frequency.

A preliminary survey was carried out in November 1994 with 42 students in one Secondary Four class, the new cohort of the students studying under the new examination, in the New Territories area of Hong Kong. Students were asked about what motivated them to learn English, and produced the following list:

- public examinations   30%
- future job   27%
- parents' concern   19%
- classmate competition   8%
- teachers' expectations   7%
- interesting textbooks   5%
- active learning activities   4%

When students were asked about aspects of their learning that were affected by the public examination, they produced the following list (in order of importance): learning strategies, emotions, motivation, self-image, and teacher-student relationships. According to the students, their examination results affected their parents in the following ways:

- parents changed the advice they gave to them
- parents became tense and anxious
- parents put more pressure on them.

Students were asked to comment on their classroom language activities according to separate skills. Listening was given as the most frequent classroom activity. The second most frequent classroom activities were those related to language exercises such as grammar or vocabulary. Reading and writing occupied similar class time, whereas the amount of time spent in speaking was ranked the least.

When asked about aspects of their teachers' talk, the students reported that their teachers talked to the whole class for 57% of class time. Only for less than 5% of the time did their teachers keep silent in their teaching. The major activities teachers carried out, according to the students, were, in rank order:

- explanation of language points
- explanation of language activities
- explanation of homework
- explanation of lesson objectives.

When students were asked to comment on the activities conducted in English in class, doing exercises was the most frequent activity, followed by asking their teacher for further explanation. Regarding their activities in English outside class, watching TV or reading newspapers and magazines in English were the most frequent activities. Communicating with teachers, classmates or parents were among the least frequent activities the students engaged in outside class.

School visits – teachers' and students' classroom behaviours

When the revised HKCEE syllabus was introduced, two versions of the examination syllabuses coexisted in Hong Kong secondary schools: the old HKCEE syllabus and the revised 1996 HKCEE syllabus. Two cohorts of F5 students were studied: one F5 cohort that took the old examination in 1995–the last year the old HKCEE was taken, and one F5 cohort that took the new examination in 1996–the first year the new 1996 HKCEE was taken. The classroom observations involved watching the same teachers teaching both cohorts of students. The preliminary observations focused on any change in the classroom activities employed by these teachers when teaching the two groups.

Classroom observations were carried out on a small scale with those teachers who were willing to be observed. As the main observations were carried out in Phase II of the study, the only changes observed at this stage lay in the different language activities teachers employed in their teaching. For example, as the old HKCEE required that students demonstrate their ability to read aloud a dialogue, teachers would teach their students the skill that was required by the examination–reading aloud. A lot of reading aloud activities were carried out using choral practice. However, with the current F4 and F5, the group of students studying for the revised 1996 HKCEE, reading aloud was replaced by role play and group discussion. Teachers no longer taught reading aloud, and more and more time was being spent on group discussions and oral presentations.

Washback on the English curriculum

Summarizing the above research findings in the initial phase, a certain degree of washback effect was perceived on the English curriculum as a whole as a result of the change of the HKCEE syllabus: on the teaching content as well as on teachers' attitudes and behaviours towards teaching and learning in Hong Kong secondary schools.

Spolsky (1994) points out that the backwash effect usually happens irrespective of test designers' intentions and is out of their control, though the reasons might be complicated in different educational settings. It is unlikely that any changes would happen in a linear manner. As Wall and Alderson (1993: 47-48) admit:

> What we did not know at the time was just how difficult it would be to determine whether washback has occurred at all, and to decide, if there were no evidence for it, whether this was because there was no such thing or because there were conditions in the educational setting that were preventing it from 'getting through...'

Even if there were favourable conditions in the educational setting in Hong Kong at the macro level, as reported above, it was still not difficult to formulate clearly the nature of the washback effect. It was even more difficult to say whether the effect was positive or negative. What teachers stated they would like to change was not necessarily the same as what they actually would do in the classroom. Therefore, exploration of the relationship between teachers' beliefs and their teaching behaviours in Phase II and Phase III of the study is important. As can be observed through school visits, although Hong Kong is a place where change is constant, teachers still worried about their students, and showed their own confusion over the changes in actual teaching as well.

This logistically leads us into the second and third phases of the study to enable detailed investigation to be carried out. Since only limited data was collected in Phase I, it is not clear whether the new examination will eventually change teachers' behaviours or, if it does, to what extent. From the preliminary classroom observations, changes were observed only in the way teachers organized classroom activities. It is difficult to judge whether the washback effect observed in the above teaching activities is simply as a result of cramming for the examination, or a genuine difference in the way skills were being taught. Cramming is obviously one level of the washback effect. It was expected by the HKEA (1994b: 80) that 'examination changes will help classroom teachers to keep a better balance between teaching and skill-building on one hand and examination preparation on the other.'

However, it would still be difficult to say whether cramming of the above kind could produce a positive or negative washback effect on teaching. To test this, more data based on classroom observations at Phase III are required. Teaching and learning should include more varied activities than the examination formats alone. Furthermore, the success of the initiative or the examination change is partly within the hands of the teachers and students in the actual teaching and learning context.

However, it is natural for teachers to employ activities similar to those required in the examinations. During school visits, teachers mentioned that it was their responsibility to prepare their students well for the examination. If they did not do enough to familiarize their students with the test formats, they would feel guilty. One teacher said in an interview,[19] 'I am very examination-oriented. And I will do whatever I can to get my students fully prepared for this public examination.'

From the results above, it can be seen that public examinations and future jobs are the main factors that motivate Hong Kong secondary students' learning. As has been mentioned above, the main role of the public examination is for selection. Passing the public examination and obtaining a good job are closely related. It is crucial, therefore, for students to get good scores in the examinations.

In Hong Kong secondary schools, normal teaching at F5 stops at the end of February or earlier. March is the month for mock examinations, and in May students sit for the certificate examinations. When students reach the F5 level, teaching and learning become more and more examination-driven. It is clearly seen from the school visits and observations that schools tend to use practice

---

19. This interview was carried out on 5 January 1995 in a Band One school on Hong Kong Island with a senior teacher after gaining agreement from the school principal and the teacher himself.

papers, not textbooks, from the beginning of F5 to the time when the students sit for the examination. Full preparation of their students for the examination is seen in Hong Kong secondary schools as the responsibility of teachers and principals. It is stated in the Teaching Syllabus of English (secondary), developed by the Curriculum Development Council, that the teaching of English at the F5 level will be heavily examination-oriented. Therefore, cramming for the examination is natural in Hong Kong schools. However, with the revised examination syllabus, which puts greater emphasis on task-based skills, it might be expected that washback on the way language activities are carried out will be positive.

Washback on textbooks

The most dramatic change due to the introduction of the 1996 HKCEE (see Appendix VI for the details of the exam changes) lay in the teaching content, an area of high washback intensity. By the time the examination syllabus affected teaching in Hong Kong secondary schools in the 1994 – 1995 academic year, nearly every school changed their textbooks for the students. Almost all textbooks were labelled specifically 'For The New Certificate Syllabus'. Publishers in Hong Kong worked extremely hard and fast to get their textbooks ready for the schools. The main reason might be related to the way in which Hong Kong society reacts rapidly, especially in relation to commercial matters.

Through interviews with teachers and textbook publishers, it was discovered that textbooks are by far the most direct teaching support teachers can obtain and rely on for their teaching. Textbook publishers in Hong Kong not only provide teaching materials but also detailed teaching and learning activities with suggested methods. They even suggest how much time should be devoted to carry out those teaching and learning activities. One textbook writer said in an interview:[20]

> Anyone who speaks some English would be able to teach English in Hong Kong as we have provided everything for them... Sometimes teachers phone us when they come across difficulties in teaching a particular unit or task and we would write a detailed plan for them.

In Hong Kong secondary schools, there is a general teaching schedule for a whole academic year called a Scheme of Work,[21] which teachers rely on in their teaching. This Scheme of Work is designed according to the layout of the

20. The interview was carried out on 27 October 1994 at the University of Hong Kong.
21. A Scheme of Work, sometimes called a teaching programme, is the overall teaching plan for a whole school academic year.

kind of textbook, which the school adopts for the school cycle or weekly system in Hong Kong secondary schools. Teaching and learning is usually based on a major textbook, together with a set of workbooks. These workbooks are specifically designed to prepare students for specific examination papers in the HKCEE. Therefore, given the teachers' reliance on textbooks, it could be assumed that the 1996 HKCEE would likely have certain washback effects on the teaching and learning of English in Hong Kong schools if those textbooks catering to the 1996 HKCEE had really integrated the underlying theories behind the change and realized this integration through the language activities in the textbooks.

Washback on teachers' attitudes and behaviours

It can be seen from the teacher survey results that the teachers generally welcomed the 1996 HKCEE. However, there was not enough evidence at this point to prove whether this would necessarily bring about positive changes in teaching methodology. They might still find it difficult to put their ideas into practice. This was evident from the written answers teachers provided in the preliminary survey, when they described their worries about their shy and quiet students. The teachers also worried about difficulties in classroom management and the use of teaching facilities, as there was a requirement to carry out more active learning activities in the revised HKCEE.

From the data obtained from classroom observations in Phase I of the study, it was clear that those teachers teaching both the old and the new syllabuses did make use of different types of activities. However, some obvious changes made in teaching related directly to the different activities in the textbooks the teachers employed. This meant that teachers changed their ways of organizing classroom activities according to the textbook publishers' understanding of the 1996 HKCEE. Also those activities or tasks were designed on the basis of only a limited sample of examination formats provided by the HKEA.

During school visits, it was seen that the teachers were very careful to arrange classroom activities to meet the requirements of the revised syllabus. In addition, they also talked about their confusion over its objectives. In effect, at this stage the teachers followed the new syllabus simply by adherence to the new textbooks, but it would be very interesting to observe how the teachers reacted in their teaching after the first cohort of students took the examination. By then, teachers might have a clearer idea of the new examination, and possibly would rely less on the proposed sample papers and textbooks. This part of the findings will be reported and discussed, based on in-depth interviews with teachers in Phase III of the study.

Summary

Research on the washback effect ought to first begin with an analysis of the nature of the test, be it a large-scale public examination or a classroom assessment, since the function and/or the importance of a particular test determines its degree of influence and the areas of its washback intensity. Then, attention should be directed to investigating the particular educational context in which the examination is taken. Only by exploring the context can the research contribute to our knowledge of how a particular examination change influences teaching and/or learning within that context, to what extent and what kind of washback occurs, either positive or negative.

Moreover, we should explore the degree of superficiality of the washback effect on teaching and learning. One of the main purposes of the HKEA in changing the present examination is that 'the new format will have favourable washback on classroom teaching' (HKEA, 1993: 5). From the preliminary results, washback on aspects of teaching can be seen, for example, in the changing of textbooks. Textbook publishers have certainly altered the format and organization of the teaching content in their books according to the new examination formats, which allows schools and teachers to have something to rely on in teaching the new examination syllabus. It is evident from the publishers' seminars[22] and workshops that teachers did not wish to buy those textbooks if they had not been specifically labelled for the new HKCEE examinations.

Similarly, changing an examination is likely to change the kind of examination practice, but not the fact of examination practice. Changing examination formats may not change the degree of emphasis on examinations, nor does it necessarily change teachers' methods in actual classroom teaching. The changes tend to be at the obvious superficial level. The intention to bring about a positive washback effect in classroom teaching by changing the major public examination is a laudable one, but it might only change the format of teaching.

This chapter has summarized the research findings in Phase I of the study, which comprised the observations and investigations made in the initial stage of the examination change. This phase of the study answered the first research question in Chapter 3. The findings showed the initial reactions of different parties within the Hong Kong educational context, thus providing a sound background for the further study carried out into the second and third phases of the study. The next two chapters will report the research findings for Phase II of the study.

---

22. One such observation was the Macmillan seminar organized on 11 March 1996 at the Sheraton Hotel, Kowloon, Hong Kong.

5 Phase II – Teachers' perceptions of the change

Introduction

The research findings of Phase II of the study–results of the Teacher Questionnaire (TQ)–will be discussed in this chapter. The questionnaire was issued twice, once in 1994 and again in 1995 to comparatively explore possible changes in teachers' attitudes to various aspects of teaching in relation to the changes in the 1996 HKCEE syllabus. This section will report the comparative findings from the two surveys. Differences in teachers' attitudes between 1994 and 1995 were tested for statistical significance using independent sample t-tests and the chi-square tests. A probability of less than 0.05 was taken as statistically significant for both tests.

There were three parts in the Teacher Questionnaire (see Appendix I: TQ). Part One consisted of eight categories of various nominal variables related to demographic information about the teachers who responded to the questionnaires. Part Two consisted of 12 categories and 95 items on a five-point Likert scale of agreement, where five = strongly agree and one = strongly disagree. Part Two explored teachers' attitudes towards the new HKCEE. Part Three consisted of 10 categories. The first six categories were nominal variables, inviting the teachers to make a choice under each category. The remaining four categories were designed on a five-point Likert scale of frequency, where five = always and one = never and were related to the teachers' everyday teaching. For clarity and simplicity of reporting, notation such as TQ 2.1.1 is used to describe the Teachers' Questionnaire, Part 2, Category 1, Item 1.

Demographic information on the teachers who responded to the questionnaires

Eight aspects of teachers' characteristics were included in the study: gender, age, academic and professional qualifications, number of years of teaching, the current form they were teaching, number of lessons taught, and the band[1] of their school.

The survey focused on 323 aided schools among 388 Anglo-Chinese[2] schools, which was based on 448 day secondary schools in Hong Kong's 19 school districts (Hong Kong Government, 1993: 55). The specific population of the survey consisted of teachers of English from 60 such Hong Kong secondary schools. These 60 schools comprised 19% of the total aided school population (i.e. 60 out of 323). F5 students from 35 of these secondary schools were surveyed. Teachers from the 35 schools who taught those students were all included in the teachers' survey in both years.

The return rate was 40% in 1994 (140 out of the 350 questionnaires issued that year) and 47% in 1995 (94 out of the 200 questionnaires issued that year). The population of teachers in Hong Kong secondary schools changes dramatically from year to year due to the rapid pace of social change in Hong Kong. One constraint on the research was that it was almost impossible to track and survey the same groups of teachers over the year. The questionnaires were, however, issued to similar overlapping groups of teachers in 1994 and 1995. As there was no guarantee that the sample was the same in each year, a chi-square test was carried out after the survey. The chi-square test was used to evaluate the discrepancy (the degree of relativity) between the means of the teachers' characteristics in the two sample years. The significance level (P <.05) of the results from the chi-square statistical analysis provided a valid basis for further sample mean comparison. The chi-square results showed that there was no significant difference among the seven categories of the two groups of teachers' characteristics (see Table 5.1), which further indicated that the two samples were similar, and satisfied the requirement for mean comparison using independent sample t-tests, i.e. to statistically compare their attitudes towards the new HKCEE in two different years. It should be noted here that the survey was conducted over a short period over two academic years (a 12-month period precisely). Therefore, changes were assumed to be limited and/or restricted in certain aspects of teaching (see Part Two of Chapter Three for more details regarding the survey design). It is, however, assumed that the limited or restricted aspects of changes observed in the survey could reflect washback effects induced by the 1996 HKCEE as this exam change was the biggest change in Hong Kong Secondary schools at the time of the research.

Only one category, however, 'forms currently taught by teachers,' showed a significant difference (p = .00016). In 1994, the survey covered teachers

---

1. School band is an indicator of the overall achievement level of a school's student intake. Banding is determined by the Secondary School Places Allocation System (SSPA) in Hong Kong. The SSPA is the process by which primary students are allocated to secondary schools.

2. Anglo-Chinese schools refer to schools whose medium of instruction is English, that is, all courses are delivered in English, except Chinese and Chinese history.

teaching all different forms, whereas the 1995 survey was more focused on teachers who were teaching Forms 1-3 and Forms 4-5 in secondary schools. The major assumption behind the 1995 survey was that those teachers were the ones who were mainly responsible for preparing students for the new HKCEE. The adjustment in the sampling should have been avoided in retrospect as it might have contributed to the mixed picture seen in the results to be reported below. Teachers in Hong Kong secondary schools teach either Forms 1-3, or Forms 4-5 and/or Forms 6-7 according to Key Stages of Teaching as set out in the CDC Teaching Syllabus. Which forms a teacher teaches is usually decided according to their qualifications and experience and assigned by their principals. Table 5.1 shows teachers' characteristics and the chi-square test of significant difference between the samples in 1994 and 1995.

It can be seen that two thirds of the teacher participants were male and one third were female. Ages ranged between 20 and 40 years old. More than 40% of the teachers had one to six years of teaching experience, and half of them had more than ten years' experience. The majority of the teachers (around 75%) were teaching between 22 to 33 periods per week. The sampled teachers came from schools of various bands in Hong Kong. This sample of teachers was better qualified academically (more than 69% held a bachelor's degree) and professionally (more than 80% held a teacher's certificate) when compared with the general population of teachers of English in Hong Kong secondary schools (Coniam, Sengupta, Tsui, & Wu, 1994). Only 18.9% were subject trained, and 14.2% were both subject and professionally trained. It needs to be stated that there are teachers of English in Hong Kong secondary schools who have a bachelor's degree, are not subject trained in English, but are still permitted to teach English. In most of the cases, their bachelor degrees were obtained from overseas universities. In one of the case study schools in Phase III, there were 14 teachers of English. None of them were subject trained in English including the panel chair, who was a chemistry major.

As the majority of the categories in the Teachers' Questionnaire (see Appendix I) were designed on a five-point Likert scale, independent sample t-tests were carried out to test the difference in teachers' attitudes in Part Two and Part Three of the questionnaire. Certain categories, such as TQ 3.1-3.7 in Part Three, were designed as multiple-choice questions depending on the nature of the variables. In this case, chi-square tests were performed to test the significance of difference among these variables. The results, however, will be reported and discussed according to the following conceptual order, rather than according to the statistical methods:

- teachers' reactions to and perceptions of the 1996 HKCEE
- washback on teaching materials
- washback on teachers' classroom behaviours

- washback on assessment and evaluation
- washback on teachers' attitudes towards aspects of learning.

Table 5.1 Characteristics of the respondents and chi-square test of significant difference in 1994 and 1995

Items	Variables	1994 (%)[3]	1995 (%)	Chi-square significance
Gender	Male	69.1	63.4	.37266
	Female	30.9	36.6	
Age	20-30	38.1	36.6	.66865
	31-40	36.0	37.6	
	41-50	20.9	17.2	
	Above 50	5.0	8.6	
Academic qualifications	B.A.	59.0	66.3	.18192
	B.Sc.	10.8	3.3	
	Master's	12.9	10.9	
	Others	17.3	19.6	
Professional qualifications	Teacher's Cert.	38.2	32.4	.22437
	P.C. Ed/Dip.	48.0	62.0	
	Advanced dip.	8.8	2.8	
	R.S.A	2.0	0	
	M.Ed.	2.9	2.8	
Years of teaching	1-3	26.9	22.3	.49256
	4-6	17.9	20.2	
	7-9	8.2	13.8	
	10+	47.0	43.6	
Major forms currently taught	F1-F3	35.1	40.4	.00016
	F4-F5	35.1	52.1	
	F6-F7	29.8	7.4	
Teaching periods per week	16-21	19.8	25.8	.18056
	22-27	35.9	38.7	
	28-33	40.5	35.5	
	Above 33	3.8		
School band	Band 1	28.1	35.9	.18852
	Band 2	26.6	22.8	
	Band 3	26.6	15.2	
	Band 4	10.9	13.0	
	Band 5	7.8	13.0	

3. Percentage reported in both survey studies is given here as valid per cent.

Teachers' reactions to and perceptions of the 1996 HKCEE

There were six categories on the questionnaire related to teachers' reactions to and perceptions of the 1996 HKCEE. One category refers to the teachers' reactions (TQ 3.1), which was designed on a four-point scale. The other five categories referred to the teachers' perceptions of the new 1996 HKCEE (TQ 2.1-2.5). These five categories were scaled from five = strongly agree to one = strongly disagree.

Teachers' reactions to the 1996 HKCEE

Teachers were asked to describe their reactions to the 1996 HKCEE in 1994 and 1995. The results are presented in Table 5.2 below.

Table 5.2 Teachers' reactions to the 1996 HKCEE

Teachers' reactions	1994 N=125	1995[4] N=89
Sceptical about the change	38.4	20.2
Neutral about the change	29.6	32.6
Welcome the change	30.4	42.7
Enthusiastically endorse the change	1.6	4.5

When the teachers were asked about their reactions to the 1996 HKCEE (TQ 3.1), it was found that there was a significant difference in their reactions to the 1996 HKCEE between 1994 and 1995. There was an increase[5] in the number of teachers who 'welcome the change,' from 30.4% in 1994 to 42.7 % in 1995, whereas a decrease in teachers who were 'sceptical about the change,' from 38.4% in 1994 to 20.2% in 1995. Teachers who 'enthusiastically endorse the change' also increased from 1.6% to 4.5%. This increase is a clear indication of teachers' positive attitudes towards the new HKCEE over the year. More teachers tended to be less sceptical about the change after the new HKCEE had been in effect for one year. There was also a slight increase in teachers who are 'neutral about the change,' from 29.6% to 32.6%. However, this difference is marginal.

---

4. The numbers for 1994 and 1995 in the table refer to the number of valid cases of the statistical analysis.
5. The use of 'increase' or 'in an increasing direction' and 'decrease' or 'in a decreasing direction' in reporting the findings in the book refers solely to the increase and decrease in the mean score comparison over the two year period for the independent t-tests.

This positive attitudinal change in teachers towards the new HKCEE is supported by the initial survey study carried out in Phase I of the study. Teachers in Hong Kong tend to have a positive and supportive attitude towards change in general (Morris, 1990b). It is only when they come across problems and difficulties in actual teaching that they confront the pressure of change. The reluctant attitude to change might be due to the practical aspects of teaching in the case of this examination change. Moreover, it is normal that teachers seldom abandon what they have been doing and embrace completely some new philosophy, methodology, or new curriculum approaches, even if they do have a positive attitude towards the examination change. It is only to be expected that teachers would modify what they have been doing to prepare their students for the new HKCEE as it is so important to both students and teachers alike. However, even if the survey showed a positive attitudinal change, this does not necessarily mean that the teachers are going to change their behaviour. Further discussion of this issue will be presented in Phase III of the study.

Teachers' perceptions

Five categories are related to teachers' perceptions of the following areas:

1. Perceptions of the reasons behind the new 1996 HKCEE.
2. Perceptions of the new format of the 1996 HKCEE.
3. Perceptions of possible extra work and pressure under the new 1996 HKCEE.
4. Perceptions of possible difficulties in teaching the new 1996 HKCEE.
5. Perceptions of the possible teaching methods teachers would like to adopt to prepare for the new 1996 HKCEE.

All these categories were designed on a five-point Likert scale with five = strongly agree and one = strongly disagree.

Change in perceptions towards the reasons behind changing the HKCEE

This category was designed to explore the extent to which teachers perceived the reasons behind the change in the HKCEE and how much they understood the underlying theories behind the change. When teachers were asked what they saw as the major reasons for the HKEA to change the present exam syllabus, the general picture ranked according to the mean scores in 1994 showed the following pattern, which explores what teachers saw as the reasons behind the HKCEE change.

	1994	**1995**
• to encourage better textbooks*	4.0413	2.5217
• to enable students to communicate more with others	3.8833	3.8602
• to narrow the gap between HKCEE and UE	3.7899	4.0108
• to motivate students to use integrated skills*	3.7333	3.9892
• to encourage students to play an active role in learning	3.6250	3.6882
• to meet the demands of tertiary education	3.6167	3.7742
• to prepare students for their future careers*	3.5583	3.8495
• to refine testing methods	3.2333	3.3011
• to widen the gap between high and low ability students*	2.9661	2.6237
• to cope with the present decline in English standards	2.9407	2.9140

Four out of the ten reasons listed above[6] indicated significant differences between 1994 and 1995, as shown in Figure 5.1 and Table 5.3.[7] These four reasons are marked with an asterisk in the list above.

It can be seen from the above table that teachers' perceptions of the reasons 'to prepare students for their future careers' and 'to motivate students to use integrated skills' changed in an increasing direction, indicating that the teachers implicitly agreed with the principles of the intended washback effect of the new HKCEE (c.f. HKEA, 1992/1993). The agreement might also suggest that teachers became more aware of the underlying theories behind the new HKCEE between 1994 and 1995. This understanding may encourage teachers in the direction of teaching for the examination.

However, teachers' perceptions of the reasons 'to widen the gap between the top and low students' and 'to encourage more good textbooks' decreased, especially with regard to textbooks. In 1994, teachers perceived 'to encourage better textbooks' as one of the main reasons behind the new 1996 HKCEE, but fewer teachers held this view in 1995. The reason for this decrease might be related to the actual quality of the revised textbooks produced for the new HKCEE. On one hand, it was the intention of the HKEA to have support from the textbook publishers for the examination change. On the other hand, teachers also expected to have something to rely on in case of changes made by the HKCEE. However, this might not necessarily indicate good textbooks. Teachers have different points of view among themselves of good textbooks. The support mentioned above might not necessarily be related to good textbooks. In fact, textbooks suitable for an examination syllabus are not necessarily good.

---

6. The categories and items in the Teachers' Questionnaire were obtained from the theoretical framework in the previous research and from the qualitative data from the earlier initial study in 1994, carried out at the beginning of the study.

7. Figures in this chapter are used to show the difference in the teachers' attitude towards the new HKCEE in 1994 and 1995. Tables are used to illustrate the significant attitudinal difference by means of statistical analysis.

Table 5.3 Differences in teachers' perceptions of the reasons behind the 1996 HKCEE

Variables	Year	Cases[8]	Mean	SD	T-Value	df	2-Tail Prob.
To prepare students for their future careers	1994	120	3.5583	1.002	-2.31	211	.022
	1995	93	3.8495	.779			
To widen the gap between the top and low students	1994	118	2.9661	1.045	2.29	209	.023
	1995	93	2.6237	1.122			
To motivate students to use integrated skills	1994	120	3.7333	.857	-2.24	211	.026
	1995	93	3.9892	.787			
To encourage better textbooks	1994	121	4.0413	.907	11.71	211	.000
	1995	92	2.5217	.978			

Figure 5.1 Teachers' perceptions of the reasons behind the 1996 HKCEE

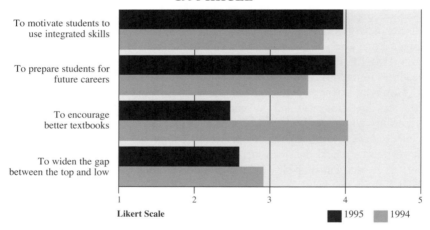

Changes in perceptions towards the changes in the HKCEE exam papers

The responses given when teachers were asked 'what are the major changes that you have perceived in the exam papers of the 1996 HKCEE?' are shown in the following pattern, listed according to the mean score for 1994. From the

8. The number of cases indicated here refers only to valid cases for statistical analysis.

general pattern, it can be seen that teachers knew what the changes were in the 1996 HKCEE. The two main changes they perceived on the lists were those changes related to the format change of the exam papers.

	1994	1995
• more role play and group discussion*	3.9741	4.2527
• more emphasis on oral activities	3.9316	4.0879
• closer to the 'Use of English'[9] in the oral paper*	3.8898	4.2000
• more integrated and task-based approaches*	3.8185	4.1758
• more practical and closer to real life*	3.5630	3.8462
• more emphasis on listening	3.4576	3.6923
• more related to Target Oriented Curriculum principles	3.3136	3.4000
• less emphasis on grammatical usage	3.0171	2.9780

Four out of the eight items, identified by an asterisk in the list above, were found to have changed significantly over the period, as illustrated in Figure 5.2 below.

Figure 5.2 Teachers' perceptions of changes made in the 1996 HKCEE

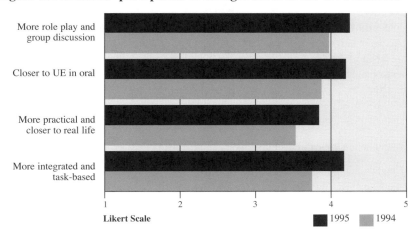

9. *The Use of English* is an English language examination taken by students at the end of Secondary Seven. The examination tests the ability of candidates to understand and use English, as it might be required in tertiary education and/or future employment. The examination consists of five sections. Four proficiency sections (A-D) focus on a range of productive and receptive skills. One section (E) concentrates on work and study skills. Section D, Oral English, tests the ability of candidates to give an oral presentation and take part in a small-group discussion. Candidates are examined in groups of four. There are two parts.

In Part One, each candidate is required to present a brief spoken account of a short written text lasting between one and a half to two minutes. The four texts are related to the same topics.

In Part Two, the candidates take part in a 12-minute discussion on a topic related to the texts they spoke about in Part One of the examination. The discussion simulates a study-related or work-related situation, where it is assumed there is a problem to be solved or a task to be addressed.

**Table 5.4 Differences in teachers' perceptions of changes
made to the 1996 HKCEE**

Variables	Year	Cases	Mean	SD	T-Value	df	2-Tail Prob.
More integrated and task-based approaches	1994	119	3.8185	813	-3.71	208	.000
	1995	91	4.1758	508			
More practical and closer to real life	1994	119	3.5630	890	-2.31	208	.022
	1995	91	3.8462	855			
Closer to the Use of English in the oral paper	1994	118	3.8898	941	-2.41	206	.017
	1995	90	4.2000	889			
More role play and group discussion	1994	116	3.9741	889	-2.37	205	.019
	1995	91	4.2527	769			

From the above results, changes can be seen in teachers' perceptions of the changes made in the new HKCEE. As a result, their attitudes matched more closely the theory and the intended washback effect over the period. The intended washback effect from the HKEA was to bring about positive change in teaching, which would enable students to perform certain real life tasks and use their language skills integratively. The four items mentioned in Table 5.4 are related to genuine language skill building. Teachers' perceptions of the rest of the items in this category remained relatively the same. This suggests that teachers' perceptions of the changes in the new HKCEE are compatible with the HKEA intended washback effect.

Extra work or pressure involved in teaching towards the 1996 HKCEE

Teachers were asked what kind of extra work or pressure (if any) they thought the 1996 HKCEE would put on their teaching. The extra work and pressure reported by teachers in the 1994 survey is listed below, which shows the general teaching pattern in Hong Kong. It can be seen that in 1994 teachers did foresee an increased workload and new challenges in relation to the 1996 HKCEE. However, in 1995, teachers' attention focused on 'employing new teaching methods.'

	1994	1995
• preparing more materials for students*	4.0579	3.7742
• following a new syllabus	3.9917	3.7742
• meeting new challenges in teaching	3.9504	3.8602
• doing more lesson preparation	3.9256	3.7957

- setting up new teaching objectives 3.8852 3.8710
- employing new teaching methods 3.8430 3.9247
- revising the existing materials 3.7951 3.6774
- organizing more exam practices 3.5785 3.4086

Only one out of the eight items in this category was found to have changed significantly, as marked by an asterisk. However, mean difference[10] for this item between 1994 and 1995 is .2837, indicating a decrease in the mean score from 1994 to 1995 as shown in Table 5.5. The result also showed that teachers initially thought, in 1994, that the change in the HKCEE would result in preparing more materials for students. However, their attitudes changed between 1994 and 1995, and there seemed to be less worry or tension in their attitudes towards preparing extra teaching material as a result of the change to the examination.

Table 5.5 Differences in teachers' attitudes regarding pressure the new exam puts on their teaching

Variables	Year	Cases	Mean	SD	T-Value	df	2-Tail Prob.
Preparing more	1994	121	4.0579	.830	2.35	212	.020
materials for students	1995	93	3.7742	.934			

This finding is in accordance with the results regarding teachers' attitudes towards textbooks when they were asked what they saw as the major reasons for the HKEA to change the exam syllabus. In 1994, teachers felt that the 1996 HKCEE would encourage better textbooks, but their attitudes changed considerably (mean difference = 1.5196) in 1995, showing a decrease in the attention to textbooks and teaching materials. Teachers in the study no longer thought that changing the HKCEE was aimed at producing good textbooks. In 1994 when teachers were first confronted with the examination change, they expressed concerns over teaching materials. One of the teachers' main worries expressed in a school survey carried out by the HKEA in 1993 was the need for new teaching materials to cope with the examination change.

In the interviews with teachers and during the school visits in Phase I of this study, the teachers showed great concern over how to carry out their teaching with the new examination syllabus. It might be normal for teachers to seek immediate teaching support when faced with change. Moreover,

10. The mean difference is obtained from the independent sample t-test on SPSS.

according to Phase I of the study, textbooks are the most direct and accessible teaching support in Hong Kong secondary schools. These attitudinal changes towards textbooks and teaching materials might suggest a positive attitudinal change towards the new HKCEE since teachers demonstrated less concern about the teaching materials in 1995 compared to 1994.

The remaining seven items listed above related to the extra work or pressure that the teachers associated with the new exam. No significant differences were shown over the year according to statistical analysis. It can be seen from the mean scores[11] that teachers did have strong feelings or worries about the examination change. These feelings about the HKCEE change remained relatively constant between 1994 and 1995. This, to some extent, suggests overall tensions and worries over the examination change, even though the mean scores for most of the items in 1995 tended to decrease. However, the mean scores of teachers' attitudes towards employing new teaching methods increased over the period. This might indicate the teachers' subconscious desire to change to new methods between 1994 and 1995, though it was not explicitly expressed on the Likert scale.

Teaching methods the teachers would change due to the 1996 HKCEE

There were eight items in this section regarding the changes the teachers would like to make in their teaching in relation to the 1996 HKCEE.

	1994	1995
• to encourage more student participation in class	4.2397	4.2527
• to put more emphasis on the integration of skills	4.1405	4.1630
• to employ more real life language tasks*	4.1074	3.9130
• to put more stress on role play and group discussion	4.1066	4.1957
• to adopt new teaching methods	4.0820	3.8901
• to use a more communicative approach in teaching	4.0413	3.8804
• to put more emphasis on the oral and listening components*	4.0165	4.2609
• to teach according to the new test formats	3.9917	4.1413

Two items in the above list (marked by an asterisk) were seen to differ significantly between 1994 and 1995. The differences are further elaborated in Figure 5.3 and Table 5.6.

---

11. Mean scores were obtained from a five point Likert scale in the teachers' questionnaire.

Figure 5.3 Changes teachers would like to make in their teaching

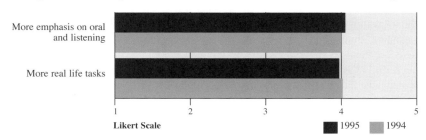

Table 5.6 Differences in teachers' attitudes to changes they would like to make in their teaching

Variables	Year	Cases	Mean	SD	T-Value	df	2-Tail Prob.
More oral and listening	1994	121	4.0165	.645	-2.91	211	.004
	1995	92	4.2609	.552			
More real life tasks	1994	121	4.1074	.668	2.03	211	.043
	1995	92	3.9130	.721			

The assumption made by the HKEA was that if the weighting of certain components in the examination was increased, there would be an increase in the emphasis on these areas reflected in teaching, which was true in this case. Regarding 'putting more emphasis on oral and listening components' due to the change in the examination, the teachers' attitudes did change in an increasing direction. Teachers were clearly aware of the increase in this case. This showed that there might be certain washback effects of the examination change on the weighting of the oral and listening components.

However, 'employing more real life language tasks' showed a significant difference between the 1994 and 1995 surveys, but changing in a decreasing direction. The teachers initially thought they would put more emphasis on real life tasks as specified in the examination, but their attitudes had changed one year later.

It is interesting to notice the discrepancy between this item and an item in Figure 5.1, which is related to teachers' perceptions of the changes made in the examination. There was a significant difference in teachers' attitudes towards the 1996 HKCEE being 'more practical and closer to real life.' However, when they were asked whether they would like to 'employ more real life language tasks,' teachers' attitudes changed in a decreasing direction over time. This discrepancy clearly demonstrates the gap between the teachers' attitudes and their actions in the classrooms. This may also indicate the nonlinear direction of making use of the public examinations to change teaching.

The remaining items listed above (i.e. those not marked with an asterisk) did not show significant differences between 1994 and 1995 according to statistical analysis. However, it would be interesting to observe the order of possible changes that teachers would like to make in terms of the new HKCEE according to the mean scores listed above. For example, 'more student participation in class,' ' more emphasis on the integration of skills,' and 'more role play and group discussion' are high on the list, with a slight increase in 1995. However, when it came to 'new teaching methods' and a 'more communicative approach in teaching,' the teachers' attitudes changed in a decreasing direction. This might also suggest another kind of discrepancy between teachers' attitudes towards adopting new classroom activities and employing new teaching methods.

Difficulties in teaching towards the 1996 HKCEE

Teachers were asked, 'What do you find the most difficult aspects of teaching the 1996 HKCEE?' Seven items are listed below according to the mean scores in 1994.

	1994	1995
• students' current English level*	3.9580	4.4409
• class size	4.3445	4.5484
• inadequate textbooks and available teaching resources*	3.9417	3.5699
• noisy learning environment*	3.4874	2.7849
• the lack of teaching and learning resources and facilities*	3.8571	3.3978
• too heavy a workload	3.8983	4.1075
• inadequate time for students to practise English outside the language classroom*	4.1186	4.6129

Five out of the seven items are seen to have significantly changed over the year as follows. Differences are shown in Figure 5.4 and Table 5.7 below.

From Figure 5.4, it can be seen that the teachers' attitudes towards items such as 'inadequate time for students to practise English outside the language classroom,' 'noisy environment,' and 'lack of teaching & learning resources' were seen to change in a decreasing direction, which indicated that there were fewer tensions and worries about those aspects of the perceived difficulties in teaching towards the 1996 HKCEE between 1994 and 1995. The three aspects concerning inadequate textbooks, noisy environment, and lack of teaching and learning resources were the teachers' main concerns when they were first informed about the change in the examination. It seems that these external or environmental worries diminished over time, especially in regard to textbook

Figure 5.4 Teachers' attitudes to the difficulties in teaching towards the 1996 HKCEE

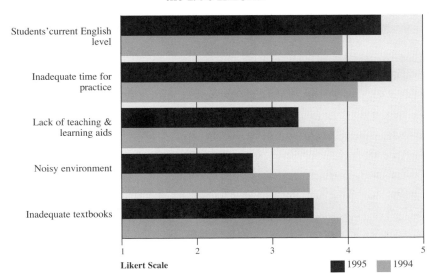

Likert Scale   ■ 1995 ▨ 1994

Table 5.7 Differences in teachers' attitudes to the difficulties in teaching towards the 1996 HKCEE

Variables	Year	Cases	Mean	SD	T-Value	df	2-Tail Prob.
Inadequate textbooks	1994	120	3.9417	.946	2.62	211	.010
	1995	93	3.5699	1.127			
Noisy learning environment	1994	119	3.4874	.982	4.99	210	.000
	1995	93	2.7849	1.062			
Lack of teaching and learning resources	1994	119	3.8571	.826	3.64	210	.000
	1995	93	3.3978	1.012			
Inadequate time for students to practise	1994	118	4.1186	.849	-4.78	209	.000
	1995	93	4.6129	.590			
Students' current English level	1994	119	3.9580	1.003	-3.90	210	.000
	1995	93	4.4409	.729			

supplies. As shown in Figure 5.4 and Table 5.7, however, there are two items–'inadequate time for practice' and 'students' current English level'–that showed significant differences in teachers' attitudes in an increasing direction over the year. These aspects are the two major concerns that the teachers most frequently commented on as being problematic in teaching the new examination syllabus, especially in Phase II and Phase III of the study. Even in the later interviews with the teachers after the first cohort of F5 students had taken the new 1996 examination, teachers still considered students' current English level as the main obstacle in teaching the new examination syllabus.

There are only two items that did not show a significant difference between 1994 and 1995 but still show a tendency towards movement in an increasing direction.

	1994	**1995**
• class size	4.3445	4.5484
• too heavy a workload	3.8983	4.1075

The above findings show that the practical aspects of teaching that received increasing amounts of teachers' attention were 'inadequate time for practice' and 'students' current English level.' The other three aspects of teachers' concerns in Figure 5.4 are seen to move in a decreasing direction from 1994 to 1995. One point needs to be emphasized here, which is that class size is perceived by teachers as the most difficult aspect in teaching towards the 1996 HKCEE in terms of mean scores. This reflects the logistical problems of teaching English in Hong Kong secondary schools, the average class size being 40 students.

Looking at teachers' reactions to and perceptions of the new 1996 HKCEE, it has been shown that teachers tended to have a more positive reaction to it in 1995 compared to 1994. Moreover, their perceptions of the reasons behind the changes to the HKCEE in relation to the changes that were actually made in the HKCEE reflected teachers' awareness of the underlying theories in teaching and learning behind the exam change and the HKEA's intended washback. The agreement between teachers' and policy-makers' perceptions could also suggest a positive attitude towards the implementation of the new HKCEE. However, whether teachers would actually alter their teaching to reflect the underlying theories in teaching and learning is still a question to be answered.

In addition, it can be seen that washback on actual aspects of teaching in the context of the examination change is very complicated as perceived by the teachers, and showed a mixed picture (see the section on Teaching Methods the Teachers Would Change due to the 1996 HKCEE). Teachers' perceptions of the teaching and learning in terms of 'more emphasis on listening and oral components' changed significantly in an increasing direction from 1994 to 1995. 'More student participation in class,' 'more emphasis on the integration of skills,' and 'more role play and group discussion' also showed a slight increase in 1995. However, teachers' perceptions in terms of adopting 'new teaching methods' and a 'more communicative approach in teaching' changed in a decreasing direction.

Another aspect of the findings was that there were, according to the mean scores on teachers' attitudes, general tensions and worries over the 1996 HKCEE related to specific aspects of teaching. However, there was less concern or worry over the new teaching materials and textbooks detected in 1995. Instead, the students' current English level and inadequate practice time had become the major concerns over the year. The actual impact of the examination change on the teachers' attitudes, however, cannot be directly determined from the survey results due to the nature of the survey study, and the relatively short period of the survey, and will be discussed further in Phase III of the study.

Washback on teaching materials

There are three categories in relation to teaching materials (TQ 3.5, 3.6, 3.10). Items in TQ 3.5 and 3.6 were designed on a multiple-choice scale. TQ 3.10 was designed on a five-point Likert scale, where five = always and one = never. The purpose of the questionnaire was to explore possible relationships between teaching materials and the examination change.

Textbook arrangements related to teaching materials

There were two categories related to teaching materials in the context of the change in the 1996 HKCEE. They were presented in a multiple-choice format as shown in Table 5.8. Neither of them changed significantly over the year according to the chi-square test of difference.

- who makes the major decision on the choice of textbooks? (TQ 3.5)
- what are the primary functions of textbooks in teaching? (TQ 3.6)

Table 5.8 Textbook arrangements in Hong Kong secondary schools

Items	Variables	1994 (%)	1995 (%)	Chi-square significance
Who makes the major decision on the choice of textbooks?	1. Principal	2.6	2.2	.22462
	2. Panel chair	40.0	28.1	
	3. English teachers together	57.4	68.5	
	4. Yourself	0	1.2	
What are the primary functions of textbooks in teaching?	1. To provide practical activities	11.6	15.1	.53810
	2. To provide a structured language program to follow	69.5	59.3	
	3. To provide language models	8.4	12.8	
	4. To provide information about the language	10.5	12.8	

From Figure 5.5 below, it can be seen that teachers of English in the Hong Kong secondary schools have much say in the choice of textbooks. Together with the panel chairs, it is normally the teachers of English who decide which textbooks to use in their teaching. As one of the panel chairs explained, it was natural and essential to choose the textbook which teachers preferred, otherwise they would not enjoy teaching it.

Figure 5.5 Decision on the choice of textbook

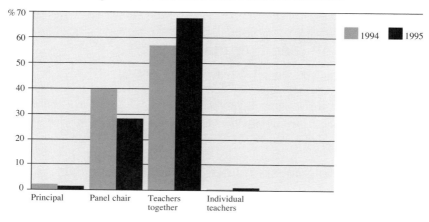

Regarding the function of the textbook in teaching, it can be seen that textbooks, by a wide margin, are 'to provide a structured language program to follow.' This is fully illustrated for the choice of textbooks in Hong Kong secondary schools, which indicates that textbooks play an important role in

Figure 5.6 Teachers' attitudes to the function of the textbook in teaching

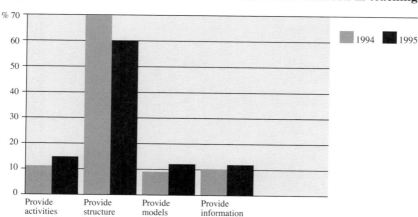

English teaching. However, a slight decrease in teachers' beliefs about this function of textbook use can be seen between 1994 and 1995 in Figure 5.6.

Teaching and learning resources

This category aimed to find out whether the teachers believed that the examination change would involve extra teaching and learning resources. This was one of the main concerns teachers expressed when they were first informed about the change. Teachers were asked to express how often they used a list of nine teaching and learning resources in their teaching (TQ 3.10). This list is arranged according to the mean scores in 1994. Textbooks and supplementary materials were rated among the most frequently used resources in teaching.

	1994	1995
• textbooks	4.1791	4.0659
• supplementary materials	3.6866	3.7802
• examination syllabus*	3.5000	3.0000
• overall lesson plan (Scheme of Work)	3.4361	3.3444
• teaching syllabus*	3.4361	2.9101
• newspapers	3.0593	3.0659
• television/radio	2.5746	2.5495
• language laboratory	2.5448	2.4111
• pictures and/or cards	2.4511	2.4333

It was found that the use of two kinds of resources changed significantly over the year. They changed, however, in a decreasing direction. The teachers used both the teaching and examination syllabuses less in 1995.

The rest of the teaching and learning resources did not change according to the mean scores in 1994 and 1995. It could clearly be seen that textbooks are the most often used teaching and learning resources, followed by supplementary materials (including workbooks for mock exams). There was a slight increase in the use of supplementary materials in 1995, which might be

Table 5.9 Differences in the teaching and learning resources used by the teachers

Variables	Year	Cases	Mean	SD	T-Value	df	2-Tail Prob.
T. Syllabus	1994	133	3.4361	.940	3.79	220	.000*
	1995	89	2.9101	1.114			
E. Syllabus	1994	134	3.5000	.964	3.57	221	.000*
	1995	89	3.0000	1.108			

due to the new HKCEE. It is quite evident throughout the study that these materials produced by textbook publishers are the most direct form of support on which teachers rely in their teaching. The HKEA informed the textbook publishers about the examination change after their decision, and they provided them with the sample papers because the HKEA believes that any curriculum change must involve a change in teaching materials as well. Textbook changes must be in accordance with changes in examinations, otherwise no schools or students would choose to buy new textbooks that bear no relevance to the HKCEE examination.

When the results were examined in detail, it was found that pictures and cards were used less in teaching than newspapers, and television and radio programmes. The teachers usually encouraged their students to buy the *Young Post,* published by the *South China Morning Post,*[12] as part of their teaching and learning activities. This is one example of the fact that the teachers use a variety of authentic materials (real life materials) in their teaching.

Summarizing the results in the area of washback on the choice of teaching materials (TQ 3.5, 3.6, 3.10), there was no clear evidence of washback in this area. The overall pattern was not seen to change in the context of the examination change. There was not an increasing amount of attention given to the examination syllabus. Moreover, the initial assumption by the teachers that the examination change would require more teaching and learning resources (due to the integrated and communicative approaches and the increase in the oral components in the 1996 HKCEE), was not proven. The teachers continued to use conventional textbooks and supplementary materials more frequently in their teaching.

Washback on classroom teaching behaviour

Questions related to aspects of daily teaching were investigated in this section. The purpose of this section was to investigate whether the introduction of the 1996 HKCEE would influence the teachers' decisions about and perceptions of their everyday teaching activities.

There were six categories in this section. The first three categories (TQ 3.2, 3.3 and 3.4) were designed in a multiple-choice format as shown in Table 5.10 below. The chi-square test was carried out to test the significance of differences among the variables between 1994 and 1995.

The next three categories (TQ 3.7, 3.8 and 3.9) were designed on a five point Likert scale of frequency, where five = always and one = never. An independent sample t-test was used for statistical analysis of differences for these items over the year. Results of this section will be reported in two parts:

35. *South China Morning Post* is one of the English language newspapers in Hong Kong.

(a) teaching arrangement and medium of instruction in English lessons (TQ 3.2, 3.3 and 3.4), and (b) lesson planning, teacher talk, and teaching activities in English lessons (TQ 3.7, 3.8 and 3.9).

Both of the above two categories are related to aspects of teacher classroom behaviours. They are reported separately in two categories because items in the first category were designed on a multiple-choice scale, and the items in the second category were designed on a five-point Likert scale.

Teaching arrangement and medium of instruction

There were three categories in this section. As they were designed on a multiple-choice scale, a chi-square test was first used to clarify the general teaching situation. The results are shown in Table 5.10, and each category will be discussed in detail below. Among the three categories in this section, only one category, 'how teachers arrange their teaching in schools' (TQ 3.4) showed a significant change between 1994 and 1995.

The greatest difference among these items was seen in teaching

Table 5.10 Chi-square tests of differences in aspects of daily teaching

Items	Variables	1994 (%)	1995 (%)	Chi-square significance
How do teachers arrange their teaching in schools?	1. According to textbooks	18.3	17.1	.01593*
	2. According to Scheme of Work	59.6	39.0	
	3. According to separate skills	9.2	24.4	
	4. According to the content	11.0	17.1	
	5. According to language activities	1.9	2.4	
Who makes the decision on the arrangement of lessons?	1. Principal	14.2	19.1	.25675
	2. Panel chair	16.7	14.6	
	3. English teachers together	40.8	29.2	
	4. Yourself	28.3	37.1	
What is the medium of instruction?	1. English only	37.8	24.4	.05198
	2. English supplemented with occasional Chinese explanation	48.9	63.3	
	3. Half English, half Chinese	12.6	8.9	
	4. Mainly Chinese	.7	3.4	

arrangement according to the Scheme of Work in the Hong Kong secondary schools. The Scheme of Work is an overall teaching plan for the whole academic year. In 1994, 56.6% of teachers arranged their teaching according to the Scheme of Work, but in 1995 there was a sharp decrease in this number to 39%. In addition, the teachers seemed to arrange their lessons in 1995 much more according to 'separate skills' (an increase from 9.2% to 24.4%) and 'content to be taught' (from 11% to 17.1%). Of the other two choices, 'textbook' and 'language tasks' remained relatively unchanged.

Figure 5.7 Ways teachers arrange their teaching in schools

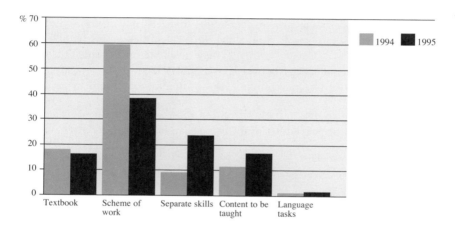

The remaining two categories did not show a significant difference between 1994 and 1995. The chi-square test results and descriptive analysis of frequency are shown in Table 5.10. Among these two categories, the item regarding medium of instruction showed an interesting pattern. As is shown in Figure 5.8 below, there were more teachers in 1995 who used English supplemented with occasional Chinese explanations as their medium of instruction, than in 1994. The increase was from 48.9% in 1994 to 63.3% in 1995. Consequently, there was a decrease in teachers' use of English only, from 37.8% in 1994 to 24.4% in 1995 (c.f. Table 5.10). This might indicate an increasing tendency for teachers to use English with occasional Chinese. One possible reason for this might be their concerns and worries over their current students' English level. They aim to get the meaning of the language across to students so that the students can pass the exam. This point was frequently mentioned by many teachers during school visits in all phases of the study.

Figure 5.8 Medium of instruction in Hong Kong secondary schools

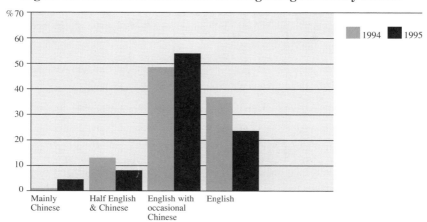

Lesson planning, teacher talk, and teaching activities in English lessons

Three aspects of teaching were placed on the Likert scale of frequency, where five = always and one = never. They are related to lesson preparation (TQ 3.7), teacher talk (TQ 3.8), and teaching activities (TQ 3.9).

Lesson preparation

Teachers were asked how often they consider seven specific aspects when they prepared their lessons. Two aspects of teaching in this category were found to have changed significantly over the year. They were ranked by respondents as the highest and the lowest ones on the list. The differences in both aspects increased between 1994 to 1995 as shown in Table 5.11 below.

	1994	1995
• the content of teaching*	4.2782	4.4725
• the tasks to be performed in teaching	4.0227	4.0659
• the skills to be taught	4.0000	4.0879
• the methods of teaching	3.9167	3.9890
• how to motivate students to learn	3.8258	3.9231
• any supplementary materials to be used	3.6641	3.6468
• homework to give to students*	3.4586	3.7912

In 1995, the teachers seemed to pay more attention to 'content of teaching' and the 'homework' to give to students. This result matches with the teachers' attitudes to their general teaching arrangement as shown in Figure 5.7. In 1995, more teachers considered the content to be taught. The increase was

Table 5.11 Aspects of teaching considered while preparing lessons

Variables	Year	Cases	Mean	SD	T-Value	df	2-Tail Prob.
Content of teaching	1994	133	4.2782	.632	-2.36	222	.019*
	1995	91	4.4725	.565			
Homework to give to students	1994	133	3.4586	.783	-2.95	222	.003*
	1995	91	3.7912	.888			

from 11% in 1994 to 17.1% in 1995 shown in Table 5.10. Other aspects such as the 'tasks to be performed in teaching' and the 'skills to be taught' received the same attention respectively in teaching between 1994 and 1995.

Moreover, teachers also paid more attention to the homework given to their students. In Phase III of the study, it was observed by the researcher that some parts of the language tasks were carried out outside the classroom and performed by students as part of their homework. For example, in one of the case studies, a teacher was observed to ask her students to write up an essay as part of the oral lesson according to the oral discussion they had in class. The students would complete the essay for homework and use it for further classroom activities in the next lesson. This might be an example of a positive washback effect of the change in the HKCEE, as part of the underlying integrated theories of teaching and learning. This result might also suggest that the change brought about as a result of the change to the examination could direct the teachers' attention more towards empowering their students to do more work at home. In addition, giving more homework to students might have indicated the pressure of the new examination.

The remaining aspects of teaching to be considered during lesson preparations showed no significant differences. It can be seen from the mean scores that 'the tasks to be performed in teaching' are ranked the second highest, followed by the 'skills to be taught,' and then the 'methods of teaching.' This suggests that these teachers of English paid more attention to teaching content than to teaching methods and other learner factors. They were more content oriented than thinking how content should be delivered to learners. The findings are also supported by Morris (1990a, 1990b) on curriculum innovation.

Teacher talk

Teachers were asked how often they did the following activities in class: (a) talk to the whole class, (b) talk to groups of students, (c) talk to individual students, or (d) keep silent. The general situation over the two academic years is shown below. There was no significant difference among all four items under the category of 'teacher talk'. The figure and table below, however, show the pattern of teacher talk in English lessons in Hong Kong secondary schools.

Figure 5.9 Teacher talk in English lessons

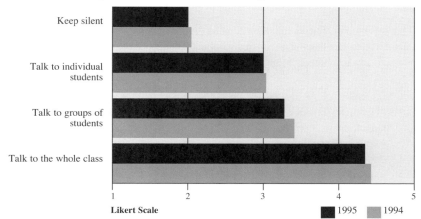

Table 5.12 Teacher talk in English lessons

Variables	Year	Cases	Mean	SD	T-Value	df	2-Tail Prob.
Talk to the whole class	1994	133	4.4436	.633	.80	222	.425
	1995	91	4.3736	.661			
Talk to groups of students	1994	133	3.3759	.831	1.12	222	.263
	1995	91	3.2527	.769			
Talk to individual students	1994	132	3.0758	.768	.72	221	.471
	1995	91	3.0000	.775			
Keep silent	1994	131	2.0305	.952	.24	218	.814
	1995	89	2.0000	.929			

The four teacher talk modes remained the same, irrespective of the examination change. However, a general pattern can be observed showing the nature of the teacher talk in their English lessons. For the great majority of the time, teachers talked to the whole class, and much less to groups and to individuals. The mean score of keeping silent for both years in 1994 and 1995 was at two (seldom) out of the five (always) scales. This, together with the mean scores shown above, indicates that teachers were talking most of the time in class. The results suggest that the teachers dominated and controlled the classroom talk for most of the lesson time. This shows that teacher talk is an area on which the change in the examination did not seen to have an impact.

Teaching activities

There are ten activities listed under this category to explore how often teachers carry out the following activities in class. None of the activities listed below were found to change significantly. They are:

		1994	1995
A1.	tell the students the aims of each lesson	3.2313	3.2667
A2.	demonstrate how to do particular language activities	3.7015	3.7000
A3.	explain the meaning of the text	3.7015	3.7556
A4.	explain specific language items	3.8881	3.9111 **(highest)**
A5.	explain textbook exercises	3.5896	3.6333
A6.	explain homework	3.5333	3.6222
A7.	explain mock exams	3.1756	3.1364
A8.	organize language games*	2.9328	2.9111 **(lowest)**
A9.	organize group work or discussion	3.3407	3.4945
A10.	organize integrated language tasks	3.2500	3.3077

Observing the pattern carefully, it can be seen that activity four (A4), 'explain specific language items, such as words or sentences,' was carried out most often by teachers. This is closely followed by 'explaining the meaning of the text' together with activities A5 and A6. All these activities are related to explaining, which might suggest the reasons why the teachers spent most of the time talking to the whole class (c.f. Table 5.12). This finding is also supported by Phase III of the study when classroom observations were carried out. The teachers spent a great deal of time explaining language points and the meanings of the text to their students in class. Some teachers[13] felt that they had not done their job well if they did not teach students explicitly. A9 and A10–demonstrating how to carry out group work or discussion and organizing language tasks, respectively–were slightly less common activities carried out by the teachers. Furthermore A8, 'organizing language games,' was ranked the lowest among the items. Comparing A8 and A4 might show that the teachers still adhered to more traditional methods. This shows the trend of how teachers carry out their classroom activities in Hong Kong secondary schools.

13. The data was obtained from the interview carried out on 5 January 1994 with a senior teacher in one secondary school on Hong Kong Island–Phase I of the study.

Summarizing the findings in washback on classroom teaching behaviours (TQ 3.2 – 3.4; 3.7 – 3.9), there is not much of an indication of washback on aspects of teaching at the micro level, which was not surprising considering the short period of the survey. General ways of teaching, such as teachers' talk, the nature of teaching, and delivery modes, remained unchanged in the context of the examination change. However, some changes were observed. There was a tendency in 1995 for teachers to pay more attention to the content and skills to be taught and homework to be given to students, which might be directly related to the new HKCEE for the increasing of the oral component and the integrated skill components. The medium of instruction was also seen to change from using English only to using English occasionally with Chinese explanations. However, these changes might not be directly related to the examination change. The medium of instruction, according to the teacher respondents, might be due to the teachers' perceptions of the current level of students' English proficiency.

Washback on assessment and evaluation

This section was designed to explore various aspects of assessment and evaluation that might have been influenced by the changes to the 1996 HKCEE. Three categories (TQ 2.10–2.12, 25 items in total) were investigated using Likert scales.

The use of mock exams

Six items were employed to explore the teachers' attitudes to the basic functions of mock exams in schools:

	1994	1995
• to prepare students for public examinations	4.2313	4.3763
• to assess students' learning difficulties	3.8571	3.8280
• to give feedback to teachers*	3.8284	4.0323
• to identify areas of re-teaching	3.6692	3.8065
• to direct students' learning	3.4851	3.5591
• to motivate students	3.3008	3.3978

Only one item above, 'to give feedback to teachers,' was seen to have changed significantly. However, it is hard to tell whether this change was due to the new examination. The reason why more teachers started to perceive the use of mock exams as a way to provide them with feedback is not clear. Maybe it was due to the reason that more exam practices were employed.

Table 5.13 The use of mock exams as perceived by teachers

Variables	Year	Cases	Mean	SD	T-Value	df	2-Tail Prob.
To give feedback to teachers	1994	134	3.8284	.741	-2.07	225	.040
	1995	93	4.0323	.714			

There was no significant change among the remaining items. The above results are arranged according to mean scores to allow better interpretation of teachers' perceptions of the use of mock exams in Hong Kong secondary schools. From the results, it can be seen that 'to prepare students for public examinations' was rated as the most important function of mock exams in schools in both years. In Hong Kong secondary schools, public examinations clearly play a very important role and, as reported in Phase I of the study, the teachers did perceive preparing students for the public examination as one of their major responsibilities.

The assessment of teaching in Hong Kong secondary schools

In this section, teachers were invited to illustrate how their teaching was assessed in their schools. The major purpose of this category was to determine the importance that is attached to the teachers' work life in schools–the key components that influenced their daily teaching. None of the seven ways of assessing teaching in their schools was seen to have changed significantly over the year according to the t-test results.

	1994	1995
• your own reflections on teaching	3.7079	3.8478
• the performance of your students on tests and public examinations	3.6992	3.6087
• the overall inspection of your students' work by your school	3.2164	3.3261
• the overall completion of the subject content	3.0758	3.0217
• anonymous student evaluation of teaching	2.8062	2.8152
• evaluation by colleagues	2.6591	2.8261
• evaluation by principal or school inspectors	3.1429	3.1739

The above results are arranged according to mean scores in 1994. 'Teachers' own reflections on teaching' came in the highest on the mean scores, closely followed by 'students' performance in examinations' and 'inspection of their students' work.' To some extent, this situation reflected how explicitly or implicitly the teachers carried out their teaching in schools, and the factors considered by teachers as important in the assessment and evaluation in their schools. It is usually believed that the more important a public examination is, the more attention teachers will give to the examination in teaching. Attaching a teacher's job evaluation to public examinations is likely to redirect the focus of the teacher's daily work. On the other hand, the fact that the teachers' attitudes towards the above items remained unchanged between 1994 and 1995 might suggest that the washback from this HKCEE was limited. Changing the examination did not reflect a change in the role and function of public examinations in teaching in Hong Kong secondary schools. No matter how the examination was changed, the function of the HKCEE and the importance it bore remained constant.

Factors that influence teaching

In this section, teachers' perceptions of a list of 12 factors that influence their teaching were explored. The results are listed according to the mean scores in 1994.

	1994	**1995**
• professional training	3.9695	3.9395
• teaching experience and beliefs*	3.9250	4.4043
• past experience as a language learner	3.9008	3.9570
• the need to obtain satisfaction in teaching	3.8397	4.0430
• the teaching syllabus	3.7519	3.8152
• learners' expectations*	3.6870	3.9140
• public examinations*	3.6718	3.9247
• academic seminars or workshops	3.3206	3.5054
• textbooks	3.2576	3.2366
• peers' expectations	3.1221	3.0968
• principal's expectations	3.1145	2.9355
• social expectations	3.0769	2.9570

The t-test results showed that teachers perceived three factors (*) differently between 1994 and 1995. All three factors were seen to change in an increasing direction.

Figure 5.10 Factors that most influence teachers' teaching

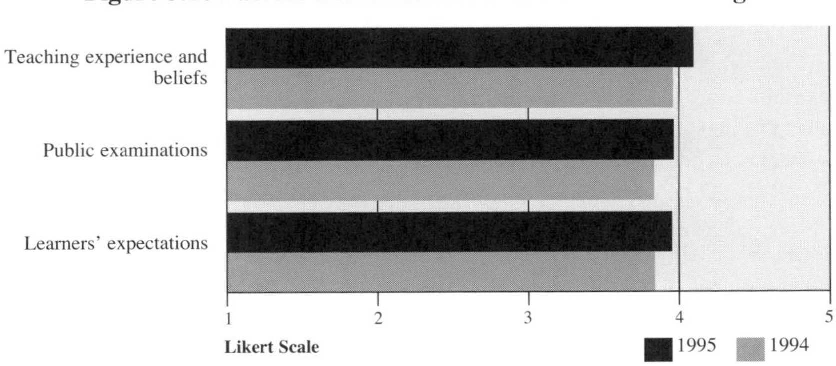

The remaining items perceived by the teachers remained unchanged, which are listed to show the perceived levels of importance of those specific factors. In Phase I of the study, textbooks were reported by the teachers as providing the most direct teaching support, but teachers regarded them as relatively less important than other factors here, such as the teaching syllabus, according to Phase II. The teachers might rely on textbooks directly and extensively, but they do not perceive textbooks as an important factor in teaching. The most noticeable finding perceived by the teachers was the public examination being one of the most important factors that affects teaching.

Table 5.14 Differences in teachers' attitudes towards factors that most influence their teaching

Variables	Year	Cases	Mean	SD	T-Value	df	2-Tail Prob.
Teaching experience and beliefs	1994	140	3.9250	1.258	-3.38	232	.001
	1995	94	4.4043	.677			
Public examinations	1994	131	3.6718	.907	-2.12	222	.035
	1995	93	3.9247	.837			
Learners' expectations	1994	131	3.6870	.860	-1.97	222	.050
	1995	93	3.9140	.830			

Summarizing the findings regarding washback from the new HKCEE on assessment and evaluation (TQ 2.10, 2.11, 2.12), there was no clear sign of an effect. In this respect, washback was seen as superficial at this stage. Teachers perceived and realized the underlying teaching and learning theories behind the exam change. They might have had a positive attitude and might have changed their classroom activities. However, teachers' attitudes towards assessment and evaluation remained unchanged in general. The aspects that changed in the teachers' attitudes that were observed between 1994 and 1995 were those influencing factors such as teaching experience and beliefs, public examinations, and learners' expectations. This might suggest that an examination change such as the new HKCEE could possibly redirect teachers' attention to the public examination itself and make them pay more attention to learners' expectations.

Changing an examination is likely to change the *kind* of exam practice, but not the *fact* of the examination practice. Changing the examination test formats does not usually tend to change the degree of emphasis on the examinations. Changing the HKCEE into formats that are more compatible with the Target Oriented Curriculum initiative could possibly change some aspects of teaching pedagogy. However, from the above results, the most important aspects that governed teachers' daily teaching in Hong Kong secondary schools remained relatively unchanged over the period.

Washback on teachers' attitudes towards aspects of learning

Four categories in Part Two of the teacher questionnaire (2.6, 2.7, 2.8 and 2.9) explored teachers' attitudes regarding: (a) the learning strategies the teachers would recommend to their students (TQ 2.6); (b) the aims of learning English in Hong Kong secondary schools (TQ 2.7); (c) the kinds of activities language learning should involve (TQ 2.8); and (d) the methods the teachers would like to use to motivate students to learn (TQ 2.9). There were 29 items all together within these four categories. All items were designed on a five-point Likert scale, where five = strongly agree and one = strongly disagree. These categories dealt with teachers' attitudes towards how aspects of learning might be influenced in terms of the change to the examination.

Learning strategies

Nine strategies were listed to explore teachers' attitudes towards the learning strategies they would recommend to their students in the context of the new HKCEE. They are listed below. Mean scores are shown in descending order for 1994 and then 1995.

	1994	1995
• to expose themselves to various English media	4.5000	4.3617
• to learn to express their opinions in class	4.4538	4.3298
• to be more active in classroom participation	4.3729	4.5000
• to communicate more in English*	4.3277	4.5213
• to use English more in their daily life	4.3025	4.2340
• to change from passive learning to active learning	4.2712	4.3404
• to put more emphasis on listening and speaking	4.2203	4.2128
• to learn to initiate questions	4.2119	4.1809
• to learn to take better notes*	3.6783	3.9149

Only two of them showed significant differences, in increasing directions, between 1994 and 1995. This finding shows teachers' increasing attention to these two strategies.

The change in the teachers' attitudes towards the above two strategies might suggest an increasing change in their attitudes towards how learners should study in the context of the 1996 HKCEE. This might also indicate pressures associated with taking the examination. Therefore, these strategies could be regarded as pragmatic ways to cope with the examination rather than a learning strategy for improving English. One of the major changes in the

Figure 5.11 Learning strategies teachers would recommend to their students

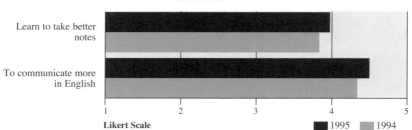

Table 5.15 Differences in the learning strategies teachers would recommend to students

Variables	Year	Cases	Mean	SD	T-Value	df	2-Tail Prob.
To learn to take better notes	1994	115	3.6783	.884	1.97	207	.050
	1995	94	3.9149	.838			
To communicate more in English	1994	119	4.3277	.726	-2.13	211	.035
	1995	94	4.5213	.563			

new HKCEE was Paper III: Integrated Listening, Reading and Writing. This paper requires students to know how to take notes, especially for the listening task, as they are required to make use of the information through listening in order to later carry out a writing task. It is natural that the teachers strongly recommended their students to learn to take notes and that the teachers paid more attention to the strategy in 1995.

Another major change in the new examination was reflected in Paper IV: Oral. On one hand, there was an increase in the weighting (from 10% to 18%) of the oral component in the new HKCEE. On the other hand, the new oral component also required students to perform interactive and communicative real life tasks. Teachers seemed to pay particular attention to these aspects in teaching in 1995. The old examination used to have structured oral activities such as a structured dialogue and a picture description. Therefore, this change in teachers' attitudes towards these two strategies suggests a direct washback effect of the new examination on teachers' recommended learning strategies to their students.

The remaining strategies that the teachers would like to recommend to their students did not change significantly over the year. Even though there was no significant difference, the priority that teachers gave to strategies they regarded as important is revealed from the results. The results also showed that these strategies were highly recommended by teachers, as all mean scores were above four.[14] This also suggests that teachers tended to recommend those strategies directly related to the exam paper. It can also be seen that the first few strategies, high on the list, are all related to the requirements of the 1996 HKCEE. This indicates a washback effect of the new examination's format on the teachers' perceptions of certain learning strategies. The teachers would suggest their students adopt those learning strategies accordingly in attempting the new 1996 HKCEE examination.

One point worthy of mentioning here is the different levels of these learning strategies. Some of them are directly related to English language studies; some of them are more general learning strategies. The major reason for this difference is because the list of strategies was directly obtained from the qualitative data provided by the teachers in the pilot studies of the questionnaire.

Learning activities

Teachers' attitudes towards what types of activities should be involved with language learning in the context of the new HKCEE were explored in this section. There were seven types of activities all together. They are listed below in descending order according to the mean scores in 1994, and show the tendency of teachers' preferred learning activities.

	1994	**1995**
• exposure to various English media	4.4030	4.3298
• using authentic materials	4.2406	4.1489
• role play and group discussion*	4.1955	4.4043
• training in basic language knowledge	4.1756	4.1702
• task-oriented activities	4.1128	4.0108
• language games	4.0522	4.0213
• doing extracurricular activities	3.7820	3.6064

Only one such learning activity (marked by an asterisk) was found to have changed significantly between 1994 and 1995. This change is very sensible in the context of the examination change as Part IV – Oral of the new HKCEE had two parts, (a) role play and (b) group discussion. It suggests a direct washback effect on the oral learning activity. Moreover, according to the results above, the teachers encouraged and recommended that their students communicate more in English. This might suggest that teachers in many ways

14. The questionnaire was designed on a five-point Likert scale.

were conscious of the changes made in the examination and paid more attention to those specific areas in their teaching and learning to meet the requirements of the new HKCEE.

The remaining learning activities, according to the teachers' responses, remained unchanged statistically from 1994 to 1995. It can be seen from the above list that learning activities that resemble real life situations were highly recommended by teachers. Although there were no significant differences between the two years, the list shows the activities in which teachers wanted their students to be engaged, which, in certain ways, reflects the underlying theories of the examination change.

Learning aims

Teachers were asked about their perceptions of the major aims of learning English in Hong Kong secondary schools. None of the five items shows a significant difference between 1994 and 1995.

	1994	1995
• to pursue further studies	4.3864	4.3298
• to pass examinations	4.1729	4.2128
• to obtain 'good' jobs	4.1716	4.1596
• to satisfy school requirements	3.9394	3.6064
• to satisfy parents' requirements	3.6515	3.2128

It was found that the mean scores of two out of the five aims decreased over the year. The teachers gave far more weighting to satisfying the school's and parents' requirements in 1994 than in 1995 as the aims of learning English in Hong Kong. As for the aim of satisfying parents' requirements, there was a big change over the year. Compared with the mean scores, the remaining aims were unchanged, yet these aims were strongly perceived by the teachers. The mean scores of the aims were all above four on the Likert scale, indicating that these aims were both regarded as important aims of learning English in Hong Kong between 1994 and 1995.

Teachers' responses to 'pursuing future studies,' which came highest on the list, were followed by 'passing examinations,' indicating a hidden agenda within the teachers' perceptions of the aims of learning English in Hong Kong secondary schools. Moreover, it was noted that there was a slight increase in teachers' rating of 'passing examinations' as a major aim of learning English. This might indicate possible pressure on their teaching whenever there is an examination change such as the 1996 HKCEE.

Motivation to learn

There were eight items under this category that asked teachers in what ways they would like to motivate their students to learn:

	1994	**1995**
• to create a positive attitude towards language learning*	4.2632	4.4624
• to give students more encouragement to learn*	4.2239	4.4301
• to provide students with effective language learning strategies	4.1791	4.3011
• to organize real life language activities*	4.0602	4.2660
• to use more authentic materials	3.9179	3.9362
• to do more interesting language games	3.8881	4.0108
• to have a better classroom discipline	3.7786	3.6237
• to do more mock exam papers	2.7463	2.9574

Three types of methods (indicated with an asterisk) changed significantly in an increasing direction between 1994 and 1995. They are shown in Figure 5.12, and are among the top few items on the list.

Figure 5.12 Teachers' perceptions of the methods to motivate their students

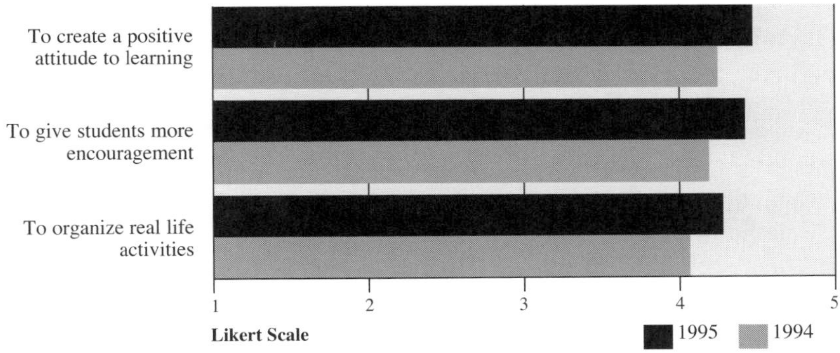

It can be seen that the teachers' attitudes towards real life language activities and positive learning increased over the year. This might be due to the change in the HKCEE, as it was influenced by this underlying theory. The teachers might have employed the above methods to motivate their students. The remaining five methods of motivating students did not show any significant difference. However, it could still be observed that teachers rated them quite highly according to the mean scores. These methods were all related to the 1996 HKCEE. 'To do mock exam papers' was not ranked very high, but there was a slight increase in 1995 over 1994. This might, in certain ways, be due to the examination change since the teachers usually see helping their students to pass examinations as one of their responsibilities.

Summarizing the area related to washback on teachers' attitudes towards aspects of learning, it can be seen that the washback effect is clear. In TQ 2.6, TQ 7.8 and TQ 7.9, whether the changes be learning strategies, learning activities, or methods to motivate students to learn, the teachers' attitudes showed a clear reflection of the intended washback effect and the underlying theories of the examination change.

Summary

It can be seen from the findings of Phase II of the study that identifying the washback effect of the new HKCEE is complicated. The following aspects of the teachers' attitudes in the context of the examination change were explored in this chapter:

- teachers' reactions to and perceptions of the 1996 HKCEE
- washback on teaching materials
- washback on classroom teaching behaviours
- washback on assessment and evaluation
- washback on teachers' attitudes towards aspects of learning.

Firstly, exploring teachers' reactions to and perceptions of the new HKCEE, it could be seen that the teachers' reactions to the new exam changed positively. There was a significant increase in the number of teachers who 'welcome the change,' from 30.4% in 1994 to 42.7 % in 1995, whereas there was a decrease in teachers who were 'sceptical about the change' from 38.4% in 1994 to 20.2% in 1995. In addition, teachers' perceptions of the reasons for changing the examination, and perceptions of the new exam formats were consistent with the underlying theories behind the changes. In terms of teaching, these changes were closely related to more integrated and task-based approaches, more practical and closer to real life language activities, and more role play and group discussion in teaching and learning. The congruence between teachers' perceptions and those of the HKEA decision-makers might suggest a positive washback effect on teaching and learning in those aspects in the Hong Kong educational context. In this sense, there was a small gap between the policy and teachers' perceptions.

Secondly, when aspects of daily teaching were explored in the context of the new examination, the situation was less clearly perceived by the teachers. The teachers' perceptions of adopting 'more real life tasks' and 'more oral and listening activities' required by the new HKCEE (also specified in the new textbooks) changed in an increasing direction from 1994 and 1995. However, teachers' perceptions of adopting 'new teaching methods' and a 'more communicative approach in teaching,' associated with the new HKCEE remained relatively unchanged over the year, which indicated reluctance in teachers to make the changes in certain aspects of teaching.

There were concerns and worries over the new HKCEE according to the mean scores on teachers' attitudes to aspects of teaching. The teachers' initial concerns or worries over the new teaching materials and textbooks in the context of the exam change decreased between 1994 and 1995, whereas concerns over their students' current English level increased. This suggests an intended washback effect on the teaching materials within the Hong Kong education context, as the HKEA informed the textbook publishers of the examination change immediately after the decision was made. Furthermore, this also suggested that there seemed to be something within the educational system that worked efficiently and effectively to provide the teachers with the new materials to deal with the examination change. Therefore, it seemed likely that the teachers would like to change their teaching activities (those tasks suggested in the textbooks) more willingly than their teaching methods, which might be largely influenced by the actual classroom teaching situations.

Thirdly, when aspects of learning were explored from teachers' perspectives, the teachers' attitudes were in accordance with the underlying theories and requirements of the new 1996 HKCEE. The teachers were more willing to encourage their students to cope with the change rather than to change their own teaching methodology. Explaining the teachers' reluctance to make changes was complicated, and will be explored through detailed classroom observations and in-depth interviews in Phase III of the study. Phase III of the study will report findings from classroom observations of the teachers' behaviours in more detail.

6

Phase II – Students' perceptions of the change

Introduction

In this chapter, the research findings of Phase II of the study–results of the Student Questionnaire (SQ) will be discussed. As explained in the methodology chapter, the questionnaire was designed to be issued twice, once in 1994 and again in 1995, to two cohorts of F5 students (one cohort of F5 students scheduled to take the old HKCEE, and one F5 scheduled to take the new HKCEE). The student survey explored possible changes in F5 students' attitudes in relation to their classroom activities within the context of the new 1996 HKCEE syllabus.

This chapter will first report the findings on the students' perceptions of their English lessons, and then the comparative findings for 1994 and 1995. Differences in the students' attitudes over the year were tested for statistical significance using independent sample t-tests and the chi-square tests. A probability of less than 0.05 was taken as statistically significant for both tests. The major reason for employing independent sample t-tests is that the survey was issued to two cohorts of F5 students. A chi-square test was conducted to guarantee that the two F5 groups of students were comparable and valid for t-test comparisons (see Chapter Three, Part Two and Table 6.1 for details). F5 students surveyed in both years were also from the same 35 schools. This could also indicate that they were taught by about the same groups of teachers assuming that the majority of teachers remained teaching in the same schools between 1994 and 1995.

The Student Questionnaire was divided into two parts. Part One consisted of five categories of variables of (a) demographic information on the students who responded to the questionnaires and (b) various elements of their learning context. All five categories were designed on a nominal scale. Students only needed to tick the appropriate choice according to their own situation. Part Two consisted of three sections (Sections A, B, & C) consisting of 11 categories and 78 items. These items were designed on a five-point Likert scale. Section A was designed on a scale of frequency. Sections B and C were designed on a scale of agreement. Part Two of the questionnaire aimed to explore the students' attitudes in 1994 and 1995 towards teaching and learning activities, inside and outside the classroom, in relation to the new HKCEE. For clarity and simplicity of reporting, a category such as SQ 2.1.1 is used here to refer to Student Questionnaire, Part 2, Category 1, Item 1.[1]

The findings are reported in two parts:

Part One: Students' Characteristics and Their Learning Contexts

Part Two: Section A: Students' Attitudes Towards Teaching Activities Inside and Outside Class

Section B: Students' Attitudes Towards Aspects of Learning

Section C: Students' Attitudes Towards Aspects of Public Examinations

Students' characteristics and their learning contexts

The survey focused on students from the 323 aided schools in Hong Kong (Hong Kong Government, 1993). The survey consisted of F5 students from 35 such Hong Kong secondary schools in 1994 and 1995, roughly 11% of the aided school population. The return rate for the student questionnaire was 76.7% in 1994 (844 out of 1100 questionnaires issued that year) and 73.8% in 1995 (443 out of 600 questionnaires issued in that year). The sampling in 1995 was smaller as the 1995 study was designed as a focus study.

Table 6.1 presents findings from Part A of the Student Questionnaire, which mainly dealt with demographic information about the students and their learning contexts. All items in this section were designed on a nominal scale, and were in a multiple-choice format. Students were required to choose one item from each category.

Table 6.1 shows that this survey consisted of similar numbers of male and female F5 students in both years. The majority of the students started learning English either in Primary One or Secondary One, indicating those students had had at least five years' learning experience prior to participating in the study. There was no statistically significant difference between the two samples in these two categories.

In terms of the medium of instruction, it can be seen that the dominant trend among their teachers when students were taught English was to teach it in

---

1. SQ 2.1.1 refers to the following item in bold.
   PART TWO Please grade the following on a 5-point scale format where 1 = never, 2 = seldom, 3 = sometimes, 4 = often, 5 = always. Put 1, 2, 3, 4 or 5 in the brackets provided.
   (1) How often does your teacher do the following in your English lessons?
   1 = never, 2= seldom, 3 = sometimes, 4 = often, 5 = always
   1[ ] Talk to the whole class
   2[ ] Talk to groups of students
   3[ ] Talk to individual students
   4[ ] Keep silent

English supplemented with Chinese–46.4% in 1994 and 51% in 1995 (c.f. Table 6.1). There was a significant difference in their medium of instruction over the two years. There was an increase in teachers' use of English only (from 18.2% in 1994 to 30.6% in 1995) and English supplemented with Chinese (from 46.4% in 1994 to 51.0% in 1995). There was a decrease in teachers using half English and half Chinese (from 28.8% in 1994 to 15.2% in 1995) and using mainly Chinese (6.6% in 1994 to 3.2% in 1995). These results indicated that more English was used in the classroom in 1995 compared with 1994 according to these F5 students in Hong Kong secondary schools. The number of student participants (cases) in the two years is given in Figure 6.1 in order to facilitate the understanding of the medium of instruction for English lessons.

Table 6.1 Students' demographic information and their learning contexts

Items	Variables	1994 (%)	1995(%)	Chi-square significance
Gender	Male	56.6	66.7	.67864
	Female	43.4	33.3	
Grade when English was taught	Primary 1-2	41.2	42.1	.83762
	Primary 3-4	4.4	4.6	
	Primary 5-6	8.9	8.4	
	Secondary 1	35.8	37.2	
	Secondary 2	9.7	7.6	
Medium of instruction	English only	18.2	30.6	.00000
	English supplemented with Chinese	46.4	51.0	
	Half English and half Chinese	28.8	15.2	
	Mainly Chinese	6.6	3.2	
Frequency their teacher mentioned the public exam	Never	3.1	4.5	.00000
	Seldom	20.0	30.4	
	Sometimes	42.2	41.0	
	Often	32.6	20.0	
	Always	2.1	4.1	
Private tutorials per week	None	59.0	49.1	.00005
	Once or twice	38.5	46.6	
	3-4 times	1.4	4.1	
	5 times & above	1.1	.2	

However, the findings from the same parallel question in the Teacher Questionnaire (TQ 3.2) revealed different results. According to the Teacher Questionnaire, there was a decrease in the teachers' use of English only, from 37.8% in 1994 to 24.4% in 1995, but an increase in using English supplemented with Chinese, from 48.9% in 1994 to 63.3% in 1995.

Figure 6.1 Medium of instruction that teachers use in the classrooms

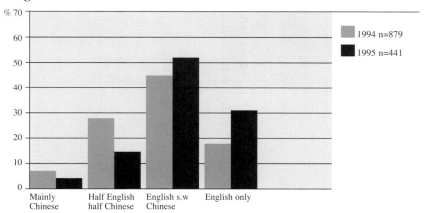

Figure 6.2 shows a general pattern of the frequency with which teachers mentioned the HKCEE to their students. A significant difference can be seen in the frequency with which teachers mentioned the HKCEE over the year. A significant decrease in the 'often' scale (32.6% in 1994 to 20% in 1995), and an increase in the 'seldom' scale (20% in 1994 to 30.4% in 1995) was observed from 1994 to 1995. This indicates that in 1994 teachers mentioned the HKCEE much more frequently than they did in 1995. Teachers spoke less about the HKCEE in 1995, which probably indicated an initial pressure in 1994 when the new HKCEE was first put into teaching.

Figure 6.3 illustrates the number of private tutorials[2] per week students attended after class in preparation for the HKCEE. The majority of the students went to tutorials once or twice each week. There was a significant increase in the number of private tutorials students attended in 1995 compared with 1994 in the categories of 1-2 and 3-4 times per week, and a decrease in the category of no tutorials. The number of private tutorials observed in 1995 might indicate that there was more exam preparation in response to the new HKCEE considering that the 1995 group had to sit for the new HKCEE in May of that year.

---

2.   'Private tutorials' refer to those paid tutorials designed specifically for examination preparation purposes. Each tutorial normally lasts about two hours.

Figure 6.2 The frequency with which teachers mentioned the HKCEE

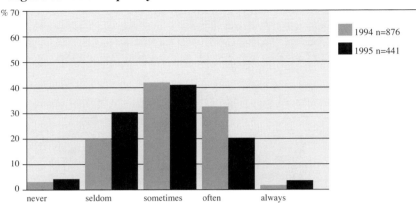

Figure 6.3 Number of private tutorials per week students attend after class

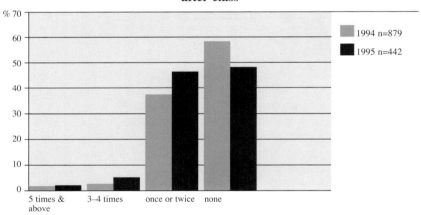

Summarizing the above three categories, firstly, English was used more in 1995 than 1994, indicating more English language input in their lessons. This might indicate more attention was given to English teaching and learning, possibly due to the influence of the new HKCEE. Secondly, students went to private tutorials more often in 1995 than in 1994. This indicates a tendency to focus more attention on the new 1996 HKCEE. Also, this result matched with the interview data collected from Ada (one of the three teachers in Phase III of the study), when she mentioned that the teachers of English in her school also organized extra tutorials for students to prepare for the new examination formats. However, when students were asked the frequency with which their teachers mentioned the HKCEE, there was a decrease. In 1995, the teachers mentioned the HKCEE less than in 1994. A possible explanation for this might be that the teachers tended to deal with the issue by employing more and more similar exam activities and mock exams rather than mentioning the HKCEE explicitly as they did at the very beginning, which was due to the nature of the change.

Students' attitudes towards teaching activities inside and outside class

This section was designed to explore the students' attitudes towards teaching activities carried out inside and outside the classroom by their teachers and by themselves in order to understand possible changes that might have taken place in the context of the new HKCEE between 1994 and 1995. There were five categories and 34 items altogether. They were Student Questionnaire: Part 2, Section A, Categories SQ 2.1, 2.2, 2.3, 2.4 and 2.5. All these categories were designed on a 5-point Likert scale, where 5 = Always, 4 = Often, 3 = Sometimes, 2 = Seldom, and 1 = Never.

Teacher talk in class

This category was designed to explore how much the teachers talked in their English lessons according to the students. The aim was to identify whether the new 1996 HKCEE reduced the amount of teacher talk and employed more task-based and integrated approaches, and consequently provided more practice opportunities for the students. The students were asked to grade how often their teachers talked to the whole class, groups of students, individual students, and kept silent in their English lessons.

The general pattern of teachers' talk over the year is shown in Figure 6.4, which illustrates how the students perceived their teacher's talk in class. Their teachers seemed to talk to the whole class the most, followed respectively by talking to groups, individual students, and keeping silent. This situation was relatively unchanged between 1994 and 1995. However, some changes were observed in teacher talk under the old and new HKCEE (c.f. Table 6.2). Table 6.2 below shows that there was a significant difference in the students' perceptions of the first two items regarding their teachers' talk in their English lessons.

Table 6.2 Differences in students' perceptions of their teachers' talk

Variables	Year	Cases	Mean	SD	T-Value	df	2-Tail Prob.
Talk to the whole class	1994	858	4.1946	.948	4.25	1296	.000
	1995	440	3.9523	1.017			
Talk to groups of students	1994	855	2.9673	.924	2.56	1285	.011
	1995	432	2.8333	.809			
Talk to individual students	1994	853	2.6436	.879	.53	1286	.597
	1995	435	2.6161	.891			
Keep silent	1994	855	1.6480	.868	-.06	1286	.948
	1995	433	1.6513	.874			

Figure 6.4 Students' perceptions of their teachers' talk

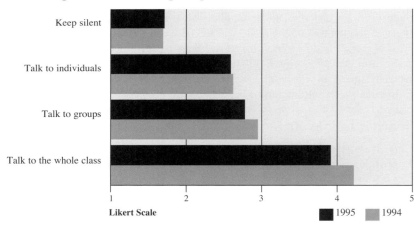

Table 6.2 and Figure 6.4 show that there was a significant decrease in teacher talk to the whole class and to groups between 1994 and 1995. However, no significant change in teacher talk to individuals and teachers' keeping silent was observed under the old and the new HKCEE. Also, from the mean scores in Table 6.2, it can be seen that the general pattern of teacher talk in class in both years is still in the order of, from most to least, 'talking to the whole class', 'talking to groups', 'talking to individuals', and finally, 'keeping silent' (c.f. Figure 6.4). Teachers were also very much in control in the context of the new HKCEE, though the new HKCEE encouraged the teachers to be more learner-centred and to provide students with more practice activities.

Students' perceptions of their teachers' teaching activities in class

This category was designed to explore the students' perceptions of their teachers' teaching activities in their English lessons. Students were asked to grade the frequency with which their teachers organized the following eight different activities in class (see Figure 6.5 and Table 6.3). Figure 6.5 shows a general pattern of the teaching activities in 1994 and in 1995.

Figure 6.5 Students' perceptions of their teachers' teaching activities

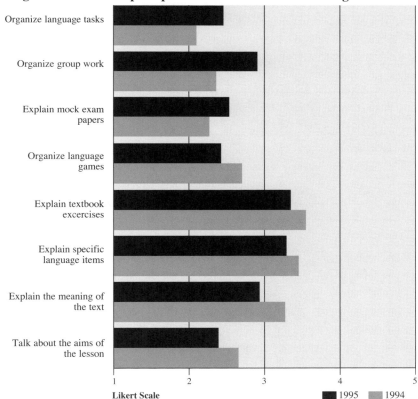

Figure 6.5 and Table 6.3 show that all eight activities changed significantly. Three items changed in an increasing direction from 1994 to 1995: organizing integrated language tasks, organizing group work and discussion, and explaining mock exam papers. These three activities were carried out significantly more often in 1995 than in 1994. All of these activities are required by the new HKCEE, thus, suggesting a positive washback effect of

the HKCEE on classroom activities. The remaining activities, such as talking about the aims of the lesson, explaining the meaning of the text, explaining specific language items, explaining textbook exercises, and organizing language games changed in a decreasing direction. These activities were carried out much less often in 1995 than in 1994, and were relatively traditional and formal teaching activities, except for language games.

Table 6.3 Students' perceptions of their teachers' teaching activities

Variables	Year	Cases	Mean	SD	T-Value	df	2-Tail Prob.
Talk about the aims of the lesson	1994	867	2.6459	1.055	3.89	1302	.000
	1995	437	2.4050	1.059			
Explain the meaning of the text	1994	866	3.1894	.999	3.91	1303	.000
	1995	439	2.9636	.957			
Explain specific language items	1994	865	3.4578	.943	4.71	1302	.000
	1995	439	3.1959	.962			
Explain textbook exercises	1994	866	3.5866	.889	5.90	1302	.000
	1995	438	3.2831	.854			
Explain mock exam papers	1994	867	2.6920	1.049	2.94	1302	.003
	1995	437	2.5126	1.022			
Organize language games	1994	884	2.6867	1.220	3.26	1325	.001
	1995	443	2.4628	1.099			
Organize group work or discussion	1994	866	2.3637	1.064	-9.40	1302	.000
	1995	438	2.9315	.961			
Organize integrated language tasks	1994	859	2.0664	.957	-6.47	1294	.000
	1995	437	2.4325	.974			

Students' classroom learning activities

This category explored the students' learning activities in their English lessons in order to see whether the new HKCEE brought about changes in their classroom learning activities. This category explored what the students did and how much practice opportunity the students had in their lessons. Usually, students in those situations did not have much control over what was going on in the classroom. Therefore, the activities they actually did in the class were the practice opportunities (learning opportunities) their teachers assigned to them. There were

10 items in this category, listed in Table 6.4. Two of the activities showed no significant difference over the year: listening and carrying out language tasks. The remaining items showed significant differences.

The remaining eight learning activities were carried out significantly differently over the period studied. Some of the activities, such as reading, writing, practising grammar items, learning vocabulary, and doing mock exams,[3] were carried out less often in 1995 than in 1994. Some activities,

Table 6.4 Students' perceptions of their classroom activities

Variables	Year	Cases	Mean	SD	T-Value	df	2-Tail Prob.
Reading	1994	865	3.1329	.930	2.342	1300	.000
	1995	437	3.0023	.900			
Listening	1994	867	3.3172	.824	-.34	1303	.734
	1995	438	3.3333	.779			
Writing	1994	869	3.1220	.744	3.20	1306	.001
	1995	439	2.9795	.792			
Speaking	1994	868	2.7224	.851	-3.79	1303	.000
	1995	437	2.9130	.871			
Practising grammar items	1994	866	3.0843	.946	3.27	1303	.001
	1995	439	2.9066	.888			
Learning vocabulary	1994	867	2.8870	.915	4.10	1304	.000
	1995	439	2.6720	.856			
Carrying out group discussion	1994	866	2.3210	1.007	-8.74	1302	.000
	1995	438	2.8242	.929			
Carrying out language tasks	1994	864	2.3542	.933	-1.81	1298	.070
	1995	436	2.4541	.947			
Doing language games	1994	859	1.9709	.894	-3.78	1294	.000
	1995	437	2.1739	.954			
Doing mock exams	1994	862	2.6265	1.097	6.10	1296	.000
	1995	436	2.2454	.995			

3. 'Mock examination' refers to the past examination papers. Taking mock exams are activities organized by teachers for their F5 students just before the actual examination season.

such as speaking, carrying out group discussion, and doing language games were carried out much more often in 1995 than in 1994, which suggested a match with the requirements of the new HKCEE oral examination. Firstly, there was an increase in the weighting of the oral component on the new HKCEE. Hence, there was a likely motivation to carry out more speaking in class. Secondly, the oral exam was changed into a group discussion format. More group discussions were also observed in class, which could also be regarded as an indication of washback effect. Both changes in the HKCEE are reflected in the classroom activities between 1994 and 1995. Also, there was an increase in mock exam activities in class. This reflected a particular approach that teachers and students coped with the examination (HKCEE) change in Hong Kong secondary schools. It seemed that when there was an

Figure 6.6 Students' perceptions of their classroom activities

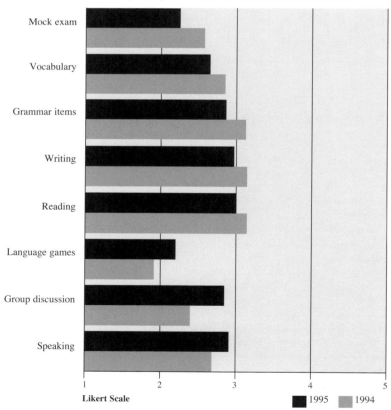

intention to use the change in the public examination to influence teaching and learning, which is the case in this context, there would very likely be a re-focus of such classroom activities to reflect the examination in the schools.

A note of caution should be mentioned here. The above results regarding students' perceptions of their teachers' teaching activities and their own learning activities in the classroom revealed certain discrepancies. According to the students, teachers organized language games less often in 1995, yet they played language games more often in 1995. Teachers explained mock exams more in 1995, yet students did mock exams less. The discrepancies here, however, demonstrated a weakness in using a questionnaire to obtain information regarding the actual teaching and learning behaviours in the classroom. Thus what was not discovered via the questionnaire was further explored via the use of classroom observations in the study, which will be discussed in the next chapter.

Students' use of English in relation to their classroom activities

This category was designed to explore the activities the students carried out in English in their English lessons. There were five items within the category. All activities were seen to be carried out significantly differently by the students in 1994 and 1995 (c.f. Table 6.5). All activities except one were carried out more in English in class in 1995 than in 1994. This indicates an increase in students carrying out learning activities in English in general over the year. There was a much greater increase in the time spent on activities in which students carried out group discussion and pair work in English in 1995. Group discussions and pair work were actually the new formats in the 1996 HKCEE Oral Paper, thus showing a direct washback effect on learning activities in the classroom. The old HKCEE Oral Paper was in the format of dialogue and guided conversation. The only activity that was carried out less often in 1995 than in 1994 was arguing for a correct answer to exercises.

Students' use of English in relation to their learning activities outside class

This category was designed to explore aspects of the students' learning activities carried out in English outside their English lessons. There were seven activities listed in this category. Only two of these activities were carried out significantly differently: talking in English to their teachers and to their classmates, both of which were carried out more frequently in 1995 than 1994 (c.f. Figure 6.8), especially talking to teachers.

Table 6.5 Students' use of English in relation to their classroom activities

Variables	Year	Cases	Mean	SD	T-Value	df	2-Tail Prob.
Carrying out group discussion and pair work	1994	865	2.5052	1.008	-4.76	1301	.000
	1995	438	2.7785	.920			
Arguing for a correct answer to an exercise	1994	869	3.0518	1.004	4.02	1305	.000
	1995	438	2.8128	1.036			
Expressing your own ideas	1994	866	2.3438	.897	-3.07	1302	.002
	1995	438	2.4703	.960			
Making a request in class	1994	866	2.3822	.935	-4.32	1302	.000
	1995	438	2.6370	1.131			
Asking for clarification	1994	866	2.4111	.933	-4.25	1302	.000
	1995	438	2.6598	1.116			

Figure 6.7 Students' use of English in relation to their classroom activities

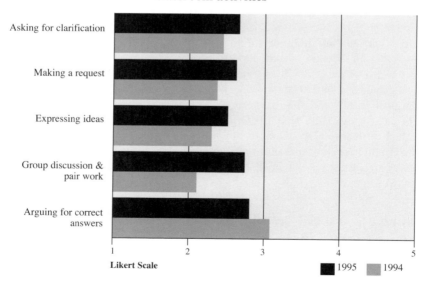

Figure 6.8 Students' use of English in relation to their learning activities outside class

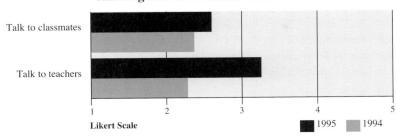

The remaining activities outside class showed no significant difference over the two years. They were as follows, and are listed here in descending order according to the mean scores in 1994 first and then 1995. This gives a general picture of the frequency of activities that students carried out in English outside class.

	1994	1995
• watching television	2.8099	2.8724
• reading newspapers and magazines	2.6164	2.5616
• listening to radio	2.0230	2.0226
• talking to other people outside school	1.5977	1.6416
• talking to family members	1.5219	1.5662

From the above list, it can be seen that watching TV was the most frequent English activity the students did outside the class, whereas talking to family members was carried out the least frequently. This indicated there were very limited communicative needs in English among family members for these students in Hong Kong secondary schools.

Summarizing the results of Part Two: Section A – Students' Attitudes Towards Teaching Activities Inside and Outside Class, firstly, there was a decrease in the amount that teachers talked to the whole class and groups in 1995, which might suggest an increase in practice opportunities for students in class. Secondly, there was an increase in the teachers' carrying out classroom activities such as those required in the new 1996 HKCEE (organizing integrated language tasks, organizing group work and discussion). Thirdly, there was also an increase in the students' carrying out learning activities such as speaking, carrying out group discussions, and doing mock examinations. These learning activities were also closely related to the new examination as well.

As for student learning activities in using English in class and outside class, there was a much greater increase in the amount of time spent on carrying out group discussion and pair work, showing a direct washback effect on classroom learning activities. Also, students talked more to their classmates and teachers in 1995 than in 1994. This result supports the information obtained from the teachers' interviews. One teacher mentioned that, in her school, an 'English Speaking Day' was set up to encourage students to communicate with other students and teachers in English. However, it can be seen from the mean score of SQ 2.5–Students' Use of English in Relation to Their Learning Activities Outside Class–that the students still did not carry out many activities in English outside class.

Students' attitudes towards aspects of learning

There were five categories in Part Two: Section B of the Student Questionnaire, designed on a five-point Likert scale where five = strongly agree and one = strongly disagree. This section aims to explore possible reasons for the students' attitudinal changes in relation to learning in the context of the new HKCEE.

Students' attitudes towards their English lessons

This category was designed to explore changes in how the students perceived their English lessons compared with other school subjects between 1995 and 1996. There were five items altogether. Figure 6.9 shows the general pattern of the students' attitudes towards their English lessons. The students' perceptions of four out of the five items in this category changed. The students' attitudes on one item as to whether or not their English lessons were full of interesting language activities remained unchanged.

Figure 6.9 Students' attitudes towards their English lessons

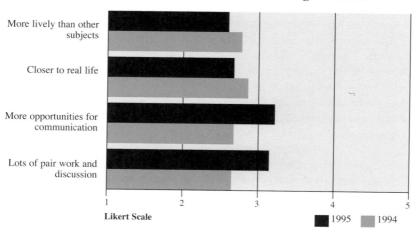

From the figure above, it can be seen that two activities were perceived by students to occur more frequently in 1995 than in 1994. These activities were 'more opportunities for communication' and 'lots of pair work and discussion'. However, the students did not perceive their English lessons to be livelier than other subjects or closer to real life in 1995 than in 1994, though encouraging lessons to be closer to real life was one of the intentions of the new HKCEE. It can be seen that more group discussions and pair work were carried out, and more opportunities for communication were provided though the students did not perceive their English lessons to be more lively or closer to real life. Although the new HKCEE is designed to bridge the gap between what happens in classrooms with that of the real world, it has not been shown that the students perceived such a change in their classroom activities.

Students' motivation to learn English

This category was designed to explore the reasons for students to learn English in Hong Kong secondary schools to see whether the new HKCEE brought about changes in the students' motivation to learn English. Nine reasons are listed in this category. Only three reasons out of the nine changed significantly between 1994 and 1995 (see Table 6.6 and Figure 6.10).

It can be seen from Table 6.6 and Figure 6.10 that the students' perceptions of fulfilling parents' expectations was seen to be less of a reason to learn English in 1995 than in 1994. However, the other two reasons–meeting the requirements of the society and watching English movies and listening to English programmes–were seen as more motivating reasons to learn English in 1995 than in 1994. This reflected the students' instrumental purposes for learning English as well as the entertainment-related purposes.

The remaining reasons did not change significantly. They are listed below in descending order according to the mean scores in 1994 and then in 1995. The mean scores of the three reasons described above that changed significantly (marked with an asterisk) are also listed below to provide a

Table 6.6 Students' perceptions of the reasons to learn English

Variables	Year	Cases	Mean	SD	T-Value	df	2-Tail Prob.
Watch English movies and listen to English programmes	1994	863	3.4623	1.047	-1.97	1299	.049
	1995	438	3.5822	1.015			
Meet the requirements of the society	1994	864	4.1088	.902	-1.97	1302	.049
	1995	440	4.2091	.797			
Fulfil parents' expectations	1994	871	3.6969	.064	5.48	1308	.000
	1995	439	3.3440	.066			

Figure 6.10 Students' perceptions of the reasons to learn English

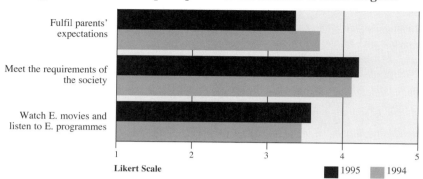

general picture of the students' reasons for learning English. The list also serves as a comparison of the reasons that students perceived as being important for learning English. The factors perceived by the students as being most important were related to instrumental reasons, such as the public exam, job, and the future. The items in this category, which followed the three instrumental reasons, were to prepare for the HKCEE and be able to go into tertiary education. The reasons perceived as less motivating were related to functional use of the English language. The list below provides a general picture of the reasons that these students learned English in Hong Kong secondary school.

	1994	1995
• to have more and better opportunities in the future	4.2130	4.2141
• to meet the requirements of the society*	4.1088	4.2091
• to get a better job	4.0218	4.0273
• to prepare for the HKCEE	3.9828	4.0091
• to be able to go into tertiary education	3.9150	3.9750
• to be able to communicate with people	3.8172	3.8341
• to acquire basic knowledge and forms of English	3.7305	3.7088
• to fulfil parents' expectations*	3.6969	3.3440
• to be able to watch English movies and listen to English programmes*	3.4623	3.5822

Students' preferred learning strategies

This category was designed to explore the students' preferred learning strategies, in order to understand whether or not the new HKCEE had an influence on the students' learning strategies. There are 11 items within this category. Four learning strategies changed significantly over the two years. These learning strategies were, however, seen to be less preferred by the students in 1995 than in 1994.

Figure 6.11 Students' preferred learning strategies

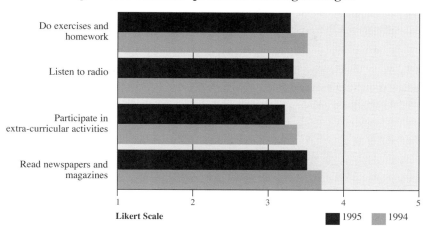

Likert Scale

Table 6.7 Students' preferred learning strategies

Variables	Year	Cases	Mean	SD	T-Value	df	2-Tail Prob.
Reading newspapers and magazines in English	1994	866	3.7517	.885	3.97	1303	.000
	1995	439	3.5444	.903			
Participating in extra-curricular activities	1994	866	3.4203	.965	2.55	1302	.011
	1995	438	3.2740	1.009			
Listening to radio programmes in English	1994	865	3.5977	.967	4.34	1302	.000
	1995	439	3.3462	1.029			
Doing exercises and homework	1994	867	3.5444	.977	4.17	1304	.000
	1995	439	3.3052	.981			

The remaining learning strategies did not change significantly. They were arranged according to the mean scores in 1994 in the list below, which presented a general picture of the degree of preferred learning strategies perceived by the students in Hong Kong secondary schools.

	1994	1995
• watching TV or videos in English	3.9264	3.9453
• reading newspapers and magazines in English*	3.7517	3.5444
• learning vocabulary	3.7126	3.6364
• listening to radio programmes in English*	3.5977	3.3462

	1994	**1995**
• doing exercises and homework*	3.5444	3.3052
• learning grammar rules	3.5426	3.5341
• learning through games	3.5098	3.5273
• expressing opinions in class	3.4919	3.4932
• taking part in group activities in class	3.4428	3.3659
• participating in extra-curricular activities*	3.4203	3.2740
• taking notes	3.1158	3.1828

Although the new HKCEE requires note-taking skills, this skill was by far the least preferred learning strategy by the students. A slight increase in the mean score was observed, from 3.1158 in 1994 to 3.1828 in 1995, but the increase was not statistically significant. This result showed that there was no direct washback effect on note-taking skills even though they were highly required skills for dealing with the 'Integrated Listening, Reading, and Writing' paper of the new HKCEE.

Students' attitudes towards whether they are influenced by the public exam

One category was designed to ask students directly whether or not they have ever been affected by their exam scores. The result is shown in Figure 6.12. A clear 'yes' answer was the dominant response in both years. A significant change in the students' attitudes towards this item was observed over the two years. In 1995, fewer students reported being affected by exam scores than in 1994, which might suggest a reduction in the initial anxiety about the new HKCEE.

Figure 6.12 Students who are and are not affected by their exam scores

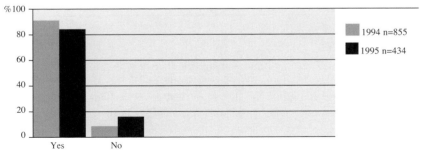

Students' attitudes towards the influence of aspects of the public exam

This category explored further those aspects of the students' lives that were affected by the HKCEE scores. There were five aspects included in this category. None of these aspects changed significantly over the two years. They are listed below according to the mean scores to show the degree of influence. The result from this category demonstrated that there was no significant change in the exam influence on aspects of the students' lives, irrespective of the new HKCEE format. Exam scores seemed to affect students in similar ways over the two years. It can also be seen that exam scores had the greatest impact on the students' motivation to learn compared with other aspects in learning.

	1994	1995
• motivation to learn	3.7115	3.7339
• future job opportunity	3.6335	3.5296
• teacher and student relationship	3.4466	3.5081
• anxiety and emotional tension	2.9187	2.9032
• self-image	2.6299	2.5175

Summarizing the results in Part Two Section B, it can be seen that there was a change in many aspects of student learning in an increasing direction between 1994 and 1995. For example, the students perceived their lessons to provide more opportunities for communication and pair work and discussion in 1995 than in 1994. All these learning activities were part of the requirements of the new 1996 HKCEE. As for the motivation of student learning, an increase was seen in 1995 over 1994 in statements such as meeting the requirements of society and watching English movies and listening to English programmes. These types of motivation were related to the requirements of the new 1996 HKCEE. The new examination syllabus specified the usefulness of the examination as well as the need 'to narrow the gap between what happens in the examination room and the real world' (c.f. Hong Kong Examinations Authority, 1993). Therefore, the above results, to some extent, reflected a washback effect on these aspects of student learning.

Regarding the students' preferred learning strategies, four out of the 11 learning strategies showed significant change, but they all changed in a decreasing direction from 1994 to 1995. No logical relationship was observed among the four changed strategies between 1994 and 1995. However, a general pattern could be seen in the mean scores of learning strategies that were most preferred by the students. In the list, the learning strategies that involved a functional use of English were, however, rated lower by the students in general. The new HKCEE did not show much effect on this aspect of learning; at least, not much effect was observed over the two years.

From the results of this section, it is clear that the students agreed that they were influenced by past examination scores (c.f. Figure 6.12), yet a decrease was observed in their perceptions of the influence of the examination from 1994 to 1995. Regarding 'students' attitudes towards the influence of aspects of the public exam,' no significant change was observed. From the list of mean scores in this category, it can be seen that motivation was clearly identified in relation to the influence of the examinations on the students. The influences of the examinations will be explored further in the following section.

Students' attitudes towards aspects of public examinations

This section–SQ Part Two: Section C–consisted of one category and 12 items. All categories were designed on a five-point Likert Scale, where five = strongly agree and one = strongly disagree. This category was designed to explore the students' attitudes towards public examinations in relation to teaching and learning in Hong Kong secondary schools. The objective of this category was to investigate whether or not the new HKCEE would have an influence on the students' attitudes over the two years. Altogether there were twelve statements. Two main themes about public examinations were included in this category. One theme dealt with the impact of the examinations on the students themselves, while the other theme dealt with the impact of the examinations on the students' learning processes and outcomes. They were arranged according to the mean scores given by the students in 1994, in descending order. The following list provides a clear picture of certain aspects of examination influences on students in Hong Kong secondary schools.

	1994	1995
8. Examinations should NOT be used as the sole determiner of students' grades*	3.9823	4.1500
11. All students work hard to achieve their best in public examinations	3.9764	3.9106
4. Examinations force students to study harder	3.7838	3.8045
2. Students' learning is improved by practising mock exams	3.7474	3.8324

1. Students dislike examinations   3.6012   3.5278
12. Examinations are one of the motivations for the
    student learning   3.5884   3.5000
7. A student's performance on an examination is a good
   indication of how well she or he will be able to apply
   what has been learned*   3.4806   3.2905
10. Mock examinations are important ways to learn   3.4210   3.5028
3. Taking examinations is a valuable learning experience   3.3549   3.3833
6. A student's score on an examination is a good indication
   of how well she or he has learned the material*   3.3482   2.9889
5. Examinations have an important effect on student
   self-image   3.3062   3.2849
9. Students perform better in an exam situation than
   in a normal teaching situation   3.0693   3.0335

The students' attitudes towards three of the above statements changed significantly over the two years. They were Items 6 and 7, which related to the processes and outcomes of their learning, and Item 8, related to the impact of the examinations on the students themselves (c.f. Table 6.8).

Table 6.8 Students' attitudes towards public examinations

Variables	Year	Cases	Mean	SD	T-Value	df	2-Tail Prob.
A student's score on an exam is a good indication of how well he or she has learned the material (SQ 2.11.6)	1994	850	3.3482	1.169	3.73	1028	.000
	1995	180	2.9889	1.196			
A student's performance on an exam is a good indication of how well he or she will be able to apply what has been learned (SQ 2.11.7)	1994	851	3.4806	1.131	2.04	1028	.042
	1995	179	3.2905	1.158			
Exams should NOT be used as the sole determiner of students' grades (SQ 2.11.8)	1994	849	3.9823	1.024	-2.00	1027	.045
	1995	180	4.1500	1.000			

Figure 6.13 Students' attitudes towards public examinations

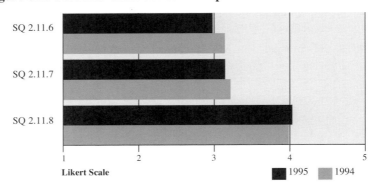

Table 6.8 and Figure 6.13 show that Items 6 and 7 changed in a decreasing direction from 1994 to 1995. Comparing the two years, the students did not seem to have strong feelings about the examination and its scores, whereas perceptions of Item 8 'Examinations should not be used as the sole determiner of students' grades' changed in an increasing direction in the same period. More students believed in 1995 that examinations should not be used as the sole determiner of students' grades, showing a healthier perception of examination practice in general. The above result showed that less attention was focused on examinations over the two years.

The students perceived the remaining statements in a similar way over the two years. All the statements were listed above according to the mean scores from the student surveys. It can be seen that Item 8 produced the strongest agreement among the students. This was, however, followed by Items 11 and 4 ('All students work hard to achieve their best in public examinations,' and 'Examinations force students to study harder' respectively). This reflected the students' mixed feelings about the examinations. On one hand, they did not think examinations were an accurate reflection of all aspects of their study; while on the other hand they were put in a position that they had to work hard to achieve the best examination scores possible. This is an understandable instrumental motivation for the students to learn English. Also, ambivalence towards the examinations was further demonstrated by the following two items: 'Students dislike examinations' (Item 1), but 'Examinations are one of the motivations for the student learning' (Item 12). On the whole, it can be seen from the mean scores (rated above three on a five-point Likert Scale) that the students did have strong feelings about aspects of public examinations in their school lives.

Summary

Findings from the Student Questionnaire in this chapter respond to the following main themes:

- students' characteristics and their learning contexts
- students' attitudes towards classroom teaching and learning activities
- students' attitudes towards aspects of learning
- students' attitudes towards the public examination.

Firstly, as for the students' learning contexts, a significant difference can be seen in the medium of instruction used in their lessons. More English was used in the classroom in 1995 compared with 1994 (c.f. Figure 6.1), indicating an increase in English language input in class. Also, in 1995 it can be observed that students attended more private tutorials than in 1994, indicating an impact of the new HKCEE on the students' learning activities outside of class and more attention being given to examination preparation. However, for the category related to the frequency with which their teachers mentioned the HKCEE, no change was observed over the year. Their teachers actually mentioned the HKCEE less in 1995 than in 1994.

Secondly, no obvious pattern was observed from their teacher talk in class (c.f. Figure 6.4). According to students, there was a reduction in teacher talk to the whole class and to groups from 1994 to 1995. But no significant difference can be seen in the other two items such as 'talking to individuals' and 'keeping silent.'

Regarding the students' attitudes towards teaching activities inside and outside class, there was a significant difference between the 1994 and 1995 surveys in all of the items under the category 'Students' Perceptions of Their Teachers' Teaching Activities in Class.' Activities such as organizing integrated language tasks, organizing group work and discussion, and explaining mock exam papers increased from 1994 to 1995. These activities are very closely related to the new HKCEE. Other more traditional and formal teaching activities decreased between 1994 and 1995 (c.f. Figure 6.5). This showed a direct washback effect on classroom activities from the students' perspectives.

Furthermore, many of the students' learning activities in class (eight out of 10) changed significantly over the year. Activities such as speaking, carrying out group discussion, and doing language games closely related to the new HKCEE were carried out more in 1995 than in 1994. In contrast, activities such as reading, writing, practising grammar items, learning vocabulary, and doing mock exams were carried out less in 1995 than in 1994. Student activities in English both inside and outside class showed a significant difference. There was a considerable increase in carrying out group discussion and pair work in 1995 compared to 1994. Moreover, students talked to their teachers and classmates more in English over the two years. All the above results showed that there was a direct washback effect on the classroom activities and the activities that students carried out inside and outside class.

The third part of the results related to the students' attitudes towards learning also showed significant change over the two years. Students perceived their English lessons to be more communicative and took part in more pair work and discussion in 1995 than in 1994. However, the students did not perceive their English lessons as being livelier than other subjects or closer to real life, which was one of the intentions of the new HKCEE. As for the students' motivation for learning English, only three out of the nine aspects changed significantly between 1994 and 1995. The aspects of motivation to learn English that increased were 'watching English movies' and 'listening to English programmes,' and 'meeting requirements of society' (c.f. Figure 6.10). In the case of the students' preferred learning strategies, four out of the 11 items changed significantly over the year, yet in a decreasing direction (c.f. Figure 6.11). The most preferred strategies according to the mean scores in this category were those related to watching TV or videos in English, reading newspapers and magazines in English, learning vocabulary, listening to radio programmes in English, and doing exercises and homework.

The last section of the findings was related to the students' attitudes towards aspects of public examinations. Only three out of the 12 items changed significantly between 1994 and 1995. This aspect of the results showed that the changes that made the new 1996 HKCEE a more integrated and task-based examination did not change the way the students perceived the public examination. In both years, the students showed mixed feelings about the examination. On one hand, they really did not like examinations. On the other hand, public examinations seemed to be one of their motivations to learn English. Therefore, changing the examination formats into a more task-based and integrated approach might have changed certain aspects of the students' attitudes towards teaching and learning, but the changes did not change the students' attitudes towards the function of the public examinations.

7 Phase III – Teachers' and students' actions and reactions to the change

Introduction

This chapter reports the findings from classroom observations and teacher interviews. This chapter complements the studies reported in Chapters 5 and 6 in answering the research questions. It will first emphasize the importance of the research framework used, and then report the baseline study, which consisted of baseline observations and interviews. Then it will report on the case studies of three teachers through classroom observations. The main issues in this phase of the study are related to the washback effect on:

- the English language curriculum within the Hong Kong context
- teaching materials used in schools
- teachers' teaching behaviours
- teachers' beliefs about teaching and learning.

The research investigated how a change in the HKCEE, a high-stakes public examination, influenced classroom teaching. The investigation was carried out in relation to the participants' reactions in the local educational context and, furthermore, to explore the effect of the change on aspects of teachers' attitudes, teaching content, and classroom interaction. This research stressed 'the importance of context, setting, and subjects' frames of reference' (Marshall & Rossman, 1989: 46). The methodology used in the study aimed to capture the reality, variation, and complexity of changes in day-to-day classroom practice within the research context.

For this study, the recommendations of Erickson (1986) and Miles and Huberman (1994) have been used. In order to understand actions and practices, the researcher engaged directly in the local scene, spent sufficient time to understand action in its specific social context, gained access to participant meanings, and showed how these meanings-in-action evolved over time. Without such a careful grounding in local cases, a more general understanding was impossible.

Furthermore, Smith et al (1994) pointed out that the definitions of the situation and the characteristics of pupils, teachers, curriculum, assessment, and educational changes held by policy-makers can be shaped and translated imperfectly by practitioners. Teachers and principals redefine and reinterpret the messages about policy that they receive. They then act (adapt, teach, learn, and evaluate) according to their own definitions of the situation (Blumer, 1986; Geisinger, 1994; Markee, 1993). For this study, in order to discover whether the new 1996 HKCEE brought about the intended washback effects on the teaching and learning in Hong Kong secondary schools, we have to explore various interacting participants in the settings and how washback, as a process, was occurring in the teaching and learning environment.

The focus of this phase of study was on the classroom. This was followed by the first two phases of the study, based on watching and asking in Phase I and by the two surveys with teachers and students in Phase II. The research question answered in this phase of study was:

- what was the nature and scope of the washback effect on teachers' behaviours as a result of the new examination?

Teachers' behaviours are operationally defined as what teachers (together with students) do in the classroom. Teachers' behaviours in the classroom were studied in relation to the following areas:

- teachers' medium of instruction, teacher talk, teaching activities
- teaching materials, aspects of lesson planning
- assessment and evaluation in relation to their teaching.

The above aspects were also studied through two comparative surveys. Teachers' classroom behaviours were further studied through detailed classroom observation in terms of activity types, practice opportunities, teacher and student talk, and interaction patterns.

As mentioned above, classroom observation is defined as the systematic, purposeful recording of interactions and events in the classroom (see Allwright & Bailey, 1991; Chaudron, 1988; van Lier, 1988). The observations in this study involved audio-taping, video-taping, taking field notes, and using a coding scheme. There were two stages of observations, the baseline and the main study.

Baseline study

The process of exploring the influence of this change in the public examination took more than three years. Due to the nature of the investigation–a study of change in teaching and learning over a period of time–this study consisted of three research phases. Four major research tools were employed through the various phases of the investigation. In Phase III of the study, classroom observations and interviews were mainly employed. The following two sections will report findings from the baseline interviews and the classroom observations. As discussed earlier and mentioned above, the purpose of the baseline study was to get a 'feel' for the research context and to focus the research questions. Both the interviews and the baseline study were carried out in the 1994–1995 academic year when the new 1996 HKCEE was first being put into the teaching and learning in Hong Kong secondary schools.

Baseline interviews

This section reports findings from the initial interviews carried out in the schools. The interviews were to investigate the decision-making process in relation to English language teaching in schools. The interviews focused on the decisions made about two aspects of teaching: materials and teaching arrangements. The interview data was all transcribed and categorized, and analysed into major themes related to the above two aspects of teaching.

Due to the nature of change in teaching over time and the choice of methodology used in this study, interviews at the school level were carried out with five panel chairs, who were responsible for making important decisions about aspects of teaching in their schools. Therefore, this part of the data showed what changes occurred as a result of the change to the HKCEE and how and why those decisions were made. All names in this study are pseudonyms. They were given to the participants instead of letters and numbers for both interview and observation to provide a human touch to the study. Table 7.1 shows details of the interviews carried out to investigate the strategies the schools used in the context of the new 1996 HKCEE. Table 7.2 summarizes the findings from the above interviews.

Table 7.1 Interviews with five panel chairs in Hong Kong secondary schools

Informant	Date and time	Method	Purpose
1. Michael	03/11/94 20:30-21:00	Telephone (taped)	To collect data on
2. Sherry	24/10/94 14:45-15:30	Field notes	actions taken by schools to tackle the
3. Sally	15/04/94 12:30-13:30	Face to face (taped)	examination syllabus
4. Patrick	05/01/95 14:00-15:00	Face to face (taped)	change
5. Cindy	09/11/94 11:30-12:30	Telephone (field notes)	

The findings showed that when the new 1996 HKCEE was first introduced, the schools changed their textbooks and included test format preparation as part of their teaching activities. The findings also showed who in the schools decided which textbooks would be used and who made the decision about teaching arrangements. It can be seen that all five schools selected revised textbooks and arranged for students to take practice tests for the new 1996 HKCEE. The situation varied among the schools as to who decided on changing the textbook, who decided on which textbook to be used, and who decided on teaching arrangements. As for the textbook change, decisions are made by panel chairs, teachers, and, in one school, by the principal. Regarding which textbooks would be used for teaching, teachers in those five schools seemed to have much say in this matter.

Table 7.2 Interviews regarding textbooks and teaching arrangements under the 1996 HKCEE

	Textbooks changed?	Test format practices in teaching?	Who decided to change textbooks?	Who decided which textbook to use?	Who decided on teaching arrangements?
Michael	Yes	Yes	Panel chair	Teachers together	Form co-ordinator[1]
Sherry	Yes	Yes	Teachers together	Teachers together	Panel chair
Sally	Yes	Yes	Teachers together	Teachers together	Panel chair
Patrick	Yes	Yes	Panel chair	Form co-ordinator	Individual teachers
Cindy	Yes	Yes	Principal	Form co-ordinator	Panel chair

Michael, one of the panel chairs interviewed, emphasized the importance of teachers' decisions in this respect. He commented that, 'if teachers don't like the textbook they are using, they won't enjoy teaching.' It can be seen from the findings above that the arrangement of teaching at the decision-making level, such as those in Table 7.2, varied according to the organizational culture of the different schools. Despite the different situations in the schools, it was found that all these schools had already been involved with a series of changes in response to the new 1996 HKCEE at the beginning of the 1994–1995 academic year.

In talking about the new HKCEE, another panel chair, Sherry, emphasized that:

> In terms of washback of the exam, lesson plans and textbooks will certainly change. But my teaching methodology won't change, as it rather depends on my belief in language teaching and my past teaching experience, which play an important role in our teachers' choice of how to teach, and which is better for our students in actual classroom settings. I am not sure about the exam change at the moment.

---

1. A form co-ordinator is a group leader. He or she is in charge of a group of teachers of English teaching at certain levels, for example F1-3, F4-5 or F6-7 levels.

Another interesting point that Sally mentioned was that the first thing the new F4 students in her school (the first cohort to sit for the new HKCEE) did was to sit for the sample papers of the new 1996 HKCEE, which was the students' goal by the end of F5. The main reason she gave to justify this practice was that students would keep asking teachers about the new exam anyway. So, it would be 'efficient' to let them experience it at the beginning of their two year study (F4 to F5). By taking the exam then, students could measure their progress during the two year period between F4 and F5. It can be seen from the above interviews that the new 1996 HKCEE had brought about certain changes in teaching, even if the changes seemed to be cosmetic. There was a need to investigate various aspects of the classroom in depth to identify the nature of the changes.

Baseline classroom observations

The researcher visited nine Hong Kong schools (23 lessons observed) as part of the preliminary classroom investigation, which was carried out between November 1994 and February 1995. Nine teachers participated in the baseline study. The main study was carried out between November 1994 and February 1995 (the first round), and between November 1994 and February 1996 (the second round). The first and second rounds were used for comparing the same teacher's teaching style and methods under the old and new HKCEE. Three out of the nine teachers in the baseline study participated in the main study, which will be reported in later sections of this chapter.

This section reports on six teachers who took part in the preliminary study (the first round of observations; c.f. Table 7.3). Different types of schools were selected initially for the baseline study based on levels of student proficiency, regional locations, religious affiliation, and education mode as in the survey studies. The main reasons behind the choice of different types of schools was that it was not clear at that time how washback would occur in schools, and whether teachers in different types of schools (schools consisting of students of higher or lower levels of proficiency) would react to the examination change differently. Studies in these areas have been well documented (see Dorr-Bremme & Herman, 1983; Fish, 1988; Fullan, 1993; Fullan with Stiegelbauer, 1991; Herman & Golan, 1991; McDonnell et al, 1990). Herman and Golan (1991) pointed out that schools serving disadvantaged students are thought to be particularly at risk of adverse effects of public examinations such as trivializing the learning and instructional process, distorting curricula, and usurping valuable instructional time. Therefore, it seemed to be appropriate to observe teachers from different types of schools for the baseline study.

Level of student proficiency is determined mainly through the banding system by Hong Kong's Secondary School Place Allocation System (SSPA). Band 1 schools have students with the highest proficiency and Band 5 the lowest (c.f. Table 7.3 for banding information). Schools at different locations were also explored. Hong Kong secondary schools are divided into 16 educational administrative 'nets' (districts) in three major geographical locations: Hong Kong Island, Kowloon, and the New Territories. Historically, the best schools tend to be located on Hong Kong Island and the Kowloon peninsula rather than in the New Territories. The religious affiliations of schools are also reflected in the school curriculum (school subjects) and through student morning assembly. Students are required to follow certain prayers at the beginning of every school day. Schools in Hong Kong are also categorized into boys', girls', or co-ed schools.

It was found through the baseline study that the differences among schools were not as pronounced as the differences among teachers. The findings of the baseline study were identical with research studies that concentrated on teachers (Katz, 1996; Harrison, 1996; Freeman, 1996). Since the schools' characteristics were not significant for this study, the schools were, therefore, simply categorized as No. 1 to No. 6 in the findings. Consequently, this study focused more on aspects of the *teachers* rather than that of schools. The teachers' names used in the findings are pseudonyms (c.f. Table 7.3).

Table 7.3 The baseline study of six schools (15 lessons) in Hong Kong secondary schools

School	Teacher	Date and Duration	Method	Form	Modality	Material
1	Lynette	07/12/94 09:50-11:10	Audio	F5	W & O	Essay & Picture talk
(Band 2-3)		07/12/94 11:25-12:45	Audio	F4	Integrated	New Effective Eng.
		28/11/94 11:25-12:45	Audio	F4	L & O	New Steps & Skills
		28/11/94 13:35-15:10	Audio	F5	Listening	New Steps & Skills
2	Yvonne	14/11/94 08:10-09:20	Audio	F4	Oral	English 2000
(Band 3-4)		14/11/94 09:55-11:10	Audio	F5	Oral	Oxford Certificate Eng.
3	Mary	05/12/94 11:15-12:45	Audio	F5	R & O	Reading & Dialogue
(Band 3-4)		04/01/95 11:15-12:45	Video	F5	R & W	Supplementary
		28/02/95 08:25-09:45	Audio	F4	Reading	Supplementary
4	Sue	22/11/94 08:45-09:55	Audio	F5	Oral	Newspaper clippings
(Band 1)						
5	Bill	01/12/94 10:55-12:15	Audio	F4	Oral	Authentic materials
(Band 3-4)						
6	Jane	12/12/94 08:30-09:10	Video	F4	Oral	New Effective Eng.
(Band 1)		12/12/94 09:10-10:30	Video	F5	Reading	Supplementary
		20/12/94 08:30-09:10	Video	F5	Listening	Authentic
		20/12/94 09:10-10:30	Video	F4	Listening	New Steps & Skills

Besides the choices of teachers in different types of schools for observations, another key purpose of the baseline study was to explore the aspects of teaching and learning within the schools in which areas of washback intensity–the degree of washback effect in an area or a number of areas of teaching and learning affected by an examination–could be detected. Therefore, lessons at both the F4 and F5 levels were observed. Information about the modality and the materials used in these lessons was obtained mainly from the teachers' lesson plans and from their Schemes of Work, an overall teaching plan for the whole academic year in Hong Kong secondary schools. The recording methods of the baseline study were either audio-taping or video-taping. Lessons at various hours during the school day were observed.

The findings from the baseline observations enhanced the understanding of the washback phenomena in Hong Kong secondary schools. They also refined the observation instrument. Two types of changes were observed. One area was in the revised teaching materials for the new 1996 HKCEE. By the time the new examination was put into teaching in Hong Kong secondary schools in the 1994–1995 academic year, nearly every school had changed their textbooks. The other area was the specific language activities teachers employed in their teaching, such as reading aloud. For example, for the F5 students under the old HKCEE, the examination required that they demonstrated their ability to read aloud a dialogue. Teachers were observed to teach their students in the method that was required by the examination. Many reading aloud activities were carried out. Under the new HKCEE, where reading aloud was replaced by role play and group discussion, F4 teachers were no longer observed to teach reading aloud, and more time was spent on activities such as role play and group discussion. However, no obvious changes in classroom interaction patterns were observed during the baseline observations. Also, observations were only undertaken between F5 classes studying towards the old HKCEE and F4 classes under the new HKCEE. The teaching of F5 and F4 had a different focus according to teachers in the study. The data in the main study would provide a close comparison of both F5 classes under the old and the new syllabus.

The following section will report an example from teacher Jane's lessons as her lessons were video recorded, the same recording method used in the main study. This example serves an illustrative purpose for the baseline study as well as guiding the main study.

Jane was pursuing an M.Ed. degree in one of the tertiary institutes in Hong Kong during the time of the study. She was in her 30s with eight years of English teaching experience in schools. The school where she was teaching was a Band 1-2 boys' school, which meant the school had an intake of among the highest proficiency of students. Students in her F5 class were very energetic and highly motivated. For the whole F5 year of teaching, she did not use any of the textbooks or practice books, which was an unusual break from the norm.

Generally F5 students in Hong Kong secondary schools are not required to buy mainstream textbooks recommended by the Education Department, although F1 to F4 students are required to do so. F5 students are instead required to buy practice books that are designed for examination preparation. Mainstream textbooks in Hong Kong schools are usually printed in colour. Therefore, it takes a long time for these textbooks to be published. Practice books, which can be black and white, are designed according to the formats of the HKCEE. They can be easily and quickly revised. Each unit of such practice books is divided into five papers for the old HKCEE and four papers for the new HKCEE. Teachers teach their F5 students according to the HKCEE format over the whole academic year. The majority of the teaching is arranged according to the above pattern. All six teachers in the baseline study followed the same pattern in terms of textbook use.

Jane's F5 classes under the old syllabus and F4 classes under the new syllabus were observed and videotaped on December 20, 1995. Both lessons focused on listening. The lessons were analysed initially by the researcher and then together with Jane for validity purposes. General agreement was achieved on the categories described in Figures 7.1 and 7.2. The segments of activities in the lessons were clear to both Jane and the researcher. All of the baseline observations were carried out in 1994 or early 1995, prior to the main study. Therefore, only F5 classes under the old HKCEE and F4 classes under the new HKCEE could be observed. The main study consequently consisted of comparative data from F5 lessons under the old syllabus and F4 and F5 lessons under the new syllabus. The following figures illustrate the findings from the F5 and F4 listening lesson conducted by Jane.

Figure 7.1 Jane's F5 lesson

F5 lesson (a 35-minute lesson)

Materials:

Type: Written

Source: School newspaper

Participant organization:

1. (57%) *20 min. – Whole class activities*

        5 min. out of 20 min. – Teacher talking to students

        15 min. out of 20 min. – Students talking amongst themselves

2. (28%) *10 min. – Group work*

3. (14%) *5 min. – Student individual work*

Figure 7.2 Jane's F4 lesson

F4 lesson (a 70-minute lesson)

Materials:

Type: Audio (listening to a recording)

Source: Textbook

Participant organization:

1. (71%)   *50 min. – Whole class activities*

        9 min. –   Teacher giving instructions before the listening exercises

        25 min. – Teacher asking students to listen to the tape, then checking the answers and explaining the answers as well as any language points to students

        4 min. –   Teacher giving instruction for group work activity

        12 min. – Students talking amongst themselves

2. (14%)   *10 min. – Group work*

3. (14%)   *10 min. – Student individual work*

        7 min. –   Students listen to the tape

        3 min. –   Students preparing before the lesson

In observing the two listening lessons that Jane carried out on the same morning, one F5 lesson under the old syllabus and one F4 under the new syllabus, it was found that she spent more time (71%) for whole class activities in her F4 lesson under the new syllabus, than her F5 lesson (57%) under the old syllabus. Also, her F5 lessons were much livelier in terms of shared laughter and more frequent interaction between the teacher and the students (c.f. Figure 7.1). However, managing the F4 class took much more effort on her part. Some students fell asleep, and some refused to participate. She commented that one of the major reasons was her familiarity with the F5 students and their respective proficiency level. Her F5 class had been with her for almost two years. They liked her teaching style and were always willing to participate in class activities. Her F4 class had only been with her for a couple of months. The class proficiency level was much lower compared with her F5 class, and the students were not yet motivated. They could not reconcile her way of teaching. However, she pointed out that if she carried on teaching this F4 class continuously as she did with her F5 class, eventually the students would be comfortable with her way of teaching.

The following transcription illustrates the interaction pattern of Jane's F5 lesson:

Figure 7.3 An excerpt from Jane's F5 lesson

Jane's F5 class at her school

One student, Bill, was presenting the results of his group's work in front of the class.

Bill:	The standard of discipline in Sing Yin is very well. (Many students said 'very good').
Teacher:	Very good. What? What is very good?
Bill:	Very good. Why? It is good. (The whole class laughs)
Teacher:	Would James (of the same group) elaborate this point?
James:	(Shakes his head)
Teacher:	It is his opinion, not your opinion.
James:	No. I don't know why.
Teacher:	Do any groups know why? Group Two. (One student from Group Two spoke up)
Student from Group Two:	There is no violence in Sing Yin.
Teacher:	There is no violence in Sing Yin. What do you mean by 'violence'?
Student from Group Two:	Fighting, er, speaking foul language.
Teacher:	Good, very good. No one speaks foul language in Sing Yin. Sorry Bill. Please continue.
Bill:	And students are good examples for other students to follow.
Teacher:	Why?
Bill:	Because... Yeah, My team member will elaborate. (The whole class laughs.)
Teacher:	Which team member will elaborate?
Bill:	You choose either one.
T:	OK. Dawson first. Dawson.
Dawson:....	
Bill:	No.5 (Discussion question No.5) Why so some students explain that some 'perfects' are always picking on them? And I don't know. (Laughter)
Teacher:	Does anyone know? Please ask someone who knows.
Bill:	Is there anybody volunteer?
Teacher:	Please choose a volunteer?
Bill:	William.
William:	There is no exact answer.
Teacher:	There is no exact answer.
William:	Er, I think that the students are in fact naughty. And they don't think about their mistakes. So when some 'perfects' punish them, they feel unfair...
Teacher:	Actually it is the students who made the mistake. What do you think, Bill?
Bill:	I don't know.
Teacher:	What do you think, Albert? Do you agree with William?
Albert:	Yes.

By comparing Jane's two lessons, one under the old HKCEE and one under the new HKCEE, it can be seen that the actual teaching situation was far more complex than the research assumptions. For example, the students' varying levels of proficiency that teachers face between classes leads to different classroom activities and teacher-student interaction. Also, even if there were no particular change observed in the early stages of the implementation of the new 1996 HKCEE, it does not preclude changes in the second year when this batch of F4 would advance to F5.

In order to minimize the differences in observation to make the teaching more comparable, only F5 classes in 1994 and 1995 were used for the main study. Furthermore, the findings from the baseline observations enabled in-depth understanding of the classroom settings. The analysis of the data in this baseline study further refined the observation instrument for the main study.

Main study

The main study began after the first round of classroom observations had been completed in 1994. It focused on selected aspects of classroom teaching. Aspects of learning were selected and studied when they were highly related to classroom interaction. The main study was carried out within the first two years of the new 1996 HKCEE being introduced into Hong Kong schools (from late 1994 to late 1995). Two kinds of classes were observed: F5 classes under the old HKCEE, and F5 classes under the new HKCEE. Classroom observations were designed to observe the same teachers in the same schools teaching the same forms of students over the two year period.

Teacher participants

Based on the above methodological considerations, the following criteria were used for identifying potential teachers who were teaching F5 classes both in 1994 and 1995 for the observation study:

- teachers who were willing to let the researcher observe their teaching
- teachers who agreed to have their lessons video-recorded
- teachers who were willing to encourage their students to ignore the video camera
- school administrators (principals and panel chairs) who had a positive attitude towards observations.

In total, nine teachers participated in the baseline and the main study. Findings from six out of the nine teachers were reported in the baseline study. Only three teachers out of the nine finally participated in the main study according to the criteria listed above. They were all female teachers. Efforts were made to include both male and female teachers in order to have a balanced representation, but none of the male teachers who were approached in the baseline study agreed to be observed for the second round in 1995. They gave various reasons for not wishing to be observed such as a 'heavy teaching workload' and 'difficulty in arranging the observation schedule'. The three female teachers who participated in the main study were willing and co-operative. In addition, the researcher tried to make this study beneficial to both parties. For example, two of the teachers made use of the video-taped lessons for their own teaching purposes. In this sense, the three teachers were willing participants. It should be noted that they were observed in this study to provide three detailed cases of teachers of English in Hong Kong secondary schools for an illustrative purpose, not for the purpose of generalization to other teachers in Hong Kong secondary schools.

The following is a brief introduction of each of the three teachers in the main study. For simplicity, and in order to provide a more human touch to the research, Ada, Betty, and Cathy are pseudonyms given to these three teachers. The information was supplied by the three teachers.

Ada was a university graduate of English literature and Chinese language. She started teaching English as a Second Language (ESL) in 1989. She wanted to incorporate both her English and Chinese language skills background into her teaching. She had been teaching in the same school for more than six years at the time of this study. During that time, she had not only taught English at every level from F1 to F7, but also lower form Geography and History.

After her first year of teaching, she applied to and was accepted by the University of Hong Kong to study (part-time) for the Postgraduate Certificate in Education (P.C.Ed.) as an English language major and an English literature minor. She realized that further training would be useful because she needed to become familiar with the Hong Kong educational system and with ESL teaching. The P.C.Ed. course not only facilitated teacher training, but also stimulated her research interests and potential in teaching. Her goal as an ESL teacher was to make English a living, functioning part of the students' learning experience, not simply a subject to be introduced and implemented, using innovative activities and approaches. She became interested in further postgraduate study and research in order to understand the present teaching situation and to be able to improve it.

Betty graduated with a Bachelor of Science degree, majoring in Chemistry. She is fluent in many Chinese dialects, such as Hokkien, Cantonese, and Mandarin. She started to teach English in the early 1990s in a Chinese school. She felt very comfortable and safe in the school environment and being a teacher came to her very naturally. She decided that teaching was suitable for her. She moved into her current school in 1993, where the principal encouraged her to begin the P.C. Ed. course. During that time, she also worked as the acting panel chair of the English Department. During her P.C.Ed. course at the University of Hong Kong, she met many teachers from different schools and enjoyed sharing their experiences as teachers. She emphasized that the teacher education course enhanced her teaching skills and developed her freedom to be creative. Most importantly, she gained more confidence in her own teaching and also made many friends who supported each other in teaching.

Betty was the panel chair of her school's English Department. She explained that she was very lucky to have co-operative and caring colleagues whom she could rely on, and an encouraging and supportive school principal. Teaching in her school was challenging and satisfying for her. The objectives of her teaching were to improve the quality of human life through education. Although she believed that every person had the ability to learn, it was quite difficult to teach English in Hong Kong. She reported that her students were very weak (her school was a low band school). She commented that students in Hong Kong were very stressed, as English was their 'examination' language. Moreover, they were not proficient in it. Their lack of exposure to English and opportunity to use the language limited their motivation and encouragement to learn the subject. She felt that English teachers nowadays needed to create more innovative teaching methods and learn how to maintain students' interest.

Cathy graduated with a Bachelor of English Language and Literature degree in 1991. She obtained her P.C.Ed. in 1995. Being a teacher was her dream, and she thought teaching suited her personality. She liked children and loved to talk to them as well. She started to teach English part-time even when she was an undergraduate. She explained that she wanted to be the one who was in control of her work. As a teacher, she believed she could achieve that control. She could plan her own schedule, teach different things to different students, and control the things she gives to her students.

She believed that nothing could replace the role of the teacher. Teachers should be facilitators. They should not tell students everything. Instead they should show students how to do self-study and help them to realize that learning can be fun. She thought teacher development was very important. Teachers needed to re-train themselves in order to provide students with what they needed. She commented that 'the world is so dynamic. If we don't change, we will be left behind and become out-dated.' She also commented that English language teaching in Hong Kong was very important. Teachers of English were essential in Hong Kong secondary schools. However, it was very difficult to teach English in Hong Kong. The current cohorts of secondary students were becoming more passive and dependent on their teachers. Students' standard of English seemed to be declining. She was also not sure about the way that English was taught. Should English be taught through English? She seemed to believe that it should not be, convinced by her success in learning English and German through Chinese.

Classroom observation scheme

The following section re-emphasizes the classroom observation scheme and the rationale behind it. Findings will be reported in the next section.

Rationale behind the observation scheme

After the initial school visits and baseline classroom observations of 23 lessons, detailed procedures for the classroom observations and an observation scheme were decided upon. Four 70-minute lessons of the selected three teachers were observed in 1994 and 1995 respectively by the researcher. Most observations took place in the winter term when a long and constant stretch of teaching[2] was under way. During those observations, a video camera was set up before each lesson in one corner of the classroom facing the students. The researcher sat at the back of the classroom and made notes as the lessons went along. The following research assumptions were made about the washback effect of the new 1996 HKCEE on classroom teaching (see Chapter One for a comparison of the two HKCEEs). Compared to teaching under the old HKCEE in 1994:

- the teacher will assign more practice opportunities to students
- the teacher will assign more class time to student activities such as role play and group discussion
- the teacher will talk less
- the students will talk more
- the teacher will use more authentic materials from real-life sources.

The observation scheme

As discussed in Chapter 3, the observation scheme was designed based on the analysis of the data from the baseline study mentioned above, and Part A of the 'Communicative Orientation of Language Teaching' (COLT) category definitions (Frohlich, Spada, & Allen, 1985: 53-56) (c.f. Table 7.4). The following five categories were designed to describe classroom activities in order to investigate such aspects as to whether the lesson was student-centred or teacher-centred, how many learning opportunities were provided, and what pedagogical materials teachers used in teaching, e.g. real life materials, main textbooks, or practice exam papers:

1. Time: How is time segmented within the lesson as a percentage of class time?

---

2. The HKCEE takes place in May every year. Intensive exam practices normally start as early as February each year. All observations were carried out before the start of such exam practices.

2. Participant organization: Who is holding the floor/talking during the segments of the lesson as a percentage of class time?
3. Activity type: What teaching and learning is realized through various activities as a percentage of class time?
4. Content: What are the teacher and the students talking, reading, or writing about, or what are they listening to?
5. Material used: What types and purposes of teaching materials were involved?

Table 7.4 Classroom observation scheme for the main study

R1 Time	R2 Participant organization					*R3 Activity Type	*R4 Activity Content	Interaction					Turn	R5 Material Used					
			Group	Individual	Choral			Teacher			Students			Type			Purpose		
	T to S/C	S to S/C						L	I	A	I	A		W	A	V	P	S	N

Note: There are five research questions explored in this observation scheme (see Chapter Three and Chapter Seven for details). R3 and R4 are not predetermined, yet guided by the theoretical framework discussed in Chapter Three Part Three. The category of *interaction* together with *turn* analysis in this scheme was adopted from The Interaction Analysis System (Flanders, 1970) and Allwright and Bailey (1991). Detailed analysis of some episodes of the *activity type* and *content* was also conducted. The data was reported together with R3 and R4 in Chapter Seven.

The above observation scheme combines the methods of real time notes and transcription of video-taped episodes of classroom activities at the level of verbal interaction between teachers and students in order to obtain both a general and a specific picture of the lessons observed. They were essential to help to explain in detail the classroom interactions and discourse. Allwright (1984: 156) sees interaction as 'the fundamental fact of classroom pedagogy' because 'everything that happens in the classroom happens through a process of living person-to-person interaction.' This scheme led the researcher to observe and describe the interactions that took place in the classrooms in order to understand how learning opportunities were created in the context of the new 1996 HKCEE. The analytical method is a post-hoc analysis of video-taped recordings. Allwright and Bailey (1991) pointed out that classroom discourse mediates between pedagogic decision-making and the outcomes of language instruction. Teachers make choices in their lesson planning with regard to what to teach (syllabus), how to teach (method), and perhaps also the nature of the social relationships they want to encourage (atmosphere). When acted on, their plans result in 'classroom interaction.' The resulting interaction is not entirely planned in advance, but rather is 'co-produced' with the learners.

Observation scale

This section introduces the scale that was used in the classroom observations in the main study. Data was analysed according to the five categories of the observation scheme above, and detailed recordings were made of episodes that occurred during the lessons. A process analysis of the five categories illustrated any differences among the lessons at the level of practice opportunities, in terms of how the lessons were segmented regarding interaction patterns, the nature of teacher talk, activity types and content, and the use of teaching materials. The analysis involved calculating the amount of time that the teachers and students spent in each of the five categories of the observation scheme. This was followed by an analysis of the classroom interaction patterns and in-depth interviews with those teachers, which enabled the researcher to explore in more detail the rationale behind the actual lessons. These findings would lead to an investigation of the teachings in the context of the new 1996 HKCEE.

The following table 7.5 shows the number of lessons observed by the three teachers both in 1994 under the old HKCEE, and in 1995 under the new HKCEE.

Table 7.5 Numbers of F5 and F4 lessons observed in both 1994 and 1995

	1994 (old HKCEE)	1995 (new HKCEE)		Total
	F5 lessons	F4 lessons	F5 lessons	Total lessons observed
Ada	4	5	6	15
Betty	2	2	4	8
Cathy	2	2	4	8
Total	**8**	**9**	**14**	**31**

The classroom observations comprised 31 lessons in total. 15 lessons were observed with Ada, and eight lessons each with Betty and Cathy. After analysing all 31 lessons, the researcher discovered that there were further differences observed between the F4 and F5 levels in both years. This was mainly due to the difference in language proficiency between students in F4 and F5. According to the three teachers, this led to different lesson planning and textbook materials for the two cohorts. Therefore, attention was given only to the F5 classes in both years of the study when the teachers were teaching the same forms (F5 students) under the old and new HKCEE. Therefore, findings (c.f. Table 7.6 below) are reported from only F5 classes over the two years.

Table 7.6 Numbers of F5 lessons observed in both 1994 and 1995

	1994 (old HKCEE)	1995 (new HKCEE)	Total
	F5 lessons	F5 lessons	Total lessons observed
Ada	4	6	10
Betty	2	4	6
Cathy	2	4	6
Total	**8**	**14**	**22**

The classroom observation data consisted of 22 lessons in total; eight F5 lessons under the old syllabus and 14 F5 lessons under the new syllabus. Ten lessons were observed for Ada. Six lessons each were observed for Betty and Cathy.

Classroom observation outcomes

The following section reports the findings from the three teachers in the main study. This section discusses whether or not the new 1996 HKCEE brought about any changes in classroom teaching as intended by the HKEA.

Participant organization

The following three figures illustrate the interaction patterns of the lessons with Ada, Betty, and Cathy teaching F5 classes under the old and the new HKCEE. Differences in interaction patterns in those lessons were observed through 'participant organization,' which is a parameter describing basic patterns of organization for classroom interactions (Allen, Frohlich, & Spada, 1984).

Three basic aspects were observed: (a) Is the teacher working with the whole class or not? (b) Are students divided into groups or are they engaged in individual work? (c) If they are engaged in group work, how is it organized? They are represented in the table as:

- T to Student/Class (teacher to students or class as a whole, e.g. in the case of lecturing)
- S to Student/Class (students to students or class as a whole, e.g. in the case of oral presentations)
- Group work (students are working on a certain task in groups of two or more)
- Individual (individual work, e.g. on exercises or listening).

'Choral' in the figures below refers to the whole class repeating a phrase provided by the textbook or the teacher. Differences between the two years can be seen from the figures.

Figure 7.4 Participant organization of lessons with Ada

	Percentage of lesson time					Total
	Whole class		Group	Individual	Choral	
	T to S/C	S to S/C				
1994 (old)	60	10	22	8	0	100%
1995 (new)	61	12	26	1	0	100%

A general pattern of classroom interaction was observed from the comparative analysis of Ada's lessons in the two different years. There was not much difference in the percentage of class time during which Ada talked to the whole class. However, differences were observed in student talk. There was an increase in student talk from 10% in 1994 to 12% in 1995. An increase in group work was also observed, from 22% in 1994 to 26% in 1995. It was seen that although teacher talk in terms of class time remained approximately the same, there were increases both in student talk and group work as a percentage of class time. Furthermore, individual work, comparatively, decreased from 8% in 1994 to 1% in 1995. For Ada, no choral work was used either in the 1994 or 1995 classes that were observed.

By looking at the findings from Betty's lessons in the two different years, it was seen that teacher talk as a percentage of class time increased from 41% in 1994 to 56% in 1995. She actually talked to the whole class more in 1995 than she did in 1994. No changes were observed in student talk. However, there was more group work in 1995 (18% of the class time observed) than in 1994 (15%). A slight decrease in class time spent on individual work was observed from 1994 (15%) to 1995 (13%). The most dramatic change observed was in the amount of choral work in Betty's lessons over the two years. There was a sharp decrease in choral work, from 21% in 1994 to 5% in 1995. The rationale for her use of more choral work in 1994 was that it was the format for the oral exam of the old HKCEE. She said she believed in teaching students in the same way as the exam format. As students were required to perform choral work by the end of their study in 1994, they needed to get familiar with the format. One of her aims and objectives in teaching F5 students was preparing them for the HKCEE. However, as choral work was not a format required by the new HKCEE, her use of the activity decreased.

Figure 7.5 Participant organization of lessons with Betty

	Percentage of lesson time					Total
	Whole class		Group	Individual	Choral	
	T to S/C	*S to S/C*				
1994 (old)	41	8	15	15	21	100%
1995 (new)	56	8	18	13	5	100%

The findings from Cathy's lessons showed that she talked less in 1995 (68%) compared with 1994 (86%). No student talk, i.e. student(s) talking (or reading aloud) to other students or student(s) speaking to the whole class at the class level, was observed in her lessons in either 1994 or 1995. Note that this category of activities was treated differently from group work. In group work, students were involved in discussion (multi-levels/parties' communication) or in conducting a group task.

Figure 7.6 Participant organization of lessons with Cathy

	Percentage of lesson time					Total
	Whole class		Group	Individual	Choral	
	T to S/C	*S to S/C*				
1994 (old)	86	0	5	9	0	100%
1995 (new)	68	0	7	25	0	100%

A slight increase was found in group work, from 5% in 1994 to 7% in 1995. However, it was found that much more individual work was assigned in 1995 (25%) than in 1994 (9%). The rationale behind the increase in individual work, according to detailed observations over the year and based on interviews with Cathy, was the time spent on certain listening activities in class. The increase, however, indicated a direct washback from the new HKCEE, as the new exam format in Paper III: Integrated Listening, Reading, and Writing stressed an integrated and task-based approach in the four skills. Therefore, textbook writers designed such activities in the revised textbooks, but there were fewer such activities in the old F5 textbooks. Another finding from the above figure was that Cathy, like Ada, never used choral work in her teaching–not in any of the lessons observed during 1994 to 1995. When they were asked about choral work, they seemed to have the same comment. They did not believe that it was a good teaching method. Even though it was required in the old HKCEE exam, they said that students could practise choral work after class. Cathy mentioned that she used to assign such homework for her students.

An overall increase in group work was seen in all three teachers' classes in 1995 compared with 1994, though the increase varied from teacher to teacher. This suggested a washback effect of the new HKCEE, as group work is required for its oral exam. Paper IV: Oral, consists of role play and group discussion whereas the old exam format consisted of Reading, Dialogue, and Conversation. From this point of view, changing the formats of the exam seems to have had an impact at this level on classroom teaching. This type of effect on classroom teaching was also observed in Betty's lessons in 1994 and 1995. There was a sharp decrease in her use of choral work in 1995, as choral work was required for the old HKCEE but not the new one. However, the nature of teacher and student talk, as a percentage of class time, did not show much difference. It seemed that the teachers still dominated most of the classroom interaction and that teacher talk was the predominate move in their classroom.

Activity types and content as a percentage of class time

The purpose of looking at activity type in classroom teaching is to explore what kinds of teaching and learning are realized through various activities as a percentage of class time. By investigating the content of those activities carried out in the classroom, we can explore the subject matter of the activities–what are the teachers and the students talking, reading, or writing about, or what they are listening to?

After each lesson was segmented and participant organization of classroom interaction patterns were analysed, it would then be possible to look more closely at the activity types carried out according to the segments analysed. Activity types were grouped into teacher activities, teacher and student activities carried out together, and student activities. Each activity was classified, such as discussion, drill, or singing. Frequently, activities consisted of two or more episodes as mentioned earlier. This section will report the above three activities as a percentage of class time. Episodes during certain activities will be reported in the next section, when excerpts of transcriptions are analysed.

Findings related to the content will be reported in this section only as a percentage of class time. Whether the content of a particular activity was management (classroom procedures or disciplinary routines) or language input (form, function or discourse) will be analysed in a later section when detailed analysis of excerpts of transcriptions of lesson episodes was carried out.

Table 7.7 shows (a) what types of activities were carried out in the lessons and how lessons were segmented according to the percentage of time (duration of time) devoted to them by the three teachers, and (b) who was holding the floor during the lessons (teacher or student), and in what ways. The analysis of the 22 lessons with the three teachers shows the following patterns. It could be seen that teacher talk as a percentage of class time increased under the new 1996 HKCEE for both Betty and Cathy.

Table 7.7 Segmented classroom activities of all three teachers' lessons by percentage of class time under the old and the new HKCEE

Activity type	Ada old	Ada new	Betty old	Betty new	Cathy old	Cathy new
Teacher: Pre-lesson activities	1	3	1	3	0	2
Teacher: Lecturing, describing, explaining, narrating, directing	59	35	40	53	14	62
Teacher & Student: Checking answers for exercises together	0	20	0	0	72	4
Teacher & Student: Reading aloud	0	0	21	5	0	0
Student: Individual work	8	1	15	8	9	12
Student: Group work	22	26	15	18	5	7
Student: Oral	10	12	8	8	0	0
Student: Listening	0	3	0	5	0	13
Total in percentage = 100%						

One of the research focuses was to explore whether, as a result of the new 1996 HKCEE, teachers could provide students with more practice opportunities, which would suggest less teacher talk. When Betty and Cathy were asked the reason for there being more teacher talk in their classes, they both explained that it was because of the new examination. As their students would take the new HKCEE, they had to explain more and provide explanations in detail in order to make sure that students could meet the new examination requirements.

One activity type specified above was teacher and student joint activities–a typical activity in Hong Kong secondary schools, as was also discussed earlier in the discussion on the findings of the baseline study. It was found that Ada and Cathy used these types of activities. When these episodes were analysed, frequent and short turns between the teachers and students were found. These are regarded as ideal for providing practice opportunities (see Allen, Frohlich, & Spada, 1984; Tsui, 1995). However, it was found that these turns were used for simple questions and answers. This type of activity was usually related to a grammar-related exercise or a comprehension exercise with multiple-choice responses. Therefore, the interaction between the teachers and students would be based on responses to choose the correct answer: A, B, C, or D. The students simply answered A, B, C, or D, according to whichever was the answer they had arrived at. Then the turn went to the teacher for the next exercise item. This type of activity looked to be interactive in terms of the frequency of turns, but little was achieved in terms of actual learning opportunities for the students, who were observed to be bored and reluctant to participate.

By cross-referencing the three student activities (excluding listening) in the lessons observed, it was found that there was little change if all three types of student activities were amalgamated. The total results would be 39% in 1994 and 39% in 1995 for Ada; 38% in 1994 and 34% in 1995 for Betty; and 14% in 1994 and 19% in 1995 for Cathy. Cathy's lessons were the most teacher-controlled of the three teachers, but she was the only teacher under whom student activity time in class actually increased under the new HKCEE.

Activity type and content: a closer look

In the above section, activity type and content were studied as a percentage of class time. The findings illustrate which kinds of teaching and learning were realized through various activities, as a percentage of class time, as well as whether those activities were carried out by teachers or students, or teachers and students together. It can also be seen from the above findings that there was so much going on in those lessons, and that the actual classroom teaching situation was very complex. This section takes a closer look at episodes in some of the activities to explore certain aspects of classroom activity in depth. Two excerpts were chosen from an oral lesson carried out in 1995, which consisted of one example of a rather long stretch of teacher-controlled talk (a 17-minute transcription), and one episode of teacher and student choral activity, which had the shortest turns observed of any of the lessons in the study. Those two excerpts serve the purpose of taking a closer look at two of the most common classroom interactions in Hong Kong secondary schools. The two excerpts were analysed for the following purposes:

- to explore what teachers and students were doing within each episode of the activities
- to explore the content within this segment in terms of management (classroom procedures or disciplinary routines) and language input (form, function or discourse)
- to explore turns within these episodes: How many turns were there? How long were the turns? What were these turns used for? When did these turns occur during the lesson?

Turn-taking was studied. 'A turn is defined as any utterance, from a single word to a multi-word response, and was coded as a single turn' (Seliger, 1977, cited in Allwright & Bailey, 1991: 67). Usually 'a turn is off-stream (i.e. discontinuing), introduces something new, or denies/disputes a proposition in a previous turn' (van Lier, 1988, cited in Ellis, 1994: 579). Turn-taking and allocation were studied together with activity type and content to investigate whether the students were actively involved in the classroom interactions.

The analysis of the classroom observations in this study focused on classroom interaction in terms of the frequency and length of turns in the lessons under the old and the new HKCEE. However, no significant pattern was observed in the frequency and the length in either year after the first round of analysis of the video-taped lessons. The frequency of turns between the 1994 and 1995 observations varied from 75 to 203. Therefore, it was felt that it would be logical to study the turns qualitatively rather than quantitatively. The following is a transcript of one of Betty's oral lessons in 1995. It was found that the longest turn in her lessons was used for lecturing students on aspects of the language or for explaining how to carry out certain tasks. The shortest turns she used were to carry out reading aloud activities. One of the longest turns was analysed in original verbatim transcription and attached as Appendix V because it is extremely long.

The excerpt from this lesson illustrates in detail how the teacher carried out her lesson. It can be seen that the teacher focused solely on the language forms and usage required for carrying out a discussion, and not on the required skills. Therefore, the teacher spent a great deal of time explaining to students about discussion, but she did not provide the step-by-step skills needed to have a discussion. The gap in that part of the lesson was that she failed to teach her students how to perform a group discussion. Group work was required by the new HKCEE, which was (a) clear to teachers and students, and (b) supported by textbook writers in their revised textbooks. However, what was not clear was whether the teacher knew how to teach the skills of group discussion to their students.

Figure 7.7 An excerpt of a series of the shortest turns observed

The shortest and the most frequent turns observed:

Teacher:	Let's read the word in the middle first, discuss
Student:	discuss
Teacher:	decide
Student:	decide
Teacher:	choose
Student:	choose
Teacher:	suggest
Student:	suggest
Teacher:	recommend
Student:	recommend
Teacher:	select
Student:	select
Teacher:	list
Student:	list
Teacher:	What is 'discuss'? _____ (Meaning in Chinese). Decide? _____ (In Chinese).

The analysis of examples of the longest and shortest turn offered samples in detail of how the lessons were carried out. It can be seen that the stretch of the lesson dominated by teacher talk with very few turns was used for explaining group discussion at the content level. The stretch of the lesson with frequent turns was used for practising and repeating certain vocabulary items aloud. From the analysis of these two excerpts, no washback of the new 1996 HKCEE was seen on classroom interaction at the methodological level. The new HKCEE did not have any impact on the process of classroom activities, but it was seen to have had an influence on what was carried out in classroom teaching. For example, the teachers were observed to organize activities such as group work or integrated listening, reading and writing. However, they still organized those activities as they did before the new exam. The new HKCEE, however, had not taught teachers how to teach their students to carry out group work. The washback effect of the new HKCEE seemed to be limited at this level unless the textbooks provided teachers with more strategies to teach conversation, or unless teachers learned, in one way or another, how to teach such activities through other means.

Teaching materials

This section summarizes the findings related to the use of teaching materials in classroom teaching. It was found that all three teachers used the same kinds of commercially written exam practice books, occasionally accompanied by audio-visual materials (cassette tapes for listening). The books were structured in the same way as the HKCEE formats, whether under the old or the new examinations. The ultimate aim of both sets of F5 teaching materials was to prepare students for the HKCEE, which was the same for both years. However, in two of the 14 lessons observed in 1995 under the new HKCEE, Ada and Cathy used the newspapers as topics for oral work and discussion.

However, no major textbooks were used in any of the F5 classes in 1994 and 1995. F5 teaching was highly examination oriented. In Hong Kong secondary schools, teachers teaching at the F4 level tended to use both main textbooks as well as practice examination books. However, for F5, only practice books (examination papers) were used. In addition, many past examination papers were used with F5 students in 1994. In 1995, past examination papers were not available at the time of the research, as the 1995 cohort of F5 students was the first group to take the new HKCEE examination. Therefore, practice books were used instead, which were designed according to the formats of the examination. For example, since the 1994 HKCEE had five exam papers, the practice books were divided into five parts. As the new HKCEE had four exam papers, the practice books automatically consisted of four books. Each book focused on each examination paper. Although examination practice books were used in both years, the formats of the practice books were quite different, especially for Paper III: Integrated Listening, Reading, and Writing, and Paper IV: Oral. Therefore, the difference in the HKCEE exam papers led to differences in classroom activities. For example, the pre-1996 HKCEE Oral paper consisted of reading aloud and picture conversation activities. The new Oral paper was in the format of role play and group discussion. Therefore, classroom activities in 1995 were based on role play and group discussion in order to reflect the new examination format.

To reiterate, the types of teaching materials for both F5s were not much different. They were both practice books but the contents were different. The new 1996 HKCEE led to changes in such activities as was required by its new format.

Classroom observations of individual teachers' oral lessons

This section reports findings from individual teachers' F5 oral lessons. These lessons were focused because the oral component on the new 1996 HKCEE underwent a major change, from (a) reading and dialogue and (b) conversation on the old examination to (a) role play and (b) group interaction on the new one. The weighting of the oral component on the new HKCEE increased from 10% to 18%. Therefore, it was necessary to explore sample oral lessons in detail to see whether there were certain washback effects.

It must be noted here that although the three teachers scheduled their lessons as oral, it was observed that there were listening, reading, and writing tasks conducted during the lessons. This illustrates the complex nature of language teaching and of classroom observations. It is important to note that findings are usually derived from a limited number of observations within certain parameters. Put simply, there is so much happening in the classrooms that needs to be observed. The complexity of the actual teaching surpassed the capabilities of most of our research instruments.

Ada

Two oral lessons taught by Ada were observed and analysed. It was discovered that in the 1994 lesson, of the 70 minutes[3] of the lesson (68 minutes[4] were recorded and analysed), Ada talked for 56% of the lesson time. Besides, she was in control 69% of the lesson time. 6% of the lesson was devoted to teacher-led activities. A total of 22% of the lesson time was used for group or pair work on dialogue reading and picture description, whereby one student was the examiner and the other was the examinee. 9% of the lesson time was used for students' oral presentations in front of the class. Most of the teacher-talk time was spent on discussing the vocabulary required to give descriptions of pictures and commenting on the language points and sentence structures before or after students' oral presentations.

In 1995, during the 70 minute lesson (69 minutes recorded), Ada talked for 36% of the lesson time, which was a decrease from 1994. 4% of her lesson in 1995 was spent on leading classroom activities. Students' pair and group activities occupied 43% of the lesson time, and 13% was devoted to student oral presentations. Students' exam practice opportunities increased from 31% of the lesson time in 1994 under the old HKCEE to 56% of the lesson in 1995 under the new one. This finding suggests a direct influence of the new HKCEE Oral paper on teaching. There was an increase between 1994 and 1995 in the amount of time that Ada spent on students' activities similar to the new HKCEE Oral paper, i.e. role play and group discussion.

Despite this, the main pattern of the lesson was the same in both years. It followed the pattern: teacher explanation – student activities – teacher comment and teacher further explanation. The atmosphere was lively as students spent most of the time working and talking in groups. Their attention was focused on the tasks they were doing. The teacher went around the

3. A stopwatch was used to record the time for classroom activities. One minute increments were used.
4. Usually most of the teachers cannot start the lesson at the exact time when the lesson is timetabled to begin. If there is no recess before the lesson, there is no time in between the last lesson and the following lesson. Even if the teacher in the previous lesson leaves the classroom exactly on time, students still need some time to relax and change textbooks, etc. Therefore, teachers usually spend the first few minutes talking to students about homework or daily news. Teachers might use this period of time to fix the tape recorder for listening, etc.

classroom to give individual comments, and then periodically commented to the whole class.

It can be seen from Table 7.8 that teacher-dominated talk and activities declined, and students' activities were on the increase. These findings indicate that the format differences between the two syllabuses might have led to certain changes in the general pattern of Ada's lessons. The new HKCEE seemed to have led to an increase in the percentage of lesson time being spent on activities required in the new exam.

Table 7.8 Comparison of two oral lessons carried out by Ada in 1994 and 1995

Activities	Teacher 1994	Teacher 1995
Pre-lesson activities	7%	4%
Lecturing and explaining	56%	36%
Leading classroom activities	6%	4%

Activities	Students 1994	Students 1995
Pair work or group work	22%	43%
Oral presentation	9%	13%

Furthermore, Ada did not assign silent individual work among her students. Instead, the major student activities were either talking in pairs, within groups, or giving oral presentations. Students received more opportunities to talk in a more creative manner in 1995 than they did in 1994. This change was due, to a large extent, to the basic requirements of the examination. Ada later commented in the interview[5] why certain changes happened in her teaching due to the exam:

> Definitely yes, there are certain changes. I think teachers are under a lot of pressure. Teachers who are teaching at the exam levels (F5) are under a lot of pressure to deliver–you know–good grades. At least, in my schools, they won't acknowledge that, but it is there. Teachers have to work for the exam.

Her colleagues, (according to Ada), made certain changes in their teaching for the new exam as their students' exam scores were related to their reputation in the school. However, Ada commented further on the possibility that the change in the exam would eventually change teaching.

> Definitely the exam will change teaching, but I don't think it will idealize it. I don't think it will make it into an ideal situation, but I think what you

---

5. All interviews were carried out in English. Interviews with the three teachers during the second year observation were audio-taped. Each of the interviews was about two hours. They were transcribed.

[the current researcher] should do is to look at the backwash [*sic*] effect into the lower forms to see the washback back down there. You know, what I would want to do is to allow more language in the classrooms, more spoken language–in that, the students can feel more. They allow the language to become a part of themselves. You know it is not something that is just a subject matter. They internalize it. That is what I want the teachers of the lower forms to do to prepare the students for the CE and A level examinations. They have to internalize the language and that is not going to come through a certain format of the exam. It has got to come through the activities.

Betty

Two of Betty's oral lessons were observed, one in 1994 and the other in 1995. It was seen that in the 1994 lesson, during the 70 minutes of the lesson (69 minutes recorded), she talked for about 39% of the lesson time. 23% of the lesson was spent on dialogue reading, where the teacher was the examiner and students were the examinees. 22% of the time was spent on individual student work, and 13% on pair work where one student acted as the examiner and the other as the examinee, and vice versa. The major interaction between the teacher and students was choral work. There was no student initiation of questions.

In the 1995 lesson, during the 70 minutes of the lesson (67 minutes recorded), Betty was observed to talk for 55% of the time. 11% of the lesson was devoted to listening activities and 18% to oral group activities. 12% of the lesson time was spent on organizing activities. The main pattern of the two lessons was *IRF: Initiation – Response – Feedback* (Cazden, 1985; Mehan, 1979; Sinclair & Coulthard, 1975), but there were many examples of interactions observed in 1995 where Betty initiated questions and students answered them. The teaching material that Betty used was confined to a practice exam workbook.

It can be seen from Table 7.9 that there was more pair work and group work carried out in the 1995 class (18%) than in 1994 (13%). The time that was devoted to individual work decreased to 11% in 1995 from 22% in 1994. However, there was an increase in the time spent on teacher talk, which was different from the previous assumption, namely a decrease of teacher talk and an increase in students' practice opportunities. Teacher talk increased from 39% in 1994 to 56% in 1995. During the interview, Betty explained the reason for this increase.

Yes. Probably it is because the old type of examination is very structured. Of course, the old type one has been there for quite some time. Being a very experienced teacher in the old Hong Kong exam format, then we all know what is the requirement of the examination. So we are very structured. We get the students to read. We get the students to look at the pictures and learn vocabulary. But with the new one, we don't really know what questions would come up. Because it emphasizes on communication, so I have to create different situations for the students. I have to teach them the basic skills.

Table 7.9 Comparison of two oral lessons carried out by Betty in 1994 and 1995

Activities	Teacher 1994	Teacher 1995
Pre-lesson activities	3%	4%
Lecturing and explaining	39%	55%
Leading classroom activities	23%	12%

Activities	Students 1994	Students 1995
Individual work	22%	11%
Pair work or group work	13%	18%

She also mentioned that she gave the new F5 students more opportunities to talk in class. When asked about whether the new HKCEE had brought some significant changes in her teaching methods, she said:

> Yes, it has. Especially I, for example, I think the biggest impact is on Paper IV, the oral part. I have started a lot of role plays. We have a lot of group discussions. That is not just in class. It is even the whole school thing. For example, the English week–then we created situations for students so that they can have an environment where they can talk or speak to other students or things like that, whereas there is no need for us to do such things in the previous year.

The biggest change observed in Betty's lessons between 1994 and 1995 was that there was much more interaction between the teacher and the students in 1995. Although Betty did not talk a lot in the 1994 lesson, that lesson was carried out according to the old examination format, i.e. practising reading a dialogue aloud. Choral reading aloud dominated the whole lesson. There was no interaction, only simulations of dialogue practice between the teacher and the students and students amongst themselves.

It is difficult to perceive changes in just a few lessons but interviewing the teacher provided insights into what had happened as a result of changing the examination. In the interview, Betty talked about the major differences in the way she taught her oral lessons between 1994 and 1995:

With the old F5 class, it is more like learning more vocabulary. This is a flower. This is a tree. You must know how to say these words. They also have to read. The oral skills for the previous F5s are reading skills, I think. Reading aloud? [Asked by the researcher] That is it. They see the words. And they must know how to pronounce it, and they have to remember intonation and stresses of certain words, but with the new CE syllabus, the emphasis is on communication. That is the problem. The students have to reveal how they would solve a particular problem. It is, I think in that way, students became more natural in their responses rather than reading aloud.

Although the interaction patterns in her class did not change much, the way that the lesson was organized changed significantly. Betty's perception of her role and her students' roles changed. The nature of the classroom activities was definitely different in 1994 to what it was in 1995, especially in the oral activities.

Cathy

Cathy's talking time decreased from 81% of the lesson in 1994 to 53% of the lesson in 1995. In the 1995 lesson, there was an increase in practice opportunities for students' individual work, pair work, and oral presentation. The increase was from 8% in 1994 to 18% in 1995 for individual work, and 3% in 1994 to 14% in 1995 for pair and group work. However, the interaction pattern observed in her lessons in both years still reflected the traditional 'Initiation – Response – Feedback' (IRF) model. The focus of Cathy's lesson was on the teacher. In both the 1994 and 1995 lessons and in the other lessons observed in that period, Cathy followed a pattern that started with assigning a language task, and then progressed through lecturing, explaining language points, and checking students' answers. During most of those lessons, she talked to the whole class. Students only provided very limited responses such as 'yes' or 'no' answers. Students did not initiate questions. The pattern of interaction did not show much change when she taught according to a different practice book or when using either of the two HKCEEs as guides.

Table 7.10 Comparison of two oral lessons carried out by Cathy in 1994 and 1995

Activities	Teacher 1994	Teacher 1995
Pre-lesson activities	4%	4%
Lecturing and explaining	81%	53%
Leading classroom activities	4%	11%

Activities	Students 1994	Students 1995
Individual work	8%	18%
Pair work or group work	3%	14%

When I asked her whether she thought teaching under the old exam syllabus and the new syllabus were different, she replied:

> Concerning the methods, no; but concerning the materials, yes. Well, I don't know about other teachers. But to me, I am still using the same methods. I am still asking the students to do the exercises. Well, take F5 for example, they are in Term Two now, they are doing, well, exam practices. I am still using the same method. I am still asking the students to do it in class. Do it as homework at home. Then they have to tell me the answers. They have to tell me where and how they get the answers, where they find the support, and where they find the proof of it, whatever. It is the same.

In her 1994 lesson, Cathy began by assigning a reading task. She led the students through the comprehension exercises of the pre-assigned reading passage one by one. The lesson continued for almost nine minutes before she started to ask the students a question. Only a few students answered the question. During the lesson (66 minutes of which was video-recorded), she talked for 81% of the class time. In the entire lesson, only 3% of the time was left for the students to work in pairs.

One year later, in 1995, under the new HKCEE, a decrease in teacher talk was observed in Cathy's lesson to 53% from 81% in 1994. Teacher-led activities accounted for 11% of the lesson, and 14% of the lesson was spent on pair work. For the remainder of the lesson, students either worked on their exercise books or carried out listening activities. There was not much change in the way Cathy organized her lessons in 1995 in comparison with 1994. From the later interview, it was clear that she believed that checking the answers and making sure students knew how to get the right answers was her major responsibility.

During the interview, she also mentioned that students' proficiency level was the key problem in implementing the new syllabus. To her, if a class of students was 'good,' (i.e. they had an overall high level of proficiency), there was no need for the teacher to talk and explain much. The students would be able to carry out tasks on their own. However, if the class level was generally low, it was her opinion that a teacher would have to spend a lot of time in the lesson explaining the theory part and then give them extra practice during lunch hour, as was the case with her 1995 F5 class.

> I would use the oral lessons teaching them the theory part first. If they want to ask questions properly, they have to do the practice in class. In F5, I am focusing on the discussion, Part Two of the oral exam. I have to give them extra lessons. In oral class, I teach them the theory. Then every afternoon, they would have extra lessons. They come to my office, group by group–and they would have a discussion just like the examination–and they have practices at that time during the lunchtime–and I tried, before I gave them extra lessons, I try to let them practice in class–but I don't think the results would be good–because I can't supervise all of them.

Comparing the three teachers between 1994 and 1995

To summarize the observations of the three teachers above, it can be seen that oral lessons were similar between the three teachers, particularly in 1994. The oral activities at that time emphasized oral reading skills; vocabulary building and sentence structures required by 'Dialogue Reading' and 'Picture Conversation' by the old HKCEE. In 1995, however, the emphasis had shifted to 'Role Play' and 'Group Discussion'. The skills emphasized in the new HKCEE focus on the expression of meaning, and were less likely to be on the linguistic accuracy of utterances. 'Dialogue Reading,' on the other hand, tended to limit students to produce isolated sentences, which are assessed for grammatical accuracy.

Each teacher's pattern of interaction in the classroom, however, did not reveal much change. The lessons were carried out in a similar fashion in both years. The lessons were highly teacher-controlled. In both years, teacher talk dominated the majority of the class time. There were two levels of changes that could be observed. First, there were changes among teachers in the allocation of time in teacher and student talk vs. teacher and student activities in both years. In Ada's 1995 lesson, student talk overtook teacher talk. For Cathy, teacher talk decreased by 21% in 1995. Second, there were differences between teachers in both years. Cathy's lessons were much more teacher-controlled, and consequently showed the least amount of student activity time compared with the other two. Table 7.11 summarizes the three teachers' lessons according to the percentage of class time spent on activities.

Table 7.11 Summary of the observations of the three teachers

	Ada		Betty		Cathy	
	1994	1995	1994	1995	1994	1995
Teacher talk	69	44	65	71	89	68
Student talk	31	56	35	29	11	32

The observations revealed that the approaches to teaching were more varied in the 1995 lessons. Teachers tried to vary their teaching activities according to their understanding of the integrated and task-based approaches encouraged by the new HKCEE. One of the reasons Betty gave was that they did not really know what the new HKCEE format would be, and they did not know how they should teach according to the new examination syllabus. Nor could they rely on any past exam papers. Thereafter, they just tried their own ideas. This washback effect was seen to occur with some of the teachers who were positive about their teaching. The change to the new exam provided an opportunity for them to try out new ideas and activities in schools. The students would not complain, as they did not know much about the new HKCEE either. Other teachers tended to rely on the practice books for the new 1996 HKCEE. In that case, they used activities suggested by the textbook writers.

Furthermore, it can be seen that there was an increase in the opportunities for student activities in 1995. Teachers provided students with much more time for activities such as role playing and group work. As a result, class time spent on student individual work decreased. However, there was no evidence in the lessons observed in this study that teachers employed more authentic materials. Teachers relied on the revised practice examination books most of the time. In the 1994 lessons, the teachers tended to use past examination papers. In 1995, however, they relied on the revised practice workbooks designed especially for the new HKCEE papers. One teacher did mention the use of English newspapers in her lessons and she requested her students to buy one. She mentioned that she needed the newspapers to help students cope with Paper III: Integrated Listening, Reading, and Writing of the new examination. However, she did not use newspapers under the old syllabus.

When comparing the three teachers' approaches to teaching between 1994 and 1995, it can be seen that the general pattern of teaching approaches did not change much. In 1995, the teachers still taught in a manner similar to that of 1994. Major changes lie in differences between teachers, not within individual teachers. It can be seen that although the change in the HKCEE could push them to change their classroom activities given the importance of this public examination, it did not change them in their fundamental beliefs and attitudes about teaching and learning, the roles of teachers and students, and how teaching and learning should be carried out.

The following interview excerpt further illustrates this point. The researcher asked the teachers individually whether they thought that the new HKCEE actually brought about any changes in teaching methodology. Their answer was in each case an unqualified 'yes'. Betty's comment exemplified this point.

> Yes, after all especially for teachers who are teaching graduate classes, F5s and F7s, of course the main guidelines are usually from the Examinations Authority. All right, no matter what we are going to say about the curriculum, we have to follow the curriculum. We have to follow the syllabus, but truly where we go, at the front line, the first thing the teachers and students are very concerned about is 'Are my students able to perform well in the exam? OK.' If the Examinations Authority is going to change something or anything, I think all teachers will be concerned about this. I think teachers will just do their best in order to make their students take the examinations well. I think most of the teachers believe this.

A key assumption behind changing a public examination in order to bring about a change in teaching is that the outcome is something that is required of all teachers, regardless of their different capacities and interpretations. The researcher found a substantial variation in teachers' beliefs about how to teach and how students learn. Teachers also varied significantly in their classroom practices. A change to a public examination can, to a large extent, change the content of teaching and even the way activities are carried out, but very little change in the interaction pattern between teachers and students could be found in this study, and might not be found within the initial couple of years of the change.

McDonnell and Elmore (1987) pointed out that reform instruments tend to depend on coercion to create uniformity. If one expects practitioners to change themselves and their students, an environment conducive to such change must be fostered. The teaching context, school environment, messages from the administration, and expectations of other teachers facilitate or detract from the possibility of change. Fullilove (1992: 131) also commented that 'the nature and strength of this washback effect and the benefits or disadvantages of the washback depend in large measure upon the educational system as a whole, upon the nature of the other participants involved in writing or establishing the competing curricular, and, of course, upon the types of examinations in question.'

Noble and Smith (1994b) concluded that to be consistent with cognitive-constructivist beliefs about learning and teaching, educational reform efforts directed towards instructional improvement should acknowledge the challenges presented by such conceptual changes. Changes of this type are not simply brought about by the acquisition of new ideas. Conceptual changes are seldom achieved without attending to the beliefs of those who are the targets of change: teachers and the environmental conditions in which they function, schools, and student levels of proficiency.

Summary

This chapter has focused on the findings from the classroom by observing teachers and students in classroom settings and by talking to those teachers about their lessons. It has focused on F5 lessons carried out by three teachers in both 1994 and 1995 under the old and new HKCEE. The findings have illustrated in detail the washback effect brought about in teaching by the new 1996 HKCEE. It was shown that participant organization of classroom interaction has changed with a definite increase in group work as a percentage of class time for all three teachers as a result of the new HKCEE. However, by segmenting those lessons into activity types, no obvious changes in the student activities were revealed when those activities were amalgamated. It could also be seen that teacher talk as a percentage of class time increased under the new 1996 HKCEE for one of the three teachers. This teacher commented that because it was a new examination, she had to explain more, and in more detail, in order to make sure that students could meet the new examination requirements. This further illustrated the complexity of washback effect on the teaching situation.

8 Washback revisited

> Plus ça change, plus c'est la même chose. The more things change, the more they remain the same. Change is everywhere, and progress is not.
>
> Karr, 1849, cited in Nunan (1996: 1)

Introduction

As this was a large study, this chapter will first synthesize the findings which were obtained by using different research methods. It will then draw a set of conclusions across all three phases of the study by re-visiting the major issues in this washback study. A discussion of the limitations of the study will follow. Lastly, recommendations for further research will be suggested.

The major aspects in this study were investigated through a washback exploratory model in the Hong Kong educational context as follows.

1. The Hong Kong Educational context at the macro level.
   i)   Hong Kong Examinations Authority
   ii) Tertiary institutions and textbook publishers
2. The Hong Kong educational context at the micro level.
   i)   School administration
   ii) A survey – teachers' and students' attitudes
   iii) School visits – teachers' and students' classroom behaviours.

A washback effect of the new 1996 HKCEE has been shown in the following areas in relation to the issues explored above:

- washback on teaching materials
- washback on teachers' attitudes towards the teaching and learning of English
- washback on students' attitudes towards the teaching and learning of English
- washback on teachers' classroom behaviours.

Synthesis of the findings

This section summarizes the findings from the three phases of the study, which were obtained using a variety of different research methods. It will discuss the findings in relation to the research questions addressed by the study.

Phase I: The decision-making stage of the examination change

Phase I of the study consisted of an investigation of the Hong Kong educational context at the macro and micro levels. The research methods employed in this phase were general observations, interviews, and document studies, which represented the research approaches of watching and asking. Phase I of the study answered the first research question: 'What strategies did the HKEA use to implement the change in the examination?' Embedded in this research are sub-questions about the strategies used by the HKEA and reactions of the participants in relation to the examination change.

The Hong Kong educational context at the macro level

In this study, the Hong Kong educational context consisted of two levels of organizations at the macro level. The first level consisted of decision-makers such as the Hong Kong Examinations Authority (HKEA), the Curriculum Development Council (CDC) and the Education Department (ED). The HKEA was the engineering body for the new 1996 HKCEE syllabus, while the CDC was responsible for the teaching syllabus. The second intervening level within the Hong Kong educational context was mainly composed of textbook publishers and tertiary institutes.

The findings showed that Hong Kong education organizations tried to provide an environment conducive to a positive washback effect on teaching and learning. The following outlines evidence of the strategies these organizations used in the case of the new 1996 HKCEE.

The new 1996 HKCEE was in accordance with a major curriculum change–Target Oriented Curriculum (TOC) in schools. Both the new HKCEE and TOC reflected a major paradigm shift in assessment in relation to teaching and learning in schools. By shifting assessment from the behaviourist belief of a multiple-choice examination system to a more task-based, integrated, and constructivist approach, the HKEA believed that the new examination could have a beneficial washback effect on teaching and learning. There was, therefore, a consensus regarding the underlying theoretical paradigm in teaching and learning, and in assessment. This was true in the Hong Kong educational context, both for the new HKCEE intended by the HKEA, and for the TOC intended by the ED and the CDC.

Consequently, the actions of these mutually supportive bodies led to a series of specific support activities provided by textbook publishers and tertiary institutions. All textbook publishers were informed about the new HKCEE. They all then revised the textbooks before the commencement of the new 1996 HKCEE. Seminars and workshops were organized by textbook publishers and tertiary institutions. These seminars and workshops to some extent helped some teachers to get ready to teach towards the new 1996 HKCEE. To emphasize, the Hong Kong educational context at the macro level had established an environment that was conducive, in theory and in practice, to beneficial washback effects from the new 1996 HKCEE.

The Hong Kong educational context at the micro level

The situation at the micro level, the actual teaching situation within the school setting, was not as clearly favourable as it was at the macro level. However, schools were observed to prepare for teaching for the new 1996 HKCEE.

Teaching towards the new 1996 HKCEE was planned at the overall school administrative level. Revised textbooks for the new HKCEE were quickly published and employed. Various preparations were undertaken within the schools for the examination. Teachers showed a positive attitude towards the new HKCEE. For example, in the 1994 survey, 84% of the teachers commented that they would change their teaching methodology. As for teaching materials, by the time the actual teaching started, nearly every school in Hong Kong whose students would sit for the 1996 HKCEE was using revised textbooks targeted towards the new examination. Teachers were also provided with the new teaching materials. To summarize, schools and teachers were prepared for teaching (in terms of teaching materials) for the new 1996 HKCEE before the start of the school year in 1994. The Hong Kong educational context showed a high level of preparation for the new 1996 HKCEE.

Phase II: Survey study – washback on teachers' and students' perceptions

This section will summarize the findings from Phase II of the study, in which two comparative survey studies of teachers and students were conducted in two separate academic years (1994 and 1995). The purpose of investigating changes in teachers' attitudes lay in the theoretical relationship between teachers' attitudes and behaviours. What teachers think (discovered via the surveys) has a great influence on what they do in the classroom, and vice versa. Changes in teachers' and students' perceptions towards the new HKCEE ought to happen prior to the changes in their classroom behaviours. The research questions explored in this phase were as follows:

- what was the nature and scope of the washback effect on teachers' and students' perceptions of aspects of teaching towards the new examination?
- what was the nature and scope of the washback effect on teachers' behaviours as a result of the new examination?

Phase II of the study focused on the first research question. The second research question was explored partially in Phase II and Phase III of classroom observations, where behaviours were observed in the classrooms.

Teachers' survey

Major issues explored in the teachers' survey in 1994 and 1995 were as follows.

1. Teachers' reactions and perceptions in relation to the new 1996 HKCEE:
   - the reasons behind the new 1996 HKCEE
   - the exam formats of the new 1996 HKCEE
   - possible extra work and pressure under the new 1996 HKCEE
   - possible difficulties in teaching towards the new 1996 HKCEE
   - possible teaching methods teachers would like to change for the new 1996 HKCEE.
2. Teaching materials:
   - textbook arrangements related to teaching materials
   - teaching and learning resources.
3. Teachers' classroom behaviours:
   - teaching planning (who plans and how to plan)
   - medium of instruction
   - lesson preparation
   - teacher talk
   - teaching activities.
4. Assessment and evaluation:
   - the use of mock exams
   - the assessment of teaching in Hong Kong secondary schools
   - factors that influence teaching.
5. Teachers' attitudes towards aspects of learning:
   - learning strategies
   - learning activities
   - learning aims
   - motivation to learn.

First, the survey showed that teachers had a positive *reaction* towards the new 1996 HKCEE. For example, fewer teachers tended to be sceptical about the change (from 38.4% in 1994 to 20.2% in 1995) after the new 1996 HKCEE was put into practice for one year. There was also an increase in the number of teachers who welcomed the change, from 30.4% in 1994 to 42.7% in 1995.

In terms of teachers' perceptions of the new 1996 HKCEE, it was clear that their perceptions of (a) the reasons behind changing the examination and (b) teachers' knowledge of the actual changes made in the new 1996 HKCEE by the HKEA matched the intended washback effect anticipated by the HKEA. The agreement between teachers' perceptions of the changes and that of the policy-makers' suggested a positive attitude towards the implementation of the new HKCEE. It can also be seen that teachers' perceptions of some teaching and learning activities behind the 1996 HKCEE changed in an increasing direction between 1994 and 1995. For example, there was a significant increase in 1995 in the teachers' use of (a) more integrated and task-based approaches, (b) more practical tasks that resembled real-life situations, and (c) more role play and group discussion. All these activities were directly related to the essence of the new HKCEE.

When teachers were asked what changes they would like to make in their teaching in the context of the examination change, however, their perceptions remained relatively unchanged between 1994 and 1995, although the above findings showed that they perceived those intended changes made in the 1996 HKCEE formats. Of the eight items explored in the area of teaching, the only one that changed significantly over the two year period was 'more emphasis on oral and listening,' which was closely related to the increase of the weighting of the two components in the new examination. Furthermore, teachers' perceptions of whether they would like to employ more real life language tasks decreased significantly in 1995 compared to 1994. Teachers seemed to have a positive attitude towards the change in the examination, but the results also suggest a reluctant attitude towards making the changes that they ought to carry out in their own teaching.

As for teachers' perceptions of the possible difficulties in teaching the new HKCEE, it is shown that there were tensions and worries over the 1996 HKCEE. Despite this, those concerns, especially regarding inadequate textbooks and teaching resources as well as the noisy environment, decreased between the 1994 and 1995 surveys. The teachers' major concerns shifted to students' current English levels and inadequate student practice time. Teachers' perceptions of different aspects of teaching towards the new HKCEE over the year changed. Initially, teachers seemed to worry about teaching materials and resources and the external teaching environment. By 1995, their concerns shifted to students' proficiency levels and the inadequate amount of time for students to practise for the examination, which are more methodological worries than concerns about the teaching content or the environment. This indicated tension in teaching to the new HKCEE, suggesting a degree of anxiety washback on teachers' teaching.

Second, in summarizing the results of how the teaching materials are decided upon for the new HKCEE, it appears that teachers in Hong Kong secondary schools had a strong voice in the choice of textbooks. According to teachers, the major function of the textbook was to provide a structured language programme to follow in their teaching. The results indicated the important function that textbooks played in the teaching of English in Hong Kong secondary schools. The initial tensions and concerns over the availability of new teaching materials for the new 1996 HKCEE decreased between 1994 and 1995, as mentioned above. The initial assumption from Phase I of the study, that the change of the examination would require the use of more teaching and learning resources due to the integrated and communicative approaches and the increase in the oral components in the 1996 HKCEE, was not proven by the findings. Teachers continued to use conventional teaching materials and supplementary practice exam materials more frequently in their teaching rather than real life materials.

Third, summarizing the findings of washback on classroom teaching behaviours, it can be seen that teacher talk remained unchanged despite the examination change. Teachers talking to the whole class was the predominant activity in the classroom. In addition, there was no significant change regarding teaching activities over the two year period. The most frequent activities that teachers carried out in class were explaining specific language items and explaining the meaning of the text. The least frequent activity was organizing language games.

Some changes were however observed. The medium of instruction (nature of teaching delivery mode) changed from using English only to using English occasionally with Chinese explanations between 1994 and 1995. A word of explanation should be provided. These changes might not be directly related to the examination change. The change in medium of instruction observed in 1995, according to the teachers, was due to the lower level of their students' language proficiency. There was also a tendency in 1995 for teachers to pay more attention to the content, skills to be taught, and homework to be given to students. This might indicate that teachers paid increased attention to the new examination, which led to coaching students through homework. Some teachers mentioned that they assigned more homework to prepare their students for the new HKCEE. The results also showed that teachers paid more attention to teaching content than teaching methods and other teaching and learning factors in their lesson preparation.

Fourth, summarizing the findings concerning washback on assessment and evaluation, it can be seen that teachers' attitudes towards assessment and evaluation in schools remained generally unchanged over the period during which this research was conducted. Two factors influencing teaching were professional training and past experience as a language learner. Certain aspects regarding teaching experience and beliefs, public examinations, and learners' expectations were observed to change between 1994 and 1995. The strength of teachers' beliefs in these factors increased significantly over the year. This might indicate that using the examination as a change agent could possibly re-direct teachers' attention to the examination, and possibly make teachers pay more attention to learners' expectations. Both could suggest a direct washback effect of the new HKCEE.

Summarizing the above four aspects of teaching in relation to the new 1996 HKCEE, the changes produced by the new HKCEE were seen to be superficial rather than substantial. Although they might have had a positive attitude and/or might have changed their classroom activities at the surface level in accordance with the examination change, substantial changes in their teaching had not occurred.

It appears that changing the examination had likely changed the *kind* of exam practice (from reading aloud to group discussion), but not the *fact* of the examination practice. Changing an examination's format does not usually tend to change the degree of emphasis on the examination. In this study, revising the format of the HKCEE so that it was in accordance with the Target Oriented Curriculum initiative possibly changed some aspects of teaching pedagogy. However, from the summary above, it can be seen that the most important aspects that governed teachers' daily teaching in Hong Kong secondary schools remained relatively unchanged over the period of this study. Teachers were examination oriented, and their teaching was content-based and highly controlled by the teachers themselves. It is important to point out that the short period of research time–the two-three years when the new HKCEE was first introduced to the Hong Kong secondary schools–could restrict the scope of the research findings that only the superficial changes were observed.

Fifth, a washback effect from the revised HKCEE seemed obvious from the teachers' perception on aspects of learning. Whether they were related to learning strategies, learning activities, or methods to motivate students to learn, teachers' attitudes clearly reflected the washback effect intended by the HKEA and the rationale and underlying theories behind the examination change. For example, as for strategies, there was a significant increase in teachers' recommending their students to learn to take better notes and to communicate more in English. On one hand, learning to take better notes could be a direct washback effect of Paper III of the new 1996 HKCEE, in which an integrated component of Listening, Reading, and Writing was required. The suggestion 'to communicate more in English,' on the other hand, showed a further washback effect, which could be related to the increased weighting given to Paper IV – Oral. Moreover, among the recommended learning activities, role play and group discussion were given increased attention by teachers between 1994 and 1995. These two activities were part of the new examination's oral format. This suggests that the new format had a direct washback effect. However, it is worthwhile pointing out that giving recommendations is not the same as helping students to develop the skills.

Students' survey

The major issues explored in the student survey over the period of this study are as follows.

1. Students' learning contexts:
   - medium of instruction
   - frequency their teachers mentioned the HKCEE
   - the number of tutorials they attend.
2. Students' attitudes towards teaching and learning activities inside and outside class:
   - teacher talk in class
   - their teachers' teaching activities in class
   - their own learning activities in class
   - their use of English in class
   - their use of English outside class.
3. Students' attitudes towards aspects of learning:
   - their English lessons
   - their motivation to learn English
   - their preferred language learning strategies.
4. Students' attitudes towards aspects of public examinations.

First, summarizing the first three categories, an increasing washback effect was observed in relation to the medium of instruction and the private tutorials students attended for preparation for the HKCEE. For example, their teachers used more English only (18.2% in 1994 to 30.6% in 1995) and English supplemented with Chinese (46.54% in 1994 to 51% in 1995). The results suggest that there was more English language input in their lessons in 1995 than in 1994. This finding might also suggest more attention was being given to English–a possible influence of the new 1996 HKCEE. Secondly, students attended private tutorials more frequently in 1995 than in 1994. More students attended tutorials[8] 1–2 and 3–4 times per week (40% in 1994 to 51% in 1995 in total). This suggests that more attention was being given to the new 1996 HKCEE, which might be the usual case whenever there is a change in the public examination.

---

8. A private tutorial is usually a two hour session in Hong Kong. Students usually talk about how many times they attend tutorials each week.

Students did indicate however that teachers mentioned the HKCEE less in 1995 than 1994. A possible explanation for this might be that teachers tended to deal with the issue by employing more exam-type activities or mock exams rather than by referring to it explicitly. This might also be due to the nature of the change in general. At the beginning of any change, certain things related to the change were mentioned much more frequently than later on.

Second, in summarizing students' perceptions of the teaching and learning activities that they undertook inside and outside class (SQ 2.1–2.5), there was a clear sign of washback effects in the following three areas. First, there was a significant decrease in teacher talk to the whole class and to groups in 1995, which might suggest an increase in practice opportunities for students in class. Second, there was an increase in the amount of time teachers spent carrying out classroom activities such as organizing integrated language tasks, organizing group work and discussion, and explaining mock exam papers. Organizing integrated language tasks and organizing group work and discussion were activities required in the new 1996 HKCEE, thus showing a direct washback effect at the surface level. The increase in explaining mock exam papers also indicates a direct washback effect brought about by the change in the examination. Third, there was also an increase in the amount of time students spent carrying out learning activities such as speaking, carrying out group discussions, and doing mock examinations. These learning activities were also closely related to the activities in the new examination.

There were however obvious discrepancies between the students' and teachers' perceptions of the exam change in relation to the above aspects, such as in the areas of teacher talk, and teaching and learning activities. For example, teachers and students had rather different views over teacher talk. According to the teacher surveys, there was no significant change in the amount of teacher talk between 1994 and 1995, but according to the student surveys, there were changes. This shows the complexity of the teachers' and students' perceptions of teacher talk. It probably also illustrates the problems of using surveys to track teachers' and students' perceptions. Teachers and students might simply have different understandings of the term itself or of the concept of teacher talk.

As for students' use of English inside and outside class, there was also a great increase over the period of this study in the amount of time students spent carrying out group discussion and pair work, which showed a direct *format* washback effect on learning activities carried out in English lessons. Although students were seen to do more talking in English to classmates and to teachers inside class in 1995 than in 1994, students still seldom used English outside class. The new 1996 HKCEE had a washback effect on activities directly related to the exam format as discussed above. However, it did not increase the number of English-medium activities that students did outside class.

Third, summarizing students' attitudes towards aspects of learning activities, there was a definite washback effect on aspects of student learning in 1995 compared to 1994. For example, in 1995, students perceived their lessons to provide more opportunities for communication and to involve more pair work and discussion than they did in 1994. These two kinds of learning activities were required by the new 1996 HKCEE. As for motivation in student learning, factors such as 'meeting the requirements of the society' and 'watching English movies and listening to English programmes' changed in an increasing direction from 1994 to 1995. These types of motivations were related to the requirements of the new 1996 HKCEE. The new examination syllabus specified the 'usefulness' of the examination and stressed the need 'to narrow the gap between what happens in the examination room and the real world' (c.f. Hong Kong Examinations Authority, 1993). With regard to students' preferred learning strategies, there were significant changes in four out of the 11 learning strategies. However, students seemed to prefer those four strategies less in 1995 compared to 1994. No logical relationship among these four strategies could be observed. Among the strategies in this category, 'watching English TV or videos' and 'reading English newspapers and magazines' were preferred most by the students in both years.

Fourth, it was definitely agreed that students were influenced by past examination scores. However, their perception of the influence of the examination decreased in 1995 compared to 1994. No significant change was observed regarding aspects of examination influence on the students over the year. One category that received students' attention was 'exams should not be used as the sole determiner of students' grades'. It can be seen from the results that students had to work hard in order to do well in the public examination. Results from both years showed the important role of public examinations in school life.

Phase III: Major issues explored in the classroom observations

This part of the findings discusses whether the new 1996 HKCEE had any washback effect on classroom teaching in terms of teacher and student behaviours. The research question explored in this phase is, 'What was the nature and scope of the washback effect on teachers' behaviour as a result of the new examination?'

The research focuses of the classroom observations were as follows. Compared with the old HKCEE:

- the teacher will assign more practice opportunities to students
- the teacher will assign more class time to students' activities such as role play and group discussion
- the teacher will talk less

- the students will talk more, and;
- the teacher will use more authentic materials from real-life sources.

The results will be summarized in terms of participant organization, activity type, content and teaching materials, and a comparison of oral lessons.

Participant organization

Compared with 1994, the interactive patterns of classroom activities carried out in the 14 lessons by Ada, Betty, and Cathy showed an increase in group work in 1995, though the degree of increase varied from teacher to teacher. This increase in group work is a clear example of a direct washback effect of the new 1996 HKCEE because group work is one of the required oral activities in the new HKCEE. A sharp decrease in choral work (required by the old HKCEE, but not by the new one) was observed in Betty's lessons between 1994 and 1995. Both of these findings demonstrated the washback effect of the new 1996 HKCEE on the participant organization of classroom teaching. As mentioned above, the new HKCEE's Paper IV: Oral consisted of (a) role play and (b) group discussion, whereas the old exam format consisted of (a) reading and dialogue and (b) conversation. From this point of view, changing the format of the examination had an impact on classroom teaching. When the new HKCEE emphasized group work, group work was observed to be carried out more often than activities that it did not require, such as choral reading. However, the nature of teacher and student talk as a percentage of class time did not show much difference from one year to the next. It seemed that teachers still dominated most of the classroom interaction despite the changes in the new HKCEE.

Activity type and content

The purpose of looking at activity type in classroom teaching was to explore aspects of teaching and learning that were realized through various classroom activities as a percentage of class time. The investigation of the content of those activities carried out in classroom teaching provided information about the subject matter of the activities. After the video recordings of each lesson were segmented and the participant organization of classroom interaction patterns were analysed, activity types were grouped into (a) teacher activities, (b) teacher and student activities, and (c) student activities.

The findings showed an increase in the percentage of time spent on students' activities in group work. When the results of all three types of student activities were amalgamated however (not including listening over the two year period), not many changes were found. When combined and calculated in terms of percentage of total class time, student activities in Ada's class accounted for 34% in 1994 and 34% in 1995, i.e. the same amount of time for both years. For Betty, 38% was observed in 1994 and 34% in 1995, i.e. a slight decrease in student activities. A slight increase from 14% in 1994 to 19% in 1995 was observed for Cathy, whose lessons were the most teacher-controlled among the three teachers, although she was the teacher who had actually increased her students' activities in 1995 as a percentage of class time under the new HKCEE.

As for teacher activity, teacher talk as a percentage of class time increased in preparation for the new 1996 HKCEE in both Betty's and Cathy's lessons. In interviews, both Betty and Cathy stated that the increase in teacher talking time was due to the new examination. They felt that they had to spend more time explaining the new examination formats in order to make sure that students were prepared for the requirements of the new HKCEE. This demonstrated that the new 1996 HKCEE had brought about changes in teaching since both teachers and students perceived the new examination to be important. The changes may not necessarily be positive in terms of the beneficial washback effect intended by the HKEA.

When classroom activities were examined closely, it was seen that teachers tended to teach in a similar manner in both years regardless of whether they were preparing their students for the old or the new examination. By looking at oral lessons carried out by the three teachers over the year, it was seen that the teachers tried to use teaching activities appropriate to their understanding of the integrated approach and task-based approach, as promoted by the new HKCEE. The changes to the new examination provided an opportunity for teachers to try out new ideas and activities in their classroom teaching. Furthermore, an increased number of opportunities for students' activities in oral lessons was observed in 1995. However, teachers still dominated classroom teaching for the majority of the time. The general pattern of teaching did not change much. Teachers in 1995 still taught in a manner similar to 1994. The main changes lay in differences between the teachers, not within the teachers themselves.

If we look back to the survey results from teachers and students, it is clear that teachers had a very clear perception of what was expected of them vis-à-vis the new HKCEE. They were aware of the changes and wanted to make changes in their teaching towards the new exam. The results from students' surveys also showed that teachers tended to carry out activities that were similar to those in the new exam. The results from the teachers' surveys did not show many changes in the teachers' activities. Besides, a further careful look at their classroom teaching revealed that the changes were superficial. In this way, the data from different sources such as surveys and classroom observations helped to provide a complete, yet complex, picture of the washback effect of the new exam on teaching and learning.

To summarize, although the change in the HKCEE syllabus encouraged the teachers to change their classroom activities given the importance of this public examination in Hong Kong secondary schools, it did not change their fundamental beliefs and attitudes about how teaching and learning should be carried out, in terms of teaching and learning in relation to the roles of teachers and students.

Teaching materials

Although Ada, Betty, and Cathy taught in three separate schools, they used the same types of teaching materials, which were commercially printed materials that were occasionally accompanied by audio-visual materials (cassette tapes for listening). These printed materials were exam practice books, which were structured in the same format as the HKCEE for both the old syllabus and the new one. Moreover, there was no evidence in the lessons observed that these three teachers employed more authentic materials over the period of this study. The teachers relied on the revised practice examination books most of the time. In the 1994 lessons, the teachers tended to use past examination papers. In 1995, however, they relied on the revised practice workbooks designed specially for the new HKCEE papers. In this sense, teaching materials in Hong Kong secondary schools were largely examination oriented. Furthermore, teachers relied heavily on these teaching materials, which led to a content washback effect of the new HKCEE.

Review of the washback model in the Hong Kong educational context

Having discussed the findings from various research phases, let us take another look at the researcher's own washback model. This model elaborates and describes how the washback effect in terms of participants, processes, and products worked in this study.

The model below was adapted from Hughes' trichotomy (cited in Bailey, 1996: 264) and Markee's model (1997: 42-47). It was also created based on the initial washback exploratory models within the Hong Kong educational context, which were described in Chapter Two. As a result of the past four years of research, the researcher believes that this model best represents the mechanisms by which the effects of washback occur on classroom teaching. Washback from the new 1996 HKCEE is seen to involve participants, processes, and products within the Hong Kong educational context.

The participants included in the model should include all those who are involved: teachers and students, administrators, material developers and publishers. They also include those who are related to the outcomes of

Figure 8.1 Model of the effect of washback within the Hong Kong educational context

	Participants	*Processes*	*Products*
Level 1 Decision-making level	ED HKEA & CDC	syllabus design ▼	new HKCEE ▼
Level 2 Intervening level	**Textbook publishers** **Teacher educators**	materials development bring about changes in teaching and learning through teacher education ▼	new materials ▼
Level 3 School level	**Principals** **Panel chairs** **Teachers & Students**	changes in attitudes towards teaching and learning; changes to teaching methodology, changes to teaching and learning activities	▼ ▼ ▼ ▼ ▼

New 1996 HKCEE ▶ ▶ ▶ ▶ ▶ ▶ **Improved Learning**

teaching and learning, such as stakeholders of the examinations, users of the examinations, parents, and the community–the 'who' in Markee's curricular innovation model. All of their attitudes towards their educational work can/may be affected by the examination (c.f. Bailey 1996: 262). In this study, three levels of participants were studied: those who initiated, developed, and implemented the new HKCEE. These parties included mainly the Hong Kong Examinations Authority for the design of the new 1996 HKCEE examination syllabus, textbook publishers and teacher educators for bridging the change process with materials and methodological support, and the teachers and students who used the exam syllabus. The combined function of these participants within the Hong Kong education system determined the nature and scope of the washback effect of this new examination. In this sense, the washback effect is seen as a more complex educational phenomenon than simply the effect of the examination on teaching and learning. It not only involved participants within the Hong Kong education context, but also a complex process of change.

Processes, according to Hughes (1993), refer to 'any actions taken by the participants which may contribute to the process of learning and teaching' (cited in Bailey, 1996: 262). He suggested that 'such processes include materials development, syllabus design, changes in attitudes towards teaching and learning, changes to teaching methodology, the use of test-taking strategies, etc.'. The processes should also include the 'adopt what, where, when, why, and how' element of Markee's curricular innovation, i.e. who (participants) adopts (process) what (the innovation), where (the context), when (the time duration), why (the rationale), and how (different approaches in managing innovation). This study thus explored what happened at the three different levels of participants involved with the new 1996 HKCEE via textbook writers and publishers to the schools. It then looked at the process of the new HKCEE being delivered from the teachers to the students during the first two years of the change when both the old and new syllabus coexisted in teaching and learning. This study focused on the processes of the washback effect on the actual classroom teaching and learning, both at the behavioural level through classroom observations and at the policy level and the theoretical or philosophical levels through the use of the teacher and student surveys.

The researcher would like to point out that the study of the washback effect as a process involved:

- a study of classroom teaching and learning
- a study of what happened in classroom teaching and learning in relation to the new 1996 HKCEE, and
- a study of classroom teaching and learning from the point of view of change.

Therefore, the processes in this study were seen in terms of attitudinal and behavioural changes in teachers and students in relation to the new HKCEE. In a sense, the washback effect being studied was seen as a process as well as a product of the processes involved. The categorization of product has a different meaning from Hughes's definition of the product (the third perspective within his trichotomy). Hughes (1993: 2) defined the product as 'what is learned (facts, skills, etc.) and the quality of the learning such as fluency, etc.' (cited in Bailey, 1996: 262). This study did not focus on the product as defined by Hughes (1993) due to its short time period. It charted and recorded the process of the washback effect in order to understand how the participants and processes interacted within the Hong Kong education system. This study, therefore, was not a washback study of the revised teaching materials, nor was it a washback study of student learning outcomes, although either of these could be a useful focus for a washback study. It was, rather, a study of the washback effect on the participants and the processes. Therefore, the changes in attitudes towards teaching and learning, the changes to teaching materials and methodology, and the changes to teaching and learning activities were treated as processes as well as products within the washback model.

Indeed, the nature and the scope of the new 1996 HKCEE affected first the perceptions and attitudes of the participants towards their teaching and learning (studied via surveys). These perceptions and attitudes, in turn, affected what participants did in carrying out their work (processes). The processes could affect the learning outcomes, and would eventually lead to the product of teaching and learning. This model is an ideal model of the washback mechanism, although rather simplistic. Whether the intended washback effect vigorously promoted by the HKEA has been realized is still partially in question. We are not sure whether all the participants' products (e.g. revised textbooks) have contributed to and facilitated the enhancement of students' learning outcomes. It would not be possible for a single study like this one to explore all the above areas in full. It would also naturally take a much longer time (beyond the initially few years of the new 1996 HKCEE) to see all possible washback effects brought about by the new 1996 HKCEE.

To emphasize, washback is a very complex educational phenomenon. It should be evaluated with reference to many 'contextual variables of society's goals and values, the educational system in which the test is used, and the potential outcomes of its use' (Bachman & Palmer, 1996: 35). It should also be evaluated with reference to aspects of assessment, curriculum, and teaching and learning theories and practices within the educational system. The researcher feels that it is not possible to illustrate the phenomenon completely within a single model such as the figure above. This model, however, can serve as a guide for future washback studies. The significance of this study lies in the contribution of the methodological considerations of identifying (a) the mechanism of the washback effect, and (b) areas of washback intensity in classroom teaching.

Implications of the study

Many implications arise from the findings of this study. Three aspects of the nature and the scope of washback need particularly to be re-addressed here.

The nature of washback as change

Andrews (1994b) pointed out that examination reform should be viewed as one of the four key components (along with curriculum development/syllabus design, materials writing, and teacher development) of any large-scale curriculum innovation involving major systemic change. Development in the four key components needs to be kept in harmony. Any attempt to innovate in relation to any one of the four components would need to ensure that the proposed innovation preserved a harmonious relationship between them. At the same time, due account would need to be taken of the features of the context and any other factors likely to promote or impede the successful adoption and implementation of the change.

Washback is an educational phenomenon in which change is central. It can be intended by policy-makers to bring about changes in teaching and learning. Therefore, washback on teachers in this context means change; change of one type or another that they feel obliged to make in their teaching for the new HKCEE. Change can be a highly personal experience as 'each and every one of the teachers who will be affected by change must have the opportunity to work through this experience' (Fullan, 1991: 117). Furthermore, change involves learning how to do something new. In this study, teachers had to cope with something new–the new 1996 HKCEE. We have to know how, as well as why, teachers changed, and likewise did not change, in order to understand the nature of the washback effect.

The scope of the intended washback

From the point of view of the HKEA, the new examination was designed to bring about positive washback effects on teaching and learning in schools. Such an intention relates to the extended construct validity concept of test design (Messick, 1989, 1996). Senior HKEA officials claimed that they have successfully changed the 'what' in teaching and learning in Hong Kong secondary schools (HKEA, 1994b). However, the extent to which this new examination has changed the 'how' of teaching and learning is limited. The changes in teaching and learning so far have been largely superficial. For example, it was seen that teachers adopted activities similar to those designed in the examination, such as group work, which reflected the new examination syllabus. But what is occurring here is the fact of the examination (examination preparation). It is the important role of that public examination in Hong Kong schools that works. The high-stakes nature of public examinations drives teaching and learning, a fact that is very well documented and can even be traced back to imperial examinations in ancient China. Examinations drive teaching in the direction of coaching and drilling for what is required in the examinations. Examples can be seen from this study of an increasing number of activities being carried out in classroom teaching and learning, which are similar to exam activities.

The washback effect of the new examination on classroom teaching is limited in the sense that it did not appear to have a fundamental impact on classroom teaching. For example, the washback effect, as a process, can occur to the extent that role play and group discussion were found to have been widely adopted in the classroom instead of reading aloud (choral work), which was observed in this study. When classroom teaching was observed closely and in detail, it was seen that teachers still spent most of the class time lecturing on group discussion or simply letting students go ahead and attempt to engage in group discussions by themselves without the necessary pedagogical preparation. No genuine teaching and/or pedagogical help was given, such as breaking group discussions into managerial language tasks or activities, and/or guiding students in *how* to begin a conversation or *how* to interrupt and/or to argue. Students might over-learn the vocabulary items for group discussion in the practice books or in the format of group discussion, but may still not learn the conversational strategies required of the language to carry out group discussion successfully. The way the teachers carried out their teaching remained more or less the same, whether the syllabus was the old one or the new one. A word of caution needs to be mentioned here. The reason that only superficial changes were observed might be due to the fact that this study was conducted at the first three to four years of the introduction of the new HKCEE. Changes are unlikely to take place overnight, particularly those involving teachers' beliefs and behaviours.

The HKCEE undoubtedly plays an important role in school teaching and learning in Hong Kong. If the HKEA changes the exam again, teachers as well as the textbook publishers will follow the new changes again, but the changes are highly likely to remain superficial and at the surface level. How teachers perceive teaching and learning might change, but not how they carry out the teaching and learning activities. The change of the examination has informed teachers *what*, but not *how*. The extended construct validity (the washback effect) can only be fully realized when all levels of the parties (participants) within the education system are involved. In this sense, there must be a genuine involvement of teacher educators and textbook writers. Only in this way can the extended construct validity be realized. A change in the examination syllabus itself will **not** on its own fulfil the intended goal. Teacher education and professional development must be involved in the process.

In this study, the washback effect is clearly limited to the surface level. The idea of changing the examination based on an 'ideal' assessment model in order to influence teaching and learning to move towards an 'ideal' direction is, in this researcher's opinion, oversimplifying the teaching and learning situation. The actual teaching and learning situation is much more complex because so much is happening in classroom teaching. To bring about a positive washback effect on teaching and learning of the kind intended by the HKEA, the process needs to be defined and collaboration agreed upon in the area of teacher education and materials development, as well as in the creation of supportive teaching and learning cultures in schools. Only when all these organizations (participants) work together can substantial changes in teaching and learning eventually be realized. Furthermore, the washback effect as 'process' takes time to occur and may occur in reciprocal cycles.

Discrepancy between stakeholders

One of the outcomes of this study is the identification of gaps between the three levels of the Hong Kong education situation, namely (a) the decision-making level, (b) the intervening level, and (c) the implementing level. The gaps show the discrepancies between levels, which might prevent washback from occurring. Shohamy et al (1996: 313-314) have pointed out in the two language tests they studied that,

> There is a discrepancy between the way teachers, students, and bureaucrats view the effects of the test. The gap is mostly evident in the fact that unlike teachers and students, the bureaucrats portray a much more positive picture of the testing event and express satisfaction with the way the test is being administered within the educational system. The bureaucrats seem to use the test both as a means to improve matters and as a device by which they control the system.

Furthermore, Andrews and Fullilove (1994) highlighted the discrepancy in their study with regard to the possibility of engineering precisely targeted pedagogical change by means of washback from public examinations between the policy-makers (the HKEA) and teachers. They noted especially the mismatch between the views of the HKEA Subject Working Party and those of the teachers. This gap was also identified in the present study as preventing the washback effect from being realized in actual teaching and learning.

As mentioned earlier, washback from the examinations can influence teaching to some extent, such as the implementation of activities similar to those required by the exam, but washback from examinations does not make teachers change their teaching. One reason is that the change of the HKCEE towards an integrated and task-based approach can show teachers something new, but it cannot automatically teach teachers how to teach something new. Moreover, the HKEA failed to specify areas in teaching and learning on which this new examination may have an impact, and how such an intended washback effect could be brought about in teaching, though references to washback can be frequently found in the HKEA documents (HKEA, 1993, 1994a, 1994b, 1996). It is clear that there must be collaboration with other education agencies, such as textbook writers and tertiary institutions, in order to bring about fundamental changes.

Furthermore, Andrews and Fullilove (1994) argue that the design of exam-related textbooks may be based on information from the HKEA for an innovation, but the final product might not be moulded according to the innovators' view of what is desirable in terms of teaching, but rather according to the publishers' view of what will sell. In the Hong Kong context, at least, this unfortunately tends to lead to the rapid production of materials which are very specific to the examination, and which represent a limiting of focus for teachers and students rather than a broadening of horizons.

Lessons learned from the study

This section will look at some of the weaknesses of the study as it progressed and as the findings were being examined in order to offer lessons to be learned. In the discussion, it is important to bear in mind the underlying purpose of the study. This purpose influenced the scope of the study, which may have necessarily entailed a sacrifice in depth. Secondly, the study was carried out within a constrained timeframe, which lasted from the birth of the new exam syllabus, to the end of the first year in which the examination was taken by the first cohort of F5 students. The time constraint had particular implications on the results of the teachers' survey study as the observed differences that were conducted amount to similar groups of teachers teaching the 1996 new HKCEE for the first and the second years. It was unlikely that substantial changes could be observed with that frame of work. The same could be true of the classroom observations. In this way, the limited amount of time and the available empirical research studies on washback contributed to the relative lack of sophistication of the research instruments used in this study. In the end, such a washback study should be on a longitudinal basis, and studied from multiple perspectives.

Scope of the study

Hong Kong is 'an examination-mad town' (Fullilove, 1992: 131). Public examinations play an extremely dominating role in the education system. Washback is a complex educational phenomenon involving many facets of teaching and learning. As this is the first such large-scale empirical study of washback in Hong Kong, the researcher has chosen a more panoramic view of the mechanism of washback within the Hong Kong educational context. By exploring the three levels of participants (decision-making, intervening, and implementing levels), the researcher sacrificed paying in-depth attention to each key participant, on the grounds that a study of any level of participants, even selected key participant teachers or students, would constitute a solid and focused washback study alone. Such an in-depth study would, to some extent, reveal more detailed information about the mechanism of the washback effect within that focus. In a way, a washback study would be a compromise, allowing investigation of both the big and small pictures unless a team of researchers, sometimes in different contexts, gather together to look at all facets of teaching and learning (Saville & Hawkey, 2004).

Refined instruments required

This study is one of the few washback studies that has employed both quantitative and qualitative data, especially classroom data, to study washback. Therefore, there were not many existing instruments in the area of washback, which could be drawn upon. No single uniform questionnaire has emerged as being widely used to survey either teachers or students about language testing washback. Bailey (1999) points out that it would be a valuable contribution to the available methodological tools for washback study to develop a widely usable questionnaire for teachers and for students.

The researcher tried to develop parallel surveys from the beginning, drawing upon theoretical underpinnings from classroom language teaching and learning studies and the teachers' initial qualitative input in Phase I of the study. Furthermore, due to the time constraints on the research, the categories and items of both survey instruments were relatively limited. The researcher to some extent achieved theoretical constructs among the categories of the survey instruments. Items within each category needed to form a more coherent construct of aspects of teaching and learning. This weakness prevented more advanced statistical analysis of the survey data. Statistical analysis was performed on the level of items for t-test comparison. This could be a good lesson for future researchers and serves as a reminder to devote as much time as possible on the development of the instrument. In that way, the instruments in this study could have been refined to a greater extent if more time had been allowed for further trials and testing of the items within each category.

The classroom observation scheme also had some limitations. The researcher tried to develop an appropriate instrument to capture classroom interaction, both at the macro level (large segments of the lessons) and at the micro level (to catch classroom interaction as brief as a single 'turn'). The research problem lay in the inquiry about the levels of classroom interaction on which washback could have an impact. This study used a classroom observation instrument that achieved a balanced focus for both the macro and micro levels of classroom teaching. The researcher feels that the classroom observation scheme could be honed further in order to provide a closer look at the micro level of classroom interaction.

Moreover, some technical aspects of the classroom observation scheme could have been improved. For example, the findings showed an increase in students' activities as a percentage of class time. The increased percentage of class time used by the students was not known. The video camera was set in the corner of the classroom to avoid interrupting the natural teaching and learning process, yet consequently it was only able to catch and record certain aspects of the detailed process of student activities. Those parts of the lessons showed us that students were working among themselves, such as in group discussions, over a certain period of time. The video recordings did not show exactly what students were doing. It would have enriched the findings to fix another video camera closer to one or two groups of student activities.

Implications for future research

This study investigated curriculum changes in relation to the impact of the new 1996 HKCEE (as the change agent) on the teaching and learning of English in Hong Kong secondary schools. Curriculum models encourage researchers to see both the big picture and the small picture in order to understand the reality, variation, and complexity of curriculum changes (Fullan, 1991). Both the big and small pictures were studied in the three phases of the study. Phase I focused on the big picture, investigating different parties within the Hong Kong education context. Phases II and III emphasized the small picture, investigating teachers' attitudinal and behavioural changes towards the new 1996 HKCEE. A combined inquiry drawing upon both quantitative and qualitative paradigms has achieved an overall investigation of the washback phenomenon.

One recommendation for a future washback study would be to closely consider the balance between the breadth and specificity of what is studied. This has to be the research issue that every researcher ponders before, during, and after any study. Take the present study for example: what else could have been investigated at the macro level of the big picture? One suggestion would be to carry out an investigation of the perceptions at the decision-making level for the new 1996 HKCEE, together with those perceptions at the intervening level and the school level. The differences in perceptions would, to a large extent, dictate the actual washback effect of the new examination. What else could have been studied in the small picture? One recommendation would be to investigate the effect of washback on teachers of different teaching styles. This study has shown that washback works for certain teachers but not others, or that it works on teachers at different levels. In order to understand the 'why' and 'how' of the above questions, a smaller and closer analysis could be undertaken. The researcher would like to recommend two research areas for future washback study.

An investigation of the washback effect of textbooks

The degree of superficiality of the washback effect, i.e. form vs. substance, could be studied. The intent of changing an examination is to effect real changes in the substance of students' proficiency and development (improved learning and more effective learning). Washback tends to change the form of teaching (the washback effect of the test formats).

In order to understand more about the nature of washback, a focus could have been given to investigate textbook washback in retrospection–the washback effect on teaching and learning via the textbooks (and teaching materials) used in classroom teaching. As mentioned in this study, a rapid change of teaching content into the revised textbooks is particularly evident in the Hong Kong context. Textbook washback was also evident through the surveys and classroom observations as one area of washback intensity in this study. The fact is that the teachers tended to rely solely on textbooks in Hong Kong secondary schools. Their Scheme of Work is subsequently determined by the structure of textbooks. The teachers would arrange their lessons on the basis of their Scheme of Work, which affects the sequencing of lessons. This is probably the main reason why examination changes can bring about direct changes in classroom teaching.

The HKEA encouraged textbook publishers to change both the form and substance of the textbooks. but textbook publishers were concerned with how changing the textbooks would affect their sales. This need would directly determine the kind of changes to be made in the revised materials. Furthermore, textbook publishers could not allow themselves sufficient time to make a thorough revision due to the commercial nature of textbook publishing in Hong Kong. Schools usually would look for materials that were highly related to the form change of the new examination. Textbook writers complained that if they only changed the substance, teachers would not wish to buy those books. This study[3] revealed that one of the textbook series in Hong Kong secondary schools (*Impact 5*) sold less than 50% of its former equivalent, *Impact 4,* because it failed to change its format in an obviously visible manner. The book cover did not explicitly indicate that it was for the new HKCEE.

Practice books for examinations always sell best. So publishers are always keen to produce those kinds of teaching materials. Analysing those textbooks currently used in Hong Kong secondary schools would provide valuable information on the extent of substance changes in the revised teaching materials for the new examination. Consequently, this will determine the extent of the changes teachers might make in their teaching. Perkinson (1985: 2) emphasized the controlling role of textbooks in teaching, saying that 'it was textbooks that established the content to be taught and delineated the methods used to teach them.' He pointed out that the domination of the textbook in curricular affairs has been evident for a long time, and continues to be so in current times.

Furthermore, the teaching situation in Hong Kong secondary schools is largely dictated by examination oriented teaching materials because teachers believe that they are handy to rely on. The washback effect of the new 1996

---

3. This part of the interview data was obtained from a textbook writer on 20 March 1995.

HKCEE may be, to a large extent, determined by textbook publishers' interpretation of the examination. Publishers want to sell their books. Teachers want something to rely upon in their teaching. A detailed analysis of the revised textbooks commonly used in Hong Kong secondary schools could then be another breakthrough point in studying the effect of washback. In retrospection, textbooks should have been studied in this study, yet it was not conducted due to the researcher's research intentions on teachers' perceptions and behaviours.

An investigation into the lower forms

Referring to the point raised above, changing an examination is likely to change the kind of examination practice, but not the substance of the examination practice. New changes in any examination will certainly re-focus and re-direct attention in teaching to the examination formats more than before, given the importance of examinations in the Hong Kong school system. Most of us believe that what is needed is not only examination practice such as drilling and coaching but a sound approach to developing language proficiency. This study has shown that changing the examination does not change the degree of emphasis on examinations nor does it necessarily change teachers' methods of teaching in any fundamental way, if teacher education and professional development is not involved. Changing the exam tends to change the content of teaching rather than the methods teachers use in teaching.

Furthermore, many proponents of academic achievement testing view 'coachability' not as a drawback, but rather as a virtue (see Heyneman, 1987; Wiseman, 1961). 'Better' examination formats enhance 'better' teaching methods. Most of the participants within the Hong Kong education context believe this. For example, the change of oral examination format from 'reading aloud' in the old HKCEE to 'role play and group work' in the new HKCEE changed to a certain extent the way teachers taught at the F5 level. Teachers did not teach 'reading aloud' any more. As the English subject committee of the HKEA mentioned, if teachers crammed their students for the exam (and they certainly did), and followed the new exam format, this was already a plus in teaching. If we wish to know whether cramming for this 'better' examination actually influenced teaching for the better, we need to look at lower forms in the secondary school education setting. The form studied here was F5, which was the year when students were heavily coached for the examination. If we wish to see whether there was really any genuine impact of the new HKCEE, it would be logical to look at lower forms such as F1, 2 or 3 to see whether the new ideas in teaching and learning built into the new HKCEE actually influenced teaching at those levels.

Conclusion

As pointed out by Glaser and Silver (1994: 28), 'there is good reason for the optimism that the oft-postponed wedding of assessment and instruction will occur.' If teachers can be empowered (depending on the role of the examination) to use new forms of assessment to improve their teaching, and if they, together with educational policy makers, can devise systemic approaches that integrate assessment into efforts to improve learning and instruction, perhaps the time for change in assessment practice to enhance its usefulness for instructional decision-making and the display of standards of competent performance will be at last upon us. Glaser and Silver's picture is obviously very positive given the many existing 'ifs' within any educational context. The findings from this study, illustrate the constraints and limitations of using an examination to influence teaching and learning.

Furthermore, the key assumption above is that the outcome is something that is required of all, regardless of their differing capacities and interpretations. Noble and Smith (1994b) found substantial variability in teachers' beliefs about themselves and about how students learn. Teachers also varied significantly in their classroom practices and their views of students and curriculum. The difference between the teachers illustrates variation in capacity to implement the mandated reform, which is also true in this study. To the researcher, in order to be consistent with cognitive-constructivist beliefs about learning and teaching, educational reform directed towards instructional improvement by using examinations should first acknowledge the challenges presented by such conceptual changes. Change of this type is not simply brought about by the acquisition or knowledge of new facts. Conceptual change is seldom achieved without attending to the beliefs of those who are the targets of change (teachers) and the conditions of the environments in which they function (schools). Not taking into account these beliefs and conditions would lead to a situation in which 'the more things change the more they remain the same. Change is everywhere, and progress is not' (Karr, 1849, cited in Nunan, 1996: 1).

In order to enable changes to occur, Noble and Smith (1994b) pointed out that consistent reform would have to first accept that teacher learning is a process of construction, and that teachers possess diverse interpretations and prior knowledge structures. We have to recognize the need for conceptual change and teacher learning in the context of classroom practice. Therefore, any change would need to include sufficient time and resources such as mentoring, peer coaching, intensive seminars/workshops, and the like. In this sense, the washback effect will take time to occur. Also, an education system should be established to encourage teachers to risk experimentation and failures in the short run. A socio-political context in which teachers feel safe trying new strategies needs to exist in order to enable changes to occur.

Changing teachers from a mastery model of content-deliverers to active constructors of knowledge and co-constructors of students' knowledge is not merely an incremental change; it is a fundamental shift. This means that the quality and intensity of curriculum and professional development, the resources to support the development, and the time to incorporate and refine the changes, should be made available for the shift to happen within the school setting and wider educational context.

High-stakes examinations such as the new 1996 HKCEE are not instruments that encourage teachers' inquiry into, or critical thinking about, the status quo of teaching and learning. On the contrary, they depend on coercion to create uniformity (see also McDonnell & Elmore, 1987; McDonnell et al, 1990). If the HKEA expects teachers to change themselves (teaching contents and methodology) and their students, an environment conducive to such change must be fostered. The Hong Kong educational context at the macro level is favourable according to this study. But the actual teaching context (school environment, messages from administration, expectations of other teachers, and students) also plays a key role in facilitating or detracting from the possibility of change.

In the end, the change is in the teachers' hands. As English (1992) pointed out, when the classroom door is shut and nobody else is around, the classroom teacher can then select and teach almost any curriculum he or she decides is appropriate irrespective of the various reforms, innovations, and public examinations.

Appendices

APPENDIX I
Teachers' questionnaire for the main study

Teachers' Perceptions of Public Examinations
in Hong Kong Secondary Schools

Dear Colleague,
We would like to ask you for your opinions of the ***new 1996*** Hong Kong Certificate
of Education Examination (HKCEE) in English and the necessary preparation you
intend to carry out in order to cope with the changes in the syllabus. To help us,
please fill in this questionnaire according to your own experience. ***All information
will be treated in the strictest confidence***. Thank you very much.

PART ONE   Please tick the appropriate answer.

(1) Your gender:
      ❑ F   ❑ M
(2) Your age:
      ❑ 20-30 ❑ 31-40 ❑ 41-50 ❑ above 50
(3) Your academic qualifications:
      ❑ BA   ❑ BSc   ❑ Masters   ❑ Others
(4) Your professional qualifications:
      ❑ Teacher's Certificate   ❑ P.C.Ed/Diploma in Education
      ❑ Advanced Diploma in Education   ❑ RSA   ❑ M. Ed
(5) Number of years you have been teaching:
      ❑ 1-3   ❑ 4-6   ❑ 7-9   ❑ 10 and above 10
(6) Major forms you currently teach:
      ❑ F1-F3   ❑ F4-F5   ❑ F6-F7
(7) Number of periods you teach English per week:
      ❑ 16-21 ❑ 22-27 ❑ 28-33 ❑ above 33
(8) The band of your school:
      ❑ Band 1 ❑ Band 2 ❑ Band 3 ❑ Band 4 ❑ Band 5

PART TWO   Please grade the following on a 5-point scale format where
*1= Strongly disagree, 2= Disagree, 3= Undecided, 4= Agree, 5= Strongly agree.
Put 1, 2, 3, 4 or 5 in the brackets provided.*

(1) What do you see as the major reasons for the HKEA (Hong Kong Examinations
Authority) to change the present HKCEE in English?
1= strongly disagree, 2= disagree, 3= undecided, 4= agree, 5= strongly agree

1❑ To meet the demands of tertiary education.
2❑ To prepare students for their future career.
3❑ To refine testing methods.
4❑ To narrow the gap between HKCEE and UE.
5❑ To cope with the present decline in English standards.
6❑ To widen the gap between the top and low students.
7❑ To motivate students to use integrated skills
8❑ To encourage students to play an active role in learning.

9❏ To enable students to communicate more with others.
10❏ To encourage better textbooks

(2) What are the major changes that you have perceived in the exam papers of the 1996 HKCEE in English?
1= strongly disagree, 2= disagree, 3= undecided, 4= agree, 5= strongly agree

1❏ More related to Target Orientated Curriculum principles
2❏ More integrated and task-based approaches
3❏ More practical and closer to real life
4❏ Closer to the Use of English in the oral paper
5❏ More role play and group discussion
6❏ More emphasis on oral activities
7❏ More emphasis on listening
8❏ Less emphasis on grammatical usage

(3) What kind of extra work or pressure if any do you think the 1996 HKCEE in English will put on you in your teaching?
1= strongly disagree, 2= disagree, 3= undecided, 4= agree, 5= strongly agree

1❏ Following a new syllabus
2❏ Doing more lesson preparation
3❏ Preparing more materials for students
4❏ Revising the existing materials
5❏ Employing new teaching methods
6❏ Setting up new teaching objectives
7❏ Meeting new challenges in teaching
8❏ Organising more exam practices

(4) What are the major changes you are likely to make in your teaching in the context of the 1996 new HKCEE?
1= strongly disagree, 2= disagree, 3= undecided, 4= agree, 5= strongly agree

1❏ To teach according to the new test formats
2❏ To adopt new teaching methods
3❏ To use a more communicative approach in teaching
4❏ To put more stress on role play and group discussion
5❏ To put more emphasis on the oral and listening components
6❏ To put more emphasis on the integration of skills
7❏ To employ more real life language tasks
8❏ To encourage more students' participation in class

(5) What do you find the most difficult aspects of teaching the 1996 HKCEE in English if any?
1= strongly disagree, 2= disagree, 3= undecided, 4= agree, 5= strongly agree

1❏ Students' current English level
2❏ Class size
3❏ Inadequate textbooks and other available teaching resources
4❏ Noisy learning environment
5❏ The lack of teaching and learning aids and facilities

6❑ Too heavy work load
7❑ Inadequate time for students' practice of English outside the language classroom

(6) What are the learning strategies you would recommend to your students in the context of the 1996 new HKCEE?
1= strongly disagree, 2= disagree, 3= undecided, 4= agree, 5= strongly agree

1❑ To learn to take better notes
2❑ To expose themselves to various English media
3❑ To learn to express their opinions in class
4❑ To put more emphasis on listening and speaking
5❑ To learn to initiate questions
6❑ To be more active in classroom participation
7❑ To use English more in their daily life
8❑ To change from passive learning to active learning
9❑ To communicate more in English

(7) What types of activities do you think should be involved with language learning?
1= strongly disagree, 2= disagree, 3= undecided, 4= agree, 5= strongly agree

1❑ Task-oriented activities
2❑ Language games
3❑ Role play and group discussion
4❑ Exposure to various English media
5❑ Authentic materials
6❑ Training in basic language knowledge
7❑ Extracurricular activities

(8) What do you think are the major aims for learning English in Hong Kong?
1= strongly disagree, 2= disagree, 3= undecided, 4= agree, 5= strongly agree

1❑ To pursue further studies
2❑ To pass examinations
3❑ To obtain jobs
4❑ To satisfy school requirements
5❑ To satisfy parents' requirements

(9) In what ways do you think you would like to motivate your students in learning English?
1= strongly disagree, 2= disagree, 3= undecided, 4= agree, 5= strongly agree

1❑ To do more mock exam papers
2❑ To use more authentic materials
3❑ To organise real life language activities
4❑ To do more interesting language games
5❑ To give students more encouragement to learn
6❑ To create a positive attitude toward language learning
7❑ To provide students with effective language learning strategies
8❑ To have better classroom discipline

(10) What do you think are the basic functions of mock tests in school?
1= strongly disagree, 2= disagree, 3= undecided, 4= agree, 5= strongly agree

1❑ To give feedback to teachers
2❑ To assess students' learning difficulties
3❑ To motivate students
4❑ To direct students' learning
5❑ To prepare students for public examination
6❑ To identify area of re-teaching

(11) How is your teaching assessed in your school?
1= strongly disagree, 2= disagree, 3= undecided, 4= agree, 5= strongly agree

1❑ Your own reflections on teaching
2❑ The performance of your students in tests and public exams
3❑ The overall inspection of your students' work by your school
4❑ The overall completion of the subject contents
5❑ Anonymous student evaluation of teaching
6❑ Evaluation by colleagues
7❑ Evaluation by principal or school inspectors

(12) The factors that most influence your teaching are?
1= strongly disagree, 2= disagree, 3= undecided, 4= agree, 5= strongly agree

1❑ Professional training
2❑ Academic seminars or workshops
3❑ Teaching experience and belief
4❑ Teaching syllabus
5❑ Past experience as a language learner
6❑ The need to obtain satisfaction in teaching
7❑ Textbooks
8❑ Public examinations
9❑ Learners' expectations
10❑ Peers' expectations
11❑ Principal's expectations
12❑ Social expectations

PART THREE   Please tick the right answer or provide written answers.

(1) What is your ***current*** reaction to the 1996 HKCEE in English?
1❑ sceptical about the change
2❑ neutral
3❑ welcome the change
4❑ enthusiastically endorse the change

(2) What is the medium of instruction you use when you teach English in the classroom?
1❑ English only
2❑ English supplemented with occasional Chinese explanation
3❑ Half English and half Chinese
4❑ Mainly Chinese

(3) Who generally makes the decision on the arrangement of lessons?
1❏ Principal
2❏ Panel chair
3❏ English teachers together
4❏ Yourself

(4) How do you arrange your teaching in your school?
1❏ According to the textbook arrangement
2❏ According to the school scheme of work
3❏ According to separate skills such as reading or listening
4❏ According to the contents and materials to be taught
5❏ According to language activities/tasks

(5) Who makes the major decision on the choice of textbooks?
1❏ Principal
2❏ Panel chair
3❏ English teachers together
4❏ Yourself

(6) What are the primary functions of textbooks in teaching?
1❏ To provide practical activities
2❏ To provide a structured language program to follow
3❏ To provide language models
4❏ To provide information about the language

Please grade the following on a 5-point scale *where 1= never, 2= seldom, 3= sometimes, 4= often, 5= always and put 1,2,3,4 or 5 in the brackets provided.*

(7) How often do you consider the following aspects when you prepare your lessons?
1= never, 2= seldom, 3= sometimes, 4= often, 5= always
1❏ The methods of teaching
2❏ The contents of teaching
3❏ The tasks to be performed in teaching
4❏ The skills to be taught
5❏ Any supplementary materials to be used
6❏ How to motivate students to learn
7❏ Homework to give to students

(8) How often do you do the following in class?
1= never, 2= seldom, 3= sometimes, 4= often, 5= always
1❏ Talk to the whole class
2❏ Talk to groups of students
3❏ Talk to individual students
4❏ Keep silent

(9) How often do you do the following activities in class?

1= never, 2= seldom, 3= sometimes, 4= often, 5= always

1❑ Tell the students the aims of each lesson

2❑ Demonstrate how to do particular language activities

3❑ Explain the meaning of the text

4❑ Explain specific language items such as words or sentences

5❑ Explain textbook exercises

6❑ Explain homework

7❑ Explain mock exams

8❑ Organise language games

9❑ Organise group work or discussion

10❑ Organise integrated language tasks

(10) How often do you use the following teaching and learning aids in your teaching?

1= never, 2= seldom, 3= sometimes, 4= often, 5= always

1❑ Textbooks

2❑ Supplementary materials

3❑ Television/Radio

4❑ Newspapers

5❑ Language laboratory

6❑ Pictures and/or cards

7❑ Teaching syllabus

8❑ Examination syllabus

9❑ Overall lesson plan (scheme of work)

—- End of Questionnaire —-
Thank you very much for your help

APPENDIX II
Teachers' questionnaire for the initial study

Dear Colleague,

We would like to hear about how you feel about the new Hong Kong Certificate of Education Examination (HKCEE) and the preparation you intend to carry out in order to cope with the changes in the new exam. Please tick the right answer or answer in words. All information you provide here will be treated as highly confidential. Thank you for your valuable time.

Part One Personal Data

1. Your gender and age:
❑ F ❑ M
❑ 20-30 ❑ 31-40 ❑ 41-50
2. Professional qualifications :
❑ BA ❑ BSc ❑ Masters ❑ below
3. Number of years you have taught English:
❑ 1-2 ❑ 3-4 ❑ 5-6 ❑ 7-10 ❑ above 10
4. Forms you currently teach. Tick more than one box if necessary:
❑ F1 ❑ F2 ❑ F3 ❑ F4 ❑ F5 ❑ F6 ❑ F7
5. The band of your school:
❑ Band 1 ❑ Band 2 ❑ Band 3 ❑ Band 4 ❑ Band 5
6. In what district is your school:

7. The medium of instruction your school has opted for in 1994:
❑ English ❑ Chinese ❑ Mixed
8. The typical size of your classes in terms of student numbers:
❑ 20-30 ❑ 31-40 ❑ 41-50 ❑ above 50
9. Textbooks you mainly use in teaching:

10. Teaching and learning aids and facilities you regularly use:
❑ TV ❑ Radio ❑ Language lab ❑ Computer lab
❑ Pictures /Cards ❑ Transparencies ❑ Slides
11. Number of hours you teach English per week:
❑ 4-8 ❑ 9-12 ❑ 13-16 ❑ above 16

Part Two Attitudinal Data

1. In what year will the proposed NEW HKCEE in English first be issued to F5 students?
❑ 1995   ❑ 1996

2. How many papers are there in the New HKCEE in English?
Please specify what they are.

_____

_____

3. What are the major changes in the different papers of the NEW HKCEE in English?

_____

_____

4. What do you see as the major reasons for the HKEA's decision (Hong Kong Examinations Authority) to change the present exam?

_____

_____

5. Do you think you will have to change your teaching in some way because of the change in the exam?
❑ yes   ❑ no
If yes, what are the major changes you will have to make?
If no, could you please give your major reasons?

_____

_____

6. Do you think your students will have to change their learning strategies because of the change of the exam?
❑ yes   ❑ no
If yes, what are the learning strategies which you recommend for your students?

_____

_____

If no, could you please give your major reasons?

_____

_____

7. What was your first reaction to the NEW exam?
❑ sceptical about the change   ❑ neutral
❑ welcomed the change   ❑ enthusiastically endorsed the change

8. What do you think of the NEW exam? Please list some good or weak points that you see in it.

_____

_____

9. Do you think the NEW exam will put extra pressure on you?
❑ yes   ❑ no
If yes, could you please specify what these pressures will be?

_____

_____

If no, could you please give your major reasons?

_____

_____

10. Do you think there is anything required in the NEW exam which is contradictory to your teaching philosophy? Please specify.
❑ yes ❑ no

_____

_____

11. What types of activities do you think should be involved in language learning?

_____

_____

12. Do you think the NEW exam will improve students' motivation? Please specify.
❑ yes ❑ no

_____

_____

13. Do you think the NEW exam will involve using more teaching aids and facilities?
❏ yes ❏ no

14. Have the test scores of your students ever been commented on negatively against you or your colleagues? ❏ yes ❏ no
If yes, could you please specify how?

Part Three Behavioural Data

1. How are the English lessons arranged in your school?
❏ separately as listening, reading or writing, etc.
❏ integrated skills
❏ according to your own arrangements

2. Could you please specify the percentage of time you spend on each skill?
[   ]% listening [   ]% speaking [   ]% reading [   ]% writing

3. Who generally makes the decision about lesson arrangements for English teaching in your school?
❏ principal ❏ panel chair ❏ English teachers together ❏ yourself

4. Who makes the major decision in the choice of English textbooks in your school?
❏ principal ❏ panel chair ❏ English teachers together ❏ yourself

5. Has your school changed textbooks because of the NEW exam?
❏ yes ❏ no

6. What are the factors that play a major role in your teaching? Please arrange them according to their importance by putting from 1 as the most important to 6 as the least important.
❏ public examinations
❏ learners' expectations
❏ peers' expectations
❏ principal's expectations
❏ your teaching views
❏ your teaching experience

7. Do you have regular opportunities to discuss with your colleagues or exchange opinions on language teaching?
❏ yes ❏ no

8. If you are teaching F5, are there any extra hours assigned to prepare the students for their coming certificate English exam besides normal teaching?

❑ yes ❑ no

If yes, how many extra hours are assigned to the students?

_____

_____

Thank you very much for your kind help.

APPENDIX III
Students' questionnaire for the main study

A: Chinese version 學　　生　　問　　卷

親愛的學生:

我們希望了解你們在學校的英語學習情況和你們對將要參加的英語會考的
想法。你在這里所提供的一切信息均會得到保密。多謝你爲此付出的時閒。

第一部分　　　　　請選擇恰當的答案打勾。

(1) 你的性別　1□男　2□女

(2) 你的課程從哪個年級開始用英文講授？
　　1□小1-小2　4□中1
　　2□小3-小4　5□中2
　　3□小5-小6

(3) 你的英文老師給你們上課時用哪種語言方式？
　　1□只用英文　　　　　2□大部分用英文,少時用中文解釋
　　3□一半英文一半中文　4□主要用中文

(4) 你的老師和你們提到英文會考的頻繁程度如何？
　　1□從不　2□極少　3□時常　4□經常　5□總是

(5) 爲參加明年的會考,你每周上几次學校課程外的英文輔導課？
　　1□無　2□一-二次　3□三-四次　4□五次以上

第二部分　請你按照五個等級來評估以下問題。其中(1)=從不 (2)=極少 (3)=時常
　　　　(4)=經常 (5)=總是,然后將相應的1, 2, 3, 4, 5填入空格中。

(1) 你的老師在給你上英文課時如何面對你們講話
　　(1)從不　(2)極少　(3)時常　(4)經常　(5)總是
　　1□面對全班同學講話
　　2□面對部份同學講話
　　3□面對個別同學講話
　　4□保持緘默

(2) 你的老師在給你們上英文課時做以下活動的頻繁程度如何?

　　(1)從不　　(2)極少　　(3)時常　　(4)經常　　(5)總是

　　1□ 講述每節課的目的

　　2□ 講解課文含義

　　3□ 講解語言現象,如單詞、句型

　　4□ 講解課文練習

　　5□ 講解模擬考試

　　6□ 組織語言游戲活動

　　7□ 組織小組討論

　　8□ 組織綜合語言活動

(3) 你們在英文課時從事以下活動的頻繁程度如何？

　　(1)從不　　(2)極少　　(3)時常　　(4)經常　　(5)總是

　　1□ 閱讀

　　2□ 聽力

　　3□ 寫作

　　4□ 會話

　　5□ 語法練習

　　6□ 詞匯學習

　　7□ 小組討論

　　8□ 綜合語言活動

　　9□ 做語言游戲

　　10□ 做模擬考試題

(4) 你們上課時用英文做以下話動的頻繁程度如何？

　　(1)從不　　(2)極少　　(3)時常　　(4)經常　　(5)總是

　　1□ 小組討論和兩人操練

　　2□ 討論練習答案

　　3□ 表述自己的觀點

　　4□ 在課上提出請求

　　5□ 請求老師重新講解

(5) 你在課堂外用英文做以下活動的頻繁程度如何？

　　(1)從不　　(2)極少　　(3)時常　　(4)經常　　(5)總是

　　1□ 和老師用英文講話

　　2□ 和同學用英文講話

　　3□ 和家里人用英文講話

　　4□ 和校外人員用英文講話

5 □ 看英文電視
6 □ 聽英文電台節目
7 □ 讀英文報紙或雜誌

請按五個等級來評估以下問題。其中(1)=完全不同意 (2)=不同意 (3)=無法確定 (4)=同意 (5)=完全同意, 然后將相應的1, 2, 3, 4, 5填入空格中。

(6) 你對目前你們的英文課看法如何？
 (1)完全不同意 (2)不同意 (3)無法確定 (4)同意 (5)完全同意
 1 □ 比其它課程活躍
 2 □ 充滿各種有趣的語言活動
 3 □ 許多兩人練習和小組討論
 4 □ 有同老師和同學交談的機會
 5 □ 接近日常生活

(7) 你對以下學習英文的動機看法如何？
 (1)完全不同意 (2)不同意 (3)無法確定 (4)同意 (5)完全同意
 1 □ 爲了學習語言的基本知識和形式
 2 □ 爲了找一份好的工作
 3 □ 爲了能夠上大學
 4 □ 爲了能和別人用英文交談
 5 □ 爲了能夠看懂英文電影和聽懂英文電台
 6 □ 爲了適應社會的需求
 7 □ 爲了將來有更多、更好的發展機會
 8 □ 爲了英文會考
 9 □ 爲了父母的期望

(8) 你喜歡使用的學習方法有哪些？
 (1)完全不同意 (2)不同意 (3)無法確定 (4)同意 (5)完全同意
 1 □ 閱讀英文報紙和雜誌
 2 □ 收聽英文電台節目
 3 □ 收看英文電視
 4 □ 參加英文小組活動
 5 □ 用英文交換意見
 6 □ 通過游戲學習
 7 □ 學習語法規則
 8 □ 學習詞匯
 9 □ 做練習和家庭作業

10 □ 練習記筆記
11 □ 參加課外英文活動

(9) 你是否受過考試成績的影響？
　1 □ 是。
　2 □ 否。

(10) 在以下哪些方面你受到考試成績的影響？
　　(1)完全不同意 (2)不同意 (3)無法確定 (4)同意 (5)完全同意
　1 □ 個人形象
　2 □ 學習動機
　3 □ 老師和學生之間的關係
　4 □ 個人情緒
　5 □ 將來的就業機會

(11) 以下問題的看法如何？
　　(1)完全不同意 (2)不同意 (3)無法確定 (4)同意 (5)完全同意
　1 □ 學生不喜歡考試
　2 □ 通過做模擬的考試題，學生的學習成績有所提高。
　3 □ 參加考試是一種有益的學習經歷。
　4 □ 考試迫使學生學習努力。
　5 □ 考試成績對學生的形象好坏起重大作用。
　6 □ 一個學生的考試成績反映他是否掌握了學過的知識。
　7 □ 一個學生的考試成績反映他是否能夠運用所學的知識。
　8 □ 考試成績不應做為衡量學生學習的唯一標準。
　9 □ 學生在考試時比日常學習情況下表現的更好。
　10 □ 模擬考試是重要的學習方法之一。
　11 □ 大部分學生都力爭在考試中取得盡可能好的成績。
　12 □ 考試是學生學習的主要動機之一。

問卷結束
衷心感謝你的幫助

B: English version
Students' perceptions of public examinations in Hong Kong secondary schools

Dear students:

We would like to hear how you feel about your English learning in school and also how you feel about the public examination you are going to sit soon. **All information you provide here will be treated in the strictest confidence.** Thank you for your valuable time.

PART ONE Please tick the appropriate answer.

(1) Your gender   1 ❑ Female   2 ❑ Male

(2) At what level did you begin to receive lessons in English?
        1 ❑ Primary 1-2   4 ❑ Form 1
        2 ❑ Primary 3-4   5 ❑ Form 2
        3 ❑ Primary 5-6

(3) What is the medium of instruction your teacher usually uses to teach you English?
        1 ❑ English only
        2 ❑ English supplemented with occasional Chinese explanation
        3 ❑ Half English and half Chinese
        4 ❑ Mainly Chinese

(4) How often does your teacher refer to the HKCEE in English, which you are going to take in school?
        1 ❑ never   2 ❑ seldom   3 ❑ sometimes
        4 ❑ often   5 ❑ always

(5) How many hours of private tutorials do you undertake for the preparation of the coming HKCEE in English?
        1 ❑ none   2 ❑ once or twice
        3 ❑ three to four times   4 ❑ more than five times

PART TWO Please grade the following on 5-point scale format where 1= never, 2= seldom, 3= sometimes, 4= often, 5= always and put 1,2,3,4,5 in the brackets provided.

(1) How often does your teacher do the following in your English lessons?
    1= never, 2= seldom, 3= sometimes, 4= often, 5= always

        1 ❑ Talk to the whole class.
        2 ❑ Talk to groups of students.
        3 ❑ Talk to individual students.
        4 ❑ Keep silent.

(2) How often does your teacher do the following activities in your English lessons?
1= never, 2= seldom, 3= sometimes, 4= often, 5= always

1 ❑ Tell your class the aims of each lesson
2 ❑ Explain the meaning of the text
3 ❑ Explain specific language items such as words or sentence structures
4 ❑ Explain textbook exercises
5 ❑ Explain mock exam papers
6 ❑ Organise language games
7 ❑ Organise group work or discussion
8 ❑ Organise integrated language tasks

(3) How often do you do the following activities in your English lessons?
1= never, 2= seldom, 3= sometimes, 4= often, 5= always

1 ❑ Reading
2 ❑ Listening
3 ❑ Writing
4 ❑ Speaking
5 ❑ Practising grammar items
6 ❑ Learning vocabulary
7 ❑ Carrying out group discussion
8 ❑ Carrying out language tasks
9 ❑ Doing language games
10 ❑ Doing mock exam papers

(4) How often do you do the following *in English in class*?
1= never, 2= seldom, 3= sometimes, 4= often, 5= always

1 ❑ Doing group discussion and pair work
2 ❑ Arguing for correct answers to an exercise
3 ❑ Expressing your own ideas
4 ❑ Making a request in class
5 ❑ Asking for clarifications

(5) How often do you do the following *in English outside class*?
1= never, 2= seldom, 3= sometimes, 4= often, 5= always

1 ❑ Talk to your teachers
2 ❑ Talk to your classmates
3 ❑ Talk to your family members
4 ❑ Talk to other people outside school
5 ❑ Watch television
6 ❑ Listen to radio
7 ❑ Read newspapers and magazines

Please grade the following on a 5-point scale where 1= strongly disagree, 2= disagree, 3= undecided, 4= agree, 5= strongly agree and put 1,2,3,4 or 5 in the brackets provided.

(6) How do you find your English lessons compared with other school subjects?
1= strongly disagree 2= disagree 3= undecided 4= agree 5= strongly agree

      1 ❑ Much more lively than other subjects
      2 ❑ Full of interesting language activities
      3 ❑ Lots of pair work and group discussion
      4 ❑ More opportunities to communicate with teachers and classmates
      5 ❑ Close to real life activities

(7) How do you agree with the following reasons for learning English?
1= strongly disagree 2= disagree 3= undecided 4= agree 5= strongly agree

      1 ❑ To acquire basic knowledge and forms of English
      2 ❑ To get a better job
      3 ❑ To be able to go into tertiary education
      4 ❑ To be able to communicate with people
      5 ❑ To be able to watch English movies and listen to English programs
      6 ❑ To meet the requirements of the society
      7 ❑ To have more and better opportunities in the future
      8 ❑ To prepare for HKCEE
      9 ❑ To fulfil parents' expectations

(8) What are your preferred strategies for learning a language?
1= strongly disagree 2= disagree 3= undecided 4= agree 5= strongly agree

      1 ❑ Reading newspapers and magazines in English
      2 ❑ Listening to radio programs in English
      3 ❑ Watching TV or videos in English
      4 ❑ Taking part in group activities in class
      5 ❑ Expressing opinions in class
      6 ❑ Learning by games
      7 ❑ Learning grammar rules
      8 ❑ Learning vocabulary
      9 ❑ Doing exercises and home work
      10 ❑ Taking notes
      11 ❑ Participating in extracurricular activities

(9) Have you ever been affected by your exam scores?
      1 ❑ yes.
      2 ❑ no.

(10) In what aspects have you been affected by exam scores?
1= strongly disagree 2= disagree 3= undecided 4= agree 5= strongly agree

      1 ❑ self-image
      2 ❑ motivation to learn
      3 ❑ teacher and student relationship
      4 ❑ anxiety and emotional tension
      5 ❑ future job opportunity

(11) How do you agree with the following opinions?
1= strongly disagree 2= disagree 3= undecided 4= agree 5= strongly agree

    1 ❑ Students dislike examinations.
    2 ❑ Students' learning is improved by practising mock exam.
    3 ❑ Taking examinations is a valuable learning experience.
    4 ❑ Examinations force students to study harder.
    5 ❑ Examinations have an important effect on student self-image.
    6 ❑ A student's score on an examination is a good indication of how well she
       or he has learned the material.
    7 ❑ A student's performance on an examination is a good indication of how
       well she or he will be able to apply what has been learned.
    8 ❑ Examination should NOT be used as a sole determiner of student
       grades.
    9 ❑ Students perform better in an exam situation than in normal teaching
       situation.
  10 ❑ Mock examinations are important ways to learn.
  11 ❑ All students work hard to achieve their best in public examinations.
  12 ❑ Examination is one of the motivations for students' learning.

End of the Questionnaire
Thank you very much for your help.

APPENDIX IV
The Hong Kong Certificate of Education Examination 1996
English Language (Syllabus B)

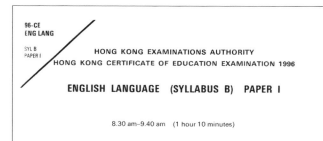

HONG KONG EXAMINATIONS AUTHORITY

HONG KONG CERTIFICATE OF EDUCATION EXAMINATION 1996

ENGLISH LANGUAGE (SYLLABUS B) PAPER I

8.30 am–9.40 am (1 hour 10 minutes)

*Write about 300 words on **ONE** of the topics.*

Write your composition in the answer book provided.

You are reminded of the importance of clear handwriting and the need for planning and proof-reading.

Do not use your real name in answering any of the questions. If names are provided in the question, you must use those names. If no name is provided and you still wish to use a name to identify yourself, then use 'Chris Wong'. You will lose marks if you do not follow these instructions.

Do not turn over this page until you are told to do so.

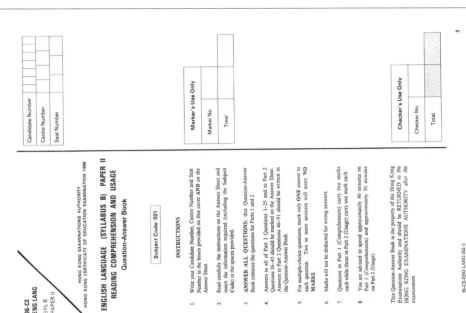

96-CE
ENG LANG
SYL B
PAPER II

HONG KONG EXAMINATIONS AUTHORITY
HONG KONG CERTIFICATE OF EDUCATION EXAMINATION 1996

ENGLISH LANGUAGE (SYLLABUS B) PAPER II
READING COMPREHENSION AND USAGE
Question-Answer Book

Subject Code: 021

INSTRUCTIONS

1. Write your Candidate Number, Centre Number and Seat Number in the boxes provided on this cover **AND** on the Answer Sheet.

2. Read carefully the instructions on the Answer Sheet and insert the information required (including the Subject Code) in the spaces provided.

3. **ANSWER ALL QUESTIONS:** this Question-Answer Book contains the questions for Parts 1 and 2.

4. Answers to all of Part 1 Questions 1–25 and to Part 2 Questions 26–45 should be marked on the Answer Sheet. Answers to Part 2 Questions 46–91 should be written in the Question-Answer Book.

5. For multiple-choice questions, mark only **ONE** answer to each question. Two or more answers will score **NO MARKS**.

6. Marks will not be deducted for wrong answers.

7. Questions in Part 1 (Comprehension) carry two marks each while those in Part 2 (Usage) carry one mark each.

8. You are advised to spend approximately 40 minutes on Part 1 (Comprehension) and approximately 50 minutes on Part 2 (Usage).

This Question-Answer Book is the property of the Hong Kong Examinations Authority and should be RETURNED to the HONG KONG EXAMINATIONS AUTHORITY after the examination.

Candidate Number
Centre Number
Seat Number

Marker's Use Only
Marker No.
Total

Checker's Use Only
Checker No.
Total

96-CE-ENG LANG BII-1

3

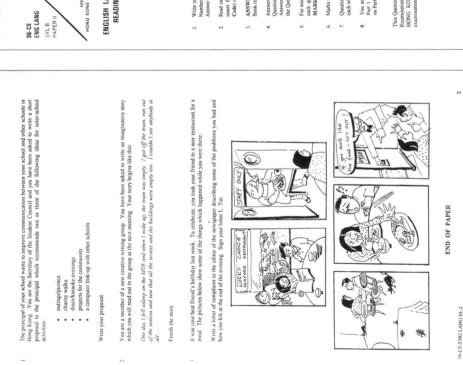

1. The principal of your school wants to improve communication between your school and other schools in Hong Kong. You are the Secretary of the Student Council and you have been asked to write a short proposal to the principal which recommends two or three of the following ideas for inter-school activities:

    • outings/picnics
    • charity walks
    • disco/karaoke evenings
    • projects for the community
    • a computer link-up with other schools

    Write your proposal.

2. You are a member of a new creative writing group. You have been asked to write an imaginative story which you will read out to the group at the next meeting. Your story begins like this:

    One day I fell asleep on the MTR and when I woke up, the train was empty. I got off the train, ran out of the station and saw that all the streets and the buildings were empty too. I couldn't see anybody at all...

    Finish the story.

3. It was your best friend's birthday last week. To celebrate, you took your friend to a new restaurant for a meal. The pictures below show some of the things which happened while you were there.

    Write a letter of complaint to the editor of the newspaper describing some of the problems you had and how you felt at the end of the evening. Sign your letter L. Tse.

END OF PAPER

96-CE-ENG LANG BII-2

2

PART 1   COMPREHENSION   (2 marks each)

Passage A   *Read the following article and then answer questions 1 – 12.*   (24 marks)

Chemicals are Killing the 'Land of Fish and Rice'

The farmers of Tai Lake have been feeding the people of China for centuries. Located where the Yangtze River crosses the ancient Grand Canal, this part of Jiangsu Province was, for a long time, one of the most
5 beautiful rice-growing regions on earth. Known as the 'Land of Fish and Rice', it is still a rice bowl for much of the country, but with its ancient ecosystem rapidly disappearing, it could be barren in 50 years.

The key to Tai Lake's success as a rice-
10 producing area was labour-intensive organic agriculture. The farms were man-made like those that Dutch engineers reclaimed from the North Sea in Europe, but as ecologically balanced as the Amazon rain forest. Sadly though, the secrets of Tai Lake are being lost. Today's
15 farmers nourish the fields of their ancestors not with traditional mulch (rotten plants and vegetation) and canal mud, but with bags of chemical fertiliser. The old ways, farmers say, waste time.

Convenient as the new methods may be, they
20 have put the entire region in peril. Although rice yields have jumped to 40 percent since large-scale fertiliser use began in 1982, the nitrogen content of the region's water has increased dramatically by 500 percent over the same period. There's been a radical transformation from total
25 organic management to total chemical management,' says Erle Ellis, an American agro-ecologist who has been doing research in the region since 1993. 'Excessive fertiliser use, he says, has polluted groundwater, threatens fish stocks and could turn the soft soil into a hard clay-
30 like crust which would be difficult to cultivate.

Tai Lake's soil drew its fertility from *oufei*, a mixture of pig manure, crop residues, canal mud and milk vetch – a kind of plant grown for fertiliser. For centuries this mixture was prepared after each harvest, then stored
35 in open pits to be applied at the next planting. For fast-acting plant food, farmers used oil-seed cakes, soybean waste or ash. F.H. King, an early advocate of organic farming from the U.S. Department of Agriculture, toured the region in 1908 and commented, 'Whatever cannot be
40 eaten or worn is used for fuel. The wastes of the body, of fuel and of fabric serve as manure for the soil or as feed for the crop. The experience so amazed King that he urged his countrymen to follow the Tai Lake way to prevent, or at least slow down, the soil erosion in
45 America's farming heartland.

However, just the opposite has happened. Like their American counterparts, Tai Lake farmers now buy fertiliser from a supplier in the village. Oil-seed cakes are fed to pigs, canals are blocked with unused mud and *oufei*

50 pits have disappeared. Aerial photos taken in the 1930s reveal milk vetch was planted on about 20 percent of all farmland. 'Now,' says Ellis, 'it's basically a weed.'

The decline of organic agriculture is the result of Beijing's grain policy. After abolishing Chairman Mao's
55 communes in the late 1970s, state planners decided that 'science' was the way to improve on rice yields. That meant subsidised fertiliser had to be provided. Suddenly chemical fertiliser, a former luxury, was supplied virtually free to countless family farmers on millions of tiny plots.
60 But it has since proved difficult for those trained in little but Chairman Mao's 'Thought to be scientific. To increase yields, most farmers apply fertiliser for too liberally, unaware that much of it ends up in their drinking water and could cause birth defects.

65 Another cause of Tai Lake's vanishing traditions is China's economic miracle. Industrialisation has transformed the east coast. Today, most farmers either have full-time factory jobs in their home village or migrate to cities between harvests to find other work. As
70 a result, farming is now only a minor task – one that is easier to manage with chemicals. At a psychological level, China's new cash economy has given farmers a short-term view of the future. Farmers are at the bottom of the social ladder. Most dream that they or their
75 children will some day quit the land. So more and more of them are out to make a quick profit by using chemicals, even those that, in the long run, could make the land infertile.

Ironically, Tai Lake, even in its present poor
80 condition, is seen as a model for the rest of China. The experts, however, warn of ecological collapse unless the government starts to control chemical farming. According to one geographer, this kind of environmental damage is happening everywhere, but none of the major
85 agricultural countries is risking more than China.

Even proponents of the government's fertiliser policy admit that unhealthy quantities are being dumped on the fields. In developed countries, fertilisation rates are based on frequent analysis of soil samples. In China,
90 however, the large number of tiny plots makes it impossible to check them all, so measuring the quantity of fertiliser being used remains guesswork. One solution is to combine China's tiny plots of cropland into large-scale commercial farms. That has begun in the Tai Lake
95 region, but there is no guarantee that even good chemical management can do better than ancient farming techniques.

(Adapted from an article by George Wehrfritz in *Newsweek*, 15th May, 1995.)

The writer has chosen to write about Tai Lake because ......
A   very special rice is grown there.
B   the future of the land is at risk.
C   it is of historical importance.
D   the lake is rapidly disappearing.

In the past, Tai Lake was successful because ......
A   it was a rain forest.
B   the farms were built by Dutch engineers.
C   the farmers kept their farming methods a secret.
D   the farmers used suitable farming methods.

In line 20, 'in peril' means ......
A   in debt.
B   in danger.
C   in advance.
D   in defence.

According to paragraph 3, the increase in rice yields is due to ......
A   the groundwater and the soft soil.
B   the use of chemicals on the land.
C   the help of agro-ecologists.
D   the better managers on the farms.

Oufei is something that the farmers ......
A   found in the soil.
B   grew to eat.
C   fed to the animals.
D   made to put on the land.

F H King thought that the Tai Lake method of farming was ...... the American method.
A   better than
B   similar to
C   not as good as
D   more old-fashioned than

From what is mentioned in paragraph 5, the writer seems to be ...... what has happened around Tai Lake
A   disappointed by
B   indifferent to
C   frightened by
D   excited about

---

8   The offer of subsidised fertiliser probably made the farmers ......
A   disappointed.
B   angry.
C   surprised.
D   worried.

9   According to paragraph 6, the farmers ......
A   put the fertiliser in the wrong places.
B   use the fertiliser scientifically.
C   use too much fertiliser.
D   are trained to use the fertiliser.

10   According to paragraph 7, the farmers use chemicals because they ......
A   have less time to spend on farming.
B   want an industrial method of farming.
C   do not have as many farms as before.
D   are more hardworking than they used to be.

11   China does not use the same methods of measuring fertilisation rates as developed countries because ......
A   the right equipment is not available.
B   the methods used are too expensive.
C   Chinese farmers use a different kind of fertiliser.
D   there are as many small farms.

12   According to the last paragraph, the writer ...... that good chemical management will do better.
A   claims
B   hopes
C   fears
D   doubts

Passage B   Read the following article and then answer questions 13 – 25.   *(26 marks)*

ASTHMA

According to the International Asthma Campaign, asthma is a chronic condition which, although treatable, is becoming more and more common. In the past 20 years, the number of asthma sufferers around the world has actually doubled, and Hong Kong is no exception. Figures for the territory show that hospital admissions for asthma and related diseases increased from 8,119 in 1991–2 to almost 10,000 in 1993–4. It is currently estimated that five percent of the territory's adults and as many as eleven percent of young people between the ages of 10 and 20 are sufferers. Asthma, bronchitis and emphysema are listed as the ninth major killer in Hong Kong.

However, asthma is not a new disease. In fact it seems to be as old as civilisation. The Greeks first used the word to describe an attack of breathlessness. The Chinese knew about it 3,000 years ago. Indian writings of 450 AD recommended treating it with herbs, acupuncture and yoga. A Jewish physician wrote a book about it in 1190 AD, and recommended a dry climate, an even temper and hot chicken soup. Today, people commonly breathe in steroids to prevent attacks.

As the number of sufferers increases, so too does the list of things known to trigger attacks. They can be brought on by throat or chest infections, exercise, cold weather, cigarette smoke, stress or allergens – things that cause unusual reactions in certain people. In Britain, about 1,000 adults develop asthma every year because of something they have been exposed to at work. And each year, somewhere between 1,500 and 2,000 people die from it.

A new study has been undertaken in Hong Kong by a team of researchers at the Chinese University to compare how common asthma and allergic diseases are among secondary school students aged between 13 and 17 in three Southeast Asian populations. These are Hong Kong, Kota Kinabalu in Malaysia and San Bu in southern China. While rates of asthma in Hong Kong children may be lower than those in countries such as Australia, they are nevertheless much higher than those of neighbouring countries. The study reveals that Hong Kong has more sufferers than either of the other populations, with San Bu having the least sufferers of all. Hong Kong actually has over five times more sufferers than this town in China.

Dr Roland Leung, who led the study, was very cautious about linking the increase in the number of asthma sufferers in Hong Kong to pollution. He said, 'Many countries in Asia are generally more polluted yet have lower numbers of asthma sufferers. Air pollution can cause chest coughs, but it is not the main reason for the large number of asthma cases in Hong Kong.'

Dr Leung went on to suggest that instead of looking at the outside environment for something to put the blame on, the real answer to the problem may actually be found in our own homes. After all, as he argues, people spend more time in their homes than on the streets of Hong Kong. Therefore, it is possible that rather than pollution being the culprit, the allergens people are exposed to at home are responsible for the increase in the number of sufferers. The ways in which flats and houses are now built is an important factor. The modern home tends to be either air-conditioned or centrally heated, the windows are kept closed so air movement is effectively stopped. Anything that is being generated within that environment is likely to accumulate rather than be removed. As a result, it is highly likely that the number of allergens people are exposed to has increased.

It has been known for a long time that one important cause of an attack is domestic dust. Doctors have discovered that one of the allergens contained in it are house dust mites, which are tiny, sightless, eight-legged animals up to 0.31mm long. They live in bedding, carpets and soft furnishings. One count through 25 grams of mattress dust has produced 40,000 of them. Many homes in Hong Kong are infested with house dust mites thanks to the humid climate, which provides the perfect breeding ground for them. People who do have an allergic reaction to dust are advised to remove soft toys, carpets and soft furnishings from the bedroom and to wash their bedding in hot water. This will certainly help to reduce the number of house dust mites in their homes.

Unfortunately, however, even if it were possible to get rid of all the house dust mites, asthma sufferers would still exist. The list of other causes is long and varied. For example, it is believed that certain dietary habits can cause asthma. Dr Leung said that the diet enjoyed by today's young people in Hong Kong could be behind the rising figures. The modern fast food diet differs greatly from the more natural diet enjoyed by earlier generations. In China, where the study showed the percentage of sufferers was very low, people's diet still relies heavily on fruit and vegetables. Dr Leung also said that fish seemed to offer some protection against the disease.

As the number of asthma sufferers continues to grow, so too does the number of studies into the causes of this debilitating illness. One conclusion which all these studies seem to come to is that, in a world of haves and have-nots, asthma looks increasingly like a disease of the rich rather than of the poor.

(Freely adapted from an article by Mariana Wan in the *South China Morning Post*, 17th May, 1995, and an article by Tim Radford in the *Eastern Express*, 11th May, 1995.)

According to paragraph 1, compared with 20 years ago, there are ...... asthma sufferers in Hong Kong today.

A. the same number of
B. half as many
C. twice as many
D. slightly more

The first paragraph aims to ...... the reader.

A. amuse
B. reassure
C. inspire
D. alarm

The second paragraph gives information about ......

A. asthma sufferers in different countries.
B. how asthma has changed.
C. different ways of treating asthma.
D. asthma and other illnesses.

Using information from paragraph 2, decide which of the following does not help asthma sufferers.

A. a dry climate
B. acupuncture
C. breathlessness
D. herbs

In line 24, 'They' refers to ......

A. attacks.
B. reactions.
C. sufferers.
D. infections.

In line 40, 'those' refers to ......

A. rats.
B. countries.
C. populations.
D. sufferers.

Using information from paragraph 4, if you suffered from asthma, which would be the best place for you to live?

A. Hong Kong
B. Malaysia
C. San Bu
D. Australia

20. According to paragraph 6, which of the following groups of people is most likely to suffer from asthma?

People who ......

A. work on the streets.
B. use air-conditioning.
C. live in polluted areas.
D. build modern houses.

21. In line 59, 'culprit' could best be replaced with ......

A. need.
B. result.
C. allergen.
D. cause.

22. According to paragraph 7, some homes in Hong Kong have lots of house dust mites because of ......

A. children's soft toys.
B. the high humidity.
C. the way the bedding is washed.
D. the soft furnishings.

23. According to paragraph 8, it is possible that there are fewer cases of asthma in China because ......

A. there are fewer dust mites.
B. the people eat healthy food.
C. there are fewer soft toys.
D. the earlier generations did not suffer from it.

24. From your reading of the article, which of the following is the allergen mainly responsible for causing asthma?

A. atmospheric pollution
B. furnishings and carpets
C. steroids
D. house dust mites

25. Another suitable title for this article would be ......

A. *Asthma: its many causes.*
B. *Pollution causes asthma.*
C. *How to treat asthma.*
D. *The History of asthma.*

PART 2   USAGE   (1 mark each)

Decide which of the choices on page 6 would best complete the letter if inserted in the blanks.   (20 marks)

LETTERS TO MABEL

This week's topic – Hong Kong restaurants

Dear Mabel,

To celebrate the end of our HKCE exams, my friends and I decided to go to a new restaurant. Although the food was very good, our evening was spoilt by the huge bill. How can a restaurant charge $4,000 for dinner for eight people?

Alan Lee
Ho Tak Yuen Secondary School

Mabel replies

Dear Alan,

I am sorry to hear that your end of end of exam celebration was not the happy occasion it should have been __(26)__. I am afraid that you cannot go into a restaurant and __(27)__ to pay just for the food which you eat. You need to remember that there are other costs __(28)__ those for food, such as staff salaries, rent, and gas and electricity bills. __(29)__, a restaurant, __(30)__ any other business, has to make a profit.

Many restaurant managers will tell you that the ideal Hong Kong restaurant budget should probably look something like this: food takes up 28%, rent 25%, a __(31)__ 22% goes on staff and 10% on utilities. Some managers may spend even less __(32)__ food, but this does not __(33)__ that you are being cheated. They could be buying very carefully or in large volumes and wasting very __(34)__. If the restaurant is full most of the time, the profit margin should be around 15%.

To get good __(35)__ for your money, I would advise you to avoid the items on the menu which some managers call the 'high power, high profit' items. French fries, __(36)__, are extremely cheap to produce. __(37)__ people will pay as much as $30 dollars for a plate of them. Similarly, vegetarians tend to pay more for less. Vegetarian food costs very little to produce, but many restaurants __(38)__ advantage of the fact that real vegetarians __(39)__ to pay a lot of money for a meat-free meal.

The high rents in Hong Kong are __(40)__ another reason why eating out can be so expensive. Restaurant owners in Hong Kong actually pay three times more than someone __(41)__ for a similar location in a city such as New York or London. Furthermore, since the 1970s, the Government __(42)__ that at least a quarter of a restaurant's space __(43)__ be given to the kitchen. Consequently, you also end up paying for the tables you sit at, the chairs you sit on, and a part of the kitchen

I hope that this has __(44)__ your question. There are a lot of restaurants around Hong Kong which are not too expensive. If you and your friends would like to __(45)__ out where they are, I suggest you buy the book *Eating Well and Cheaply in Hong Kong*, which is available in most good bookshops.

Mabel

8

---

26. A. Moreover
     B. Besides
     C. However
     D. Consequently

27. A. believe
     B. expect
     C. refuse
     D. think

28. A. except
     B. for
     C. besides
     D. of

29. A. Although
     B. As a result
     C. Furthermore
     D. Despite

30. A. so
     B. similar
     C. like
     D. same

31. A. more
     B. higher
     C. further
     D. bigger

32. A. on
     B. to
     C. in
     D. at

33. A. say
     B. mean
     C. tell
     D. claim

34. A. small
     B. less
     C. few
     D. little

35. A. value
     B. price
     C. cost
     D. amount

36. A. in addition
     B. for example
     C. such as
     D. by comparison

37. A. then
     B. so
     C. if
     D. but

38. A. take
     B. make
     C. get
     D. bring

* 39. A. prepared
       B. are preparing
       C. are prepared
       D. have prepared

40. A. fortunately
     B. obviously
     C. luckily
     D. accurately

* 41. A. was
       B. did
       C. ought
       D. would

42. A. is demanding
     B. has demanded
     C. has been demanded
     D. demands

43. A. must
     B. may
     C. can
     D. might

44. A. answered
     B. replied
     C. responded
     D. solved

45. A. look
     B. discover
     C. search
     D. find

* These items were deleted in the live paper as they were found to be unsuitable.

9

279

Fill in each blank in the passage with ONE word only which best completes the meaning. Write your answers in the spaces provided. The first two have been done for you as examples.
(20 marks)

The International Centre

What is it?

Up __(a)__ now, there have been very few places in Hong Kong __(b)__ young people can go in their __(46)__ time without having to spend lots of money. The International Centre, which has recently opened in Tsim Sha Tsui, is a brand new centre for young people. It aims to provide people __(47)__ a relaxing, fun, safe environment where they __(48)__ go after school and at the weekends.

What is there at the centre?

There is a wide __(49)__ of things for people to choose from at the centre. We try hard to make __(50)__ that there is something that will interest everyone.

The Cafe

Come to the cafe where you can relax with friends. On Saturday nights we usually have a live band playing and __(51)__ the week we show people's favourite films.

The Sports Centre

__(52)__ the more active members, we have a swimming pool, squash and tennis courts, and a small gymnasium.

Activities and Classes

We organise lots of different __(53)__ of activities such as English lessons and fashion-design classes. What we offer depends on what members want. If you would like __(54)__ particular class to be run, we will try to arrange it.

Trips

During the school holidays and also at the weekends, we arrange trips. Once again, it is __(55)__ to the members to decide what kind of trip they would like. Things that have been organised so __(56)__ include a camping and water-skiing weekend up in Sai Kung, a 'Clean the Beach' day on Lantau to __(57)__ money for charity, and a weekend in Guangzhou.

a. *until*
b. *where*
46.
47.
48.
49.
50.
51.
52.
53.
54.
55.
56.
57.

10

Who can join?

Anyone between the ages of 12 and 18 can become a member. We welcome people of all nationalities. If you join, you will have the chance to make __(58)__ with people from all over the __(59)__ and get involved in lots of exciting activities.

How much does it cost?

In order to join the centre, you need to pay an annual membership __(60)__ of $300. Unfortunately, we will have to charge for some of the activities, __(61)__ we will do our __(62)__ to keep things as cheap as possible.

Where is it?

The centre is conveniently __(63)__ in the old police station on Hankow Road, Tsim Sha Tsui.

For further __(64)__ , just come round to the centre or call us __(65)__ 2337 4562.

58.
59.
60.
61.
62.
63.
64.
65.

Marks

11

280

Right page (13)

You are the editor of your school magazine. The following article needs to be corrected as there are a number of mistakes in it. No line has more than one mistake and some lines are correct. Do not make unnecessary changes or changes to punctuation. If you think there is no mistake in a line, put a (✓) at the end of the line in the right-hand margin of the article (example c).

Corrections must be done as follows:

Wrong word: underline the wrong word and write the correct word above it (example a).

Missing word: mark the position of the missing word with a ' ∧ ' and write the missing word above it (example d).

Extra word: delete the extra word with a ' ✗ ' (example b).

The first four lines have been done for you as examples.

(13 marks)

CHIC WINNERS DRESS FOR LESS

	Marker's Use Only
Most young people these days are ~~interesting~~ *interested* in fashion and care	a.
about how they ✗look. This is not very surprising when you consider	b.
the importance society places on personal appearance. Magazines are ✓	c.
full ∧*of* movie stars and pop singers in 'designer' clothes. On TV, fashion	d.
programmes are becoming more more popular. Many young people.	79.
however, feel that cannot afford to be fashionable.	80.
To prove it that money is not as important as people	81.
think it is, the Joint School Fashion Appreciation Competition is	82.
organised in every year in Hong Kong. Teams entering the competition	83.
must dress one of their team members in fashionably clothes for	84.
under $300. This year's competition attracted over than fifty teams	85.
from all over Hong Kong. Fifteen of the teams were selected	86.
for the finals, where were held at the Plaza Hotel last week.	87.
The eight judges all agreed that it been difficult to	88.
choose a winner and said that the students had shown	89.
that they was not necessary to have a wardrobe full of	90.
expensive clothes in order to be look good.	91.

(Freely adapted from an article by Mimi Chau in the *Young Post*, 3rd April, 1995.)

96-CE-ENG BII-11

END OF PAPER

TOTAL MARKS:

Marks:

13

Left page (12)

Choose one of the half-sentences from the list below (A–N) to complete each blank in the passage. Write the letters in the spaces provided. You can use each letter ONCE only. One has been done for you as an example.

(13 marks)

Lessons in what to learn

Parents in the 1990s are always looking out for activities which will encourage their children's development. But which one should they choose? Ballet? Football? Sewing? Many activities are good for developing skills, but what (66) . Dr Edward Schor, an expert in child-care, says that it is important for parents to see what kinds of things interest their children so that they provide them with activities (67) . If the children do not like it, (68) .

66. ___
67. ___   a. [F]
68. ___

In addition to the children's interests, the choice of activities should be guided by their physical and mental abilities. It is therefore important to consider a child's age and (69) . Parents can then look for activities that (70) . For example, by just playing together, children between the ages of two and five can learn social skills such as (71) . If parents would like to introduce their children to something more structured, experts suggest activities (72) . Painting, singing or dancing classes, for example, would be ideal.

69. ___
70. ___
71. ___
72. ___

However, games with rules are not suitable for children under the age of six (73) . When they are old enough though, team sports such as basketball and football are a good way of (74) . Skills like self-discipline and self-reliance can be learnt through (75) . For those who are not very sporty, (76) . such as piano-playing and stamp-collecting, which can develop the same kind of skills.

73. ___
74. ___
75. ___
76. ___

Regardless of which activities parents choose, the key point to remember is that the activity should (77) . As one family therapist says, 'Focusing on these activities to learn the skills is one thing, but parents should not forget that childhood (78) .

77. ___
78. ___

A   should also be a time for their children to have fun
B   the experience will have a negative effect on their development
C   is good for one child may not be good for another
D   there is a wide variety of other activities to choose from
E   will help develop the appropriate skills and characteristics
F   their parents think it will be good for them
G   not be seen as a test which children must pass
H   since the concept of rules can be very difficult to understand
I   which will help rather than hinder their development
J   how to co-operate and get along with others
K   the development that is associated with that period
L   which do not involve right or wrong answers
M   individualised sports or games like kung fu or gymnastics
N   learning about competition and co-operation

(Freely adapted from an article by Darry Owens in the *South China Morning Post*, 25th April, 1995.)

Marks: ___

96-CE-ENG BII-10

12

1996 CE English Language (Syllabus B) Paper II

Key

PART 1

1. B	6. A	11. D	16. C	21. D
2. D	7. A	12. D	17. A	22. B
3. B	8. C	13. C	18. A	23. B
4. B	9. C	14. D	19. C	24. D
5. D	10. A	15. C	20. B	25. A

PART 2

26. C	31. C	36. B	*41. D
27. B	32. A	37. D	42. B
28. C	33. B	38. A	43. A
29. C	34. D	*39. C	44. A
30. C	35. A	40. B	45. D

46. free / leisure / spare
47. with
48. can / could
49. range / variety
50. sure / certain
51. during / throughout
52. For
53. kinds / sorts / types
54. a / one / any
55. up / left
56. far
57. raise / collect
58. friends
59. world / place
60. fee
61. but / though / although
62. best
63. located / situated
64. details / information
65. at / on

* These two items were deleted in the live paper as they were found to be unsuitable.

14

66. C	71. J	76. D
67. I	72. L	77. G
68. B	73. H	78. A
69. K	74. N	
70. E	75. M	

79. more ∧ more (and) / much more (more)
80. they that ∧ cannot / they that
81. ✗
82. ✓
83. ✗ fashionable → fashionably
84.
85. then → more over
86. ✓
87. which → where
88. was → been / had / it ∧ been
89. ✓
90. it → they
91. ✗

NOTE: For the open cloze (items 46–65) and the proofreading exercise (items 79–91), there were a number of alternate correct answers. Only the more common ones are included in this key.

15

282

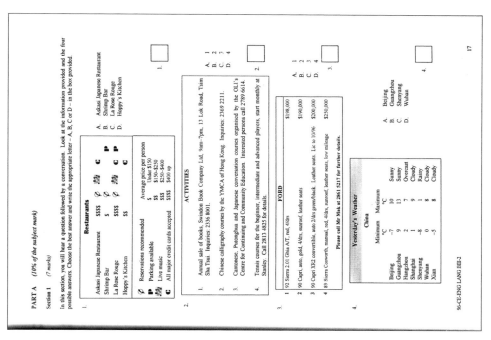

PART A *(10% of the subject mark)*

Section 1 *(7 marks)*

In this section, you will hear a question followed by a conversation. Look at the information provided and the four possible answers. Choose the best answer and write the appropriate letter – A, B, C or D – in the box provided.

1.

Restaurants

Askasi Japanese Restaurant	$$$$
Shrimp Bar	$
La Rose Rouge	$$$$
Hoppy's Kitchen	$$

Average price per person
$ Under $150
$$ $150–$250
$$$ $250–$400
$$$$ $400 up

Reservations recommended
Parking available
Live music
All major credit cards accepted

1. A. Askasi Japanese Restaurant
   B. Shrimp Bar
   C. La Rose Rouge
   D. Hoppy's Kitchen

ACTIVITIES

1. Annual sale of books, Swindon Book Company Ltd, 9am–7pm, 13 Lok Road, Tsim Sha Tsui. Inquiries: 2336 8001.
2. Chinese calligraphy courses by the YMCA of Hong Kong. Inquiries: 2369 2211.
3. Cantonese, Putonghua and Japanese conversation courses organised by the OLI's Centre for Continuing and Community Education. Interested persons call 2789 6614.
4. Tennis courses for the beginner, intermediate and advanced players, start monthly at Stanley. Call 2813 4825 for details.

2. A. 1 B. 2 C. 3 D. 4

FORD

1	92 Sierra 2.0i Ghia A/T, red, 4/drs	$198,000
2	90 Capri, auto, gold, 4/drs, sunroof, leather seats	$190,000
3	90 Capri XR2 convertible, auto 2/drs green/black, Leather seats. Lic to 10/96	$200,000
4	89 Sierra Cosworth, manual, red, 4/drs, sunroof, leather seats, low mileage	$250,000

Please call Mr Mak at 2861 5217 for further details.

3. A. 1 B. 2 C. 3 D. 4

Yesterday's Weather

China

	Minimum °C	Maximum °C	
Beijing	–7	10	Sunny
Guangzhou	9	13	Sunny
Hangzhou	2	7	Overcast
Shanghai	1	9	Cloudy
Shenyang	–8	1	Rainy
Wuhan	0	8	Cloudy
Xian	–5	8	Cloudy

4. A. Beijing B. Guangzhou C. Shenyang D. Wuhan

96-CE-ENG LANG BIII-2

17

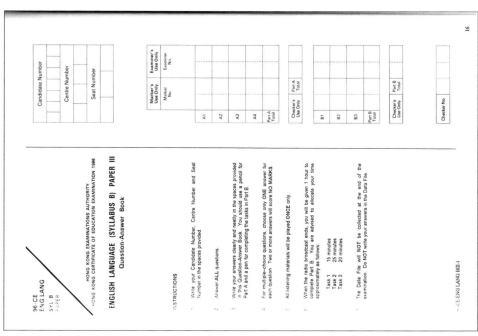

96-CE
ENG LANG
SYL B
PAPER

Candidate Number

Centre Number

Seat Number

HONG KONG EXAMINATIONS AUTHORITY
HONG KONG CERTIFICATE OF EDUCATION EXAMINATION 1996

ENGLISH LANGUAGE (SYLLABUS B) PAPER III
Question-Answer Book

Marker's Use Only	Examiner's Use Only
Marker No.	Examiner No.
A1	
A2	
A3	
A4	
Part A Total	

Checker's Use Only	Part A Total
B1	
B2	
B3	
Part B Total	

Checker's Use Only	Part B Total
Checker No	

INSTRUCTIONS

1. Write your Candidate Number, Centre Number and Seat Number in the spaces provided.

2. Answer ALL questions.

3. Write your answers clearly and neatly in the spaces provided in this Question-Answer Book. You should use a pencil for Part A and a pen for completing the tasks in Part B.

4. For multiple-choice questions, choose only ONE answer for each question. Two or more answers will score NO MARKS.

5. All listening materials will be played ONCE only.

6. When the radio broadcast ends, you will be given 1 hour to complete Part B. You are advised to allocate your time approximately as follows:
   Task 1   15 minutes
   Task 2   25 minutes
   Task 3   20 minutes

7. The Data File will NOT be collected at the end of the examination. Do NOT write your answers in the Data File.

96-CE-ENG LANG BIII-1

16

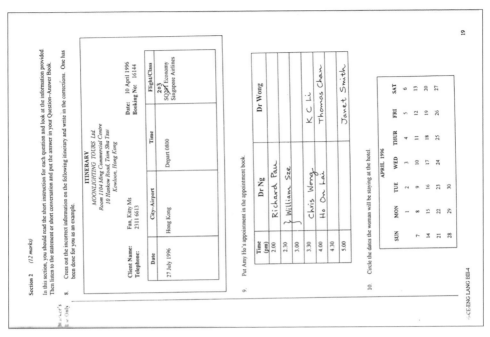

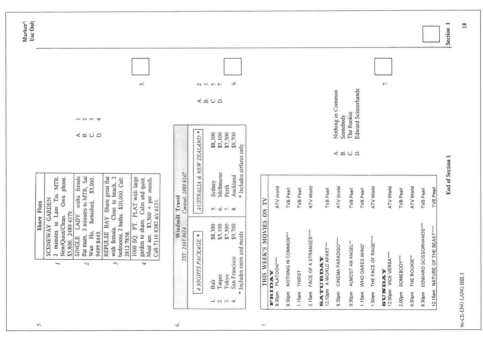

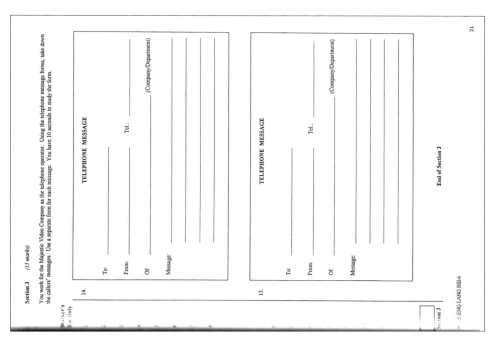

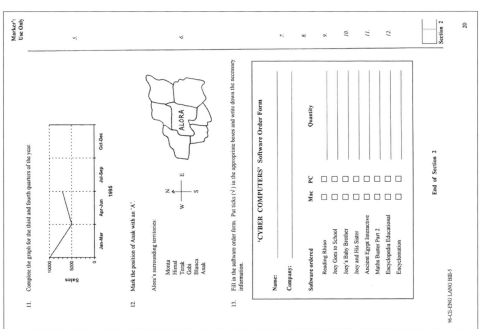

PART B (22% of the subject mark)

Situation

You are Peter Chan. Today is 12th August, 1996. You have just received your HKCEE results and now you are thinking about a career. You should listen to the radio programme, which includes a telephone call from you, make notes about how to apply for a job, what information to give and how to present it. Then you should read the job advertisement and decide which job you want to apply for.

You are required to do the following tasks:

1) Fill in an application form.   (18 marks)

2) Write a letter of application.   (27 marks)

3) Write a letter in reply to your cousin, Julia.   (21 marks)

Read everything carefully, including the instructions. You will find there is relevant information in the Question–Answer Book as well as in the Data File.

You have four minutes to study Part B of the Question–Answer Book in order to familiarise yourself with the situation and the tasks.

As you listen to the radio programme, make notes on the note sheet on page 7 of the Data File. You have one minute to study the note sheet before the radio programme begins

96-CE-ENG LANG BII-8

23

Section 4   (22 marks)

Put ticks (✓) in the appropriate boxes and write down the necessary information. You have 30 seconds to study the form. One box has been filled in for you as an example.

Marker's Use Only

1.
2.
3.
4.
5.
6.
7.
8.
9.
10.
11.
12.
13.
14.
15.
16.
17.
18.
19.
20.
21.
22.

HONG KONG TOURIST ASSOCIATION
TOURISM SURVEY

Personal details

Mr ✓
Mrs ☐
Miss ☐
Ms ☐

Surname _____   Other name(s) _____

Nationality: _____

Address: _____

Age: 20 or below ☐   21–30 ☐   31–40 ☐   41–50 ☐   51 and above ☐

Details of visit to Hong Kong

Reason for visit: Business ☐   Holiday ☐   Others ☐

Length of stay: 1–7 days ☐   8–14 days ☐   15–31 days ☐   More than a month ☐

Trip organised by: Self/Family ☐   Tour operator ☐   Company ☐

Arriving from: _____   Travelling to:

Places visited: 1. _____   2. _____
                  3. _____

Items bought: 1. _____   2. _____
                3. _____

Opinion of Hong Kong

Which aspects of Hong Kong have you enjoyed?

Shopping ☐   Nightlife ☐   Scenery ☐   Food ☐   Culture/Festivals ☐

Others ☐ (specify: _____)

Which aspects of Hong Kong have you not enjoyed (if any)?

Shopping ☐   Nightlife ☐   Scenery ☐   Food ☐   Culture/Festivals ☐

Others ☐ (specify: _____)

Ranking of tourist venues (rank in order of preference, 1 = most liked, 4 = least liked)

Hong Kong ___   Singapore ___   Tokyo ___   Beijing ___

End of Part A

96-CE-ENG LANG BII-7

Section 4

22

Task 2   *(27 marks)*

You also have to write a letter to the bank, to go with your application form, explaining why you want to work for the bank and why you want to work in Singapore. Use the space below to write the letter. Make sure that you follow the advice given in the radio broadcast. Use the information in the Data File, in the Question-Answer Book, and in the radio broadcast. Date your letter 12 August, 1996. You should use a pen.

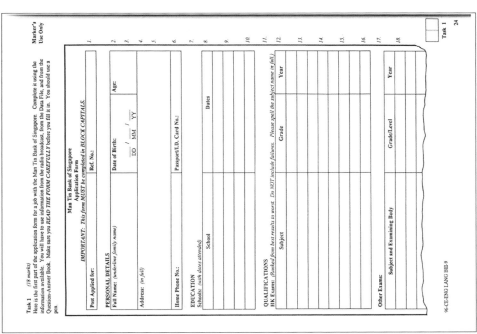

96-CE-ENG LANG BIB-10   25

Task 1   *(18 marks)*

Here is the first part of the application form for a job with the Man Tin Bank of Singapore. Complete it using the information available. You will have to use information from the radio broadcast, from the Data File, and from the Question-Answer Book. Make sure you *READ THE FORM CAREFULLY* before you fill it in. You should use a pen.

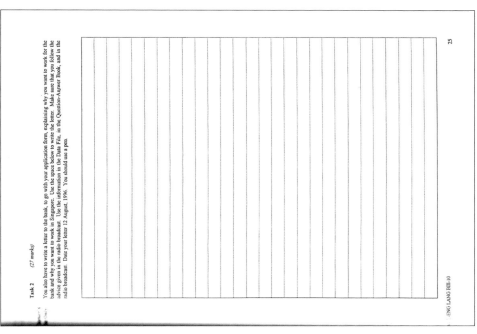

Man Tin Bank of Singapore
Application Form

IMPORTANT: This form MUST be completed in BLOCK CAPITALS.

Post Applied for:	Ref. No.:		

PERSONAL DETAILS

Full Name: *(underline family name)*	Date of Birth:	Age:
	DD / MM / YY	

Address: *(in full)*

Home Phone No.:   Passport/I.D. Card No.:

EDUCATION
Schools: *(with dates attended)*

School	Dates

QUALIFICATIONS
HK Exams: *(Ranked from best results to worst. Do NOT include failures. Please spell the subject name in full.)*

Subject	Grade	Year

Other Exams:

Subject and Examining Body	Grade/Level	Year

Marker's Use Only

1.
2.
3.
4.
5.
6.
7.
8.
9.
10.
11.
12.
13.
14.
15.
16.
17.
18.

96-CE-ENG LANG BIB-9   Task 1   24

Task 3   *(21 marks)*

Having filled in the application form and written the letter of application, you are now going to write a reply to the letter from your cousin, Julia, which is on page 5 of the Data File. Read Julia's letter carefully first. Be sure to reply to all of her questions using information from the Data File and from the Question-Answer Book. You should use a pen.

Flat 5 D
2 Lok Yu Path
Shatin, N.T., Hong Kong
Tel. 2688 5391

12ᵗʰ August, 1996

Dear Julia,

Thank you for your letter. I'm

Yours,
Peter

END OF PAPER

96-ENG LANG BIII-12   3   27

Marker's Use Only

a.
b.
c.
d.
e.

1.
2.
3.
4.
5.
6.
7.
8.
9.
10.
11.
12.
13.

L	C	S	I	O

96-CE-ENG LANG BIII-11   Task 2   26

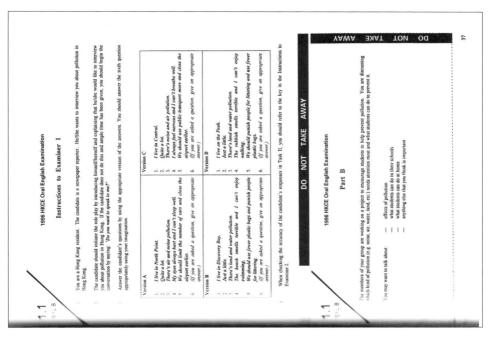

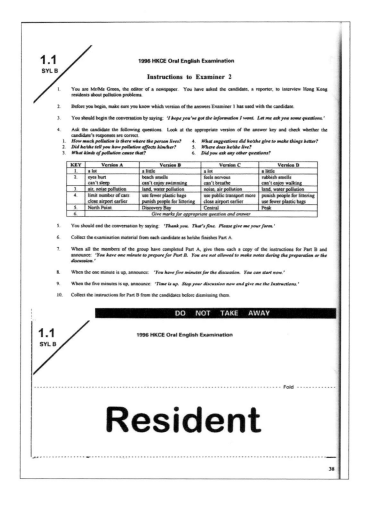

APPENDIX V
An excerpt of one of the longest turns observed

This typically long turn is at the beginning of the lesson.

Today *[framing]*, we are going to look at Part Two–discussion. If you remember when we have the final year examination, there are four people in your group. *[Pause]* And you sit together to discuss a topic. Today *[focus]*, we are going to look at how to start a discussion. If you have the paper–the career paper, you may... have a look then. We are going to have a look at Chapter Two. Chapter Two. Giving suggestions. //So yesterday Mr. Hut was trying to collect the Council letter from you. It is a visit to the Career Information Centre. Have you given it to me? Because if you haven't given it to me, then you can not go to the Career Centre.// *[Management: Discipline routine]* Please look at page 15. Page 15 please. A group discussion. Everybody has a book. Page 15 please. //No other books on your table please, no ice cream, no maps. // *[Management: Discipline routine]* OK.*[frame: indicating to the students that one transition has ended and another is beginning]* What I would like you to do is, because it is oral today, I would like you to use your mouth. Open your mouth. OK, discussion skills. Let us read this together. (2 minutes) *[Management: Classroom procedure]*.

[Up to this part, the teacher has been talking for 2 minutes in one turn–the introduction to the lesson. No language input has been given in terms of content–two kinds of management have been used–discipline and classroom procedures.]

//In this lesson, we are going to suggest ways for your schools to raise money for charity, and plan a fund-raising event.// *[Topic of discussion]* //You will look again at how to prepare for a group interaction or discussion, and revise things you can say to open a discussion. You will practise making suggestions and supporting them with reasons. You will also learn to respond to other people's suggestions and give alternative ideas.// *[content of the lesson–discussion]* (40 seconds)

[Second turn. Teacher and students reading aloud together. The topic of the discussion was introduced.]

//Before we start, I would like you to remember during the discussion what words do we use in the discussion? What things can you say in the discussion? For example, somebody says something. You say that is a good idea. What is your opinion? *[Some laughter observed. There might be a private turn, but the video camera did not catch it]*. Yes? Let's start. Oh, never mind, today in this group in this picture, we are going to learn how to discuss, to raise money for charity. To raise money for the charity. // *[The teacher wrote this on the blackboard, 'Tips for discussion']*. //Firstly, do you know what is charity? Charity means there are some people who don't have the money, who don't have enough money so we want to give them the money by donation. For example, I think the Youngchai [made up names used in the textbook] hospital is having a charity collection at the moment. So you have the Youngchai Hospital form. Then you ask people to sponsor your walk. Do you know what is the word 'sponsor'? _____ *[in Chinese].* That is correct. Sponsor for a walk? So what they do is they give you the money and you walk somewhere. Then you collect the money to help the hospital. The word charity means to give people money when they need it. Because you are kind and you are helpful. To raise money means to collect the money for the charity. There are different kinds of charity. It can be for the old people, for the elderly, for the hospital, anything else? For the schools, for children, orphanage, things like that.// *[Topic of the discussion]* Anyway, *[frame]* let's look at exercise one. In Part B of the HKCEE paper IV Oral Exam, you will be given instructions for your group interactions. You will be given a piece of paper to tell you the aims of the discussion. What is the topic of the discussion? To prepare for this, you should firstly read the instructions carefully. To find the topics, and the purpose of the discussion. OK. Can you look at the paper in Part B. See the Part B of the paper, you see the paper. Can you look at it for a while. OK, *[frame]* let's read it together. *[4 minutes]*

You and three other members. Let's read it together. [They start again from the beginning] of your group are committee members of your school's Social Club. Your Club wants to organize an event to raise money for famine relief in the African country of Bawanda. *[30 minutes] [By reading aloud together, the teacher involved her students in the process of the lesson].*

All right, let's look. So you and three members of your groups, so altogether four, are members of your school's Social Club.// *[tips for discussion]* //What is a social club? What is a club? A club is a society. For example, we have English club, math club, the student union, OK. That is called a social club. I think it is club who tell people. People in school or outside school is called a social club. All right. Let us see if the club wants to organize an event. That means to organise an activity to raise money for famine relief. What is famine relief? *[turn]* That means in Africa, there is a country in Africa called Bawanda. The people there are very very poor so poor that they famine. That means what? *[turn]* So poor that they? They don't have a car? Good. So poor they have nothing to eat. That is called a famine. They have nothing to eat. For us to help to collect the money to buy food for them is called famine relief. Relief means to help them in this problem. No food to eat. All right. So we want to organize activities for this.// *[content for discussion]*

Right. *[frame]* What are we going to discuss in the discussion. What are we going to talk about in the class. The task? So what type or what event your club should like to organize? What type of activities we are going to organize? The moderator of the class, that is the teacher, Mr. Li, has said that the we should probably raise about HK$5000. So the target, the money we want, is 5000. Involve a large number of students. Large number of people mean how many people? 10 people? What does it mean involving? One class? Do you have any suggestion? A large number of students means about how many people? *[turn]* 1000, thank you, that is right. About the whole school. I think you want to organize an activity, which involves many, and many students in the school. Be fairly easy to organize. Not too difficult to organize. And must be interesting for the students. What type of activities can we organize? You may consider the following types of events, a sponsored walk. What does that mean? *[turn]* _____ *[in Chinese]* Just like the Youngchai Hospital they have a sponsored walk. So you ask people for the money, and then you walk. And then you collect the money. Or a jumbo sale. You know what is a jumbo sale? That means you sell something. But where do you get the things from? *[turn]* _____ *[in Chinese].* That is correct. That means you ask your friends to give you something. And you sell the things to get the money. And the money you will give it to the famine relief. What is a lucky draw ? *[turn]* _____ *[in Chinese]* How do you think you can organize a _____ *[lucky draw in Chinese].* You ask people to _____ *[sponsor in Chinese].* They may pay a ticket, pay a ticket. Maybe \$1 a ticket so that they can have a lucky draw.

All right, now let's have a look at the next page. This is a very easy version of the paper B, Part B. Before we start, we must be careful what is the topic, *[focusing still on the topic not the skills for taking part in discussion]* what is the purpose of the discussion? Can you tell me from the paper you saw just now? What is your topic for discussion? The topic of the discussion _____ (*in Chinese*). Can you see any? You can get some idea from the blackboard. Can you see the blackboard? What is topic of the discussion? The topic of the discussion. What are we talking about? To raise money for famine relief in the African country of Bawanda. So our topic today is to raise money for an African country called Bawanda. Topic means ____ (*in Chinese*). And it is very important to remember the topic all the time so that you don't talk about Youngchai hospital. You don't say anything else. Finish. What is the purpose of the discussion? Purpose means _____ (*in Chinese*). (7 minutes)

[13 minutes of teacher's talk were recorded so far, with 2 short changes of turns–30 seconds and 40 seconds–for reading aloud together. She went on to explain the rest of the introduction to group discussion in a similar way as shown above for another 7 minutes, then she said:]

OK, *[frame]* //so I want to stop here. And then what I like you to do is we listen to a model conversation.// *[Management: Classroom procedure].* //In this conversation, there are four people. Their names are Ada, Ben, Carol and David. Do you think Ada is a boy or girl? *[turn]* A girl. All right. Four people are going to talk about the discussion. I'd like you to listen to their ideas. And then they will tell you about their reasons. Why they want that particular activity? Why? Is there any reason for that activity? Ready. OK. This bit is listening, so you must write in your listening book. // [1 minute]. *[instruction for listening activity].*

[Tape listening activity. Students continued to listen to tape recording.]

References

Alderson, J C (1986) Innovations in language testing, in Portal, M (Ed.) *Innovations in language testing: Proceedings of the IUS/NFER Conference,* Windsor, UK: NFER-Nelson, 93–105.

Alderson, J C and Hamp-Lyons, L (1996) TOEFL preparation courses: A study of washback, *Language Testing* 13, 280–297.

Alderson, J C and Scott, M (1992) Insiders and outsiders and participatory evaluation, in Alderson, J C and Beretta, A (Eds) *Evaluating second language curriculum,* Cambridge: Cambridge University Press, 25–60.

Alderson, J C and Wall, D (1993) Does washback exist? *Applied Linguistics* 14, 115–129.

Allen, P, Frohlich, M and Spada, N (1984) The communicative orientation of language teaching: An observation scheme, in Handscombe, J, Oren, R A and Taylor, B P (Eds) *On TESOL'83: The question of control,* Washington, DC: TESOL, 231–252.

Allwright, D (1983) Classroom-centred research on language teaching and learning: A brief historical overview, *TESOL Quarterly* 17, 191–204.

Allwright, D (1984) Why don't learners learn what teachers teach? The interaction hypothesis, in Singleton, D M and Little, D G (Eds) *Language learning in formal and informal contexts,* Dublin, Ireland: IRAAL, 3–18.

Allwright, D (1988) *Observations in the language classroom,* London: Longman.

Allwright, D and Bailey, K (1991) *Focus on the language classroom: An introduction to classroom research for language teachers,* Cambridge: Cambridge University Press.

Andrews, S (1994a) The washback effect of examinations–Its impact upon curriculum innovation in English language teaching, *Curriculum Forum* 4, 44–58.

Andrews, S (1994b) Washback or washout? The relationship between examination reform and curriculum innovation, in Nunan, D, Berry, V and Berry, R (Eds) *Bringing about change in language education,* Hong Kong: University of Hong Kong, Dept. of Curriculum Studies, 67–81.

Andrews, S and Fullilove, J (1993) Backwash and the use of English oral speculations on the impact of a new examination upon sixth form English language testing in Hong Kong, *New Horizons* 34, 46–52.

Andrews, S and Fullilove, J (1994) Assessing spoken English in public examinations –Why and how?, in Boyle, J and Falvey, P (Eds) *English language testing in Hong Kong,* Hong Kong: The Chinese University Press, 57–86.

Arnove, R F, Altbach, P G and Kelly, G P (Eds) (1992) *Emergent issues in education: Comparative perspectives,* Albany, NY: State University of New York Press.

Aschbacher, P R (1990) *Monitoring the impact of testing and evaluation innovations projects: State activities and interest concerning performance-based assessment,* Los Angeles: University of California, National Center for Research on Evaluation, Standards, and Student Testing.

References

Aschbacher, P R, Baker, E L and Herman, J L (Eds) (1988) *Improving large-scale assessment,* Resource Paper 9, Los Angeles: University of California, CRESST.

Bachman L F (1990) *Fundamental considerations in language testing,* Oxford: Oxford University Press.

Bachman, L F (1991) What does language testing have to offer? *TESOL Quarterly* 25, 671–747.

Bachman, L F and Palmer, A S (1996) *Language testing in practice,* Oxford: Oxford University Press.

Bailey, K M (1985) Classroom-centred research on language teaching and learning, in Celce-Murcia, M (Ed.) *Beyond basics: Issues and research in TESOL,* Rowley, MA: Newbury House, 96–121.

Bailey, K M (1996) Working for washback: A review of the washback concept in language testing, *Language Testing* 13, 257–279.

Bailey, K M (1999) *Washback in language testing,* Princeton, NJ: Educational Testing Service.

Bailey, K M and Nunan, D (Eds) (1996) *Voices from the language classroom: Qualitative research in second language education,* Cambridge: Cambridge University Press.

Baker, E L (1989) *Can we fairly measure the quality of education?* Centre for Study of Evaluation, Technical Report 290, Los Angeles: University of California, Centre for Study of Evaluation.

Baker, E L (1991) *Alternative assessment and national policy,* paper presented at the National Research Symposium on Limited English Proficient Students' Issues: Focus on Evaluation and Measurement, Washington, DC, November 1991.

Baker, E L, Aschbacher, P R, Niemi, D and Sato, E (1992) *Performance assessment models: Assessing content area explanations,* Los Angeles: University of California, CRESST.

Biggs, J B (1992) The psychology of assessment and the Hong Kong scene, *Bulletin of the Hong Kong Psychological Society* 27/28, 1–21.

Biggs, J B (1993) The quality of teaching and learning in an expanding tertiary system, *New Horizons* 34, 102–104.

Biggs, J B (1995) Assumptions underlying new approaches to educational assessment, *Curriculum Forum* 4 (2), 1–22.

Biggs, J B (Ed.) (1996) *Testing: To educate or to select? Education in Hong Kong at the cross-roads,* Hong Kong: Hong Kong Educational Publishing Co.

Blenkin, G M, Edwards, G and Kelly, A V (1992) *Change and the curriculum,* London: P. Chapman.

Blumer, H (1986) *Symbolic interactionism: Perspective and method,* Berkeley, CA: University of California Press.

Borko, H, Flory, M and Cumbo, K (1994) *Teachers' ideas and practices about assessment and instruction: A case study of the effects of alternative assessments in instruction, student learning and accountability practices,* CSE Technical Report 366, Boulder: University of Colorado at Boulder, CRESST.

Boyle, J and Falvey, P (Eds) (1994) *English language testing in Hong Kong,* Hong Kong: Chinese University Press.

Bracey, G W (1987) Measurement-driven instruction: Catchy phrase, dangerous practice, *Phi Delta Kappa* 68, 683–686.

Bracey, G W (1989) The $150 million redundancy, *Phi Delta Kappa* 70, 698–702.

Brandt, R (1989) On the misuse of testing: A conversation with George Madaus, *Educational Leadership* 46 (7), 26–29.

Brannen, J (1992) Combining qualitative and quantitative approaches: An overview, in Brannen, J (Ed.) *Mixing methods: Qualitative and quantitative research,* Burlington, VT: Ashgate, 3–37.

Breen, M (1989) The evaluation circle for language learning tasks, in Johnson, R K (Ed.) *The second language curriculum,* Cambridge: Cambridge University Press, 187–206.

Brooke, N and Oxenham, J (1984) The influence of certification and selection on teaching and learning, in Oxenham, J (Ed.) *Education versus qualifications?* London: Allen & Unwin, 147–175.

Brown, G (1975) *Microteaching,* London: Methuen.

Brumfit, C and Mitchell, R (1989a) The language classroom as a focus for research, in Brumfit, C and Mitchell, R (Eds) *Research in the language classroom,* Great Britain: Modern English Publications, in association with the British Council, 3–15.

Brumfit, C and Mitchell, R (Eds) (1989b) *Research in the language classroom,* Great Britain: Modern English Publications in association with the British Council.

Bryman, A (1992) Quantitative and qualitative research: Further reflections on their integration, in Brannen, J (Ed.) *Mixing methods: Qualitative and quantitative research,* Burlington, VT: Ashbury, 57–80.

Buck, G (1988) Testing listening comprehension in Japanese University entrance examinations, *JALT Journal* 10, 12–42.

Byrne, D (1987) *Techniques for classroom interaction,* London: Longman.

Calderhead, J (1996) Teachers: beliefs and knowledge, in Berliner, D C and Calfee, R C (Eds) *Handbook of educational psychology,* New York: Macmillan Library Reference, 709–725.

Cannell, J J (1987) Nationally-normed elementary achievement testing in America's public schools: How all 50 states are above the national average, *Educational Measurement: Issues and Practice* 7 (4), 12–15.

Cazden, C B (1985) Classroom discourse, in Wittock, M C (Ed.) *Handbook on Teaching,* New York: Macmillan, 432–63.

Cazden, C B, John, V and Hymes, D (1972) *Functions of language in the classroom.* New York: Teachers' College Press.

Chaudron, C (1986) The interaction of quantitative and qualitative approaches to research: A view of the second language classroom, *TESOL Quarterly* 20, 109–17.

Chaudron, C (1988) *Second language classrooms: Research on teaching and learning,* Cambridge: Cambridge University Press.

Cheng, L Y (1997) How does washback influence teaching? Implications for Hong Kong, *Language and Education* 11, 38–54.

Cheng, M C (1993) *Testing and re-testing in Hong Kong F5 and F6 English secondary classes,* Hong Kong: University of Hong Kong Press.

Cohen, L (1976) *Educational research in classrooms and schools: A manual of materials and methods,* London: Harper & Row.

Cohen, L and Manion, L (1989) *Research methods in education,* London: Routledge.

References

Coniam, D, Sengupta, S, Tsui, A B M and Wu, K Y (1994) Computer-mediated communication and teacher education: The case of TELENEX, in Bird, N, Falvey, P, Tsui, A B M, Allison, D A and McNeill, A (Eds) *Language and learning,* Hong Kong: Institute of Language in Education, 352–369.

Cooley, W W (1991) State-wide student assessment, *Educational Measurement: Issues and Practice* 10, 3–6.

Coulthard, M (1977) *An introduction to discourse analysis,* London: Longman.

Cronbach, L J (1988) Five perspectives on the validity argument, in Wainer, H and Braun, H I (Eds) *Test validity,* Hillsdale, NJ: Erlbaum, 3–17.

Crooks, T J (1988) The impact of classroom evaluation practices on students, *Review of Educational Research* 58, 438–481.

Dalton, T H (1988) *The challenge of curriculum innovation–A study of ideology and practice,* London: The Falmer Press.

Davies, A (1968b) Oral English testing in West Africa, in Davies, A (Ed.) *Language Testing Symposium: A psycholinguistic approach,* London: Oxford University Press, 151–179.

Davies, A (Ed.) (1968a) *Language testing symposium: A psycholinguistic approach.* London: Oxford University Press.

Davies, A (1985) Follow my leader: Is that what language tests do? in Lee, Y P, Folk, A C Y Y, Lord, R and Low, G (Eds) *New directions in language testing,* Oxford: Pergamon Press, 3–12.

Dorr-Bremme, D and Herman, J (1983) Use of testing in schools: A national profile, in Hathaway, W (Ed.) *Testing in the schools: New directions for testing and measurement,* San Francisco: Jossey Bass, 3–17.

Dorr-Bremme, D and Herman, J (1986) *Assessing student achievement: A profile of classroom practices* (CSE Monograph Series in Evaluation 11), Los Angeles: University of California, CSE.

Dunkin, M J and Biddle, B J (1974) *The study of teaching,* New York: Holt, Rinehart and Winston.

Dunn, S S (1989) *Public accountability in Australian education: A discussion paper* (Occasional Paper No. 11), Curtin, Capital Territory: Australian Collections of Education. (ERIC Document Reproduction Service No. ED 321 354)

Eckstein, M A and Noah, H J (Eds) (1992) *Examinations: Comparative and international studies,* Oxford: Pergamon Press.

Eckstein, M A and Noah, H J (1993a) *Secondary school examinations: International perspectives on policies and practice,* New Haven, CT: Yale University Press.

Eckstein, M A and Noah, H J (1993b) The politics of examinations: Issues and conflicts, in Eckstein, M A and Noah, H J (Eds) *Secondary school examinations: International perspectives on policies and practice,* New Haven, CT: Yale University Press, 191–216.

Edelsky, C (1981) Who's got the floor? *Language in Society* 10, 383–421.

Education Department, Hong Kong (1989) *Report of the working group set up to review language improvement measures,* Hong Kong: Author.

Education Department, Hong Kong (1990) *Report of the working group set up to review language improvement measures,* Hong Kong: Education Department.

Ellis, R (1984) *Classroom second language development,* Oxford: Pergamon Press.

Ellis, R (1994) *The study of second language acquisition,* Oxford: Oxford University Press.

English, F W (1992) *Deciding what to teach and test: Developing, aligning, and auditing the curriculum,* Newbury Park, CA: Corwin Press.

Erickson, F (1986) Qualitative methods in research on teaching, in Wittock, M (Ed.) *Handbook of research on teaching,* New York: Macmillan, 119–161.

Erickson, F and Shultz, J (1981) What is a context? Some issues and methods in the analysis of social competence, in Green, J and Wallat, C (Eds) *Ethnography and language in educational settings,* Norwood, NJ: Ablex, 147–60.

Falvey, P (1991a) English language teaching in secondary schools in Hong Kong: From the 80's into the 90's, *Curriculum Forum* 1, 61–65.

Falvey, P (1991b) Language curriculum and behavioural problems in schools: The connection, in Crawford, N and Hui, E K P (Eds) *The curriculum and behavioural problems in schools,* Hong Kong: University of Hong Kong, Faculty of Education. 79–84.

Falvey, P (1994) The Target Oriented Curriculum–Issues in assessment, in Nunan, D, Berry, R and Berry, V (Eds) *Bringing about change in language education: Proceedings of International Language in Education Conference 1994,* Hong Kong: University of Hong Kong, Department of Curriculum Studies, 34–41.

Falvey, P (1996) The Education of Teachers of English in Hong Kong: A Case for Special Treatment, in Lopez-Real, F (Ed.) *Proceedings of An International Conference: Teacher Education in the Asian Region* 1995, Hong Kong: The University of Hong Kong and the Hong Kong Institute of Education, 107–114.

Fish, J (1988) *Responses to mandated standardised testing,* Unpublished doctoral dissertation, University of California, Los Angeles.

Flanders, N A (1970) *Analysing teaching behaviour,* Reading, MA: Addison-Wesley.

Forbes, D (1973) Selling English short, *English Language Teaching Journal* 27, 132–137.

Frederiksen, N (1984) The real test bias: Influences of testing on teaching and learning, *American Psychology* 39, 193–202.

Frederiksen, J R and Collins, A (1989) A system approach to educational testing, *Educational Researcher* 18 (9), 27–32.

Freeman, D (1996) Redefining the relationship between research and what teachers know, in Bailey, K M and Nunan, D (Eds) *Voices from the language classroom: Qualitative research in second language education,* Cambridge: Cambridge University Press, 88–115.

Frohlich, M, Spada, N and Allen, P (1985) Differences in the communicative orientation of language classrooms, *TESOL Quarterly* 19, 27–56.

Fullan, M G (1983) *The meaning of educational change,* New York: Columbia University, Teachers' College.

Fullan, M G (1993) *Change forces: Probing the depth of educational reform,* London: Falmer Press.

Fullan, M G [with Stiegelbauer, S] (1991) *The new meaning of educational change,* London: Cassell.

Fullilove, J (1992) The tail that wags, *Institute of Language in Education Journal* 9, 131–147.

Gaies, S J (1983) The investigation of language classroom processes–Classroom-centred research: State of the art, *TESOL Quarterly* 17, 205–217.

Gardner, H (1992) Assessment in context: The alternative to standardised testing, in Gifford, B R and O'Connor, M C (Eds) *Changing assessments: Alternative views of aptitude, achievement and instruction,* London: Kluwer Academic Publishers, 77–119.

Geisinger, K F (1994) Cross-cultural normative assessment: Translation and adaptation issues influencing the normative interpretation of assessment instruments, *Psychological Assessment* 6, 304–312.

Genesee, F (1994) Assessment alternatives, *TESOL Matters* 4 (5), 2.

Gergen, K J (1985) The social constructionist movement in modern psychology, *American Psychologist* 39, 93–104.

Gifford, B R and O'Connor, M C (Eds) (1992) *Changing assessments: Alternative views of aptitude, achievement and instruction,* London: Kluwer Academic Publishers.

Gipps, C V (1994) *Beyond testing: Toward a theory of educational assessment,* London: The Falmer Press.

Glaser, R and Bassok, M (1989) Learning theory and the study of instruction, *Annual Review of Psychology* 40, 631–666.

Glaser, R and Silver, E (1994) *Assessment, testing, and instruction: Retrospect and prospect,* CSE Technical Report 379, Pittsburgh, PA: University of Pittsburgh, CRESST/Learning Research and Development Centre.

Gu, Y Q, Wen, Q F and Wu, D X (1995) How often is *often*? Reference ambiguities of the Likert-scale in language learning strategy research, *Occasional Papers in English Language Teaching* 5, 19–35.

Gullickson, A R (1984) Teacher perspectives of their instructional use of tests, *Journal of Educational Research* 77, 244–248.

Haggstrom, M A, Morgan, L Z and Wieczorek, J A (Eds) (1995) *The foreign language classroom–Bridging theory and practice,* New York: Garland Publishing.

Haladyna, T M, Nolen, S B, and Haas, N S (1991) Raising standardised achievement test scores and the origins of test score pollution, *Educational Research* 20 (5), 2–7.

Halfpenny, P (1979) The analysis of qualitative data, *Sociological Review* 27, 799–823.

Hammersley, M and Atkinson, P (1983) *Ethnography: Principles and practice,* London: Routledge.

Hargreaves, A and Fullan, M G (Eds) (1992) *Understanding teacher development,* London: Cassell.

Harrison, B (Ed.) (1990) *Culture and the language classroom,* London: Modern English Publications.

Harrison, I (1996) Look who's talking now: Listening to voices in curriculum renewal, in Bailey, K M and Nunan, D (Eds) *Voices from the language classroom: Qualitative research in second language education,* Cambridge: Cambridge University Press, 283–303.

He, A E (1996) *Teaching English at China's tertiary universities: Policy, practice and future prospective,* Unpublished doctoral dissertation, Monash University, Melbourne, Australia.

Herman, J L (1989) *Priorities of educational testing and evaluation: The testimony of the CRESST National Faculty*, CSE Technical Report 304, Los Angeles: University of California, CRESST.

Herman, J L (1992) *Accountability and alternative assessment: Research and Development issues,* CSE Technical Report 384, Los Angeles: University of California, CRESST.

Herman, J L and Golan, S (1991) *Effects of standardised testing on teachers and learning–Another look,* CSE Technical Report 334, Los Angeles: University of California, CRESST.

Heyneman, S P (1987) Use of examinations in developing countries: Selection, research, and education sector management, *International Journal of Education Development* 7, 251–263.

Heyneman, S P and Ransom, A W (1990) Using examinations and testing to improve educational quality, *Educational Policy* 4, 177–192.

Hivela, A and Law, E (1991) A survey of local English teachers' attitudes towards English and E L T, *Institute of Language in Education Journal* 8, 25–28.

Hogan, T P (1986, April) *The relationship between the curriculum and test development: Some considerations for the future,* Paper presented at the Annual Meeting of the American Educational Research Association, San Francisco.

Hong Kong Curriculum Development Committee (1983) *Syllabus for English (Forms I-V)* Hong Kong: Author.

Hong Kong Curriculum Development Council (1995) *Target Oriented Curriculum Programme of Study for English Language,* Hong Kong: Author.

Hong Kong Examinations Authority (1992/1993) *HKCE English Language Subject Committee (1992/93)–Restricted Documents,* Hong Kong: Author.

Hong Kong Examinations Authority (1993) *Hong Kong Certificate of Education Examination 1996–Proposed English Language Syllabus,* Hong Kong: Author.

Hong Kong Examinations Authority (1994a) *Hong Kong Certificate of Education Examination 1996–English Language,* Hong Kong: Author.

Hong Kong Examinations Authority (1994b) *The work of the Hong Kong Examinations Authority–1977-93,* Hong Kong: Author.

Hong Kong Government (1984) *Education Commission Report No.1,* Hong Kong: Hong Kong Government Secretariat.

Hong Kong Government (1986) *Education Commission Report No.2,* Hong Kong: Hong Kong Government Secretariat.

Hong Kong Government (1990) *Education Commission Report No.4,* Hong Kong: Hong Kong Government Secretariat.

Hong Kong Government (1993) *Enrolment Survey 1993,* Hong Kong: Education Department Government Secretariat.

Honig, B (1987) How assessment can best serve teaching and learning, *Assessment in the service of learning: Proceedings of the 1987 ETS Invitational Conference,* Princeton, NJ: Educational Testing Service.

Howe, K and Eisenhart, M (1990) Standards for qualitative (and quantitative) research: A prolegomenon, *Educational Researcher* 19 (1), 2–9.

Hu, C T (1984) The historical background: Examinations and controls in pre-modern China, *Comparative Education* 20, 7–26.

References

Huberman, M and Miles, M (1984) *Innovation up close,* New York: Plenum.

Hughes, A (1988) Introducing a needs-based test of English language proficiency into an English medium university in Turkey, in Hughes A (Ed.) *Testing English for university study: ELT Documents* 127, Great Britain: Modern English Publications, 134–153.

Hughes, A (1993) *Backwash and TOEFL 2000,* unpublished manuscript, University of Reading, UK.

Ingulsrud, J E (1994) An entrance test to Japanese universities: Social and historical contexts, in Hill, C and Parry, K (Eds) *From testing to assessment: English as an international language,* London: Longman, 61–81.

Jaeger, R M (1988) Survey research methods in education, in Jaeger, R M (Ed.) *Complementary methods for research in education,* Washington, DC: American Educational Research Association, 303–330.

Johnson, F and Wong, C L K L (1981) The interdependence of teaching, testing and instructional materials, in Read, J A S (Ed.) *Directions in Language Testing,* Singapore: Regional Language Centre, 277–302.

Johnson, K R (1983) *Report on the ELTU study of the oral medium of instruction in Anglo-Chinese secondary school classrooms,* Hong Kong: University of Hong Kong, English Language Teaching Unit.

Johnson, K R (1989) A decision-making framework for a coherent language curriculum, in Johnson, K R (Ed.) *The second language curriculum,* Cambridge: Cambridge University Press, 1–23.

Johnson, K R (1992) The instructional decisions of pre-service ESL teachers: New directions for teacher preparation programs, in Flowerdew, J, Brock, M and Hsia, S (Eds) *Perspectives on second language teacher education,* Hong Kong: City Polytechnic of Hong Kong.

Johnson, K R (1993/1994) Language policy and planning in Hong Kong, *Annual Review of Applied Linguistics* 14, 177–199.

Katz, A (1996) Teaching style: A way to understand instruction in language classrooms, in Bailey, K M and Nunan, D (Eds) *Voices from the language classroom: Qualitative research in second language education,* Cambridge: Cambridge University Press, 57–87.

Kellaghan, T and Greaney, V (1992) *Using examinations to improve education: A study of fourteen African countries,* Washington, DC: The World Bank.

Kellaghan, T, Madaus, G F and Airasian, P W (1982) *The effects of standardised testing,* London: Kluwen, Nijholf Publishing.

Khaniya, T R (1990a) *Examinations as instruments for educational change: Investigating the washback effect of the Nepalese English examinations,* Unpublished doctoral dissertation, University of Edinburgh, UK.

Khaniya, T R (1990b) The washback effect of a textbook-based test, *Edinburgh Working Papers in Applied Linguistics* 1, 48–58.

King, R (1994) Historical survey of English language testing in Hong Kong, in Boyle, J and Falvey, P (Eds) *English language testing in Hong Kong,* Hong Kong: Chinese University Press, 3–29.

Krashen, S (1981) *Second language acquisition and second language learning,* Oxford: Pergamon.

Kubiszyn, T and Borich, G (Eds) (1996) *Educational testing and measurement: Classroom application and practice,* New York: Harper Collins College Publishers.

Lai, C T (1970) *A scholar in imperial China,* Hong Kong: Kelly & Walsh.

Lam, H P (1993) *Washback–Can it be quantified? A study on the impact of English Examinations in Hong Kong,* Unpublished master's thesis, University of Leeds, UK

Lam, H P (1994) Methodology washback–An insider's view, in Nunan, D, Berry, V and Berry, R (Eds) *Bringing about change in language education,* Hong Kong: University of Hong Kong, Dept. of Curriculum Studies, 83–99.

Larsen-Freeman, D (Ed.) (1980) *Discourse analysis in second language research,* Rowley, MA: Newbury House.

Latham, H (1877) *On the action of examinations considered as a means of selection,* Cambridge: Deighton, Bell and Company.

Li, X J (1990) How powerful can a language test be? The MET in China, *Journal of Multilingual and Multicultural Development* 11, 393–404.

Linn, R L (1983) Testing and instruction: Links and distinctions, *Journal of Educational Measurement* 20, 179–189.

Linn, R L (1992) *Educational assessment: Expanded expectations and challenges,* CSE Technical Report 351, Boulder: University of Colorado at Boulder, CRESST.

Linn, R L, Baker, E L and Dunbar, S B (1991) Complex, performance-based assessment: Expectations and validation criteria, *Educational Researcher* 20 (8), 15–21.

Linn, R L, Grave, M E and Sanders, N M (1989) *Comparing state and district test results to national norms: Interpretations of scoring "above the national average",* CSE Technical Report 308, Boulder: University of Colorado at Boulder, CRESST.

Long, M H (1980) Inside the 'black box': Methodological issues in classroom research on language learning, *Language Learning* 30, 1–42.

Long, M H (1983) Does second language instruction make a difference? *TESOL Quarterly* 17, 359–382.

Long, M H (1984) Process and product in ESL program evaluation, *TESOL Quarterly* 18, 409–425.

Long, M H and Porter, P (1985) Group work, interlanguage talk, and second language acquisition, *TESOL Quarterly* 19, 207–228.

Lord, R (1987) Language policy and planning in Hong Kong: Past, present and (especially) future, in Lord, R and Cheng, H N L (Eds) *Language education in Hong Kong,* Hong Kong: The Chinese University Press, 3–24.

Lord, R and Cheng, H . L (Eds) (1987) *Language education in Hong Kong,* Hong Kong: The Chinese University Press.

Low, G D (1988) The semantics of questionnaire rating scales, *Evaluation and Research in education* 22, 69–79.

Luijten, J M A (Ed.) (1991) *Issues in public examinations–A selection of the proceedings of the 1990 IAEA Conference,* Utrecht, Netherlands: Lemma.

Macintosh, H G (1986) The prospects for public examinations in England and Wales, in Nuttall, D L (Ed.) *Assessing educational achievement,* London: The Falmer Press, 19–34.

Madaus, G F (1990) The distortion of teaching and testing: High stakes testing and instruction, *Peabody Journal of Education* 65 (3), 29–46.

Madaus, G F (1985a) Public policy and the testing profession: You've never had it so good? *Educational Measurement: Issues and Practice* 4 (4), 5–11.

Madaus, G F (1985b) Test scores as administrative mechanisms in educational policy, *Phi Delta Kappa* 66, 611–617.

Madaus, G F (1988) The influence of testing on the curriculum, in Tanner, L N (Ed.) *Critical issues in curriculum: Eighty-seventh yearbook of the National Society for the Study of Education*, Chicago: University of Chicago Press, 83–121.

Malamah-Thomas, A (1987) *Classroom interaction*, Oxford: Oxford University Press.

Markee, N (1993) The diffusion of innovation in language teaching, *Annual Review of Applied Linguistics* 13, 229–43.

Markee, N (1997) *Managing curricular innovation*, Cambridge: Cambridge University Press.

Marris, P (1986) *Loss and change*, London: Routledge & Kegan Paul.

Marshall, C and Rossman, G B (1989) *Designing qualitative research*, Thousand Oaks, CA: Sage Publications.

Martyn, H (1992) Deconstructing the qualitative-quantitative divide, in Brannen, J (Ed.) *Mixing methods: Qualitative and quantitative research*, Burlington, VT: Ashgate, 39–56.

Mathison, S M (1987) *The perceived effects of standardised testing on teaching and curriculum*, Unpublished doctoral dissertation, University of Illinois at Urbana-Champaign.

Matthews, A, Spratt, M and Dangerfield, L (Eds) (1985) *At the chalkface: Practical techniques in language teaching*, London: Arnold.

McDonnell, L M and Elmore, R F (1987) Getting the job done: Alternative policy instruments, *Educational Evaluation and Policy Analysis* 9, 133–152.

McDonnell, L M, Burstein, L, Ormseth, T, Catterall, J M and Moody, D (1990, June) *Discovering what schools really teach: Designing improved coursework indicators*, Prepared for the Office of Educational Research and Improvement, US Department of Education.

Mehan, H (1979) *Learning lessons: Social organisation in the classroom*, Cambridge, MA: Harvard University Press.

Messick, S (1975) The standard problem: Meaning and values in measurement and evaluation, *American Psychologist* 30, 955–966.

Messick, S (1989) Validity, in Linn, R (Ed.) *Educational Measurement*, New York: Macmillan, 13–103.

Messick, S (1992, April) *The interplay between evidence and consequences in the validation of performance assessments*, Paper presented at the annual meeting of the National Council on Measurement in Education, San Francisco.

Messick, S (1994) The interplay of evidence and consequences in the validation of performance assessments, *Educational Researcher* 23 (1), 13–23.

Messick, S (1996) Validity and washback in language testing, *Language Testing* 13, 241–256.

Miles, M B (1979) Qualitative data as an attractive nuisance: The problem of analysis, *Administrative Science Quarterly* 24, 590–601.

Miles, M B and Huberman, A M (1994) *Qualitative data analysis: An expanded sourcebook*, Thousand Oaks, CA: Sage Publications.

Mitchell, R (1988) Research into communicative language teaching, *Annual Review of Applied Linguistics* 8, 109–125.

Mitchell, R, Parkinson, B and Johnstone, R (1981) *The foreign language classroom: An observational study,* Stirling Educational Monographs 9, Stirling, Scotland: University of Stirling, Department of Education.

Morris, P (1990a) *Curriculum development in Hong Kong: Education Paper 7,* Hong Kong: University of Hong Kong, Faculty of Education.

Morris, P (1990b) Teachers' perceptions of the barriers to the implementation of a pedagogic innovation, in Morris, P (Ed.) *Curriculum development in Hong Kong,* Hong Kong: Hong Kong University Press, Faculty of Education, 45–60.

Morris, P (1991) Assessment, in Marsh, C J and Morris, P (Eds) *Curriculum development in East Asia,* London: Falmer Press, 37–57.

Morris, P (1995) *The Hong Kong school curriculum: Development, issues and policies,* Hong Kong: Hong Kong University Press.

Morrow, K (1986) The evaluation of tests of communicative performance, in Portal, M (Ed.) *Innovations in language testing: Proceedings of the IUS/NFER Conference,* London: NFER/Nelson, 1–13.

Mosback, G (1994) A communicatively-oriented syllabus and textbook design for a national school system: English Every Day, in Flavell, R H (Ed.) *ELT policy and impact: A case study,* London: Modern English Publications in association with the British Council, 50–66.

Moskowitz, G (1968) The effects of training foreign language teachers in Interaction Analysis, *Foreign Language Annuals* 1, 218–235.

Moskowitz, G (1971) Interaction analysis–A new modern language for supervisors, *Foreign Language Annals* 5, 221–221.

Nagy, P and Traub, R E (1986) *Strategies for evaluating the impact of province-wide testing,* Toronto, Canada: Ontario Institute for Studies in Education.

Naiman, N, Frohlich, M, Stern, H H and Todesco, A (1978) *The good language learner: A report,* Research in Education Series 7, Toronto, Canada: Ontario Institute for Studies in Education.

Noble, A J and Smith, M L (1994a) *Measurement-driven reform: Research on policy, practice, repercussion,* CSE Technical Report 381, Tempe, AZ: Arizona State University, CSE.

Noble, A J and Smith, M L (1994b) *Old and new beliefs about measurement-driven reform: 'The more things change, the more they stay the same',* CSE Technical Report 373, Tempe, AZ: Arizona State University, CSE.

Nunan, D (1988) *The learner-centred curriculum,* Cambridge: Cambridge University Press.

Nunan, D (1989a) *Understanding language classrooms: A guide for teacher-initiated action,* Upper Saddle River, NJ: Prentice Hall.

Nunan, D (1989b) *Designing tasks for the communicative classroom,* Cambridge: Cambridge University Press.

Nunan, D (1996) The more things change the more they stay the same: Or why action research doesn't work, in Nunan, D, Berry, V and Berry, R (Eds) *Bringing about change in language education,* Hong Kong: University of Hong Kong, Dept. of Curriculum Studies, 1–19.

Oller, J W (1979) *Language tests at school: A pragmatic approach,* London: Longman.

Oxenham, J (Ed.) (1984) *Education versus qualifications? A study of relationships between education, selection for employment and the productivity of labour,* London: Allen & Unwin.

Patton, M Q (1987) *How to use qualitative methods in evaluation,* Beverley Hills, CA: Sage Publications.

Pearson, I (1988) Tests as levers for change, in Chamberlain, D and Baumgardner, R J (Eds) *ESP in the classroom: Practice and evaluation,* Great Britain: Modern English Publications, 98–107.

Perkinson, H J (1985) American textbooks and educational change, in Svobodny, D (Ed.) *Early American textbooks 1775–1900,* Washington, DC: Government Printing Office, ix–xv.

Perrin, G (1996) *Report on the trailing of a questionnaire designed to investigate the extent of use of multiple choice questions in classes at the Federal Language Centre (Hurth, Germany) and its affiliated institutions,* Unpublished manuscript.

Petrie, H G (1987) Introduction to evaluation and testing, *Educational Policy* 1, 175–180.

Piaget, J (1973) *To understand is to invent: The future of education,* New York: Grossman Publishers.

Pierson, H D, Gail, G S and Lee, S (1979) An analysis of the relationship between language attitudes and English attainment of secondary students in Hong Kong, *Language Learning* 30, 289–316.

Popham, W J (1983) Measurement as an instructional catalyst, in Ekstrom, R B (Ed.), *Measurement, technology, and individuality in education: Proceedings of the 1982 ETS Invitational Conference,* New Directions for Testing and Measurement, 17, San Francisco: Jossey-Bass, 19–30.

Popham, W J (1987) The merits of measurement-driven instruction, *Phi Delta Kappa* 68, 679-682.

Popham, W J (1991) Appropriateness of teachers' test preparation practices, *Educational Measurement: Issues and Practice* 10, 12–15.

Popham, W J, Cruse, K L, Rankin, S C, Standifer, P D and Williams, P L (1985) Measurement-driven instruction: It is on the road, *Phi Delta Kappa* 66, 628–634.

Postiglione, G A and Leung, J Y M (Eds) (1992) *Education and society in Hong Kong: Toward one country and two systems,* Hong Kong: Hong Kong University Press.

Rein, M (1983) *From policy to practice,* Armonk, NY: M. E. Sharpe.

Resnick, D P (1982) A history of educational testing, in Wigdor, A K and Garmer, W R (Eds) *Ability testing: Uses, consequences, and controversies, Part II: Documentation section,* Washington, DC: National Academy Press, 173–194.

Resnick, L B (1989) Toward the thinking curriculum: An overview, in Resnick, L B and Klopfer, L E (Eds) *Toward the thinking curriculum: Current cognitive research/1989 ASCD Yearbook,* Reston, VA: Association for Supervision and Curriculum Development, 1–18.

Resnick, L B and Resnick, D P (1992) Assessing the thinking curriculum: New tools for educational reform, in Gifford, B R and O'Connor, M C (Eds) *Changing assessments: Alternative views of aptitude, achievement and instruction,* London: Kluwer Academic Publishers, 37–75.

Richards, J C, Tung, P and Ng, P (1992) The culture of the English language teacher, A Hong Kong example, *RELC Journal* 23, 81–102.

Romberg, T A, Zarinnia, A and Williams, S R (1989) *The influence of mandated testing on mathematics instruction: Grade 8 teachers' perceptions,* Monograph, Madison: University of Wisconsin, National Center for Research in Mathematical Sciences Education.

Saville, N and Hawkey, R (2004) The IELTS Impact Study: Investigating washback on teaching materials, in Cheng, L and Watanebe, J with Curtis, A (Eds) *Washback in Language Testing: Research Contexts and Methods,* New York: Lawrence Erlbaum Associates, 37–75.

Schon, D A (1971) *Beyond the stable state: Public and private learning in a changing society,* London: Maurice Temple Smith.

Seliger, H W (1977) Does practice make perfect? A study of interaction pattern and L2 competence, *Language Learning* 27, 263–78.

Shepard, L A (1990) Inflated test score gains: Is the problem old norms or teaching the test? *Educational Measurement: Issues and Practice* 9, 15–22.

Shepard, L A (1991) Psychometricians' beliefs about learning, *Educational Researcher* 20 (6), 2–16.

Shepard, L A (1992) What policy makers who mandate tests should know about the new psychology of intellectual ability and learning, in Gifford, B R and O'Connor, M C (Eds) *Changing assessments: Alternative views of aptitude, achievement and instruction,* London: Kluwer Academic Publishers, 301–327.

Shepard, L A (1993) The place of testing reform in educational reform: A reply to Cizek, *Educational Researcher* 22 (4), 10–14.

Shohamy, E (1992) Beyond proficiency testing: A diagnostic feedback testing model for assessing foreign language learning, *The Modern Language Journal* 76, 513–21.

Shohamy, E (1993) *The power of test: The impact of language testing on teaching and learning,* Washington, DC: National Foreign Language Centre Occasional Papers.

Shohamy, E, Donitsa-Schmidt, S and Ferman, I (1996) Test Impact revisited: Washback effect over time, *Language Testing* 13, 298–317.

Simon, A and Boyer, E G (Eds) (1967–1970) *Mirrors for behaviour: An anthology of classroom observation instruments,* Vols. 1-14, Philadelphia: Research for Better Schools.

Sinclair, J McH and Coulthard, R M (1975) *Towards an analysis of discourse,* London: Oxford University Press.

Smallwood, I M (1994) Oral assessment: A case for continuous assessment at HKCEE level, *New Horizon* 35, 68–73.

Smith, M L (1991a) Meanings of test preparation, *American Educational Research Journal* 28, 521–42.

Smith, M L (1991b) Put to the test: The effects of external testing on teachers, *Educational Researcher* 20 (5), 8–11.

Smith, M L, Edelsky, C, Draper, K, Rottenberg, C and Cherland, M (1990) *The role of testing in elementary schools,* CSE Technical Report 321, Los Angeles: University of California, CSE.

Smith, M L, Noble, A J, Cabay, M, Heinecke, W, Junker, M S and Saffron, Y (1994) *What happens when the test mandates change? Results of a multiple case study,* Technical Report 380, Tempe, AZ: Arizona State University, CRESST.

Somerset, A (1983) *Examination reform: The Kenya experience,* Washington, DC: World Bank.

Spada, N (1989) A look at the research process in classroom observation: A case study, in Brumfit, C and Mitchell, R (Eds) *Research in the Language Classroom,* Great Britain: Modern English Publications in association with the British Council, 81–93.

Spolsky, B (1994) The examination of classroom backwash cycle: Some historical cases, in Nunan, D, Berry, V and Berry, R (Eds) *Bringing about change in language education,* Hong Kong: University of Hong Kong, Dept. of Curriculum Studies, 55–66.

Spolsky, B (1995) *Measured words,* Oxford: Oxford University Press.

Sproull, L and Zubrow, D (1981) Standardised testing from the administrative perspective, *Phi Delta Kappa* 62, 628–634.

Stake, R E (1988, September) *The effect of reforms in assessment in the USA,* Paper presented at the annual meeting of the British Educational Association at the University of East Anglia, United Kingdom.

Stern, H H (1983) *Fundamental concepts of language teaching,* Oxford: Oxford University Press.

Stern, H H (1989) Seeing the wood AND the trees: Some thoughts on language teaching analysis, in Johnson, R K (Ed.) *The second language curriculum,* Cambridge: Cambridge University Press, 207–221.

Stern, H H (1992) *Issues and options in language teaching,* Oxford: Oxford University Press.

Stevenson, D K and Riewe, U (1981) Teachers' attitudes towards language tests and testing, in Culhane, T, Klein-Braley, C and Stevenson, D K (Eds) *Practice and problems in language testing,* Occasional Papers 26, Essex, UK: University of Essex, 146–155.

Stiggins, R and Faires-Conklin, N (1992) *In teachers' hands,* Albany, NY: State University of New York Press.

Stodolsky, H (1988) *The subject matters: Classroom activity in math and social studies,* Chicago: University of Chicago Press.

Sudman, S and Bradburn, N M (1982) *Asking questions,* San Francisco: Jossey-Bass.

Swain, M (1984) Large-scale communicative language testing: A case study, in Savignon, S J and Berns, M (Eds) *Initiatives in communicative language teaching* Reading, MA: Addison-Wesley, 185–201.

Tsui, A B M (1995) *Introducing classroom interaction,* London: Penguin Books.

Van Lier, L (1988) *The classroom and the language learner: Ethnography and second language classroom research,* London: Longman.

Van Lier, L (1989a) Classroom research in second language acquisition, *Annual Review of Applied Linguistics* 10, 173–186.

Van Lier, L (1989b) Ethnography: Bandaid, bandwagon, or contraband? in Brumfit, C and Mitchell, R (Eds) *Research in the language classroom,* Great Britain: Modern English Publications in association with the British Council, 33–53.

Vernon, P E (1956) *The measurement of abilities,* London: University of London Press.

Wall, D (1996) Introducing new tests into traditional systems: Insights from general education and from innovation theory, *Language Testing* 13, 334–354.

Wall, D and Alderson, J C (1993) Examining washback: The Sri Lankan Impact Study, *Language Testing* 10, 41–69.

Wall, D, Kalnberzina, V, Mazuoliene, Z and Truus, K (1996) The Baltic States Year 12 Examination Project, *Language Testing Update* 19, 15–27.

Watanabe, Y (1996a) Investigating washback in Japanese EFL classrooms: Problems of methodology, in Wigglesworth, G and Elder, C (Eds) *The language testing circle: From inception to washback,* Australian Review of Applied Linguistics Series S, 13, Australia: Applied Linguistics Association of Australia, 208–239.

Watanabe, Y (1996b) Does grammar translation come from the entrance examination? Preliminary findings from classroom-based research, *Language Testing* 13, 318–333.

Weir, C and Roberts, J (1994) *Evaluation in ELT,* Oxford: Blackwell.

Wesdorp, H (1982) Backwash effects of language-testing in primary and secondary education, *Journal of Applied Language Study* 1, 40–50.

Wiggins, G (1989a) A true test: toward more authentic and equitable assessment, *Phi Delta Kappa* 70, 703–713.

Wiggins, G (1989b) Teaching to the (authentic) test, *Educational Leadership* 46 (7), 41–47.

Wiggins, G (1993) Assessment: Authenticity, context, and validity, *Phi Delta Kappa* 75, 200–214.

Wigglesworth, G and Elder, C (1996) *The language testing circle: From inception to washback,* Australian Review of Applied Linguistics Series S, 13, Australia: Applied Linguistics Association of Australia.

Wiseman, S (Ed.) (1961) *Examinations and English education,* Manchester: Manchester University Press.

Woods, A, Fletcher, P and Hughes, A (1986) *Statistics in language studies,* Cambridge: Cambridge University Press.

Workman, G B (1987) Cohesion or conflict? An analysis of the views of examiners and teachers of Hong Kong's Use of English Examination, with the aim of contributing towards improvement in the learning outcomes of Hong Kong students from their Form Six and Seven English course, *Institute of Language in Education Journal* 3, 82–102.

Yin, R K (1984) *Case study research: Design and methods,* Beverly Hills, CA: Sage Publications.

Index

Index